MONTANA ALMANAC

Andrea Merrill

Judy Jacobson

FALCON®

HELENA, MONTANA

© 1997 by Falcon® Publishing, Inc., Helena, Montana.
A division of Landmark Guidebooks, Inc.

Front cover photos: bucking bronco by Dave Black, all other photos by Michael Sample.

Printed in Canada.

Library of Congress Cataloging-in-Publication data:
Merrill, Andrea L.
     Montana almanac / by Andrea Merrill and Judy Jacobson.
          p.   cm.
     Includes bibliographical references and index.
     ISBN 1-56044-493-2
     1. Montana—Miscellanea. 2. Almanacs, American—Montana.
     I. Jacobson, Judy, 1939–   . II. Title.
     F731.M5 1997
     978.6—dc21   97-13198
                                                                           CIP

To Montanans, past and present.

CONTENTS

ACKNOWLEDGMENTS

WRITING THIS BOOK WAS A LABOR OF LOVE, not just because we love the place we write about, but because so many people loved us while we were laboring. If we could name, individually, all the people who assisted us during the past year, we would have another "almanac" just dedicated to outstanding Montanans. We offer first thanks to our families, those wonderful mates, parents, children, and grandchildren, who seem to still be around even after we abandoned them for a while. We also want to thank the many friends who cheered us on and had great faith in us. Your support, advice, and comfort mean more than words can say.

We offer our deepest appreciation to the many helpful, knowledgeable, and courteous people in government agencies who helped us in a variety of ways. This book would not be possible except for the many excellent public servants who are dedicated to compiling reports and information on their area of expertise within Montana state government. You deserve thanks from all Montanans for your industriousness, integrity, and competence in doing your part to make Montana work for all of us. We hope that all of you who helped us at the following state agencies will know that you have our sincerest appreciation: Montana Historical Society; Montana State Library; Vital Statistics Bureau of the Department of Public Health and Human Services; Montana Department of Fish, Wildlife & Parks; Department of Administration; Department of Corrections; Board of Crime Control; Montana Arts Council; Montana Agricultural Statistics Services; the former Department of Natural Resources and Conservation; Montana Lottery; Office of the Commissioner of Higher Education; Office of Public Instruction; Department of Labor and Industry; Department of Justice and its Gambling Control Division and Motor Vehicles Division; and Department of Transportation. There are many wonderful folks to thank at the Department of Commerce and its divisions: the Census and

Economic Information Center, the Business Development Center, and Travel Montana. We also thank those who helped at the library at Montana Tech of The University of Montana; the Lewis and Clark City-County Library; Bureau of Economic Research at The University of Montana; USDA Forest Service; United States Geological Survey; and Healthy Mothers, Healthy Babies.

We also want to express our gratitude to the helpful individuals at Montana Snowmobile Association, Montana Wilderness Association, Montana Association of Realtors, Montana High School Association, Montana Farmers Union, Montana Education Association, Rocky Mountain Elk Foundation, and Montana Association of Counties.

Some people need special recognition for invaluable help above and beyond the call of friendship or requests for assistance: Valerie Jaffe, Bob Trent, Gail Moser, Bill Darcy, John Fitzpatrick, Lillian Stover, Dan Connors, Jo Berg, Teresa Record, John Shontz, and Diana Dowling. And to the many talented and helpful friends at Legislative Services Division of the Montana Legislative Council (you know who you are), deepest thanks for all kindnesses. And a big thank you to all the talented people who shared their favorite things about Montana for the chapter on the arts in Montana.

We acknowledge the wonderful folks at Falcon, who were so positive and encouraging about the project. Jeff Wincapaw contributed his design talents. Dana Kim did maps and charts, and Janet Bukantis helped Jeff lay out the chapters. Allison Ledbetter and Arik Ohnstad created charts and maps, respectively. Joyce Brusin and Neil Sexton worked on proofreading the book. Paige Moriarty and Peter Grosshauser provided illustrations. Special thanks to Chris Cauble, Rick Newby, Eric Keszler, Susan Samson, Noelle Sullivan, Kathy Springmeyer, Erin Turner, Josh Corey, Sue Murray, Amy Kelley, and especially Ric Bourie for his great ideas, patience, and fine eye for detail.

Special thanks to the following experts who reviewed sections of the manuscript:

Michael Malone, President, Montana State University
Mike Cooney, Secretary of State
Dave Walter, Montana Historical Society
Grayson Cordell, former state climatologist, retired
Dave Alt, University of Montana Geology Department
Dick Dodge, economic and demographic consultant, Helena
Bob Brown, former state senator
Dori Neilson, data specialist, Office of Public Instruction
Taylor Brown, President of Northern Ag Network, Billings
Dave Jackson, University of Montana School of Forestry
Mark Bruno, Office of the Commissioner of Higher Education
Bill Lannan, former Deputy Commissioner of Higher Education

PREFACE

PEOPLE HAVE BEEN INTERESTED in statistical and essential information about this special place since Captains Meriwether Lewis and William Clark offered the first travel guide to Montana and the Indians planned their summer hunts among the buffalo herds. This book provides condensed information on the history of the state, the workings of government, the extent of the state's excellent education systems, the economic vital signs, the recreational opportunities, and the statistical health and wealth of the population, to name just a few topics.

In the opening chapter, we quote John Steinbeck on his love of Montana. This same affection for our state motivated this project. Both authors have worked for many years with the facts, figures, and people that make Montana special, and the urge to share this bounty of fascinating information with the world was irrepressible. Granted, it was a daunting task to attempt to compile comprehensive yet succinct information about Montana's past and present. For help and inspiration, we tapped into the work of those who have produced respected state histories, comprehensive state reports and data banks, excellent state and local travel promotion items, and other fine publications about Montana. The work was more fun than difficult, because of the opportunity to visit with and to learn from so many interesting and interested state citizens.

We thought it would take months, but the months have stretched into years. We have gathered the latest data available, some of it in the early weeks of 1997. Other figures and statistics date back to 1995, 1994, and earlier. For the most part, these statistics had not been updated before publication of this book, so we have provided them as the last best figures to cite.

"Montana is a remote hinterland about as well known to the average eastern seaboard citizen as East or West Africa and quite a bit like such ill-starred captive

'empires' in other ways." Joseph Kinsey Howard said that in his popular 1943 book, *Montana: High, Wide, and Handsome.* He would perhaps be surprised to find Montana in the news so much in recent years, and he might be amazed to hear there are as many as 400,000 requests for Montana travel information each year. A demand exists for accessible, comprehensive information about Montana not only for our millions of annual visitors but for new Montana residents, students of all ages, educators, government agencies, and citizens in general who need Montana facts for a variety of reasons.

This book is intended to be an accessible compendium of basic information about Montana. The intention is to provide a brief overview of what is here and to offer quick facts and trivia to educate, delight, and entice to further investigation. We hope the book is an essential household and classroom resource that imparts some of the fascination and love we feel for our state. Beyond that, the reader is invited to use this book as a yardstick with which to measure the true dimensions of the great state of Montana.

Andrea Merrill
Helena

Judy Jacobson
Butte

JULY 1997

THIS *is* MONTANA

FEW HAVE EXPRESSED what many feel about Montana better than John Steinbeck: "I am in love with Montana. For other states I have admiration, respect, recognition, even some affection, but with Montana it is love, and it's difficult to analyze love when you're in it."

Images of Montana are tucked into the hearts of the people who live here or visit, and beckon those who hope to do one or the other someday. Some people just like to know that many icons of the Old West endure and thrive here. Montana still has ranches with front gates 20 miles from the ranch house porch, amber waves of grain, and majestic mountains under skies just like the ones that Charlie Russell painted. People here still share stories at cozy roadside saloons complete with glassy-eyed animal heads guarding the bar. And they still stop for deer, elk, and other creatures along the roadways.

Montana has its share of New West icons too. It is home to airfields seemingly in the middle of nowhere, golf courses with majestic views, corny roadside attractions, glittering casino lights, and 5-acre ranchettes along blue-ribbon trout streams. Freeways stretch across the 550 east-west miles of the state, and logging roads amble through its forests.

Old and new, there is much that is special about Montana. For instance, did you know that, on the average, only six persons share each of the state's 145,556 square miles of land? (That's not counting 1,490 square miles of water, most of which we share as well.) Or that our state has forty-one state parks and more than six hundred campgrounds? The average working person in Montana earns

photo: Michael Sample

less than the national average and pays some of the highest gasoline prices in the nation. Our state has about 12.5 million acres of wilderness to nourish the soul, about 3.5 million acres of it protected by law. Conveniently, we have only one area code: 406.

People work, create, and recreate in this place of awesome beauty, incredible dimensions, and great diversity, forging a pageant of events, institutions, and traditions.

People have been interested in statistical and essential information about Montana ever since explorers Meriwether Lewis and William Clark wrote the first travel journal about the West. But few know much about us here in what some still think is a hinterland. We hope *Montana Almanac* will be a source of accessible, basic information about our state today, supplementing about 400,000 requests for travel information each year and helping Montana students, government agencies, and citizens find the facts they need. We hope it imparts some of the love we feel for Montana, and that it serves as a suitable yardstick to measure its fascinating physical and social dimensions.

notable
Montanans

Calamity Jane (ca. 1850-1903)

Born in Princeton, Missouri, as Martha Jane Canary, she came to Virginia City as a teenager with her parents. She claimed to have been a pony express rider and scout for Lieutenant Colonel George Armstrong Custer's Seventh Cavalry, but it was hard to distinguish her claims from her reality. The love of her life was Wild Bill Hickok, whom she claimed to have married and had a daughter by. Her wish to be buried beside him in Deadwood, South Dakota, was fulfilled by friends.

Montana Historical Society

notable
Montanans

 ### Plenty Coups (1848-1932)

This distinguished Crow Indian leader became chief of the Mountain Crow at age 25 and planned treaties with the United States government on behalf of the Crow people. In 1883, he successfully claimed payment on Crow lands that had been given to the railroads. In 1904, he was made chief of all the Crow. After his death, the title of tribal chief was retired. Plenty Coups worked closely with white people but practiced the traditions of the Crow. During the ceremony of dedication for the Tomb of the Unknown Soldier at Arlington National Cemetery, Chief Plenty Coups represented the Indian nations as a head of state.

Montana Historical Society

Wallace D. "Wally" McRae (1936-)

He is one in a long family line of Scottish ranchers, but into that mix add equal parts philosopher, environmentalist, and renowned cowboy poet. Wally was the first cowboy poet to receive the National Endowment for the Arts' National

Heritage Award, in 1990. Five years later, President Clinton appointed him to the National Council on the Arts. He has also been honored with the Montana Governor's Award for the Arts and the H.G. Merriam Award for distinguished contributions to Montana literature. In the 1970s, he helped found and later chaired the Northern Plains Resource Council, a group concerned with natural resource extraction in eastern Montana. In *The Cowboy Encyclopedia*, author Richard W. Slatta calls McRae "a poetic conscience for the West, the land, and the people." McRae runs a 30,000-acre family ranch in Rosebud County.

Big Sky Country in Brief

- **Admitted to the Union:** November 8, 1889, the 41st state
- **Population:** 879,372 *(est. 1996)*
  52.5% urban, 47.5% rural (1990)
  6.04 persons per square mile
  44th most populous state
- **Capital City:** Helena, in west-central Montana; population: 26,339 *(est. 1994)*
- **Largest City:** Billings, population: 86,578 *(est. 1994)*
- **State Name:** Derived from the Latin word for "mountainous region"
Nicknames: Officially known as the Treasure State, Montana is also known as Big Sky Country. Other nicknames include Land of the Shining Mountains, Mountain State, and Bonanza State
- **Size:** Total Area: 145,338 square miles (380,850 square km)
  Rank: 4th largest state
  Land Area: 145,556 square miles
  Inland Surface Water: 1,658 square miles
  Total Acres: 94,109,440
  Greatest Distance from East to West Boundary: app. 550 miles
  Greatest Distance from North to South Boundary: app. 320 miles in
    western Montana, app. 280 miles in eastern Montana
- **USGS Physiographic Regions:** Rocky Mountain region in the west,
  Great Plains in the east
- **Geographic Center:** In Fergus County, about 11 miles west of Lewistown
- **Number of Counties:** 56
- **Number of Incorporated Towns and Cities:** 126
- **Longitude and Latitude:** Between 44° 26' and 49° North Latitude and 104° 2'
  and 116° 2' West Longitude
- **Highest Point:** 12,799 feet (3,901 meters) above sea level at summit of
  Granite Peak in Park County near south-central boundary
- **Lowest Point:** 1,820 feet in Lincoln County in the northwest
  corner, where the Kootenai River enters Idaho
- **Mean Elevation:** 3,400 feet
- **Time Zone:** Mountain Standard
- **Area Code:** 406
- **Postal Abbreviation:** MT
- **Resident:** Montanan
- **Motto:** Oro y Plata, Spanish for "gold and silver"

Sources: 1996 World Almanac, Mahwah, N.J.: World Almanac Books, 1995. Microsoft Encarta.

The names of some Montana places aren't pronounced the way they're spelled.
As a courtesy to the visitor who'd rather not stand out after
botching the local place names, here is a brief tutorial:

a Visitor's
Pronunciation
—— *Guide* ——

1. The town of **Glasgow** is pronounced like the Scottish city, GLAS-ko or GLAS-go, but in Montana, typically without the lilting Scottish brogue.

2. Don't say **Havre** like the French pronounce their city on the English Channel. For the town on Montana's Milk River, just say HAV-er.

3. Don't pronounce **Missoula** with a hard S. It should sound like a popular corn oil, but with an "oo" in the middle: Mizz-OO-luh.

4. Pronounce the county of **Pondera** pon-dur-AY. It is derived from the name of an Indian tribe, which is spelled Pend d'Oreille (French for "hanging ear"), also pronounced pon-dur-AY.

5. **Meagher** County is pronounced like the fourth planet from the sun, without the S: MAR.

6. Leave off the "X" when you pronounce the town and county of **Wibaux**, both along the North Dakota border. Just say WEE-bo.

7. **Butte**, the city and the landform, sounds like the word you might use to describe a nice-looking horse or pickup truck, as in "she's a BYOOT"; not the word to describe a backside.

8. Montana's state capital is pronounced HELL-un-uh. The common mispronunciation of hell-EE-nuh will attract unwanted attention in **Helena** and elsewhere in the state.

9. **Twodot** does not get a French pronunciation, as in two-DOE. Say it TOO-dott. Another numerical name that has caused problems is **Ninepipe**, a reservoir and wildlife refuge in the Mission Valley. You'll be met with smirks if you call it NINN-ee-pipp-ee. Just say 9-pype.

10. The town of **Choteau** and the county of **Chouteau**, both along the Rocky Mountain Front, are pronounced SHO-toe or SHO-doe.

Incidentally, you'll save yourself a lot of confusion by remembering that the town of **Choteau** is not in **Chouteau** County. It's in **Teton** (TEE-tawn) county. Likewise **Deer Lodge**, the town, is not in **Deer Lodge** County, but in **Powell** County. There is no town of Powell in Montana, but there is a **Power**, northwest of **Great Falls**. The town of **Lincoln**, which gained national attention when the Unabomber suspect was found there, is in **Lewis and Clark** county, about 200 miles from **Lincoln County**, which is in the northwest corner of the state. Clear?

Montana by County

County Names and Origins

- Population based on 1995 estimate
- Area listed in square miles

BEAVERHEAD

POP: 9,008
AREA: 5,542.6
PEOPLE/SQ MI: 1.6

BEAVERHEAD
Dillon

Established: 1865
An alphabetical list of Montana's counties begins with the largest, in terms of area. The county name is from the Shoshone, given by Sacajawea's people to a rock formation shaped like a beaver's head, along the Beaverhead River, 12 miles southwest of Twin Bridges. The county seat was the gold mining town of Bannack until 1881, when it was changed to Dillon. The Big Hole River, famous for its blue-ribbon trout fishing, runs through this county. Montana's sheep industry originated in this county, as did one of the state's first registered cattle brands, the square and compass belonging to Poindexter and Orr, one of the state's early cattle ranches.

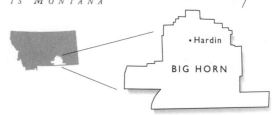

BIG HORN

POP: 12,215
AREA: 4,994.8
PEOPLE/SQ MI: 2.4

Established: 1913

The dominant river, mountain range, and county were named for the Rocky Mountain bighorn sheep. John Bozeman blazed his pioneer trail through this area. Today, the Crow Reservation covers most of the county, where the Battle of the Little Bighorn was fought. Both Indians and non-Indians engage in the main industries of farming and cattle ranching. The county seat of Hardin was named for Samuel H. Hardin, a Texas cattleman.

BLAINE

POP: 7,032
AREA: 4,226.2
PEOPLE/SQ MI: 1.7

Established: 1912

This county is mountainous in the south, the site of the Bears Paw Mountains, and dominated by prairie in the north. The county is named for James G. Blaine, a U.S. secretary of state from Maine. The county seat, Chinook, is named for the warm winds that sometimes blow across this area and throughout the state in winter. Fort Belknap College, a tribal school, and most of the Fort Belknap Indian Reservation, home to Assiniboine and Gros Ventre Indians, are within this county's boundaries.

BROADWATER

POP: 3,885
AREA: 1,191.5
PEOPLE/SQ MI: 3.3

Established: 1897

Colonel C. A. Broadwater was a prominent figure in the early commerce of the state. He was president of the Montana Central Railroad and built Helena's Broadwater Hotel and Natatorium in 1889. Canyon Ferry Lake, behind the Canyon Ferry Dam, stretches 25 miles through this county. The county seat of Townsend was named for the wife of an official of the Northern Pacific Railroad.

CARBON

POP: 9,029
AREA: 2,048
PEOPLE/SQ MI: 4.4

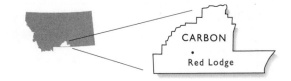

Established: 1895

Coal deposits and coal mining gave this county its name. There are several theories for the origin of the name of the county seat, Red Lodge. The most romantic and generally accepted story is that the lodges of the Crow were colored by red clay found in the area. The county includes the Beartooth Plateau and Granite Peak, the highest elevation in the state. In 1915, the first commercial oil well in the state was drilled in the Elk Basin field east of the mountains.

CARTER

POP: 1,464
AREA: 3,339.7
PEOPLE/SQ MI: 0.4

Established: 1917

Named for Montana's first U.S. congressman, Thomas H. Carter, the territory was home to the Sioux tribe
before the arrival of white people. Ekalaka, the county seat,
was named for an Indian woman whose great-uncle was the Sioux leader Sitting Bull. The woman, whose name is spelled Ijkalaka, meaning "swift one," was also the spouse of D. H. Russell, a famous scout and frontier settler. Medicine Rocks State Park is in this county.

CASCADE

POP: 81,091
AREA: 2,698
PEOPLE/SQ MI: 30.1

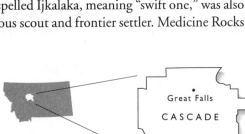

Established: 1887

The county and the county seat of Great Falls were named
for the Great Falls of the Missouri River. This was Blackfeet Indian terri-
tory at the time of Lewis and Clark's journey through the area in 1805-1806. The town of Great Falls was founded and planned by engineer and entrepreneur Paris Gibson. It has grown into Montana's second largest city. Many Cascade County residents work in agriculture.

Chouteau

POP: 5,492
AREA: 3,973.4
PEOPLE/SQ MI: 1.4

CHOUTEAU

•Fort Benton

Established: 1865

One of the original nine counties of the Montana Territory, it was named in 1882 for Auguste and Pierre Chouteau, fur traders and founders of Fort Benton, today's county seat. Fort Benton, named for U.S. Senator Thomas H. Benton of Missouri, was once an important port on the Missouri River. The area was Blackfeet Indian territory and home to vast herds of bison before the open-range cattle era. It is the state's largest winter wheat producer, at the heart of the rich wheat country in north-central Montana known as the Golden Triangle.

Custer

POP: 12,193
AREA: 3,783.3
PEOPLE/SQ MI: 3.2

• Miles City

CUSTER

Established: 1877

Originally part of the old Big Horn County, Custer was renamed in 1877, after Lt. Col. George A. Custer was killed in the 1876 Battle of the Little Bighorn. The county seat of Miles City was named for General Nelson A. Miles, a veteran of the Civil War and Indian wars. It was the range destination of many large Texas cattle drives. Today, it is cattle ranching and dry land farming country.

Daniels

POP: 2,140
AREA: 1,426.1
PEOPLE/SQ MI: 1.5

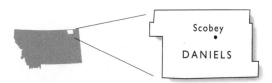

Scobey
•

DANIELS

Established: 1920

This prairie county was named for Mansfield A. Daniels, a local pioneer, rancher, and storekeeper. Scobey, the county seat, is named for Major C. R. A. Scobey, an agent of the Fort Peck Indian Reservation. In the 1920s, there was an intense baseball rivalry between Scobey and Plentywood, to the east in Sheridan County. The two towns hired professional baseball players, and for a while the competition between the towns was fierce. This area is cattle and dry land wheat country, and Scobey is a shipping and trade center for the alfalfa, livestock, wheat, and sugar beets produced in northeastern Montana.

DAWSON

POP: 9,095
AREA: 2,373.3
PEOPLE/SQ MI: 3.8

Established: 1869

Dawson County was named for Major Andrew Dawson of the
American Fur Company. The county seat of Glendive was named
by the first Montana tourist, Sir St. George Gore, an English sportsman who
was reminded of a stream named Glendale in Ireland. Gore came to hunt in
1856 and slaughtered so much game it alarmed and irritated the area Indians.
This area is now mostly dry land grain farming country but also includes coal
mines, gas and oil wells, and livestock ranches.

DEER LODGE

POP: 10,149
AREA: 737
PEOPLE/SQ MI: 13.8

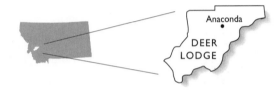

Established: 1865

Deer Lodge was one of the original nine territorial counties, once extending from
the Beaverhead County line to the Canadian border. Today, it is the second-smallest
county, with only 737 square miles. Indians called the Deer Lodge Valley the "lodge
of the white-tailed deer" because animals were attracted to the natural salt licks in
the area. Much of the Deer Lodge Valley was ceded to Powell County in 1901.
Anaconda, the county seat, was platted in 1883 as the site for Marcus Daly's copper
smelter. It was named to honor Daly's Anaconda Copper Mining Company in
Butte. Anaconda/Deer Lodge County is a consolidated city-county government
with executive management.

FALLON

POP: 3,003
AREA: 1,620.3
PEOPLE/SQ MI: 1.9

Established: 1913

This county was named for Benjamin O'Fallon, a U.S. Indian agent
and a nephew of William Clark, the explorer. The grasslands of this prairie county,
which lies within the oil-rich Williston Basin, are now dotted with the workings
of oil and gas production. The county seat of Baker, originally a train station
called Lorraine, was named for A. G. Baker, an engineer with the Chicago,
Milwaukee, St. Paul & Pacific Railroad.

FERGUS

POP: 12,689
AREA: 4,339.3
PEOPLE/SQ MI: 2.9

Established: 1885

This county was named for James Fergus, a pioneer, miner, cattleman, and territorial legislator. Some say its county seat, Lewistown, was named for Captain Meriwether Lewis of the Lewis and Clark Expedition, but more likely the name was taken from Camp Lewis, established in 1874 by Major William H. Lewis of the Seventh Infantry. Fergus County is home to three "island" mountain ranges, the Big Snowy, Judith, and Moccasin Mountains.

FLATHEAD

POP: 69,512
AREA: 5,098.6
PEOPLE/SQ MI: 13.6

Established: 1893

This county and its famous river and large freshwater lake bear the name of the "Flathead" Indian tribe, so named by early explorers, but who were actually Salish Indians. These Indians called the area "the park between the mountains." The county seat of Kalispell, originally called Ashley, was named for the Kalispel, another Salish Indian group that inhabited the area. Big Mountain ski area at Whitefish and Glacier National Park are popular tourist attractions.

GALLATIN

POP: 59,406
AREA: 2,506.8
PEOPLE/SQ MI: 23.7

Established: 1865

Gallatin was one of the original nine counties established by the Territory of Montana. The Gallatin River was named by Lewis and Clark for Albert Gallatin, U.S. secretary of the treasury at the time of the expedition. The county seat, Bozeman, was named for John M. Bozeman, who led the first white settlers into the Gallatin Valley in 1864. This county is a top producer of alfalfa hay, and was once a key national source of canning peas.

GARFIELD

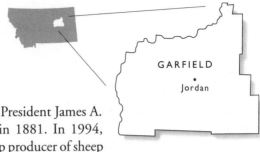

POP: 1,419
AREA: 4,668.2
PEOPLE/SQ MI: 0.3

GARFIELD
•
Jordan

Established: 1919

This county was named for U.S. President James A. Garfield, who was assassinated in 1881. In 1994, Garfield County was the state's top producer of sheep and lambs. Other chief products are cattle and winter wheat. The county seat of Jordan was founded by pioneer Arthur Jordan. This is one of the most isolated parts of the state, but not as isolated as it was before phone service was established in 1935.

GLACIER

POP: 12,677
AREA: 2,994.7
PEOPLE/SQ MI: 4.2

GLACIER

Cut Bank •

Established: 1919

Glacier National Park was the inspiration for the name of this county bordering the park's eastern edge. The Blackfeet Indian Reservation covers much of the county. Cut Bank, the county seat, was named for a deep gorge made by the Cut Bank Creek. The Blackfeet described the creek as "the river that cuts into the white clay banks." Oil, grain, and livestock production are the basic industries.

GOLDEN VALLEY

POP: 980
AREA: 1,175.5
PEOPLE/SQ MI: 0.8

GOLDEN
VALLEY
•
Ryegate

Established: 1920

This county was cut from Musselshell and Sweet Grass Counties and given the picturesque name to attract settlers to the area. One possible source for the name of the county seat of Ryegate is the rich rye grass in its stream bottoms, but another story says it was named by surveyors who camped near a rye field. The most intriguing story is the version that says it was so named because of a fenced field of rye that ran across a road, requiring travelers to open and close gates. The first white settlers were English and Scottish cattle ranchers. A railroad official named the rail station that served this area Golden Valley after observing "a fine field of rye."

GRANITE

POP: 2,619
AREA: 1,727.5
PEOPLE/SQ MI: 1.5

GRANITE

Philipsburg

Established: 1893

Granite Mountain, whose mines produced more than
$40 million worth of gold and silver in the late 1800s, gives
the county its name. The county seat, Philipsburg, was named
for Philip Deidesheimer, the first superintendent of the St. Louis-Montana Gold
and Silver Mining Company, later known as the Philipsburg Mining Company.

HILL

POP: 17,668
AREA: 2,896.4
PEOPLE/SQ MI: 6.1

HILL

Havre

Established: 1912

This county was named for James J. Hill, builder
of the Great Northern Railway and promoter of
homesteading in Montana. Havre, the county seat, was
named for the French seaport of Le Havre by railway offi-
cials, but in Montana it is pronounced HAV-er. Fort Assiniboine was constructed
in the area to police the Blackfeet and Assiniboine tribes in the late 1870s. The
fort was maintained until 1911, when it was sold to the state for an agricultural
experiment station. This county encompasses part of the Rocky Boy's Indian
Reservation.

JEFFERSON

POP: 9,233
AREA: 1,656.7
PEOPLE/SQ MI: 5.6

Boulder

JEFFERSON

Established: 1865

One of the original nine counties of the Montana
Territory, Jefferson County holds the Jefferson River, named
by explorers Lewis and Clark in 1805 for President Thomas
Jefferson. The county seat was first at Jefferson City, then Radersburg, and
finally, Boulder. The Boulder River, known for the large rocks in its streambed
(and strewn around the valley), is the source of the town's name. Jefferson County
boasts the well-preserved ghost town of Elkhorn.

JUDITH BASIN

POP: 2,281
AREA: 1,869.9
PEOPLE/SQ MI: 1.2

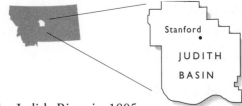

Stanford

JUDITH
BASIN

Established: 1920

Captain William Clark named the Judith River in 1805
to honor his cousin, Miss Judith (Julia) Hancock of
Virginia, whom he later married. Although this county is best known for the
mining of Yogo sapphires, its mainstays are wheat and cattle. The county seat of
Stanford was named either for Major James T. Stanford of Great Falls, or for
Stanfordville, New York, the hometown of J. E. Bower, an early rancher and
sheepman.

LAKE

POP: 24,479
AREA: 1,493.8
PEOPLE/SQ MI: 16.4

LAKE

• Polson

Established: 1923

Flathead Lake inspired the name of this county, one of
the last counties to be formed in Montana. The town of St.
Ignatius was originally St. Ignatius Mission, founded by Jesuit missionaries in
1854. The county seat of Polson was named for David Polson, a stockman from
the Mission Valley. The area is famed for its annual crop of sweet cherries.

LEWIS AND CLARK

POP: 52,785
AREA: 3,461
PEOPLE/SQ MI: 15.3

LEWIS
AND
CLARK

Helena
•

Established: 1865

When originally created as one of the first nine
territorial counties, this county was called Edgerton
County after Sidney Edgerton, first territorial governor. The
county seat of Helena is also the capital of the state. The city was
named after Helena, Minnesota, by John Somerville, formerly a
resident of that Midwestern town. The site of early gold discoveries, the city was
originally called Last Chance City; today, Helena's south Main Street is called
Last Chance Gulch.

LIBERTY

POP: 2,246
AREA: 1,429.8
PEOPLE/SQ MI: 1.6

Established: 1920

The name most likely reflects the patriotic feelings of the inhabitants. The early white settlers were stockmen, followed by homesteaders. Wheat growing and oil and gas production have been important industries. The county seat of Chester was named by a railroad telegraph operator after his hometown of Chester, Pennsylvania.

LINCOLN

POP: 18,678
AREA: 3,612
PEOPLE/SQ MI: 5.2

Established: 1909

This county was named for President Abraham Lincoln. The first white settlement in this part of the state was Libby, now the county seat. Libby is thought to be named for the daughter of an early settler, George Davis. The first commerce of this area was fur trapping and trading. Today, logging operations and sawmills dominate; more than 90 percent of this county is within two national forests, Kootenai and a small part of Kaniksu.

McCONE

POP: 2,121
AREA: 2,642.6
PEOPLE/SQ MI: 0.8

Established: 1919

State Senator George McCone worked to create this county out of Dawson and Richland counties during World War I. Before the homesteading era, this was cattle country. Today, the area economy is based in wheat, ranching, and oil production. Circle, the county seat, was named for the circle brand of the Cross and Twiggly cattle outfit. South of Circle are the Big Sheep Mountains.

Madison

POP: 6,662
AREA: 3,568.6
PEOPLE/SQ MI: 1.9

MADISON

• Virginia City

Established: 1865
Lewis and Clark named the Madison River in honor of
then U.S. Secretary of State James Madison. Virginia City,
hub of the prosperous area gold fields, was incorporated as
Montana's first town in 1864. First called Varina in honor of the
spouse of Jefferson Davis, president of the Confederacy, the name was changed
to Virginia by G. G. Bissell, a local judge and strong Unionist. Fly-fishing
outfitters, shops, and guides are some of the county's leading businesses.

Meagher

POP: 1,826
AREA: 2,391.8
PEOPLE/SQ MI: 0.8

MEAGHER

• White Sulphur Springs

Established: 1866
This county is named for General Thomas Francis Meagher
(pronounced MAR), an Irish patriot, Union army general,
and acting governor of Montana Territory. He mysteriously disappeared from a riverboat on the Missouri River at Fort Benton. The county seat
of White Sulphur Springs was named for the white deposits around local hot
sulfur springs, which local Indians used as medicinal waters.

Mineral

POP: 3,626
AREA: 1,219.9
PEOPLE/SQ MI: 3.0

Superior •

MINERAL

Established: 1914
The many mines and mining prospects in this mountainous
area inspired the name. In 1870, as many as three thousand miners flocked to the Cedar Creek mining district, only to leave for
more prosperous gold fields a few years later. The Clark Fork River
cuts through the center of the county seat of Superior, named by early white
settlers after Superior, Wisconsin.

MISSOULA

POP: 87,130
AREA: 2,598.2
PEOPLE/SQ MI: 33.5

MISSOULA

• Missoula

Established: 1865
Created as part of Washington Territory in 1860,
then incorporated into Montana Territory in 1864,
Missoula County was officially recognized as a county
by the legislature in 1865. The source of the county
name and that of its main town and county seat, Missoula, remains in dispute.
One version says that Indians used to call Hellgate Canyon "Issoul," meaning
"horrible." Another theory is that it is an Indian word meaning "sparkling waters." *The Montana Almanac* of 1959 suggests it is a contraction of the Indian
word, "Im-i-sul-e-etikee," meaning "by or near the place of fear or ambush." A
fourth version says it is a Salish word meaning "river of awe."

MUSSELSHELL

POP: 4,491
AREA: 1,867.2
PEOPLE/SQ MI: 2.4

MUSSELSHELL

• Roundup

Established: 1911
This county got its name from the Musselshell River,
which was named in 1805 by Lewis and Clark, who found mussel shells along
the riverbank. This region was home to the Crow tribe before the arrival of
white settlers. The county seat of Roundup was an annual gathering point for
cattle that grazed on the open ranges of the valley.

PARK

POP: 15,856
AREA: 2,656.2
PEOPLE/SQ MI: 6.0

• Livingston

PARK

Established: 1887
Park County was named for its proximity to
Yellowstone National Park. The most important gold
find in this county was in Emigrant Gulch. One of the
hot springs in the area, near the old town of Chico, is also a
favorite destination for gourmet diners. The county seat is
Livingston, named after Crawford, Charles, or Johnson Livingston, all former
directors of the Northern Pacific Railroad.

PETROLEUM

POP: 527
AREA: 1,653.9
PEOPLE/SQ MI: 0.3

Established: 1925

Petroleum production in the area, particularly in the
Cat Creek oil field discovered in 1920, inspired the name.
Originally Crow Indian territory, it became cattle country in
later years. It was the last county to be formed in the state. The
county seat is Winnett, named for Walter John Winnett, a local cattle owner,
freighter, and store owner. The 1990 census counted fewer citizens here than in
any other Montana county, 519. The 1995 estimate added eight, still the fewest
in the state.

PHILLIPS

POP: 5,151
AREA: 5,139.9
PEOPLE/SQ MI: 1.0

Established: 1915

This county was carved from parts of Blaine and
Valley counties and named for Senator Ben D.
Phillips, a well-known area cattle rancher and mine
owner. An official with the Great Northern Railway named Malta, the county seat, after the Medi-
terranean island.

PONDERA

POP: 6,274
AREA: 1,624.7
PEOPLE/SQ MI: 3.9

Established: 1919

The county was created from parts of Chouteau
and Teton counties. This was Blackfeet territory prior to the
arrival of fur traders, stock-raisers, and agricultural settlers; the Blackfeet Reservation now occupies the northern corners of the county. Most of the available
land was homesteaded by 1912. Wheat production is the county's main industry today. The county seat, Conrad, was named for W. G. Conrad of the Conrad
Investment Co., a major landowner, banker, and politician.

POWDER RIVER

POP: 2,011
AREA: 3297.3
PEOPLE/SQ MI: 0.6

POWDER RIVER

• Broadus

Established: 1919

The Powder River, running through the county
that shares its name, is thought to be named for
the gunpowder-colored sand on its banks. Explorers Lewis and Clark called it the Red Stone River
because of the color of the streamside rocks. Said to be "a mile wide and an inch
deep," it often runs dry. During World War I, Montana soldiers overseas were
known by their battle cry: "Powder River, let 'er buck!" The county seat, Broadus,
is named for the Broaddus family, Powder River settlers. The current spelling is
the result of a misspelling in Washington, D.C., when the town's post office was
established. This is cattle and oil country.

POWELL

POP: 6,859
AREA: 2,326
PEOPLE/SQ MI: 2.9

POWELL

Deer Lodge
•

Established: 1901

In this area, so important in Montana's
earliest days of white settlement, gold was discovered as early as 1852. A few years later, James
and Granville Stuart claimed an official gold find that
developed into a major placer mining operation, Gold
Creek. While miners combed the many drainages and
valleys of this area for their fortunes, others, such as rancher
John Grant, saw treasure in the rich grass of the valleys. This
county was separated from Deer Lodge County, but the town of Deer Lodge
remained the county seat—a source of confusion even today. The town is the
site of the first territorial prison and the present-day state penitentiary. Mount
Powell provided the county with its name, but accounts differ on whether the
mountain, west of Deer Lodge, was named for a county resident or Major John
Wesley Powell, the early geologist and explorer.

PRAIRIE

POP: 1,342
AREA: 1,736.6
PEOPLE/SQ MI: 0.8

PRAIRIE

•Terry

Established: 1915

The name of this county well describes its terrain. Here,
the Powder River joins with the Yellowstone River near the
county seat of Terry. The town is named for General Alfred H. Terry, who
commanded an expedition in 1876 against the Cheyenne and Sioux Indians in
connection with Lt. Col. George A. Custer's campaign. Sheep raising and coal
mining are the county's main industries.

RAVALLI

POP: 32,230
AREA: 2,394.3
PEOPLE/SQ MI: 13.5

Hamilton
•

RAVALLI

Established: 1893

Formed from a portion of Missoula County,
it was named for Father Anthony Ravalli, a Jesuit
missionary who came to the region in 1845.
Stevensville was the first county seat, but Hamilton re-
placed it in 1898. Hamilton probably got its name from
J. W. Hamilton, an early pioneer from whom the right of way for the
Northern Pacific Railroad was acquired. Some believe it was named after J. T.
Hamilton, who surveyed the townsite.

RICHLAND

POP: 10,351
AREA: 2,084.1
PEOPLE/SQ MI: 5.0

RICHLAND

Sidney•

Established: 1914

Like other Montana counties created during the homesteading
era, the name was chosen to attract settlers to the area. An important
fur-trading area in the early 1800s, this county was first settled by stockmen,
who were followed by homesteaders after the turn of the twentieth century. The
county seat of Sidney was named for Sidney Walters, the son of a pioneer family
in the area. This county is a top producer of sugar beets. The county also has
dairy and grain farms and a sugar beet processing facility.

ROOSEVELT

POP: 11,243
AREA: 2,355.6
PEOPLE/SQ MI: 4.8

ROOSEVELT
Wolf Point

Established: 1919

This county was cut from Sheridan County and named for Theodore Roosevelt, president of the United States and ranch owner in neighboring North Dakota. The Fort Peck Reservation, home to the Assiniboine and Yankton Sioux Indians, covers much of the county. The county seat is Wolf Point, whose name might have come from a stack of frozen gray wolf carcasses left by fur trappers along the river where the steamboats landed. Other sources say the town could have been named for a hill that resembled a wolf or for the point where Wolf Creek meets the Missouri.

ROSEBUD

POP: 10,881
AREA: 5,012.4
PEOPLE/SQ MI: 2.2

Forsyth

ROSEBUD

Established: 1901

The Rosebud River and the county were named for the profusion of wild rose bushes along the riverbanks. The county seat of Forsyth was named for General James W. Forsyth, one of the first U.S. Army officers to land in this area by steamer. The town of Colstrip grew up around what was once known as the largest "open pit" coal mine in the world.

SANDERS

POP: 10,089
AREA: 2,762.3
PEOPLE/SQ MI: 3.7

SANDERS
Thompson Falls

Established: 1905

Wilbur Fisk Sanders, pioneer, vigilante, and U.S. senator from Montana, inspired the name for this county. The county seat, Thompson Falls, was named for David Thompson, a fur trader, and for the natural falls of the Clark Fork River. Sanders was formed from part of Missoula County. The Noxon Rapids Dam and Reservoir are located in this county. Wild horses once found good winter range in the protected areas near Plains, formerly called Horse Plains.

SHERIDAN

POP: 4,431
AREA: 1,676.7
PEOPLE/SQ MI: 2.6

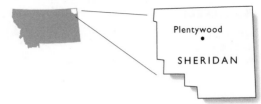

Established: 1913
This county was one of the last areas to be settled in Montana. It was named for General Philip H. Sheridan. The county seat of Plentywood is said to have been named when a cattle outfit seeking wood as it crossed the treeless prairie was directed to a place of "plenty wood." Sheridan County's main industries are wheat and oil production.

SILVER BOW

POP: 34,795
AREA: 718
PEOPLE/SQ MI: 48.5

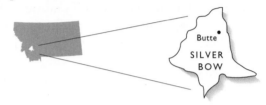

Established: 1881
The county of Silver Bow and the city of Butte are consolidated under an elected-executive form of government. The name might have originated from Silver Bow Creek, where legend has it that three prospectors saw a shaft of sun shining on the curves of the creek. The county seat, first called Butte City, was known for a century as "the richest hill on earth." Miners named the city for the peak called "Big Butte," which rises 6,369 feet above sea level. Although Silver Bow is the smallest county in land area, it has been of great economic importance to the state for more than 100 years. The mines of the Atlantic Richfield Company (formerly owned by the Anaconda Company) were closed in 1983, but mining operations were reopened in 1985 by Montana Resources, a division of the Washington Corporation.

STILLWATER

POP: 7,466
AREA: 1,794.7
PEOPLE/SQ MI: 4.2

Established: 1913
The name of the Stillwater River is reputed to have come from a Crow legend about a beautiful woman and her betrothed who died there. Stillwater County was organized from parts of Carbon, Sweet Grass, and Yellowstone Counties. The entire county was once Crow Indian Reservation land. Stillwater's county seat, Columbus, began as a stage station on the Yellowstone Trail. It is a shipping center for the farm and ranch lands around it. The Columbus quarry furnished stone for the State Capitol in Helena.

SWEET GRASS

POP: 3,374
AREA: 1,855.2
PEOPLE/SQ MI: 1.8

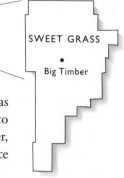

Established: 1895

This county, named for the rich grassland in the area, was originally Crow Indian Reservation land, but was opened to non-Indian settlement in 1891. The county seat, Big Timber, was probably named for the very large cottonwoods that once grew along the creek of the same name.

TETON

POP: 6,371
AREA: 2,272.6
PEOPLE/SQ MI: 2.8

Established: 1893

Teton County was cut from Chouteau County and named for the ridge and river. In pre-pioneer days, the area was controlled by the Blackfeet Indians. Choteau, the county seat, grew up around two trading posts, which moved to the site in 1876. Although named for the same early entrepreneurial family that inspired the name for the county of Chouteau, the spelling of the town differs.

TOOLE

POP: 5,103
AREA: 1,910.9
PEOPLE/SQ MI: 2.7

Established: 1914

Joseph K. Toole, the first governor of the state of Montana, inspired the name for this county, which was formed from parts of Hill and Teton counties. Wheat and oil are its main industries.
The county seat of Shelby is named for Peter Shelby, a railroad executive. The Kevin-Sunburst oil field, discovered in 1920, turned this homesteading area into a wild boom town. The town gained fame after it hosted a world championship heavyweight boxing match in 1923 between Jack Dempsey and Tommy Gibbons.

TREASURE

POP: 837
AREA: 978.9
PEOPLE/SQ MI: 0.9

Established: 1919
This county, originally Sioux Indian territory, was named to attract
settlers to the area. All of its towns are located on the banks of the
Yellowstone River. The county seat of Hysham is named for Charles Hysham, a
Texas trail herder with the Flying E Ranch. The main agricultural products of
the county are cattle, hay, and sugar beets.

VALLEY

POP: 8,462
AREA: 4,920.9
PEOPLE/SQ MI: 1.7

Established: 1893
Named for its location in the Milk River Valley,
this county is one of the largest (in area) in the
state. This region was a major homesteader destination in the early 1900s. Glasgow, the county seat
on the Milk River, is one of the oldest communities in northeast Montana. During the building of
the Fort Peck Dam, it was a bustling area. An
official of the Great Northern Railway named the community after Glasgow,
Scotland. The Fort Peck Indian Reservation covers the eastern part of the county.

WHEATLAND

POP: 2,425
AREA: 1,423.2
PEOPLE/SQ MI: 1.3

Established: 1917
Before the days of extensive wheat fields, the area that is
now Wheatland County was Crow Indian country. A gold
find in the Little Belt Mountains brought prospectors to the area in 1870. Stock
growing began in the 1870s, and with the establishment of two railroads in the
early 1900s, the homesteaders arrived. The county seat of Harlowton was named
for Richard Harlow, who built the Montana Railroad, affectionately known to
its riders as "The Jawbone."

WIBAUX

POP: 1,170
AREA: 889.3
PEOPLE/SQ MI: 1.3

Wibaux

WIBAUX

Established: 1914

An early Montana cattle baron, Pierre Wibaux (pronounced WEE-bo), inspired the name for this county and its county seat. In the late 1800s, the Northern Pacific Railroad built a stock-yard here and stimulated the economy. The town of Wibaux was originally known as Mingusville, supposedly after two early pioneers, Minnie and Gus.

YELLOWSTONE

POP: 124,655
AREA: 2,635.2
PEOPLE/SQ MI: 47.3

YELLOWSTONE

Billings

Established: 1883

Early French trappers called the Yellowstone River the Roche Jaune, for "yellow rock." Yellowstone is Montana's most populous county and the largest farm-producing area in the state. The farming is diversified, but the main products are sugar beets, wheat, beans, and livestock. Billings, the county seat, is named for Frederick Billings, lawyer, former president of the Northern Pacific Railroad, and philanthropist. Captain William Clark spotted an unusual pillar of rock near Billings and called it Pompy's Tower, for Sacajawea's son Baptiste, whom he nicknamed "Little Pomp." Today it is known as Pompeys Pillar, renamed when the Lewis and Clark journals were published, and is a national historic landmark.

Sources for population and land area figures from U.S. Bureau of the Census, compiled by Census and Economic Information Center, Montana Department of Commerce.

notable
Montanans

Sacagawea (1789-1812?)

Born in Idaho, one of the most romantic persons in American history is the Shoshone Indian woman who lived with her people near the Three Forks of the Missouri River until she was captured by another tribe and taken east to Hidatsa-Mandan villages in present-day North Dakota. Married to French-Canadian trapper Toussaint Charbonneau, she accompanied her husband when he joined the Lewis and Clark Expedition as guide and translator. Sacagawea proved fearless and helpful as she traveled with her infant son and was particularly vital in helping the Corps of Discovery acquire horses from Lemhi Shoshone relatives, so that the corps could cross the Rockies. She later received a Jefferson peace medal; the date and place of her death are uncertain.

This statue of Sacagawea was sculpted by Leonard Crunelle in 1910 and now belongs to the State Historical Society of North Dakota.

Charles M. Russell (1864-1926)

"Charlie" Russell was one of America's best-known Western artists, but he was also a storyteller with firsthand knowledge of a large portion of Montana's history. Russell's drawings, paintings, and sculptures capture the spirit of life on the Western frontier. Though born in Oak Hill, Missouri, he wandered to Montana to work at age 16 as a hunter and cowboy. With a photographic vision, he rendered vivid scenes of the West in the 1880s that gained fame outside Montana by the early 1900s. He is the only artist to be honored in Statuary Hall in the Capitol in Washington, D.C.

Montana Historical Society

State Symbols

The following descriptions of Montana's state symbols appear in chronological order, according to when the legislature designated them as "official."

The Great Seal

The official Great Seal of the State of Montana is kept under the custody of the Secretary of State and is used to validate all official state documents. It is directly impressed or embossed on the documents.

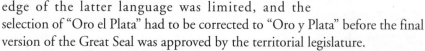

The designing of the seal was one of the first acts of the Montana territorial government, established in 1865. After choosing "gold and silver" as the state motto, a special committee debated whether to denote the phrase in English or in Spanish. Unfortunately, the group's knowledge of the latter language was limited, and the selection of "Oro el Plata" had to be corrected to "Oro y Plata" before the final version of the Great Seal was approved by the territorial legislature.

The seal shows the Great Falls of the Missouri River; mountain scenery; a central depiction of a miner's pick, a shovel, and a plow; and the state motto along the bottom of the circle.

The seal pays tribute to major components of the history of the state. Agriculture, mining, mountains, water, and timber have been and will continue to be the source of wealth, controversy, and development in Montana.

A tiled replica of the Great Seal can be found on the floor of the rotunda at the State Capitol.

Bitterroot

The bitterroot, *Lewisia rediviva*, was selected as Montana's first official symbol in 1895 and is the floral emblem of Montana. The state flower is a member of the purslane family of New World herbs and shrubs. It was highly valued for food by the Indians of the Northwest long before Meriwether Lewis and William Clark collected the exquisite lily-like, pink blossoms on their 1806 homeward trip through the valleys of western Montana.

Though universal suffrage was many years away, women were allowed to vote with the men on the question of the state flower in late 1894. It was no contest. The bitterroot garnered 3,621 votes. Evening primrose finished a distant second with 787, followed by wild rose with 668.

The bitterroot was such an important part of the diet of the Flathead, Kalispel, Pend d'Oreille, Spokane, and Nez Perce tribes that spring tribal migrations were planned to find the plant along familiar riverbanks and hillsides. The women of the tribes used a digging stick to gather the root, prized for its starch and sugar content.

The bitterroot can be found on slopes and ridges on both sides of the continental divide of western Montana. It can thrive on little moisture through the summer but likes lots of sunshine. The low-set blossoms flower in late spring and early summer. The rosette of twelve to eighteen leaves ranges from deep rose-red to the more typical pink, and the blossoms turn white after a few days in the sun.

The Flag

In the spring of 1898, Colonel Harry C. Kessler mustered and trained a group of volunteers at Fort William Henry Harrison, west of Helena, for the war against Spain. Kessler commissioned a special banner to distinguish the First Montana

Infantry, U.S.V., from other units in the "Philippine Insurrection." An unknown seamstress embroidered her interpretation of the state's Great Seal on the dark blue background of a 60- by 44-inch silk flag. The 1905 Legislative Assembly honored the First Montana Infantry by establishing an exact rendition of their flag as the official state flag.

In 1981, the word "Montana" was added to the flag, above the seal.

Western Meadowlark

Explorer Meriwether Lewis noted the western meadowlark, *Sturnella neglecta*, in the June 22, 1805, entry of his journal made while crossing what is now Montana. Lewis described the meadowlark's similarities with the eastern meadowlark of his homeland but commented that the song of the western cousin was richer and more varied. It consists of a loud, clear, melodic warble.

The chunky, brown-speckled bird has a bright yellow vest and black, V-shaped necklace. There is a patch of white on each side of its short, white tail. Its flight pattern consists of several short, rapid wing beats alternated with brief periods of sailing.

In 1930, Montana's schoolchildren were polled to select the bird that most represented their state. The responses overwhelmingly favored the western meadowlark. The 1931 Legislature agreed with the choice and declared the western meadowlark the official bird of Montana. The states of Kansas, Nebraska, North Dakota, Oregon, and Wyoming also designated the meadowlark as state bird.

Ponderosa Pine

The majestic ponderosa pine can be found on many hills and mountains of Montana. It is the dominant pine of the entire Rocky Mountain region, from Canada to Mexico. *Pinus ponderosa* was invaluable to settlers, who harvested millions of board feet of ponderosa lumber for railroad ties, mining braces, telegraph poles, bridges, and homes.

At maturity (about 150 years), a ponderosa pine is approximately 20 to 30 inches in diameter and from 60 to 200 feet tall. Its seed cones are 3 to 5 inches long, and its needles measure 8 to 10 inches. The species has a number of other popular names, including bull pine, black jack pine, western pitch pine, and western yellow pine.

In 1908, Helena's schoolchildren picked the ponderosa pine as the tree that best represented Montana, but it was not until the Montana Federation of Garden Clubs waged a yearlong campaign that the 1949 Legislature passed a resolution to officially honor this "king of the forest."

The largest known ponderosa pine in Montana stands at a Department of Fish, Wildlife & Parks viewing site about 3.4 miles up Fish Creek Road off Interstate 90 between Alberton and Superior. It measures 78 inches in diameter and is more than 194 feet tall.

Montana, The Song

The song "Montana" was virtually an overnight sensation when it was first introduced in 1910. A well-known songwriter and theatrical producer, Joseph Howard, had written several musical hits of the day, including "Shuffle Off to Buffalo" and "I Wonder Who's Kissing Her Now." He and his troupe were touring the state with a performance of *The Goddess of Liberty*. At an after-theater party in Butte, Howard accepted a challenge by his hostess to write a song about Montana. He retired to the music room and worked out a tune. Another guest, Charles C. Cohen, city editor for the *Butte Miner*, helped pen the lyrics.

When Howard got to Helena later that month with his troupe, he found an audience eager to hear the catchy "Montana" song. They requested twelve encores of the new song before proceeding with the play. At a social gathering following the performance, Governor Edwin L. Norris enthusiastically proclaimed the tune Montana's official song. The Legislature made it official in 1945.

The lyrics go, in part:

Tell me of that Treasure State,
story always new.
Tell of its beauties grand
and its hearts so true....

Montana, Montana—
glory of the West.
Of all the states from coast to coast
you're easily the best.

Copies of "Montana" can be obtained for $3.50 from Shodair Hospital, Box 5539, Helena, MT 59604.

Bluebunch Wheatgrass

Of the many official Montana symbols, the official grass—bluebunch wheatgrass—was the most important to Montana's first inhabitants as well as the later settlers. Both depended on the wildlife and domesticated animals that were nourished by this important native grass. The 1973 Legislature officially recognized the grass, with encouragement from a community development group from Havre.

Bluebunch wheatgrass (*Agropyron spicatum,* or pursh) also has the widest range of all Montana's official symbols. It is found from border to border in all types of soil. It greens up early in spring and peeks out from under the earliest fall snows to provide wildlife habitat, valuable forage for all types of animals, and protection of the watershed.

Grass *roots*

Some seventy Montana place names (cities, rivers, mountains) have "grassy" names, like Grassrange, Haystack Butte, Lodge Grass, and Grassy Mountain.

Sapphire and Moss Agate

The 1969 Montana Legislature honored both the sapphire and the moss agate as the state gemstones.

Many variations of the exquisite moss agate are found in abundance along the Yellowstone River and are sought after by hobbyists and jewelry makers. Contrary to its name, a moss agate does not really contain fossilized moss.

It also goes by the names landscape agate, scenic agate, Montana agate, plume agate, and Yellowstone River agate. The best spot to find the agate is in terraced gravel deposits on the hills above and on sand and gravel bars along the Yellowstone River, from Billings to Sidney.

The world-famous Yogo sapphires are one of Montana's most stunning exports, with over $40 million in precious gemstones over the years. The beautiful cornflower-blue gems even grace the Royal Crown Jewel Collection in London. The world's largest cut Yogo, 10.2 carats, is housed in the Smithsonian Institution in Washington, D.C.

The Yogo sapphire is unique for its ability to retain its brilliance under artificial light. Other types of sapphires generally absorb such light and appear black and lusterless.

Blackspotted Cutthroat Trout

A poll of the state's 200,000 resident fishing enthusiasts inspired the 1977 Legislature to designate the blackspotted cutthroat trout as the official Montana state fish.

The cutthroat species, *Oncorhynchus clarki,* bears the name of Captain William Clark. The taxonomy also honors his partner, Meriwether Lewis, by naming the westslope cutthroat *Oncorhynchus clarki lewisi.* The journals of the Lewis and Clark Expedition mention a "sumptuous" meal of 16- to 23-inch-long

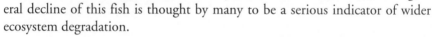

blackspotted cutthroat trout caught at the Great Falls of the Missouri River.

Today, the number of blackspotted cutthroat trout is depressed in much of the Upper Missouri River drainage, and it has been designated a sensitive species by the USDA Forest Service. The general decline of this fish is thought by many to be a serious indicator of wider ecosystem degradation.

Cutthroats have been overfished in many areas because they are generally easier to catch than other trout species. They are also highly vulnerable to competition from other species and to hybridization with rainbow trout.

The Grizzly Bear

In 1982, more than 55,000 students in 425 schools joined in the selection of an official state animal. They nominated seventy-four animals, compiled voter registration lists, conducted lively campaigns, and staged primary and general elections. In the final statewide tally of votes, the grizzly bear, *Ursus arctos horribilis,* won by a large margin over the runner-up, elk.

Montana Melody

A proposal was made in 1983 to replace "Montana" with a more recently com-posed song, "Montana Melody," written by Carleen Harvey and LeGrande Harvey. Lawmakers were reluctant to trade in the old song for the newer model, even though most state residents admit knowing only the refrain of the old one. As a compromise, "Montana Melody" was declared the official state ballad.

Sheet music for "Montana Melody" is available for $5 from Grant Hill Records, P.O. Box 4682, Missoula, MT 59806.

Duck-billed Dinosaur

The duck-billed dinosaur, *Maiasaura peeblesorum*, was se-lected by the 1985 Legislature as the official Montana state fossil after middle school students from Livingston collected eight thousand petition signatures from sixty schools in the state.

The name *Maiasaura* means "good mother lizard"; *peeblesorum* honors the Peebles family, on whose Choteau-area ranch the discoveries were made. The area, known as Egg Mountain, has the world's largest known accumulation of dinosaur fossils.

The unearthing of the remains has provided valuable evidence that duck-billed dinosaurs nested in extensive colonies and had nests 6 feet in diameter that contained as many as 20 eggs. The duck-billed dinosaur, when newly hatched, was not quite 14 inches long and weighed about 1.5 pounds but matured to measure more than 30 feet long and weigh about 3 tons.

Legal State Holidays

Each Sunday
New Year's Day, January 1
Martin Luther King, Jr. Day, the third Monday in January
Presidents Day, the third Monday in February
Memorial Day, the last Monday in May
Independence Day, July 4
Labor Day, the first Monday in September
Columbus Day, the second Monday in October
Veterans' Day, November 11
Thanksgiving Day, the fourth Thursday in November
Christmas Day, December 25
State general election day, the first Tuesday after the first Monday in November

If any of the holidays above falls upon a Sunday, the Monday following is a legal holiday. All other days are business days, including the Friday before a holiday that occurs on a Saturday.

*Mon*table *ontanans*

Gary Cooper (1901-1961)

One of America's favorite movie stars was born Frank James Cooper in Helena. Cooper began as a silent film extra during the 1920s and by 1937 was America's highest-paid entertainer. He appeared in more than 90 movies and won Academy Awards for his performances in *Sergeant York* (1941) and *High Noon* (1952). One of his last roles as a Western hero was as Doc Frail in *The Hanging Tree*, in a script by Montana author Dorothy M. Johnson. Some of his other time-honored films include *The Virginian, For Whom the Bell Tolls, Mr. Deeds Goes to Town, The Pride of the Yankees,* and *A Farewell to Arms.*

Montana Historical Society

Dorothy M. Johnson (1905-1984)

Born in Iowa, she grew up in Whitefish and became one of the most beloved portrayers of the history and heroes of the American West. The movies *The Man Who Shot Liberty Valance, The Hanging Tree,* and *A Man Called Horse* are based on Johnson's stories, which appeared regularly in many national magazines, including the *Saturday Evening Post*. After a 15-year career as a book and magazine editor in New York, she came home and worked as an editor at the *Whitefish Pilot*, later teaching journalism at The University of Montana in Missoula. She died at her home there.

Montana Historical Society

Further Reading:

Ashby, Norma B., and Rex C. Myers. *Symbols of Montana*. Helena: Montana Historical Society, 1989.

Cheney, Roberta Carkeek. *Names on the Face of Montana: The Story of Montana's Place Names*. Missoula: Mountain Press Publishing Company, 1983.

DeSanto, Jerry. *The Montana State Flower Bitterroot*. Babb, Mt.: LERE Press, 1993.

Eagle Walking Turtle. *Indian America*. Santa Fe: John Muir Press, 1991. **Tribal histories and cultural information for visitors.**

Federal Writers' Project of the Work Projects Administration. *Montana: A State Guide Book*. New York: Hastings House, 1949. **Recently reissued by The University of Arizona Press as The WPA Guide to 1930s Montana.**

Guthrie, A. B., Jr. *The Big Sky*. Boston: Houghton Mifflin, 1947.

McRae, W.C. and Judy Jewell. *Montana Handbook*. Third edition. Chico, Ca.: Moon Publications, Inc., 1996.

Montana: The Last Best Place. Helena: Falcon Publishing Co., 1993.

Montana On My Mind. Helena: Falcon Publishing Co., 1991. **A book for the coffee table. Color photos by Michael S. Sample and quotes from A. B. Guthrie, Chet Huntley, Jeannette Rankin, Mike Mansfield, and other Montanans.**

Montana Writers' Project. *Montanans' Golden Anniversary, Humorous History, Handbook and 1940 Almanac*. Helena, State Publishing Co., 1940.

Murphy, Alexandra. *Graced by Pines*. Missoula: Mountain Press Publishing Company, 1994. **Essays on the cultural and natural history of the ponderosa pine.**

Tirrell, Norma. *Montana*. Oakland: Compass American Guides, Inc., 1991. **A thoughtful description of Montana culture and places.**

Toole, K. Ross. *Twentieth Century Montana: A State of Extremes*. Norman, Ok.: University of Oklahoma Press., 1972.

Wilson, Gary. *Honky-Tonk Town: Havre's Boot-legging Days*. Havre: High-Line Books, 1986. **Old-time Havre comes to life in this good read.**

And for Reference:

Montana Atlas and Gazetteer. Freeport, Maine: DeLorme Mapping Co., 1994.

Montana State University. *The Montana Almanac, 1959-60*. Missoula: Montana State University Press, 1958.

CLIMATE *and* WEATHER

MONTANA HISTORIAN HARRY FRITZ declared Montana to be a "land of contrasts," and nowhere are those contrasts more apparent than in the state's diverse topography and the vicissitudes of weather caused by the terrain.

The boundary of Montana forms a rough rectangle that contains parts of two major physiographic regions of North America. The western third of the state (about 49,000 square miles) contains the Rocky Mountain region. Montana's portion of the Rockies consists of long, roughly parallel mountain chains oriented along a northwest-to-southeast axis. This area of the state is covered with forests, mountain ranges, lakes, basins, and valleys. The largest of the valleys are from 10 to 20 miles wide, and from 25 to 100 miles long. The Continental Divide meanders along ridges of the western mountains, entering from the north in Glacier National Park, continuing south, then taking a slow arc to the west near Helena and Butte before heading along the Anaconda and Pintler mountains to the Idaho border.

The eastern edge of Montana's Rockies gives way to the central portion of the state: some isolated or "island" mountain ranges (the Belts, the Snowies, the Crazies), broad benchlands and valleys, and an expanse of prairie—the Great Plains—that extends through eastern Montana and beyond the state's eastern, northeastern, and southeastern borders. The geological history of the non-mountainous parts of the state includes vast lakes and semitropical marshes, inhabited by dinosaurs. The valley lakes dried up and left fertile ground for high plains vegetation like bunch grass and bluejoint. This soil, though much has been turned

photo: Michael Sample

over and blown away, is still a tremendous resource, contributing to the third of Montana that is considered arable.

The size and topography of Montana contribute to wide climatic variations across the state. The barrier created by the high elevations of the Rocky Mountains has an inescapable effect on Montana's weather.

Winds from the Pacific Ocean temper the climate west of the Rocky Mountains. The winters are generally milder and the summers cooler there than on the eastern plains. To the east, the semi-arid Great Plains are influenced by humid air moving north from the Gulf of Mexico in late spring and summer, from the Pacific in the fall, and from Canada in the winter.

Montana's weather has a reputation for being extreme and unpredictable. Our temperature extremes certainly are noteworthy, with the lows dipping below minus 35 degrees (all temperatures in this chapter are given in Fahrenheit) in the high mountains and the northeast in winter, and the highs topping 100 degrees, most often in the middle and lower Yellowstone Valley.

In measurable reality, though, Montana's temperatures are no more severe than in other states along the northern tier of the U.S. Duluth and Minneapolis/St. Paul, Minnesota, for example, are on average colder than most of Montana's major cities. Although Montana weather can be temperamental any given day in any season, our overall climate is generally milder than the extremes reported from some of the state's more infamous recording stations such as West Yellowstone, which often records the lowest temperature in the continental U.S. on national weather charts.

Compared to the U.S. average, the state's relatively low precipitation and low relative humidity take the edge off the hottest days of summer and the coldest days of winter.

The Big Skies

The following pie charts represent 365 days of weather (sunrise to sunset) and are divided into the mean number of days of each condition —clear (white), partly cloudy (gray), and cloudy (black).

Billings

mean based on 1939-90

Great Falls

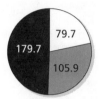

mean based on 1937-90

Miles City

mean based on 1972-90

Helena

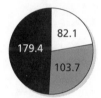

mean based on 1940-90

Glasgow

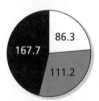

mean based on 1955-90

Kalispell

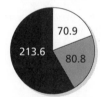

mean based on 1949-90

Havre

mean based on 1971-90

Missoula

mean based on 1944-90

Source: Joseph M. Caprio and Gerald A. Nielsen. Climate Atlas of Montana—1992.
Bozeman: Montana State University Extension Service.

Hottest Places in Montana*

Location	County	Average Daily High in July (°F)
1. Hardin	Big Horn	91.7
2. Yellowtail Dam	Big Horn	90.7
3. Lame Deer	Rosebud	89.9
4. Birney	Rosebud	89.8
5. Hysham	Treasure	89.6
6. Jordan	Garfield	89.5
7. 11 miles northeast of Ingomar	Rosebud	89.4
8. Ballantine	Yellowstone	89.2
9. water plant at Billings	Yellowstone	89.1
10. Plevna	Fallon	89.0
11. Crow Agency	Big Horn	88.9
12. Roundup	Musselshell	88.9
13. 24 miles northeast of Roy	Fergus	88.6
14. Glendive	Dawson	88.3
15. Loma	Chouteau	87.9
16. 9 miles southwest of Otter	Powder River	87.9
17. Circle	McCone	87.5
18. Colstrip	Rosebud	87.4
19. 2 miles east of Poplar	Roosevelt	87.4
20. power plant at Fort Peck	Valley	87.2
21. Joliet	Carbon	87.2
22. 18 miles southwest of Haxby	Garfield	87.3
23. ranger station at Libby	Lincoln	87.3
24. Savage	Richland	87.3
25. Columbus	Stillwater	87.0

* Based on maximum normal temperatures, 1961-1990, for reporting weather stations.
Source: James R. Owenby and D. S. Ezell, Monthly Station Normals of Temperature, Precipitation, and Heating and Cooling Degree Days, 1961-90, Montana. *Asheville, N.C.: National Climatic Data Center, 1992.*

Hottest Readings

The mercury rose to 117 degrees in Glendive on July 20, 1893, and again in Medicine Lake, in the northeastern corner of the state, on July 5, 1937.

Rain and Snowfall

As a consequence of its interior position on the continent, and because the west winds lose moisture over the mountains, Montana has relatively light precipitation. The annual average precipitation (rain and melted snow) for the entire state is 15 inches.

In the valleys on the westward side of the Continental Divide, the annual average is just under 20 inches. The annual average for the eastern side of the divide is about 13 inches, but local averages vary widely. Along the Clarks Fork of the Yellowstone River in southern Carbon County is the driest spot in the state, receiving less than 6 inches a year. Fort Benton receives close to the state's average of 15 inches. An unmanned weather station near Grinnell Glacier in Glacier National Park is the wettest place measured in the state, with an annual average of nearly 120 inches.

The wettest months in Montana also vary across the state: December and January in the mountains either side of the Continental Divide, May and June for the plains and valleys. The driest months are January and February in the eastern plains and valleys, and July in the west and in the mountains east of the divide.

Summit, on U.S. Highway 2 south of Glacier Park, holds several records for moisture. It received 55.5 inches of precipitation in 1953. Summit was also hit by Montana's greatest snowfall ever, in January 1972. The storm lasted

Wettest Places in Montana*

Location	County	Annual Average Precipitation (in inches)
1. 12 miles northeast of Bozeman	Gallatin	35.15
2. 18 miles north of Troy	Lincoln	34.90
3. Hungry Horse	Flathead	34.48
4. 2 miles northwest of Heron	Sanders	33.86
5. Hebgen Dam	Gallatin	30.11
6. Trout Creek Ranger Station	Sanders	29.72
7. West Glacier	Flathead	34.48
8. 7 miles south of Shonkin	Chouteau	28.68
9. East Glacier	Glacier	28.56
10. Swan Lake	Lake	28.43
11. 3 miles east of Haugan	Mineral	27.60
12. Lindbergh Lake	Lake	27.58
13. Red Lodge	Carbon	25.82
14. 32 miles southeast of Libby	Lincoln	25.55
15. 2 miles west of Cooke City	Park	25.54
16. Mystic Lake	Carbon	25.14
17. Troy	Lincoln	25.18
18. 10 miles south of Lewistown	Fergus	24.18
19. Olney	Flathead	23.04
20. Thompson Falls	Sanders	22.97
21. 10 miles southwest of Gallatin Gateway	Gallatin	22.84
22. Whitefish	Flathead	22.51
23. 13 miles south of Bigfork	Flathead	22.41
24. West Yellowstone	Gallatin	22.14
25. Polebridge	Flathead	21.88

* Based on annual precipitation normals, 1961-1990, for reporting weather stations near populated areas.
Source: James R. Owenby and D. S. Ezell, Monthly Station Normals of Temperature, Precipitation, and Heating and Cooling Degree Days, 1961-90, Montana. Asheville, N.C.: National Climatic Data Center, 1992.

six days and dropped more than six feet of snow (77.5 inches), including a one-day record of 44 inches on January 20. Summit normally gets about 40 inches of precipitation a year. The record for 24-hour rainfall belongs to Circle, where 11.5 inches fell on June 20, 1921.

For total snowfall during one winter, Cooke City is tops. Almost 35 feet (418.1 inches) of the white stuff fell during the winter of 1977-1978.

Winter

 The truth is the infamous Montana winter rarely settles in for keeps. Montana's cold spells, blasts of arctic air that can bring blizzards and whose chill can hang in the valleys for days, are frequently broken up by a sunny mildness and refreshingly warm, dry chinook winds from the west.

Winters in the Great Plains are generally colder than in the west. North-central and eastern Montana are subject to waves of that frigid arctic air from six to twelve times each winter; the entire state can become enveloped by such cold waves about twice each winter. Some of the cold waves, often referred to as the "Siberian Express," can push temperatures to 50 below zero, but extremes like that do not occur in most winter seasons.

Source: Climatological Data for Montana, annual reports 1980-89, *National Oceanic and Atmospheric Administration, U.S. Dept. of Commerce*

The winter of 96

A few weeks in January and February 1996 illustrate the weather extremes that are possible during a Montana winter. On January 14, much of the state experienced a tropical heat wave. Winter heat records fell with readings like 61 degrees at Billings and 52 degrees at Butte. A few days later, a blizzard buried much of the state in more than 10 inches of snow. The following near record low temperatures were recorded February 2:

Helena	-42	Cut Bank	-37
Belgrade	-40	Great Falls	-35

By February 5, warm winds blew in, and two days later, most of the snow in the valleys was all but melted. The downside of the balmy weather was a destructive four days of flooding.

Coldest Reading

The state record cold temperature also stands as the lowest temperature ever recorded in the lower 48 states: 70 degrees below zero. It was recorded January 20, 1954, by an unpaid observer for the United States Weather Bureau who saw the mercury plummet to 69.7 degrees below zero at a mining camp just west of Rogers Pass along the Continental Divide. Based on the observer's written remarks about the condition of the thermometers, and subsequent laboratory tests in Washington, D.C., the official temperature was pegged at 70 below. The previous record of minus 66 degrees was recorded at West Yellowstone, Montana.

Coldest Places in Montana*

Location	County	Average Daily Low in Jan. (°F)
1. Westby	Sheridan	-5.8
2. 10 miles north of Opheim	Valley	-3.3
3. 12 miles southeast of Opheim	Valley	-2.9
4. Redstone	Sheridan	-2.7
5. Culbertson	Roosevelt	-2.0
6. border station at Raymond	Sheridan	-2.0
7. 3 miles southeast of Medicine Lake	Sheridan	-1.3
8. 4 miles northeast of Forks	Phillips	-0.5
9. West Yellowstone	Gallatin	0.2
10. 2 miles east of Poplar	Roosevelt	0.0
11. Berdette	Roosevelt	0.1
12. Lakeview	Beaverhead	0.1
13. Simpson	Phillips	0.2
14. Terry	Prairie	0.5
15. Cooke City	Park	1.0
16. 35 miles south of Malta	Phillips	1.0
17. Wibaux	Wibaux	1.1
18. Glasgow (airport)	Valley	1.2
19. 4 miles northwest of Lustre	Valley	1.3
20. Glendive	Dawson	1.4
21. Harlem	Blaine	1.4
22. Hebgen Dam	Gallatin	1.6
23. Wisdom	Beaverhead	1.7
24. Sidney	Richland	1.8
25. 4 miles northwest of Mizpah	Custer	2.0

* Based on minimum normal temperatures, 1961-1990, for reporting weather stations.
Source: James R. Owenby and D. S. Ezell, Monthly Station Normals of Temperature, Precipitation, and Heating and Cooling Degree Days, 1961-90, Montana. Asheville, N.C.: National Climatic Data Center, 1992.

Growing Season

The growing season varies from 39 days a year in the high mountain valleys of the southwest to 150 in scattered areas of the Yellowstone River basin. These figures were averaged over a 40-year period:

Frost-free Days

City	Average Last Frost Date	Average Earliest Frost Date	Average Annual Frost-free Days
Augusta	May 29	September 10	104
Big Timber	May 20	September 20	123
Billings	May 15	September 25	133
Bozeman	May 28	September 12	107
Bridger	May 20	September 23	126
Browning	June 7	August 30	84
Butte	June 8	August 28	81
Choteau	May 30	September 12	105
Columbia Falls	June 1	September 8	99
Cut Bank	May 27	September 12	108
Darby	June 4	September 10	99
Deer Lodge	June 4	September 7	95
Dillon	May 31	September 7	99
Ennis	June 2	September 11	101
Forsyth	May 19	September 26	130
Glasgow	May 19	September 20	124
Glendive	May 10	September 27	139
Great Falls	May 14	September 26	135
Hamilton	May 24	September 23	122
Harlowton	June 3	September 7	96
Havre	May 9	September 23	138
Helena	May 12	September 23	134
Jordan	May 24	September 9	108
Kalispell	May 12	September 23	135
Lewistown	June 2	September 17	107
Libby	June 8	August 27	79
Livingston	May 26	September 18	116
Miles City	May 5	October 3	150
Missoula	May 18	September 23	112
Ovando	June 19	July 28	39
Philipsburg	June 16	August 10	55
Polson	May 10	September 28	142
Red Lodge	June 5	September 17	104
Roundup	May 16	September 22	129
Shelby	May 27	September 14	126
Sidney	May 18	September 21	126
Springs	June 6	September 11	97
St. Ignatius	May 21	September 17	119
Superior	June 5	August 30	85
Thompson Falls	May 25	September 17	115

Source: Sandra Perrin. Organic Gardening in Montana and the Northwest. *Missoula: Montana Reconnaissance Project, 1981.*
Note: Averages based on approximately 40-year records.

Precipitation Total and Growing Season, 1994-1995

County	Station	Annual Precip. (inches)		Length of Growing Season (days)	
		1994	1995	1994	1995
Beaverhead	Dillon	9.03	19.16	99	106
Big Horn	Hardin	11.57	13.37	161	130
Blaine	Chinook	11.60	19.27	142	116
Broadwater	Townsend	6.90	9.64	143	116
Carbon	Joliet	14.80	N/A	158	N/A
Carter	Ekalaka	21.14	20.96	141	121
Cascade	Great Falls	10.57	15.43	155	115
Chouteau	Ft. Benton	9.58	15.42	NA	130
Custer	Miles City	9.77	12.90	160	129
Daniels	near Scobey	11.15	16.54	89	104
Dawson	Glendive	13.16	14.23	161	146
Deer Lodge	N/A				
Fallon	Plevna	13.76	14.02	144	83
Fergus	Lewistown	13.91	22.82	140	117
Flathead	Kalispell	12.64	22.82	96	105
Gallatin	Bozeman	17.77	N/A	155	N/A
Garfield	Jordan	11.51	10.23	114	119
Glacier	Cut Bank	9.60	16.73	97	116
Golden Valley	Barber	10.02	14.14	131	119
Granite	N/A				
Hill	Havre	10.45	16.59	158	120
Jefferson	N/A				
Judith Basin	Stanford	11.59	24.58	96	115
Lake	near Bigfork	16.04	25.86	178	143
Lewis & Clark	Helena	7.47	12.41	145	102
Liberty	Chester	6.86	16.38	97	116
Lincoln	N/A				
Madison	Virginia City	12.56	20.60	108	92
McCone	Circle	14.09	9.86	119	119
Meagher	N/A				
Mineral	N/A				
Missoula	Missoula	11.64	16.22	161	117
Musselshell	Roundup	14.01	17.61	141	121
Park	Livingston	14.77	15.64	121	103
Petroleum	near Flatwillow	10.94	13.52	147	119
Phillips	near Malta	10.12	13.15	140	115
Pondera	Valier	8.86	16.83	156	120
Powder River	Broadus	N/A	N/A	N/A	101
Powell	N/A				
Prairie	Terry	10.25	12.43	116	119
Ravalli	Hamilton	11.70	18.53	163	117
Richland	Sidney	13.43	15.58	119	117
Roosevelt	Culbertson	11.90	12.29	108	103
Rosebud	Forsyth	14.89	16.29	161	130
Sanders	Thompson Falls	17.50	31.57	162	140
Sheridan	Plentywood	12.48	14.52	136	117
Silver Bow	Butte	12.08	19.26	16	50
Stillwater	Columbus	19.41	15.95	141	119

Precipitation Total and Growing Season, 1994-1995 (cont.)

County	Station	Annual Precip. (inches)		Length of Growing Season (days)	
		1994	1995	1994	1995
Sweet Grass	Big Timber	18.89	18.58	141	119
Teton	Fairfield	7.87	15.80	155	115
Toole	N/A				
Treasure	Hysham	11.78	14.36	161	122
Valley	Glasgow	10.02	13.17	156	118
Wheatland	Harlowton	13.15	14.13	105	117
Wibaux	near Wibaux	12.60	15.22	136	118
Yellowstone	Billings	13.65	16.73	176	131

N/A - data not available
Growing season = days between last frost (32 degrees) in spring to first frost after June 30.
Source: National Weather Service, Great Falls - National Oceanic and Atmospheric Administration.

Average Temperatures and Snowfall, 1980-89

Town	Average Daily High (°F) July	Average Daily Low (°F) January	Average Jan. Snowfall (inches)
Anaconda	79.0	15.3	13.6
Big Timber	87.0	13.3	9.7
Billings	87.0	13.3	9.3
Bozeman	75.7	7.8	40.8
Butte	80.1	4.2	8.1
Cut Bank	78.9	5.0	6.2
Deer Lodge	82.2	8.3	6.3
Dillon	84.0	10.0	4.2
Ennis	82.9	13.2	N/A
Glendive	89.4	2.1	7.2
Great Falls	83.6	12.3	10.0
Hamilton	84.1	16.3	12.5
Havre	84.2	3.5	8.2
Helena	82.1	10.7	8.9
Kalispell	80.6	13.7	18.0
Libby	87.9	14.7	N/A
Miles City	88.9	5.7	5.6
Missoula	84.8	14.0	12.7
Polson	82.3	17.9	11.2
Red Lodge	79.3	11.2	21.4
Shelby	82.5	4.8	N/A
Virginia City	81.3	10.6	9.1

N/A - data not available
Source: Montana Department of Commerce, Travel Montana, 1995

High Winds

The eastern region tends to be windier than the region west of the divide (excluding mountain ridge areas), with Whitehall, Livingston, and Judith Gap recording average daily wind speeds of 14.4 to 15.7 mph.

Great Falls holds the official state record for the strongest wind at a National Weather Service station, where it raced at 82 mph in December 1956. It is widely accepted that wind speeds have unofficially beaten this record at several locations east of the divide. On December 5, 1995, hurricane-force winds were recorded on both sides of the divide, with 110 mph clocked by a weather observer at Plains and 100 mph at Ulm, near Great Falls. In 1973, an observer in Big Timber clocked the wind at 120 mph. These three observations remain unofficial.

The Chinooks

Severe winter temperatures east of the Continental Divide are sometimes modified by warm chinook winds from the eastern slopes of the Rockies. Indians called these winds "snow eaters," and it's true that the warm winds can gobble up the snowdrifts of the most severe storms within days or even hours.

> This weather phenomenon begins over the Pacific Ocean and moves east as a warm, moist air mass. As the air moves up and over the mountains, it cools and causes the moisture to condense. Now here's the weird part. While cooling causes condensation, condensation generates heat—thus the air that slides down the east side of the mountains is warmer than it was at a similar elevation on the west side, plus the rush downhill further warms the air.
>
> from *Trail of the Great Bear*
> by Bruce Weide, Falcon

Chinooks occur most often in the "chinook belt," a zone from Browning and Shelby in the north, along the Front Range, 75 to 100 miles to the Yellowstone Valley and Billings to the southeast.

THE
temperatures,
they are a-
changing

Sudden and dramatic temperature changes under the Big Sky are tall tales come true. One of the quickest changes in the U.S. occurred in Great Falls, when on January 11, 1980, the temperature rose from 32 below zero to 15 above—a change of 47 degrees—in only seven minutes.

In a 24-hour period on January 23 and 24, 1916, the temperature in Browning dropped exactly 100 degrees, from 44 degrees above zero to 56 degrees below zero. This is the world record for a 24-hour temperature change.

Historic Weather Disasters

One cowboy described the winter of 1886-1887 as "hell without the heat." It all started when there wasn't enough rain during the spring and summer of 1886. The grass, streams, and water holes dried up, but cattlemen kept on bringing in more herds from Texas, Washington, and Oregon. The summer was abnormally hot. Vegetation shriveled in the searing wind. Prairie fires roared across the land. The scant water remaining in the shallow streams was so foul with alkali that thirsty horses refused to drink it. There were signs of a hard winter to come. Wild geese and ducks flew south early, and the cattle grew shaggy coats. Winter came, and it was a hard one, with snowfall drifted by wild blizzards. Cold bit down, and strong young steers froze to death in a series of bitter storms between mid-November and March, one of which lasted for ten days without a letup. When a thaw came, cold followed it, so that everything was topped by a sheet of ice.

When a March chinook melted the snow and ice like magic, cattlemen surveyed their losses and it wasn't a pretty picture. The coulees were filled with rotting carcasses of cattle that had starved or frozen. Some stockmen lost two-thirds of their herds; a few lost 90 percent. To add to the ruin, the price of beef bottomed out because so many owners had to sell their diminished herds to raise money. There were bankruptcies. The dream of the open range ended in a nightmare.

Other weather-related disasters:

March 24, 1869	Seventeen soldiers returning with supplies to Fort Shaw from Fort Benton die near present-day Vaughn in a severe blizzard that lasts only a few hours.
June 19, 1938	A flash flood weakens a trestle, causing a Milwaukee Road passenger train to plunge into Custer Creek; 49 people are killed, 65 injured.
January 25, 1962	Severe winds along the Rocky Mountain Front are blamed for the crash of a National Guard C-47 near Wolf Creek. Governor Donald Nutter loses his life in the crash.
June 7-8, 1964	After a week of heavy rains, dams fail and devastating floods along the Rocky Mountain Front claim twenty-eight lives and inundate towns from the Flathead Valley to Great Falls.
April 24, 1969	More than 100,000 livestock are killed in freezing rain and snow in southeastern Montana.

Under Ice

In the past five decades, Flathead Lake has frozen over only seven times—

in **1946,**

1962, 1969,

1972, 1985,

1986, and 1989.

Weather Reports

Montana residents and visitors can call the following numbers to receive up-dated regional weather reports.

Statewide	449-5204
Billings	652-1916
Glasgow	228-4042
Great Falls	453-5469
Havre	265-6424
Helena	443-5151
Kalispell	755-4829
Missoula	721-3939

Weather reports for the following three cities can be found at these web sites:
http://nimbo.wrh.noaa.gov/Greatfall
http://nimbo.wrh.noaa.gov/Billings
http://nimbo.wrh.noaa.gov/Missoula

Weather Radio

The National Weather Service maintains a nationwide network of weather radio transmitters known as NOAA Weather Radio (NWR), which broadcasts weather information twenty-four hours a day, 365 days a year. The broadcasts, including local forecasts and observations and severe weather watches and warnings, can be received over much of Montana with a special radio receiver available at many electronics stores on the following frequencies.

Great Falls	162.55	Helena	162.40	Havre	162.40
Butte	162.55	Kalispell	162.55	Missoula	162.40
Glasgow	162.40	Miles City	162.40		

Further Reading:

Caprio, Joseph M., and Gerald A. Nielsen. *Climate Atlas of Montana: Mapping Montana's Weather.* Bozeman: Montana State University Extension Service., 1992. *For those intently interested in mean temperatures, annual potential evaporation, solar radiation in langleys per day, etc., these maps tell the story of Montana's climate.*

For Gardeners:

Hackett, Molly, and Georgianna Taylor. *The Compleat Gardener.* Missoula: The Missoulian, 1995.

Perrin, Sandra. *Organic Gardening in Cold Climates.* Missoula: Mountain Press Publishing, 1991.

chapter three

NATURAL *Treasures*

MONTANA IS A VAST TREASURE TROVE of mountains, canyons, river valleys, forests, grassy plains, and badlands. As the 4th largest state in the nation, the 147,046 square miles (land and water) of Big Sky Country account for about 4 percent of the total U.S. land area. Montana's borders are big enough to fit Connecticut, Delaware, New Hampshire, Vermont, Massachusetts, Maine, South Carolina, and Ohio within them. If we had 23 more square miles, we could also squeeze in Rhode Island. Montana's boundary with the provinces of Saskatchewan, Alberta, and British Columbia spans one-seventh of the international border between Canada and the lower 48 states.

The eastern two-thirds of the state consists of high plains cut by numerous major rivers, several isolated mountain ranges, and rolling hills. The western third is mountainous, with broad, fertile valleys, watered by streams and rivers. It is this geography that makes Montana's history so interesting. This raw land influenced the exploits of those who came here and shaped the currents of life in this area. To conquer the elements and topography, it took nerve, knowledge, and perseverance. The steep mountains and impassable rivers made discovery difficult but yielded great resources like beaver pelts, gold, and water power. The oceans of grass that attracted the buffalo later lured the cattlemen and farmers. Even the great expanses of drier plains proved to be passable grazing for sheep.

Montana is famous for its endless blue skies and a landscape painted with many other hues of nature's palette. In fall, its forests may not flaunt all the gaudy colors of the eastern woodlands, but its tamaracks are bright yellow against

49

Wildflowers and Apikuni Mountain in Glacier National Park. Michael Sample

the evergreens, and its aspen groves are a dazzling gold. In winter, the bare branches of red-osier dogwood retain their tint along streambeds. Sagebrush provides subtle grays, greens, and whites all year long. Spring brings wildflowers of all hues, set against the stark white of bear grass in high mountain meadows. In summer, there are all the tones of green in a giant box of crayons. And to be sure, there are purple mountains, full of majesty, and amber waves of grain.

Geology

Montana's remarkable and varied landscape contains evidence of many geologic events. The earth under the prehistoric Big Sky was vastly different than it is today, at times roamed by dinosaurs or covered by shallow seas.

During the Paleozoic era, which lasted from 600 to 240 million years ago, much of the northern Rocky Mountain area was flooded by shallow seas at various intervals. The rise and fall of great seas occurred again during the Mesozoic era, which lasted until about 65 million years ago. The shallow seas, sometimes stretching from northern Canada to Mexico, laid down thick layers of sediment that hardened to rock. Dinosaurs of many types inhabited this area during the Mesozoic time. Cretaceous rocks deposited during the last part of the Mesozoic era, between about 135 and 65 million years ago, contain bones of many kinds of dinosaurs.

Around 80 million years ago, masses of molten rock rose beneath western

North America and lifted, stretched, and heated the continental crust. The crust broke up into the long, narrow blocks of mountains that run north and south throughout much of the western and southwestern parts of Montana. Large volumes of volcanic rock erupted in western Montana.

Volcanoes erupted and molten magma rose upward into the earth's crust and, about 50 million years ago, created many of the isolated mountain ranges that dot the prairies well into the eastern half of the state. Great swamps flooded and dried, compacting the remains of vegetation into the great coal seams of today. Montana's coal beds are part of what may be the largest coal basin on earth, the Fort Union formation. Reaching into parts of Wyoming, North Dakota, and Saskatchewan, it is between 60 and 65 million years old.

Throughout the Tertiary period, from about 65 million years ago until the great ice ages began some 2 million years ago, there were long periods of dry, desert climate. There may have been enough precipitation to assist with erosion, but not enough to flush away the gravels and mud we can see today in many road cuts of the broader valleys. The eastern plains and badlands of Montana are remnants of high, smooth expanses of water-washed surfaces, where deposits of gravel tell a tale of great flash floods. Streams continue to cut through the rock layers.

When the Tertiary period ended about 2 million years ago, the great Pleistocene ice ages began. Part of Montana's modern landscape has been carved by glacial ice and the subsequent movement of great quantities of glacial meltwater. At least twice during the last 150,000 years, great glaciers blanketed northern Montana east of the Rocky Mountains and north of the Missouri River. It was not so much a time of intense cold, as many suppose, but a time when the winter snowfalls were so heavy that they could not melt during the summer.

Laccoliths

Many of Charlie Russell's paintings feature flat-topped buttes which the artist could see for miles south and southwest of Great Falls—Cascade Butte, Square Butte, Fort Shaw Butte, and Crown Butte. These formations are technically known as laccoliths. They form when magma rises into a volcano but cannot break through to the surface. The magma hardens into rock, which is slowly revealed by erosion.

Russell's beloved buttes remain, on his canvasses and on the landscape. Laccoliths can be found east of the Rocky Mountain Front and north of Helena along the Missouri River and in the Adel, Highwood, Bears Paw, and northern Crazy mountains. The laccoliths contain shonkinite, a very rare rock similar to basalt, named for Shonkin, a small settlement between Great Falls and Geraldine.

Glaciers covered the mountain peaks and scoured the Seeley, Swan, Flathead, and Bull Lake valleys. They blocked northerly flowing rivers like the Missouri to create ancient glacial lakes near Great Falls, Cut Bank, Roundup, Jordan, and Glendive. The great rivers of glacial melt scoured sediments on the valley floors that had been building for eons. The climate and vegetation between the glacial periods probably resembled those of modern times.

The glacier of 10,000 years ago was the last. It left moraines that can be seen in the rolling hills of Blaine, Phillips, and Hill counties; at the southern end of Flathead Lake; and across the Ovando Valley floor south of the Bob Marshall and Scapegoat wilderness areas. A moraine is a low ridge made by mud, sand, gravel, and boulders, deposited at the edge of a glacier.

The glaciers that ventured onto the northern third of eastern Montana did not change the landscape to a great degree. The ice was not thick enough or moving fast enough to do much eroding. As the last of the ice melted, shallow lakes disappeared and the Missouri River flowed in a new easterly course along the former front of the glacier. Modern types of vegetation adapted to the new conditions, and ice-free corridors allowed great prehistoric mammals and humans to migrate throughout the plains. The woolly mastodon roamed through portions of the state during the last ice age, as did the imperial mammoth and saber-toothed tiger.

Today, the northern Rocky Mountains are still subject to intense geological activity. Streams practice the art of erosion on a daily basis. In Yellowstone National Park, hot mud bubbles up and geysers erupt over the top of an enormous volcano. Though it has been decades since a serious earthquake struck, the earth is moving under us more often than we think.

Before the Flood

Dams of glacial ice once held back the Clark Fork River at the present site of Lake Pend Oreille in Idaho. A giant lake, 1,000 feet deep in many places, formed recurrently throughout the Clark Fork River drainage, east into the lower Deer Lodge Valley, beyond Darby, and north to the ice that filled the Seeley-Swan Valley. Evidence of Glacial Lake Missoula can be seen in the horizontal shorelines on Mount Sentinel and Mount Jumbo, the two mountains that flank Interstate 90 as it enters Missoula, and on hundreds of other mountains.

Between 15,000 and 13,000 years ago, the ice dam formed and broke at least thirty-six times, sending the contents of the giant lake down the Columbia River to the Pacific Ocean in what geologists think may have been the world's greatest flood.

Sperry Glacier. Michael Sample

WHERE THE
Glaciers *Are*

Some sources count as many as fifty small glaciers in Glacier National Park today. These are not part of the ancient glaciers that the park was named for, but formed later. Many have shrunk to half or one-third of the size they were a century ago. Many others have disappeared during that time.

Grinnell Glacier is the largest glacier in the park. It can be reached at the head of Grinnell Valley on a physically demanding trail, 5.5 miles from the Many Glacier campground. Gem and Salamander Glaciers can also be seen from the trail. Sperry Glacier is similar in size to Grinnell. It can be seen from the Sperry Chalet Trail, a 6.2-mile hike from the trailhead at Lake McDonald Lodge. Like the walk to Grinnell Glacier, it is somewhat strenuous.

In the Absaroka-Beartooth Wilderness Area, one of the largest ice fields in the U.S., Grasshopper Glacier is named for millions of grasshoppers frozen beneath its surface. The insects, whose species is now extinct, can only be seen when snow melts enough to expose the ice on an 80-foot cliff.

Earthquakes

Montana is the fourth most geologically active state, behind Alaska, California, and Hawaii. A narrow strip of the state, from Yellowstone Park to Kalispell, is at high risk of earthquake damage. History confirms this fact.

A series of 1,200 shocks struck Helena and western Montana in 1935, beginning in October and lasting into December. Another round of about six hundred more shocks hit in February 1936. Two of the October quakes were particularly powerful. One, on October 12, shook half of Montana. The most severe was centered near Helena. It occurred the evening of October 18 and was recorded as a magnitude of 6.3 on the Richter scale. Four people were killed and total property damage reached $3.5 million. The new Helena High School, completed in August, suffered the greatest damage. The Kessler Brewery and St. Joseph's Orphanage were also damaged.

The earthquake at Hebgen Lake on August 17, 1959, was one of the most severe ever recorded in the United States, with a magnitude variously reported between 7.1 and 7.5. It was felt throughout the Pacific Northwest and southwestern Canada. The world feels only about ten quakes of this magnitude each year. The Madison River valley in the Hebgen Lake area near West Yellowstone dropped by as much as 22 feet. The quake also triggered a landslide of some 80 million tons of rock and earth. The slide filled 1.5 miles of the Madison River Canyon, backing up the river to create Quake Lake. Large waves rolled across Hebgen Lake and sloshed over the top of Hebgen Dam. As many as 250 people were thought to have been camping in the area, and 28 of them lost their lives in the earthquake.

Visitors to the area, about 40 miles south of Ennis on U.S. Highway 287, can see the effects of this earthquake on the mountains and surroundings. At the

Montana's Major Earthquakes

Date	Center	Magnitude	Effects
05/22/1869	Helena	6.7	Only minor damage
12/10/1872	8 mi. east of Deer Lodge	—	Buildings shaken violently; shocks in Philipsburg, Helena, and Blackfoot Valley
06/27/1925	Three Forks area	6.75	Rock slides block railroad tracks and dam stream; slight damage to chimneys and buildings
10/12/1935	Helena	—	Very minor damage
10/18/1935	Helena	6.3	Four people killed; extensive property damage
11/23/1947	Madison-Beaverhead county line	6.2	No reported damage
08/17/1959	West of Yellowstone National Park	7.5	28 people killed
06/30/1975	Yellowstone National Park	6.4	No reported damage

top of the slide is a visitor center with educational exhibits. The USDA Forest Service has built a new campground nearby.

Minor Quakes

• During July 1995, over 550 small quakes were recorded in the vicinity of Yellowstone National Park. In October, over one hundred were centered in the southern end of the park. No one knows what all this rattling of the plumbing means for this beloved park's geothermal features.

• Montana experienced 778 earthquakes in 1993, 748 in 1994, and 731 in 1995. The largest quake in 1995 was also the largest for nearly a decade. It occurred on May 2 near Kila in northwest Montana and registered a magnitude of 4.5 on the Richter scale. It did no damage.

Many Are Better Than One

Consider us lucky that every year, frequent small earthquakes lightly jostle the state's populated areas within the earthquake belts of western Montana. Although these may be unsettling, the positive view holds that the seismic energy is being released in many small shocks instead of suddenly—in one large, destructive earthquake.

Seismic Zones

The U.S. Geological Survey ranks the part of Montana near Yellowstone National Park in Zone 4, the highest seismic risk category. Parts or all of sixteen counties are in Zone 3, which are high-risk seismic areas. The risk of earthquakes is nearly insignificant in eastern Montana.

Zone 4   Greater Yellowstone region
(Highest Risk)   Parts of Gallatin, Madison, Beaverhead,
                    and Park counties

Zone 3   Beaverhead County   Lake County
(High Risk)   Broadwater County   Lewis and Clark County
                    Butte/Silver Bow County   Lincoln County
                    Deer Lodge County   Madison County
                    Flathead County   Missoula County
                    Gallatin County   Park County
                    Granite County   Powell County
                    Jefferson County   Sanders County

For more information on Montana earthquakes and seismic zones, call the Earthquake Studies Office, Montana Bureau of Mines, Butte, at 496-4332, or Montana Disaster and Emergency Services, Helena, at 444-6982.

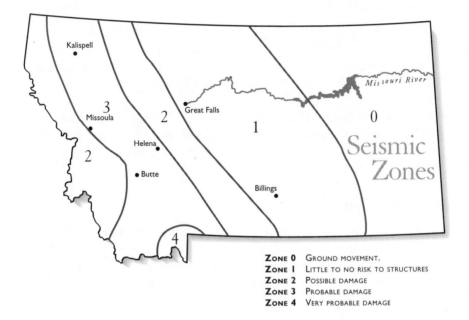

ZONE 0	GROUND MOVEMENT.
ZONE 1	LITTLE TO NO RISK TO STRUCTURES
ZONE 2	POSSIBLE DAMAGE
ZONE 3	PROBABLE DAMAGE
ZONE 4	VERY PROBABLE DAMAGE

Dinosaurs and Fossils

The first dinosaur fossil discovered and described in the western hemisphere was a single tooth found in beds near the mouth of the Judith River, east of Fort Benton, in 1854. The creature was given the name of *Troödon.* In 1902, the first fossil remains of a *Tyrannosaurus rex* were found in a dig near Hell Creek, outside of Jordan. The remains suggested an animal 40 feet long, weighing about 16,000 pounds. Based on the size of the teeth, *Tyrannosaurus rex* was thought to be a vicious predator. Montana's own dinosaur expert, Jack Horner, the director of paleontology for the Museum of the Rockies, suggests the creature was an opportunistic scavenger. *T. rex* would have been hard pressed to catch anything with its small arms, but it had strong legs for going great distances to find animals that were wounded or dead. With a good sense of smell, it could follow the duck-billed dinosaurs, or "cows of the Cretaceous period," which roamed the same areas in large herds. In 1988, Kathy Wankel, a Montana rancher out for a walk, discovered what turned out to be the most complete *T. rex* skeleton yet found.

At Egg Mountain near Choteau in north-central Montana, nests and eggs of the duck-billed dinosaur, *Maiasaura peeblesorum,* and the small plant-eater *Orodromeus makelai* have been found. The 1978 discovery of fourteen dinosaur

Vertebrate fossils and other fossils of "recognized scientific interest" are protected by federal law. Removing them from federal lands is prohibited, unless authorized by the agency that manages the land in question. It is also illegal to destroy "any historic or prehistoric ruin or monument, or any object of antiquity."

When exploring the state's geological and archaeological wonders, respect all natural resources as well as the rights of private property owners.

notable Montanans

John R. "Jack" Horner (1946-)

Though recognized all over the world as a paleontologist, Jack Horner did not have to go far from his hometown of Shelby for his most important find. Near Choteau, he found the first dinosaur nests ever uncovered. The discovery enabled Horner to solve truly ancient mysteries and change long-held ideas about dinosaur behavior. He is the recipient of major research grants from the National Science Foundation, the MacArthur Foundation, and other sources. He serves as curator of paleontology for the Museum of the Rockies in Bozeman. When he's not on a dig, he keeps busy conducting other research, lecturing, or writing articles and books. He has contributed articles to *Nature* and *Scientific American*, and was an advisor to Steven Spielberg's production of *Jurassic Park*.

Museum of the Rockies/Bruce Selyem

nests by Jack Horner helped convince other paleontologists that dinosaurs built vast colonies in order to better care for their young in a manner similar to birds. It is now widely believed that all dinosaurs reproduced by laying eggs. The fossils of numerous other plant-eating dinosaurs have been discovered in herds made up of both adults and young. Inside many of these dinosaur nests were found fossilized eggshell fragments that were thoroughly crushed, as by the feet of baby dinosaurs, leading Horner to conclude that the babies stayed in the nests and were fed and cared for by their parents. If the young had left the nests immediately after hatching, the eggshells would have stayed more intact.

Recent finds suggest there may be as many as thirty fossilized bones per square yard in the area of Egg Mountain. This site has yielded the largest collection of dinosaur remains in the world.

Mountains

Depending on who's counting and how they're counting, Montana contains between 25 and 30 mountain peaks higher than 12,000 feet, all in the Beartooth Range, west of Red Lodge and south of Big Timber. Granite Peak (12,799 feet) and the next 56 highest peaks in Montana are in the Beartooths. Hundreds of peaks in the western part of the state rise higher than 10,000 feet.

Numerous isolated mountain ranges, associated plateaus, and buttes dot the central and eastern plains. Examples of these mountains include the Pryor Range, the Crazy Mountains, and the Little Belts.

Major Montana Mountain Ranges

Absaroka Range
This range west of the Beartooths has more than 65 peaks over 10,000 feet. The Absarokas are considered the most rugged mountains in Montana—128 major summits in the range have no official names.

Anaconda Range
This range rises south of Anaconda and makes the Continental Divide for 40 miles. It borders the eastern side of the Big Hole. Two-thirds of the many 10,000-foot peaks of this range lie within the Anaconda-Pintler Wilderness Area on the western side of the range.

Beartooth Range
This is the only range in the state with peaks over 12,000 feet—almost 30 of them. Eleven plateaus reach higher than 10,000 feet. The easy way to see these peaks is along the Beartooth Highway, a National Forest Scenic Byway between Red Lodge and Cooke City.

Beaverhead Mountains

This range borders Idaho, running between the Bitterroot Range and the Big Hole Valley.

Big Belt Mountains

The range features limestone cliffs and other rock formations above the Missouri River and Canyon Ferry Reservoir.

Bitterroot Range

Montana's longest mountain range, it extends into Idaho. Eighteenmile Peak is the highest peak on the Continental Divide in Montana.

Bridger Range

The crest of this range to the north of Bozeman towers nearly 10,000 feet. Bridger Bowl Ski Area is famous for its excellent powder skiing.

Cabinet Mountains

The Cabinets are the dominant range of northwestern Montana, extending along the Idaho border. Within this range is the 100,000-acre Cabinet Mountain Wilderness Area. The highest point, Snowshoe Peak, is only 8,738 feet, but the range appears stunningly high because surrounding areas are some of the lowest elevations in Montana.

Centennial Mountains

The spine of these east-west oriented mountains forms the Continental Divide and the Montana-Idaho border. The Centennials are noted for diversity of flora and fauna.

Crazy Mountains

This west-central Montana range rises abruptly from ranchlands north of Big Timber and features 23 majestic peaks above 10,000 feet. Fifteen of these do not have names.

Flint Creek Range

The Flint Creeks separate the Deer Lodge Valley on the eastern side from the Philipsburg Valley on the western edge. The highest of these peaks is Mount Powell, which reaches higher than 10,000 feet.

Gallatin Range

The Gallatins stretch for 60 miles south of Bozeman into Yellowstone National Park. The range's highest point, Electric Peak (10,992 feet), lies just inside the park. Also includes the Gallatin River and its canyon, waterfalls, lakes, and creeks.

Gravelly Range

The Gravelly Range, south of Virginia City, is an imposing plateau with several 10,000-foot peaks.

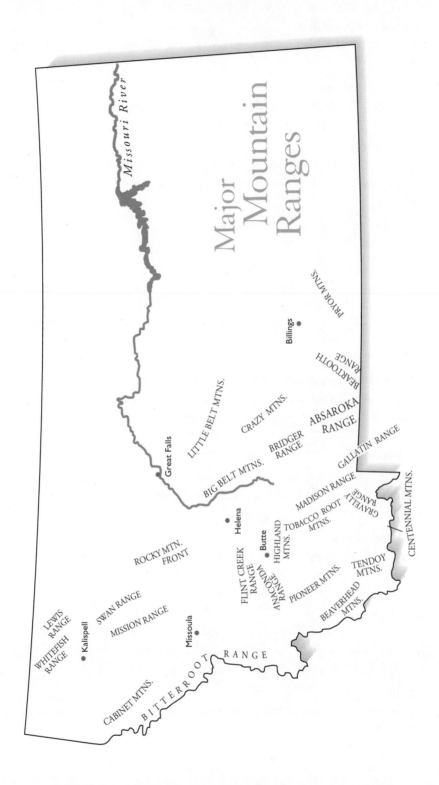

Highland Mountains
This small range, just south of Butte, includes a 10,000-foot plateau known as Table Mountain.

Lewis Range
The forested lower slopes of these mountains in Glacier National Park lead to magnificent heights. The road that winds among many of these peaks and through spectacular Logan Pass is aptly called Going-to-the-Sun.

Little Belt Mountains
This range starts 20 miles south of Great Falls and runs for some 60 miles to the Judith Basin area. The Little Belts offer abundant grazing and timber lands, excellent elk habitat, and a variety of winter fun at Showdown Ski Area. The world-famous Yogo sapphire mines are at the eastern end.

Madison Range
With six peaks over 11,000 feet, this range is considered the second highest in the state. Only 48 of its 122 peaks that exceed 10,000 feet have names. The 11,316-foot Hilgard Peak is the loftiest peak outside the Beartooth Range, yet it is only the 61st highest in the state. The range runs from south of Bozeman for 50 miles to the western entrance to Yellowstone National Park. It includes the Spanish Peaks at its northern end.

Mission Range
This 60-mile-long wall of rugged peaks separates the Swan Valley from the Mission and Flathead Valleys. The Mission Mountains rise sharply from the valley floors and appear higher than they are. There are remnants of several small

The Great Divide

The Continental Divide enters the state at the Canadian border, bisecting Glacier National Park. It then winds through the state's western counties. It defines the border of Montana and Idaho from Lost Trail Pass in southwestern Montana to the Wyoming border at Yellowstone National Park.

Every land mass has divides—a ridge of land from which water sheds in different directions. The Continental Divide is also known as the Great Divide, since it separates the continent's mass into its major watersheds. All water that falls east of the Continental Divide drains into the Gulf of Mexico and the Atlantic Ocean or Hudson Bay and the Arctic Ocean. The water that falls on the west side runs into the Pacific Ocean.

glaciers and more than one hundred high lakes. Much of the range is in the Mission Mountains Tribal Wilderness, managed by the Kootenai-Salish Indians.

Pioneer Mountains

These mountains have a western and eastern flank, split by the Wise River and a National Forest Scenic Byway, which provides access to trailheads leading into the backcountry. Fifty summits in the Pioneers reach higher than 10,000 feet.

notable
$\mathcal{M}$ontanans

James Willard Schultz (1859-1947)

Schultz came to Montana from the state of New York at the age of 17 and worked at the Fort Conrad Trading Post. He soon was living with the Blackfeet. He married a Piegan woman, was given the Piegan name *Apikuni,* meaning "Far Off White Robe," and even participated in raids against other tribes. Schultz shared his knowledge of Indian life, hunting, and the Montana wilderness by writing about them. He published more than thirty books, including *My Life As An Indian* (1907) and *Blackfeet Tales of Glacier National Park* (1916).

In 1885, the naturalist George Bird Grinnell read one of Schultz's articles in *Forest and Stream* magazine after visiting northwestern Montana. Grinnell soon returned to the area and, with Apikuni as his guide, visited the lakes, rivers, and peaks that inspired Grinnell to crusade for their preservation. In 1910, the area that Schultz wrote of was designated Apikuni Mountain, north of Lake Sherburne in the park, was named in his honor.

Schultz's son, Hart Merriam Schultz, also known as "Lone Wolf," became a respected painter and provided a visual equivalent of his father's documentation of life as a Blackfeet Indian.

Montana Historical Society

Pryor Mountains

This unglaciated range is characterized by flat benches, high deserts, mesas, buttes, and deep limestone canyons. Portions of the range, much of which is on the Crow Indian Reservation, are desert-like and only partially forested.

Rocky Mountain Front

This range is sometimes known as the Sawtooths and aptly so. Its sharp, often irregular peaks rise abruptly from the plains on the far eastern border of the Bob Marshall and Scapegoat wilderness areas. The range features many precipitous limestone cliffs and deep canyons.

Swan Range

This rugged range borders the western side of the Bob Marshall and Scapegoat wilderness areas for over 100 miles. The abrupt rise of much of the range limits access but provides several spectacular waterfalls.

Tendoy Mountains

In the southwestern corner of the state, this range stretches more than 30 miles west of Interstate 15. Its eastern canyons drain into the Red Rock River.

Tobacco Root Mountains

This range rises like a fortress on the plains south of Whitehall. Its deeply glaciated high peaks contain dozens of sparkling glacial lakes.

Whitefish Range

Extends northwest from the town of Whitefish and Big Mountain ski resort to the Canadian border. Woodland caribou have been seen in the Ten Lakes area, northeast of Ksanka Peak (7,505 feet).

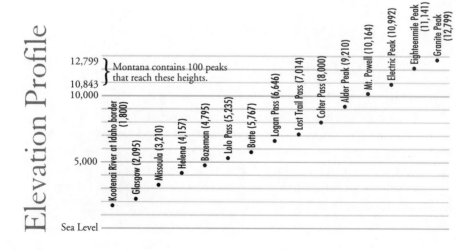

Elevation Profile

12,799	Montana contains 100 peaks
10,843	that reach these heights.
10,000	
5,000	
Sea Level	

Kootenai River at Idaho border (1,800) • Glasgow (2,095) • Missoula (3,210) • Helena (4,157) • Bozeman (4,795) • Lolo Pass (5,235) • Butte (5,767) • Logan Pass (6,646) • Lost Trail Pass (7,014) • Colter Pass (8,000) • Alder Peak (9,210) • Mt. Powell (10,164) • Electric Peak (10,992) • Eighteenmile Peak (11,141) • Granite Peak (12,799)

Highest Peaks in Selected Ranges

Peak	Elevation (in feet)	Range
Granite Peak	12,799	Beartooth Range
Hilgard Peak	11,316	Madison Range
Crazy Peak	11,214	Crazy Mountains
Mount Cowan	11,206	Absaroka Range
Tweedy Mountain	11,154	East Pioneer Mountains
Eighteenmile Peak	11,141	Bitterroot Range
Electric Peak	10,992	Gallatin Range
West Goat Peak	10,793	Anaconda Range
Mount Jefferson	10,604	Tobacco Root Mountains
Sunset Peak (in the Snowcrest Range)	10,581	Gravelly Range
Mount Cleveland	10,466	Lewis Range
Table Mountain	10,223	Highland Mountains
Mount Powell	10,164	Flint Creek Range

Highs and Lows

Montana's elevations, measured from sea level, range from 1,820 feet, where the Kootenai River exits the state in the northwest corner, to 12,799-foot Granite Peak, near the south-central border. Almost all of the plains area of the state is 4,500 feet or less, with most locations below 3,000 feet. Most agricultural activities west of the Continental Divide are confined to areas under 4,500 feet.

Source: Joseph Caprio and Gerald Nielsen, Climate Atlas of Montana. *Bozeman: Montana State University Extension Service, 1992.*

Lower
ranges

The Mission Mountains, the Cabinets, the Swan Range, ranges in the Bob Marshall Wilderness Area, and the Sawtooths of the Rocky Mountain Front make a majestic appearance on the landscape, but, surprisingly, they are not among the highest ranges in the Rockies. These ranges actually have fairly low (8,000-foot to 9,600-foot) summits in comparison to other Rocky Mountain ranges.

Elevations of Selected Cities

City	Elev. (in feet)	City	Elev. (in feet)
Butte	5,767	Missoula	3,210
Anaconda	5,288	Billings	3,117
Dillon	5,406	Whitefish	3,037
Bozeman	4,795	Kalispell	2,959
Deer Lodge	4,531	Polson	2,917
Livingston	4,487	Havre	2,670
Helena	4,157	Miles City	2,371
Lewistown	3,963	Glasgow	2,095
Hamilton	3,524	Glendive	2,069
Great Falls	3,312		

Elevations of Selected Mountain Passes

Pass	Location	Elev. (in feet)
Colter Pass	US 212, east of Cooke City	8,000
Chief Joseph Pass	MT 43, west of Wisdom	7,264
Targhee Pass	US 20, west of West Yellowstone	7,072
Lost Trail Pass	US 93, Montana-Idaho border	7,014
Monida Pass	I-15, Montana-Idaho border	6,870
Raynolds Pass	MT 87, southwest of Hebgen Lake	6,836
Logan Pass	Going-to-the-Sun Road, Glacier National Park	6,646
Homestake Pass	I-90, east of Butte	6,375
Elk Park Pass	I-15, north of Butte	6,368

MacDonald Pass	US 12, west of Helena	6,320
Flesher Pass	County 279, northwest of Helena	6,130
Bozeman Pass	I-90, east of Bozeman	5,760
Rogers Pass	MT 200, northeast of Lincoln	5,710
Marias Pass	US 2, west of East Glacier	5,280
Lolo Pass	US 12, southwest of Missoula	5,235
Lookout Pass	I-90, Montana-Idaho border	4,700

Source: Montana Department of Commerce, Official Montana Highway Map.

Rivers

Montana has within its borders portions of three major river drainage systems of North America.

• West of the Continental Divide, the streams eventually drain into the Columbia River, which flows into the Pacific Ocean. Major rivers of this system within the state are the Kootenai, Clark Fork, Blackfoot, Bitterroot, and Flathead.

• East of the divide, the Missouri River collects numerous tributaries, including the Marias, Milk, and Yellowstone rivers. From its headwaters at Three Forks, the Missouri flows 2,546 miles to the Mississippi River, and joins waters emptying into the Gulf of Mexico.

• In parts of Glacier National Park and Teton County, streams drain via the Belly and St. Mary rivers into Canada's Saskatchewan-Nelson drainage, flowing northeastward into Hudson Bay.

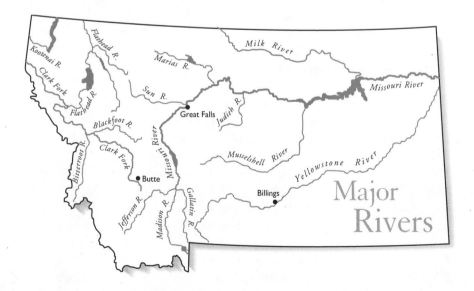

The Missouri River is 2,546 miles long, a distance longer than the main stem (2,340 miles) of the Mississippi River into which it flows near St. Louis, Missouri. Had surveyors considered the Missouri River to be the upper stem of the Mississippi, what are today considered two rivers would be one, stretching 3,710 miles from Beaverhead County to the Louisiana Delta. It would rank as the fourth longest river in the world after the Nile (4,160 miles), the Amazon (4,000 miles), and China's Chang Jiang (3,964 miles). Instead, surveyors took Lake Itasca, Minnesota, as the source of the Mississippi. The Upper and Lower Mississippi total 2,340 miles and form the world's twelfth largest river.

The waters of the Missouri begin their journey in the Red Rock River, flowing into the Beaverhead River, a tributary of the Jefferson. The Jefferson, Gallatin,

Three Ways
Sea TO THE

From Triple Divide in Glacier National Park, raindrops that fall only a few feet apart take widely differing routes to the seas. Depending on which side of the three-sided point of land they fall on, the raindrops flow **east** into the Missouri and Mississippi rivers, the Gulf of Mexico, and the Atlantic Ocean; **west** to the Columbia River and the Pacific, or **north** and **east** into the rivers that lead to Hudson Bay.

Short
STORY The Roe River, which flows between
Giant Springs and the Missouri River near Great Falls, competes with the D River in Lincoln City, Oregon, for the title of world's shortest river. Both rivers have been measured on different occasions, with lengths varying from 58 feet to 200 feet. Great Falls schoolchildren successfully campaigned to get the Roe into the *Guinness Book of World Records*.

The source of this smallest of rivers, Giant Springs, is the largest freshwater spring in the U.S.

Deep thought

Some people believe the deep waters of Flathead Lake are the home of the "Flathead Lake monster," a distant cousin of that other famous mythical creature of the deep, the Loch Ness monster.

and Madison rivers merge around Three Forks to form the main stem of the Missouri. The Missouri River receives the Yellowstone River near the Montana-North Dakota border. Other great Montana rivers that join the Missouri flow include: the Dearborn, Teton, Sun, Marias, Musselshell, Smith, Judith, Milk, and Poplar rivers, to name a few.

Montana cannot claim all of the great Yellowstone River, as it begins some 30 miles south of Yellowstone National Park in Wyoming before it winds its 670 miles to the Missouri River. Along the Yellowstone's 570-mile course through Montana, it collects water from the Shields, Boulder, Stillwater, Clarks Fork (of the Yellowstone), Tongue, Powder, and Bighorn rivers.

The Clark Fork (of the Columbia) River is the major drainage of western Montana. It begins as Silver Bow Creek near Butte and flows northwestward to the Idaho border near Noxon, Montana, and Sandpoint, Idaho. On its deep and relentless course through Montana to the Columbia, it collects Rock Creek and the Blackfoot, Bitterroot, Flathead, and Thompson rivers. The Kootenai River, a tributary of the Columbia, makes a short loop through the northwestern corner of Montana. When it enters at the Canadian border near Eureka, it is as Lake Koocanusa, a 40-mile-long reservoir behind Libby Dam. The Kootenai leaves at the state's lowest elevation—1,820 feet.

Montana's Ten Longest Rivers (in miles)

1. Missouri	1,029	5. Clark Fork *(in Montana)*	340
(to N. Dakota border)		6. Jefferson	220
2. Yellowstone	570	7. Powder	217
(in Montana)		8. Flathead	216
3. Milk	538	9. Tongue	210
4. Musselshell	364	10. Marias	170

National Wild and Scenic Rivers

Montana has 368 miles of federally designated Wild and Scenic Rivers. The federal Wild and Scenic Rivers Act of 1968 preserves these waters in their free-flowing condition for the "enjoyment of present and future generations." A stretch of river may be granted status as "Wild and Scenic" if it is free-flowing and contains at least one "outstandingly remarkable value." This standard can include scenery, recreational potential, wildlife, fisheries, or cultural, historic, or geological significance. It takes an act of Congress or the Secretary of the Interior, upon a request by a state governor, to declare a river "Wild and Scenic."

Upper Missouri

149 miles, from Fort Benton to the Fred Robinson Bridge on US 191

North Fork of the Flathead

58 miles, from the Canadian border to its confluence with the South Fork

Middle Fork of the Flathead

101 miles, from the confluence of Strawberry and Bowl Creeks to its confluence with the South Fork

South Fork of the Flathead

60 miles, from the confluence of Young's and Danaher Creeks downstream to Hungry Horse Reservoir

Up
THE
Crick
Trivia Quiz

The answers can be found at the end of the chapter.

In what drainages can the following Montana "cricks" and lakes be found?

1. Yourname Creek
2. Uncle George Creek
3. Leaky Raft Lake
4. Hanging Woman Creek
5. Whale Creek
6. Froze to Death Lake
7. Dirty Ike Creek
8. Dirty Face Creek
9. Jack the Ripper Creek
10. Mutt and Jeff Lakes

Lake McDonald, Glacier National Park. Michael Sample

Lakes

Montana has over 1,400 square miles of inland water. Much of this is held in the hundreds of natural and man-made lakes that dot the high mountain terrain, valley bottoms, and "potholes" on the prairies. Most of the natural lakes are in the Rocky Mountain region, but there are a few in the north-central and north-eastern parts of the state.

Flathead Lake, in the mountain valley south of Glacier National Park, is the state's largest natural lake, with 188 square miles of surface area. Ice age glaciers carved the trench that now holds Flathead Lake. The year-round mild weather that backs up against the Mission Mountains to the east of the lake, along with fertile glacial soils, have created an excellent environment for growing the famous Flathead sweet cherries.

Lake McDonald, in Glacier National Park, is 10 miles long and 400 feet at its deepest. Medicine Lake, in northeastern Montana, is what remains of an ancient channel of the Missouri River.

Other large natural lakes include Big, Kintla, Mary Ronan, Placid, Seeley, Salmon, Swan, Whitefish, and Georgetown.

Selected Montana Waterfalls

NAME	NEAREST TOWN
Beartooth	Red Lodge
Crazy Creek	Cooke City
Crow Creek	Townsend
Double Falls	Augusta
Falls Creek	Augusta
Holland Falls	Seeley Lake
Lost Creek	Anaconda
Natural Bridge	Big Timber
Palisade	Bozeman
Silver Staircase	Essex
Skalkaho	Hamilton
Warm Springs	Deer Lodge
Yaak	Libby

Source: Montana Dept. of Commerce, Travel Montana.
Montana Production Guide. *Helena: 1995.*

Native Plants and Trees

The Lewis and Clark Expedition compiled the first catalogue of Montana flora and fauna along its route to the Pacific Ocean. Today, more than 2,500 species of wildflowers and non-flowering plants can be found in Montana. They can be classified into the following three categories:

sub-alpine   occurring at 6,000- to 7,000-feet elevations in northwestern Montana; the zone between mountain forests and areas above timberline

montane   mountain forests beginning at 5,000-feet elevation east of the Continental Divide; 2,500 feet on the western slopes

plains   found in open terrain of desert, plains, open valleys, and foothills.

Great expanses of native grasslands on public and private lands in Montana provide some of the best cattle and sheep grazing opportunities in the nation.

A Sampling of Montana's Common Grasses

Bluebunch Wheatgrass — *Agropyron spicatum*
The official state grass, it grows 24 to 40 inches tall in erect bunches that appear bluish. This native perennial is one of the leading forage species in many areas of the state and withstands grazing well.

Rough Fescue — *Festuca scabrella*
This relatively short perennial grows 6 to 8 inches tall in prairies, hillsides, and open woods throughout the state. It is considered highly palatable forage and makes good winter range because it remains high in protein throughout that season.

Idaho Fescue — *Festuca idahoensis*
This is one of the most common grasses in the northwest, especially in foothills and open wooded areas on a wide variety of soil types. It has good palatability and can withstand overgrazing.

Blue Grama — *Boutelous gracilis*
This grass, which grows 6 to 18 inches tall, is well adapted to compacted soils. It is found in mixed prairie and shortgrass areas throughout central and eastern Montana.

Sandberg Bluegrass — *Poa sandbergii*
This plant, generally growing about 12 inches tall, is found on foothills, slopes, and plains and can also grow where the land has been disturbed.

Little Bluestem — *Schizachyrium scoparium*
This 23- to 26-inch-tall plant is found on prairies and dry slopes, generally on sandy or gravelly soils.

Bluejoint — *Clamagrostis canadensis*
Livestock and game seem to like the blades of this plant, which stands 2 to 4 feet high. It is found in marshes, wet meadows, hay meadows, and pastures.

A Sampling of Montana Wildflowers and Edible Plants

Shooting Star
A rosy purple flower banded with a red and yellow ring that points downward. Elk and deer eat this plant, which is found in moist and wet soil in the open spaces of hills, plains, and mountainsides. Shooting stars bloom from late April to July.

Fireweed
A perennial with stems that are simple and unbranched, reaching heights from 3 to 9 feet. The leaves are long and narrow, and the flowers are spikes ranging from rose to purple. The young shoots can be gathered when they are 4 to 6 inches tall and used for salad or cooked in casseroles. The flowers can be used in salads or in molds. The leaves can be dried to make tea.

Shooting Stars. Michael Sample

Lupine
Also called silky lupine, this plant has six to twenty 4-inch stems with blue cluster flowers. The leaves are seven to nine narrow, hairy leaflets. The flower blooms from late June to early August in the moist soil of hillsides and meadows. These plants are poisonous to livestock and humans during part of the growing season.

Cattail
The cattail is a large, creeping rhizome with simple, erect stems and long, broad, flat leaves. It is found in wet and marshy soil. In the early spring, as the new leaves are forming, the young shoots can be pulled loose from the root stock. When the outer leaves are peeled, a tender, light-colored core is exposed, which can be eaten raw or sautéed in butter. The pollen spikes ripen later in the season and can be collected and added as a source of protein to recipes for pancakes, biscuits, muffins, and the like.

Mountain Heath

A small evergreen shrub with needle-like leaves and clusters of pink flowers shaped like urns or bells. It is seen high in the mountains and around glacial lakes in moist to wet soil, blooming from late June to early August. Mountain heath or heather is a relative of Scotch heath.

Wild Rose

This shrub grows from 3 to 8 feet tall and has alternate compound leaves with 3 to 7 leaflets. It flowers in spring and early summer with pink blossoms. In the fall, the fruits, orange or red rose hips, ripen. The petals can be harvested to make a number of delicious foods, but the white base of the petal must be snipped off because of its bitter taste. The rose hips are dried to make rose hip tea, high in vitamin C.

Indian Paintbrush

Flowerlike leaves, usually red, but also can be white, yellow, pink, or violet, depending on the species, temperature, altitude, soil conditions, and time of year. Sixteen species are found in Montana. They bloom from June to early August in dry to moist soils.

Wood Violet

The violet comes in a variety of colors from white to purple. The most common in this area is the purple wood violet. It blooms in early spring in wooded flood plains and on slopes and ledges of deciduous forests. As with the viola and pansy, the petals of this herb can be eaten in salads or made into syrup, jelly, jam, or candy. The young leaves can also be eaten but should be harvested when the plant is in bloom to avoid harvesting poisonous look-alikes. The violet blossoms can also be dried to use as a tea.

Huckleberry Heaven

On August 14, 1805, Meriwether Lewis and his party of explorers held off starvation with huckleberry pancakes while waiting to meet up with Captain William Clark after crossing the Continental Divide into Idaho. While most of us think of huckleberries as a delightful treat, they may have served as Lewis and his corps' salvation.

The Indians they met knew all about the purple treasures. The berries held an important place in Kootenai and Salish Indian tradition. Well into this century, the Salish had a ceremony in July, around powwow time, in which two sisters would go into the woods and pick a bucket of berries. The berries would be passed among tribal members until everyone had two berries. It was then deemed the appropriate time for everyone to go picking. The Indians dried huckleberries for use in stew with venison and bitter-root.

In general, huckleberries are pea-sized, with smooth skin, an indent on their base, and seeds no bigger than a pepper flake. The bushes are knee to chest high and the green leaves are occasionally tinged with red.

The berries grow best on a north slope, with a preference for elevations of 3,500 to 7,000 feet. They require moisture and the acidic soil typical to coniferous forests. Hand-picking is the preferable way to harvest the berry. Other means can damage the plant.

Throughout the 1930s and 1940s, the legendary huckleberry crops of western Montana provided a free food supply and critical economic activity during tough times. Old-timers tell of the great "huckleberry camps," where Indian and white families would bring camping and canning equipment into woods and stay until the berries were gone. In certain good drainages, there were sometimes five hundred tepees, an improvised store, and a general boomtown atmosphere.

Huckleberry Facts

- A grown bear can eat 80 to 90 pounds of food per day, and in the fall, before the long winter's nap, that diet may consist of as much as 15 percent huckleberries.

- Late July is a good time to start hunting huckleberries. The season can go into late September or October at the highest elevations.

- An industry based on huckleberry products could be a very lucrative, sustainable addition to the Montana economy. Studies are being conducted to determine whether the wild berry can be cultivated without the loss of its unique flavor. In 1996, a gallon of berries sold for eighteen to twenty dollars. One acre of wild berries can produce 20 to 50 gallons of berries worth anywhere between $300 and $1,000 a year. That exceeds the income of an acre of the best timberland in the state.

- Since 1994, commercial picking permits are required for adults who plan to sell berries gathered on national forest lands. In 1996, the permit cost $8 for 2 days, up to $80 for the season.

Morel Mushrooms

The coveted morel mushroom flourishes in recently burned areas of the forest. More than 31,000 acres of the Kootenai National Forest are designated for commercial mushroom harvesting from mid-May through July. A permit is now required for commercial picking.

The morel mushroom looks like a cross between a brain and a cow pie, but it is a high-class delicacy that is fetching top dollar across the U.S. and the world. Morels sprout when conditions of moisture, sunlight, and soil disturbance are just right. They seem to like the edges of forests. Though morels can be found in a variety of conditions, they really thrive the year after a forest fire. After the bad fires of 1988, one commercial seller of wild mushrooms sold 80,000 pounds of morels.

WARNING The inexperienced should not attempt finding, picking, and especially consuming morels or any other wild mushrooms. Doing so can be hazardous to your health, or possibly fatal. Non-poisonous mushrooms are difficult to distinguish from the poisonous species. Careful study and perhaps a lesson from a naturalist or botanist is recommended before trying it on your own.

Weeds

The spread of noxious weeds is a big problem in Montana. Each person who engages in activities in the forests and recreation areas is a potential "carrier" of destructive weed seeds, like those of knapweed. Seeds can be transported long distances before they shake loose and become buried in the soil to germinate in a future weed patch that edges out native wild grasses, flowers, and other plants.

Knapweed is one of Montana's most undesirable noxious weeds. One plant can send out as many as 100,000 seeds. Its root system puts chemicals into the nearby ground that kill native plants. The spread of this noxious weed has ruined extensive public and private pasture lands.

It is illegal to permit certain weeds to grow on private land. Landowners are considered in noncompliance with the law if they make no attempt to control the following weeds:

Canada thistle	field bindweed	dyers woad
whitetop	leafy spurge	purple loosestrife
Russian knapweed	spotted knapweed	yellow starthistle
diffuse knapweed	Dalmatian toadflax	common crupina
Saint-John's-wort	sulfur cinquefoil	rush skeletonweed

Source: Montana State University Extension Service.

Forests and Trees

Nearly one fourth of Montana, 22.5 million acres, is forested. Nearly 11.4 million acres of forest are administered by the USDA Forest Service and 3.4 million acres are protected in wilderness areas, national parks, and monuments.

Most of the forests occur west of the Continental Divide, where the moist Pacific Coast air mass and the mountainous topography provide favorable climatic conditions for the growth of some twenty-seven types of forest trees and other vegetation. East of the divide, the drier climate results in more scattered forests, mainly found at elevations of 6,000 feet or more. At lower elevations in eastern Montana, there are considerable areas of open "coniferous woodland" along the outer margins of the forests. Douglas-fir is the predominant forest type.

Our forests provide the timber for the lumber and wood-products industries. They also serve an important function as a watershed, storing and releasing water for irrigation, hydroelectric power, and industrial and domestic uses. Annual precipitation on forested land is considerably greater than it is on nonforested. Seventy percent of the state's runoff or stream flow originates in forested areas.

Montana's Most Common Trees

Conifers: Douglas-fir
Subalpine fir
Grand fir
Mountain hemlock
Western hemlock
Rocky Mountain juniper
Utah juniper
Subalpine larch
Western larch
Limber pine
Lodgepole pine
Ponderosa pine
Western white pine
Whitebark pine
Western redcedar
Engelmann spruce
White spruce

Deciduous: Quaking aspen
Paper birch
Black cottonwood
Narrowleaf cottonwood
Plains cottonwood
Willow
Thinleaf alder
Black chokecherry
Black hawthorn
Bigtooth maple
Rocky Mountain maple
Western mountain ash
Curlleaf mountain mahogany

notable
$\mathscr{M}$ontanans

Arnold Bolle (1912-1994)

Todd Goodrich

A forester, conservationist, educator, and avid bird watcher, Bolle served as dean of The University of Montana Forestry School in the 1960s and 1970s. With six colleagues, he offered scientific evidence of the destruction wrought by clearcutting in the Bitterroot National Forest, paving the way for passage of the National Forest Management Act of 1976. Consequently, extraction of our natural resources was subjected to much closer scrutiny by public officials and lawmakers. Bolle was well liked by students and respected by his peers and many of his opponents for the knowledge and wisdom that supported his strong defense of wild lands. Of his many honors, Bolle is said to have most prized the Bob Marshall Award, the highest honor bestowed by The Wilderness Society.

Rutledge Parker (1877-1969)

Parker was a forester and administrator. He was appointed state forester in 1925 and served for twenty-eight years. In 1929, with the support of Montana's Kiwanis Clubs, he proposed a state park system to the Legislature, which responded with little enthusiasm to the idea. It was the eve of the Great Depression and Montana already had seventeen national forests and two national parks. Many officials thought the state could not afford to reserve more land, removing it from possible agricultural use and requiring an agency to manage the parks.

It took years of determination and compromise to get what Parker (and many others) wanted.

In 1936 Lewis and Clark Caverns became Montana's first state park. The land around the caverns was set aside through trades and donations, with little help from the Legislature, which had given Parker the additional title of Director of State Parks but made no appropriations for acquisition and development of land for parks. Parker kept the park system afloat and, in 1947, the Legislature finally appropriated funds for Montana's state parks.

Forest Fires

Prior to modern settlement, the forests and prairies were naturally "cleaned and groomed" by periodic forest fires, in a cycle that many believe to be beneficial to the health of the forest. But for decades, Montanans were hard pressed to find anything positive about the terrible forest fires of 1910—the worst on record for the northern Rocky Mountains. The fires that raged all across western Montana and northern Idaho that year destroyed 2.6 billion board feet of timber in Montana alone and have come to be remembered as "The Great Burn." The effort to blanket the public and private land of Montana with adequate fire protection started shortly after that frightening event. In 1994, 3,617 fires burned 306,955 acres of national forest in Montana at a cost of $104 million.

Effectiveness of Fire Control Efforts, 1910-1949

YEARS	ACRES BURNED *(state and national forest land)* BY WILDFIRES
1910-19	1,834,000
1920-29	364,000
1930-39	150,000
1940-49	53,000

Major Forest Fires

Fire Name	Year	Location	Cause	Acres Burned	Deaths/ Damage
Mann Gulch	1949	Gates of the Mountains	lightning	5,000+	12 smokejumpers 1 FS employee killed
Sleeping Child	1965	Darby		28,000	
Pattee Canyon	1977	Missoula			6 homes destroyed
Hawk Creek	1984	near Roundup		180,000	44 homes destroyed
North Hills	1984	N.E. of Helena		27,000	cabins burned, 2 towns threatened
Canyon Creek	1988	Scapegoat Wilderness- Augusta	lightning	247,000	outbuildings and cattle burned; fire- fighters receive burns
Storm Creek	1988	Yellowstone Park- Custer NF-Absaroka Wilderness	lightning	107,000	Cooke City and Silver Gate evacuated
Red Bench	1988	Flathead NF		37,500	Polebridge evacuated; firefighter killed by falling snag
Warm Springs	1988	Elkhorn Mountains	human-caused	47,000	2 homes destroyed, others burned
Shephard Mtn.	1996	East Rosebud Lake	lightning	12,800	$2 million in property damage; 32 homes destroyed; Luther and Roscoe evacuated

State Lands Fire Fighting Statistics, 1985-94

Year	Number of Fires	Acres Burned	Cost to the State
1985	384	4,996	$3.5 million
1986	319	4,181	$437,792
1987	406	7,471	$1.1 million
1988	566	118,136	$10 million
1989	391	2,579	$424,754
1990	408	48,741	$2 million
1991	441	212,333	$2.3 million
1992	417	7,769	$1.6 million
1993	260	7,864	$173,586
1994	744	37,919	$23 million

*Smoke*jumpers

Through 1995, more than 5,000 smokejumpers had learned to fight forest fires at the Smokejumper Training Center in Missoula. They have made hundreds of thousands of jumps to save forests.

Twelve smokejumpers and a USDA Forest Service employee lost their lives in the Mann Gulch fire of August 1949. The fire burnt 5,000 acres near the Gates of the Mountains on the Missouri River. The 1952 movie *Red Skies Over Montana* is based on the tragedy. Norman Maclean's book *Young Men and Fire* (1992) is an exhaustive, painstakingly researched account of the blaze and its aftermath.

Wildlife

In 1805, when the Lewis and Clark Expedition first reached Montana, they noted vast herds of buffalo, elk, and antelope on the prairies along the Missouri River. The number and varieties of waterfowl and other birds astonished them. In one journal entry, Captain Clark vowed to stop talking about the quantity of game and other animals, as no one would believe the claims.

They encountered the fearsome grizzly bear near the present-day North Dakota border. They saw moose as far east as the Milk River. By the time the

Mountain goat. Michael Sample

Corps of Discovery got to the area that would become Montana, its members had to subsist on the bounty of the land, but Captain Lewis would not allow the party to kill more animals than were needed. Captain Clark noted that it required four deer, or an elk and a deer, or one buffalo to supply the troop for 24 hours.

The Indians who made Montana home had always counted on wildlife for food, shelter, clothing, and trade items, and so did those adventurers who followed on the heels of Lewis and Clark. When the golden age of fur trapping ended in the 1850s, the beaver population was all but gone, and interest turned to a thriving trade in elk, deer, and buffalo hides. When the gold strikes of the early 1860s brought in a flood of prospectors, game was still plentiful near the mining camps and became an important source of food. That would soon change.

After the 1870s, the Indian tribes could no longer protect their hunting grounds from the buffalo hunters who slaughtered the bison for sport and profit. In addition, stockmen valued the verdant plains as rangeland for cattle driven up from Texas.

By the turn of the century, Montana's wildlife resources presented a sorry picture. Only a few bands of elk remained in the high mountains, and deer were diminishing in areas where they had formerly flourished. Mountain sheep and antelope diminished, some herds all but disappearing. Millions of buffalo had been reduced to a few stragglers in the Yellowstone National Park region.

Fur-bearing animals of any importance to man were becoming rare. The people of Montana finally realized that an important resource of the state could be wiped out. Some of the first laws enacted in the new state of Montana were aimed at protecting big game, waterfowl, fur-bearing animals, birds, and fish.

Research by wildlife biologists has advanced our understanding of habitat, ecology, and population control. Combined with law enforcement, that research has helped improve the state of most of our wildlife populations. Today, Montana is one of the best places in the lower forty-eight states for wildlife watching and hunting opportunities. According to a 1993 report by the Department of Fish, Wildlife & Parks, there are more hunters and anglers per capita here than in any other state.

Offices of Montana Department of Fish, Wildlife & Parks

State Office
1420 E. Sixth Avenue
Helena, MT 59620-0701
444-2535

Region 1, Kalispell
490 North Meridian
Kalispell, MT 59901
752-5501

Region 2, Missoula
3201 Spurgin Road
Missoula, MT 59801
542-5500

Region 3, Bozeman
1400 South 19th
Bozeman, MT 59715
994-4042

Region 4, Great Falls
4600 Giant Springs Road
Great Falls, MT 59406
454-5840

Region 5, Billings
2300 Lake Elmo Drive
Billings, MT 59106
247-2940

Region 6, Glasgow
Rural Route 1-4210
Glasgow, MT 59230
228-3700

Region 7, Miles City
P.O. Box 1630
Miles City, MT 59301
232-0932

Helena Area Resource Office
930 Custer Ave.
Helena, MT 59620
444-4720

The Montana Department of Fish, Wildlife & Parks can be reached on the World Wide Web at http://fwp.mt.gov. The site includes information on fishing, hunting, wildlife, parks, education, a kid's page, and resources. In addition, the site provides links to Travel Montana, the U.S. Fish and Wildlife Service, the National Park Service, Trout Unlimited, Ducks Unlimited, and various news and weather links.

A Montana Mammal Sampler

Here is a listing of some of the mammals that can be found, in varying habitats, within the state's borders.

Common Name	Scientific Name	Habitat & Occurrence
Badger	Taxidea taxus	Throughout the state, common.
Beaver	Castor canadensis	Along streams and lakes throughout the state, common.
Bighorn sheep	Ovis canadensis	In scattered bands in the western half of the state.
Bison	Bison bison	Formerly occurred throughout the state, now confined to Yellowstone Park, the National Bison Range, and in scattered bands on private ranches.
Black bear	Ursus americanus	Forested areas, rather common.
Black-footed ferret	Mustela nigripes	Originally across most of E. MT; reintroduced at UL Bend NWR.
Black-tailed prairie dog	Cynomys ludovicianus	Formerly abundant in eastern Montana, now much reduced by poisoning and the plague.
Bobcat	Lynx rufus	In many areas of the state, common.
Big brown bat	Eptesicus fuscus	Throughout the state; may hibernate in buildings during the winter.
Little brown bat	Myotis lucifugus	Throughout the state, common.
Canada lynx	Lynx canadensis	Heavily forested areas in western part of the state, rare.
Coyote	Canis latrans	Throughout the state, common.
Elk	Cervus canadensis	Certain areas in central and western Montana, common.
Fisher	Martes pennanti	Northwestern portion of the state, very rare.
Gray wolf	Canis lupus	Originally present throughout the state; recently reintroduced in Yellowstone Park; found in Glacier National Park and locally in NW Montana, rare.
Grizzly bear	Ursus arctos horribilis	Remote wilderness areas; originally throughout state, rare.
Hoary marmot	Marmota caligata	Above timberline in Glacier National Park and neighboring high mountain ranges, rare.
Montane vole	Microtus montanus	Dry grasslands of western and central Montana, uncommon.
Moose	Alces americana	Suitable areas in western half of the state, fairly common.
Mountain goat	Oreamnos americanus	High mountain ranges of western Montana; successfully transplanted in the Crazy Mountains.
Mountain lion	Felix concolor	Western counties, uncommon, rare in the eastern half of the state.
Mule deer	Odocoileus hemionus	Suitable habitats throughout the state, common.
Northern bog lemming	Synaptomys borealis	Only in wet meadows locally in western Montana, rare.
Northern flying squirrel	Glaucomys sabrinus	Dense forest in western counties, common.
Northern grasshopper mouse	Onychomys leucogaster	Grasslands of eastern mountains.
Norway rat	Rattus norvegicus	Known only in some of the cities.
Otter	Lutra canadensis	On large streams, mostly in western portion, uncommon.
Pygmy rabbit	Sylvilagus idahoensis	Found locally in sagebrush of SW Montana, rare.
Pika	Ochotona princeps	Slide rock areas in higher mountains, common.
Porcupine	Erethizon dorsatum	Throughout the state, common.
Prairie jumping mouse	Zapus hudsonius	Known only in southeast Montana, rare.
Pronghorn antelope	Antilocapra americana	Most of eastern and central Montana, common.
Red fox	Vulpes fulva	Across most of the state, common.
Sagebrush mouse	Lagurus curtatus	Sagebrush areas in eastern and central Montana, rare.
Snowshoe hare	Lepus americanus	Forested areas in western half of the state, common.
Western jumping mouse	Zapus princeps	High mountain meadows and wet woods near water in the western half of the state.
White-tailed deer	Odocoileus virfinianus	Forested areas in western Montana and brushy river bottoms in eastern Montana.
White-tailed prairie dog	Cynomys leucurus	Known only in Carbon County.
Wolverine	Gulo gulo	Wilder portions of western mountains, very rare.
Yellow-bellied marmot	Marmota flaviventris	Rocky areas and mountains of most of the western part of the state, uncommon.

Birds of Montana

The following 294 species have been documented as reliably occurring in Montana.

Common Loon
Pied-billed Grebe
Horned Grebe
Red-necked Grebe
Eared Grebe
Western Grebe
Clark's Grebe
American White Pelican
Double-crested Cormorant
American Bittern
Great Blue Heron
Snowy Egret
Cattle Egret
Black-crowned Night-Heron
White-faced Ibis
Tundra Swan
Trumpeter Swan
Mute Swan
Greater White-fronted Goose
Snow Goose
Ross' Goose
Canada Goose
Wood Duck
Green-winged Teal
Mallard
Northern Pintail
Blue-winged Teal
Cinnamon Teal
Northern Shoveler
Gadwall
Eurasian Wigeon
American Wigeon
Canvasback
Redhead
Ring-necked Duck
Greater Scaup
Lesser Scaup
Harlequin Duck
Oldsquaw
Surf Scoter
White-winged Scoter
Common Goldeneye
Barrow's Goldeneye
Bufflehead
Hooded Merganser
Common Merganser
Red-breasted Merganser
Ruddy Duck

Turkey Vulture
Osprey
Bald Eagle
Northern Harrier
Sharp-shinned Hawk
Cooper's Hawk
Northern Goshawk
Broad-winged Hawk
Swainson's Hawk
Red-tailed Hawk
Ferruginous Hawk
Rough-legged Hawk
Golden Eagle
American Kestrel
Merlin
Peregrine Falcon
Gyrfalcon
Prairie Falcon
Gray Partridge
Chukar
Ring-necked Pheasant
Spruce Grouse
Blue Grouse
White-tailed Ptarmigan
Ruffed Grouse
Sage Grouse
Sharp-tailed Grouse
Wild Turkey
Virginia Rail
Sora
American Coot
Sandhill Crane
Whooping Crane
Black-bellied Plover
Lesser Golden Plover
Semipalmated Plover
Piping Plover
Killdeer
Mountain Plover
Black-necked Stilt
American Avocet
Greater Yellowlegs
Lesser Yellowlegs
Solitary Sandpiper
Willet
Spotted Sandpiper
Upland Sandpiper
Whimbrel

Long-billed Curlew
Marbled Godwit
Ruddy Turnstone
Sanderling
Western Sandpiper
Least Sandpiper
Baird's Sandpiper
Pectoral Sandpiper
Dunlin
Stilt Sandpiper
Short-billed Dowitcher
Long-billed Dowitcher
Common Snipe
Wilson's Phalarope
Red-necked Phalarope
Franklin's Gull
Bonaparte's Gull
Ring-billed Gull
California Gull
Herring Gull
Caspian Tern
Common Tern
Forster's Tern
Least Tern
Black Tern
Rock Dove
Mourning Dove
Black-billed Cuckoo
Yellow-billed Cuckoo
Eastern Screech-Owl
Western Screech-Owl
Great Horned Owl
Snowy Owl
Northern Pygmy-Owl
Burrowing Owl
Barred Owl
Great Gray Owl
Long-eared Owl
Short-eared Owl
Boreal Owl
Northern Saw-whet Owl
Common Nighthawk
Common Poorwill
Black Swift
Chimney Swift
Vaux's Swift
White-throated Swift
Ruby-throated Hummingbird

Black-chinned Hummingbird
Calliope Hummingbird
Broad-tailed Hummingbird
Rufous Hummingbird
Belted Kingfisher
Lewis' Woodpecker
Red-headed Woodpecker
Red-naped Sapsucker
Williamson's Sapsucker
Downy Woodpecker
Hairy Woodpecker
Three-toed Woodpecker
Black-backed Woodpecker
Northern Flicker
Pileated Woodpecker
Olive-sided Flycatcher
Western Wood-Pewee
Willow Flycatcher
Least Flycatcher
Hammond's Flycatcher
Dusky Flycatcher
Cordilleran Flycatcher
Say's Phoebe
Cassin's Kingbird
Western Kingbird
Eastern Kingbird
Horned Lark
Tree Swallow
Violet-green Swallow
Northern Rough-winged
   Swallow
Bank Swallow
Cliff Swallow
Barn Swallow
Gray Jay
Steller's Jay
Blue Jay
Pinyon Jay
Clark's Nutcracker
Black-billed Magpie
American Crow
Common Raven
Black-capped Chickadee
Mountain Chickadee
Boreal Chickadee
Chestnut-backed Chickadee
Red-breasted Nuthatch
White-breasted Nuthatch
Pygmy Nuthatch
Brown Creeper
Rock Wren
Canyon Wren

House Wren
Winter Wren
Sedge Wren
Marsh Wren
American Dipper
Golden-crowned Kinglet
Ruby-crowned Kinglet
Eastern Bluebird
Western Bluebird
Mountain Bluebird
Townsend's Solitaire
Veery
Swainson's Thrush
Hermit Thrush
American Robin
Varied Thrush
Gray Catbird
Northern Mockingbird
Sage Thrasher
Brown Thrasher
American Pipit
Sprague's Pipit
Bohemian Waxwing
Cedar Waxwing
Northern Shrike
Loggerhead Shrike
European Starling
Solitary Vireo
Warbling Vireo
Red-eyed Vireo
Tennessee Warbler
Orange-crowned Warbler
Nashville Warbler
Yellow Warbler
Yellow-rumped Warbler
Townsend's Warbler
Blackpoll Warbler
Black-and-white Warbler
American Redstart
Ovenbird
Northern Waterthrush
MacGillivray's Warbler
Common Yellowthroat
Wilson's Warbler
Yellow-breasted Chat
Western Tanager
Rose-breasted Grosbeak
Black-headed Grosbeak
Lazuli Bunting
Indigo Bunting
Green-tailed Towhee
Rufous-sided Towhee

American Tree Sparrow
Chipping Sparrow
Clay-colored Sparrow
Brewer's Sparrow
Field Sparrow
Vesper Sparrow
Lark Sparrow
Lark Bunting
Savannah Sparrow
Baird's Sparrow
Grasshopper Sparrow
Le Conte's Sparrow
Sharp-tailed Sparrow
Fox Sparrow
Song Sparrow
Lincoln's Sparrow
White-throated Sparrow
White-crowned Sparrow
Harris' Sparrow
Dark-eyed Junco
McCown's Longspur
Lapland Longspur
Chestnut-collared Longspur
Snow Bunting
Bobolink
Red-winged Blackbird
Western Meadowlark
Yellow-headed Blackbird
Rusty Blackbird
Brewer's Blackbird
Common Grackle
Brown-headed Cowbird
Orchard Oriole
Northern Oriole
Rosy Finch
Pine Grosbeak
Purple Finch
Cassin's Finch
House Finch
Red Crossbill
White-winged Crossbill
Common Redpoll
Hoary Redpoll
Pine Siskin
American Goldfinch
Evening Grosbeak
House Sparrow

Source: The Birder's Guide to Montana,
Falcon Publishing, 1993.

Bison

The bison once roamed over one-third of the North American continent, in numbers exceeding any other large mammal of recent times. Montana's Indian tribes pursued the great beasts on their southward migration to the central Great Plains in the late fall and met them with bows and arrows on their return to the rich grasslands of the state in the spring. Scattered across Montana are a number of the "pishkuns," or cliffs where Indians killed large portions of the herds by driving them over the edge.

The skilled hunters and their tribes used nearly every part of the bison. Bison meat was a food staple, the hides became clothing and tepees, and the bones were used for knives and scraping tools. The white men who came to the plains of the West slaughtered all but a few of this species from the 1870s to 1883. In 1881-82, one steamship captain claimed that he hauled over 250,000 hides from Montana to Bismarck, North Dakota, for further dispersion. The hides sold for three or four dollars, and there was some market demand for the horns as Victorian-era hat racks and other decorations.

Bison. Michael Sample

The bison in Montana were the last of the nation's great herds to be slaughtered. They survived longer than their counterparts in other western states because the cold winters and the hostile Blackfeet discouraged many buffalo hunters. Also, the railroads were comparatively late in coming to Montana and providing a means of exporting hides and other parts. After the greatest animal annihilation ever documented, some of the dried and bleached bison bones were gathered up and sold as fertilizer for $5 a ton. A few wild bison remained in Yellowstone National Park, forming the only wild herd left in the U.S.

The bison, *Bison bison*, is a member of the cattle family and is not accurately a "buffalo," which has no hump and is found mainly in Asia and Africa. A mature bull bison can weigh close to 2,000 pounds, stand 6 feet high at the shoulder, and measure up to 12^1/$_2$ feet from his nose to the end of his tail. Calves are born in May and are a brick-red color for the first year of life. The animal sheds its shaggy, winter-damaged coat each March and can appear relatively trim and sleek until the new coat grows in.

Buffalo Bill

In July 1996, the Museum of the Northern Plains in Fort Benton opened a Hornaday exhibition wing, named for the noted zoologist William Temple Hornaday, to house a stuffed bison that served as the model for the bison that graced the ten-dollar bill at one time. The beast was shot in "the big open" of Musselshell River country by Hornaday in 1886 and displayed until recently at the Smithsonian Institution in Washington, D.C.

A *Home* on a RANGE

The bison, the largest mammal native to North America, was almost extinct in the early years of the twentieth century when the American Bison Society collected forty-one of them from private herds in Montana and elsewhere to stock the National Bison Range near Moiese. The land, 18,540 acres, was bought from the Flathead Indians, and the reserve opened in 1908. The number of bison in the herd has increased over the years. The calves that are born there every spring can bring the herd's population to about four hundred by October. Some of the bison are sold after a fall roundup.

Bison are large animals and a close encounter with one is likely to be very dangerous, perhaps fatal. Visitors to the refuge at Moiese can observe them from the safety of a motor vehicle on a 19-mile self-guided tour open during the summer months.

The National Bison Range is also home to mule and white-tailed deer, elk, bighorn sheep, and pronghorns.

BIG *Medicine*

In 1933, a remarkable bison calf was born at the National Bison Range. He was almost an albino, white except for a dark brown "hat" between his horns. White buffalo are very rare, and Montana's Indians considered them sacred, so this one was given an Indian name: Big Medicine. At full maturity, he weighed 1,900 pounds and measured 12 feet long. You can still see him, but not at the refuge. He died at the great age of 26 and is now on display in the state Historical Society Museum in Helena, on the second floor. The taxidermy is the work of Bob Scriver, who is also a renowned bronze sculptor.

Elk

Montana is home to more than 150,000 Rocky Mountain elk. The elk, sometimes referred to by its Shawnee name, "wapiti," is a large, grazing and browsing animal that prefers coniferous forests and mountain meadows. Bull elk can weigh from 700 to 850 pounds. Cows weigh in between 400 and 700 pounds. Mature bulls drop their antlers in March. By July, their new antlers may weigh up to 50 pounds.

By the turn of the last century, the Montana elk population was nearly decimated by loss of habitat, food hunters, and collectors of the "ivory teeth." In 1910, 6,000 elk from Yellowstone National Park were transplanted to suitable habitat across the state. Since that time, the state has been dedicated to protecting and increasing elk habitat, especially appropriate winter range. Montana is one of the premier hunting grounds for this most prized big game animal.

Rocky Mountain Elk Foundation

Founded in 1984, the Rocky Mountain Elk Foundation is a nonprofit wildlife conservation organization that works to conserve, restore, and enhance natural habitats. Based in Missoula, the foundation also publishes *Bugle* magazine and boasts more than 98,000 members in 50 states and 27 countries.

In just one of its successful efforts, the foundation teamed with individuals and county, state, and federal agencies to purchase more than $10 million of land to protect 9,000 acres of critical migration corridors and wildlife winter range north of Yellowstone National Park. The project started following the Yellowstone fires of 1988, when several landowners near the park expressed interest in protecting wildlife.

The foundation can be reached by phone at (800) CALL ELK.

Wolves

Most of the wolves in Montana had been exterminated by the early 1900s. From 1870 to 1877, an estimated 700,000 wolves were shot, trapped, or poisoned. While those estimates may be overstated, records suggest that some 80,000 wolves were killed from 1883 to 1918 by the bounty-hunting "wolfers" or "wolf-getters" in the service of livestock owners eager to see their industry thrive. Federal government predator control programs removed another 24,000 from 1915 to 1942.

In recent decades, several wolf packs, with members numbering from fifteen to thirty, have survived in Glacier National Park and the extreme northwestern corner of Montana. In 1989, wildlife biologists studied the first pack known to den outside Glacier National Park in 60 years. Today there are as many as nine natural wolf packs in Montana, ranging as far south as the Deer Lodge and Boulder valleys.

In the early 1990s, intense public debate and legal wrangling arose over plans for the reintroduction of breeding packs to Yellowstone National Park and central Idaho. In March 1995, twenty-nine Canadian wolves were finally released into the wilds of those areas. In January and April 1996, another seventeen Canadian wolves were set free in Yellowstone and nine were released in central Idaho. By that spring, the wolves released in Yellowstone had produced nine pups. Two of the original wolves had been killed—one by a truck; the other was illegally shot.

Troubled Species

The following species, which occur in Montana, are considered by the U.S. Fish and Wildlife Service to be endangered (in danger of extinction throughout all or a significant part of its range) or threatened (likely to become endangered in the foreseeable future).

Endangered	Gray wolf, *Canis lupus*
	Black-footed ferret, *Mustela nigripes*
	Pallid sturgeon, *Scaphirhynchus albus*
	Peregrine falcon, *Falco peregrinus*
	Whooping crane, *Grus americana*
	Interior least tern, *sterna antillarum athalasso*
	White sturgeon, *Acipenser transmontanus*
	(Kootenai River population)
Threatened	Grizzly bear, *Ursus arctos horribilis*
	Piping plover, *Charadrius melodus*
	Bald eagle, *Haliaeetus leucocephalus*

In an effort to maintain biological diversity in our state, the Montana Natural Heritage Program conducts an inventory of plant and animal populations, focusing on species and communities that are rare, threatened, endangered, or vulnerable throughout their range in Montana. The list is constantly updated and is accessible on the internet via the World Wide Web at http://nris.mt.gov. MNHP can be contacted at 444-3009.

Watching Wildlife

The numbers of U.S. citizens and, especially, Montanans who look for native birds and animals along trails and roadsides is increasing annually. The National Watchable Wildlife Program combines the efforts of public management agencies and private environmental groups to mark and preserve habitat where wildlife can be observed. Montana has more than one hundred Wildlife Viewing Areas, marked by brown and white signs with a "binoculars" logo. To learn more about designated wildlife viewing sites in Montana, see the *Montana Wildlife Viewing Guide* (Falcon®, 1995), available from most booksellers or by calling (800) 582-2665.

Public Lands

Approximately 26.14 million acres (28 percent) of Montana's 93.156 million acres are owned, held in trust, or leased by the federal government for use by all U.S. citizens. The USDA Forest Service and the Bureau of Land Management together administer nearly 25 million acres.

State land accounts for more than 5 million acres (5.4 percent).

The diverse values of public lands include recreation, range, timber, minerals, watershed, fish and wildlife, and wilderness. Other values placed on public lands include scenic, scientific, and cultural resources.

National Wildlife Refuges in Montana

Refuge Name Address/Phone	Location	Size (in Acres)	Terrain	Wildlife Viewing
Benton Lake NWR P.O. Box 450 Black Eagle, MT 59414 727-7400	14 mi north of Great Falls on US 87, the Bootlegger Trail	Land: 12,383 Water: 5,000	marshy glacial lake bed on semiarid shortgrass prairie; low hills, coulees	nesting waterfowl, inc. tundra and whistling swan, snow geese, ibis, peregrine falcon; deer and smaller prairie mammals
Bowdoin NWR HC65, Box 5700 Malta, MT 59538 654-2863	7 mi east of Malta off old US 2	Land: 15,500 Water: 3,700	prairie pothole marshes on semiarid plain	on Central Flyway; duck nesting groups; over 200 bird species, antelope, and white-tailed deer
Charles M. Russell NWR P.O. Box 110 Lewistown, MT 59457 538-8706	Between MT 24 and US 191, south of Glasgow and Malta, north of Jordan	1,009,000 Fort Peck Lake	35 mi of Missouri River and Breaks	upland game birds; 45 species of mammals inc. elk, bighorn sheep, prairie dogs
Hailstone NWR P.O. Box 110 Lewistown, MT 59457	35 mi west of Billings, N of Rapelje	Land: 1,988 Water: 660	prairie marshes, sagebrush, native grasses, some private land	breeding grounds for grouse, shorebirds, and waterfowl; antelope, mule deer
Halfbreed NWR P.O. Box 110 Lewistown, MT 59457	5 mi south of Hailstone NWR	Land: 3,886	prairie marshes, sagebrush, native grasses, some private land	breeding grounds for grouse, shorebirds, and waterfowl; antelope, mule deer
Lake Mason NWR P.O. Box 110 Lewistown, MT 59457	6 mi NW of Roundup	Land: 18,600	marshes, open water, riparian habitat, shortgrass prairie	waterfowl, shorebirds, and upland game bird nesting area; peregrine falcon, bald eagle; prairie dog, rattlesnakes, lizards
Lee Metcalf NWR Box 257 Stevensville, MT 59870 777-5552	East of Stevensville, off US 93	Land: 2,800	forested river bottom in mountain valley	waterfowl, raptors, shorebirds, falcon, bald eagle, osprey, owls, muskrats, black bear, river otter
Medicine Lake NWR 223 North Shore Rd. Medicine Lake, MT 59247 789-2305	24 mi N of Culbertson, off MT 16	Land: 31,457 Water: 21,500+	prairie potholes (glacially-formed lakes)	white pelicans nesting area; other waterfowl and upland, whooping and sandhill cranes, cormorants, gulls, heron; small prairie and game mammals

National Wildlife Refuges in Montana (cont.)

Refuge Name Address/Phone	Location	Size (in Acres)	Terrain	Wildlife Viewing
Ninepipe NWR National Bison Range Moiese, MT 59824 644-2211	49 mi N of Missoula on US 93	Land: 2,062 Water: 1,770	over 800 potholes in marshes upland grasses, W of Mission Mtns.	migratory waterfowl, nesting area; 180 species, inc. Canada geese, heron, avocets, gulls
Pablo NWR National Bison Range Moiese, MT 59824 644-221	49 mi N of Missoula on US 93	2,542	pothole marshland, upland grass W of Mission Mtns.	migratory waterfowl, nesting area; Canada geese, heron, whistling swan, avocets, gulls
National Bison Range 132 Bison Range Rd. Moiese, MT 59824 644-2211	N of Missoula on US 93 to Ravalli west 6 miles	18,541	steep hills, canyons, upland grasslands, river bottomland	some 500 American bison; mule deer, elk, bighorn sheep, mountain goat, and antelope
Red Rock Lakes NWR Monida Star Rt. Box 15 Lima, MT 59739 276-3347	115 to N of Idaho border	Land: 42,525 Water: 9,000	6,600 elev., N of Centennial Mtns., lake marshes	resident trumpeter swans, 250 species of birds, inc. sandhill crane; wide range of large and small mammals
Swan River NWR 780 Creston Hatchery Rd. Kalispell, MT 59901 755-4375	south end of Swan Lake off MT 83	1,569	wooded bottomlands, marshes	best viewing from canoe; 171 species of birds, inc. great blue heron, bald eagle, waterfowl; moose, grizzly and black bear
UL Bend NWR P. O. Box 110 Lewistown, MT 59457 538-8706	40 mi south of Malta on country roads	56,049	within Charles M. Russell NWR	elk in their native prairie habitat; prairie dogs, sage grouse, pronghorn, deer, and bighorn sheep
War Horse NWR P.O. Box 110 Lewistown, MT 59457 538-8706	40 mi east of Lewistown on MT 200	Land: 3,192 Water: 900	marshy lakes in upland grasslands and sagebrush	waterfowl and upland game bird habitat; bald eagle, antelope, mule deer

State and Federal Land (in acres)

County	County Acreage	State Trust Lands	Montana FW&P	Forest Service	Bureau Land Mgmt.
Beaverhead	3,549,870	332,647	13,017	1,370,363	662,396
Big Horn	3,235,200	87,794	3,660	——	27,646
Blaine	2,730,880	180,728	221	——	454,464
Broadwater	796,800	23,805	25	186,491	66,049
Carbon	1,327,360	41,220	1,092	324,818	215,111
Carter	2,120,320	143,035	——	89,384	506,895
Cascade	1,710,720	76,934	953	178,658	24,764
Chouteau	2,508,800	267,177	104	30,713	111,278
Custer	2,416,000	140,822	562	——	339,073
Daniels	923,520	220,596	65	——	200
Dawson	1,523,200	87,499	4,206	——	64,795
Deer Lodge	474,240	7,561	2,024	177,450	5,697
Fallon	1,045,120	67,416	359	——	119,238
Fergus	2,721,920	155,421	87	94,971	354,411
Flathead	3,379,200	129,984	2,423	1,787,379	——
Gallatin	1,709,440	51,516	10,715	607,392	8,514
Garfield	3,079,680	167,112	——	——	493,491
Glacier	1,923,840	8,339	——	28,688	1,083
Golden Valley	753,920	48,602	——	23,693	7,961
Granite	1,111,680	20,423	108	662,466	44,908
Hill	1,872,640	155,864	2,436	——	14,204
Jefferson	1,058,560	32,150	3,257	463,507	97,276
Judith Basin	1,203,200	98,605	6,407	297,427	11,850
Lake	1,059,200	55,154	6,155	156,602	——
Lewis & Clark	2,218,240	133,798	40,270	986,964	71,676
Liberty	920,960	86,578	——	——	7,413
Lincoln	2,385,920	65,316	2,744	1,762,173	——
McCone	1,697,280	94,559	——	——	200,822
Madison	2,266,240	126,645	27,490	804,638	255,123
Meagher	1,507,840	90,077	3,581	479,047	8,629
Mineral	782,720	21,960	24	646,889	——
Missoula	1,679,360	74,122	11,556	693,027	14,295
Musselshell	1,207,040	76,324	——	——	104,583
Park	1,772,160	33,388	5,366	816,632	10,003
Petroleum	1,056,000	63,470	——	——	336,102
Phillips	3,383,680	189,426	674	——	1,089,053
Pondera	1,058,560	57,347	——	106,630	1,289
Powder River	2,102,400	140,793	——	339,689	260,637
Powell	1,497,600	56,792	6,994	640,968	85,548
Prairie	1,105,280	76,699	2	——	447,462
Ravalli	1,528,320	29,464	8,662	1,116,162	——
Richland	1,321,600	81,400	2,849	——	52,528
Roosevelt	1,535,360	20,233	1	——	4,197
Rosebud	3,226,880	178,062	36	95,822	234,129
Sanders	1,804,160	62,985	1,579	914,714	——
Sheridan	1,100,800	45,147	——	——	261
Silver Bow	458,240	13,234	60,743	190,045	45,390
Stillwater	1,152,640	46,522	966	186,320	6,120
Sweet Grass	1,183,360	47,091	585	287,563	16,392
Teton	1,468,160	103,863	17,454	234,988	19,884

State and Federal Land (cont.)

County	County Acreage	State Trust Lands	Montana FW&P	Forest Service	Bureau Land Mgmt.
Toole	1,248,000	100,028	—	—	27,688
Treasure	638,080	37,394	1,172	—	12,108
Valley	3,175,040	214,830	257	—	1,019,645
Wheatland	918,080	73,434	1,591	64,919	1,275
Wibaux	570,240	32,839	—	—	26,995
Yellowstone	1,621,000	79,038	544	—	85,811
TOTALS	93,826,550	5,153,262	253,079	16,847,192	8,075,362

National Forests

The USDA Forest Service, Northern Region, manages nine national forests in Montana, containing 16.8 million acres—18 percent of all lands in the state. USDA Forest Service lands are located throughout the state, though most are in western Montana. National forests were established on conservation principles, based on wise use of natural resources. By congressional mandate, they are managed for multiple use, the combination of interests that best serves the public.

USDA Forest Service Offices

Northern Region Headquarters
Public Affairs Office
Federal Bldg., 200 East Broadway
P.O. Box 7669
Missoula, MT 59807
329-3511
FAX 329-3411

Beaverhead-Deerlodge National Forest   3.3 million acres

Dillon Supervisor's Office
420 Barrett Street
Dillon, MT 59725
683-3900

Deerlodge Supervisor's Office
Federal Building
P.O. Box 400
Butte, MT 59703
496-3400

Butte Ranger District 494-2147
Dillon Ranger District 683-3900
Madison Ranger District 682-4253
Deerlodge Ranger District 846-1770
Jefferson Ranger District 287-3223 or (800) 433-9206
Philipsburg Ranger District 859-3211
Sheridan Ranger District 842-5432
Wise River Ranger District 832-3178
Wisdom Ranger District 689-3243

Bitterroot National Forest 1.1 million acres
1801 North 1st Street
Hamilton, MT 59840
363-3131

Stevensville Ranger District 777-5461
Darby Ranger District 821-3913
Sula Ranger District 821-3201
West Fork Ranger District 821-3269

Custer National Forest 1.1 million acres
2602 First Ave. North
P.O. Box 2556
Billings, MT 59103
657-6361

Beartooth Ranger District 446-2103
Ashland Ranger District 784-2344
(other ranger districts in North and South Dakota)

Flathead National Forest 2.35 million acres
1935 Third Ave. East
Kalispell, MT 59901
755-5401

Spotted Bear Ranger District 758-5376 (Summer) 387-5243 (Winter)
Swan Lake Ranger District 837-5081
Hungry Horse Ranger District 387-5243

Glacier View Ranger District 892-4372
Tally Lake Ranger District 862-2508

Gallatin National Forest 1.8 million acres
Federal Bldg., 10 East Babcock
P.O. Box 130
Bozeman, MT 59771
587-6701

Big Timber Ranger District 932-5155
Livingston Ranger District 222-1892
Gardiner Ranger District 848-7375 or -7376
Bozeman Ranger District 587-6920
Hebgen Lake Ranger District 646-7369

Helena National Forest 975,407 acres
2880 Skyway Drive
Helena, MT 59601
449-5201

Townsend Ranger District 266-3425
Helena Ranger District 449-5490
Lincoln Ranger District 362-4265

Kootenai National Forest 1.8 million acres
506 U.S. Highway 2 West
Libby, MT 59923
293-6211

Rexford Ranger District 296-2536
Fortine Ranger District 882-4451
Three Rivers Ranger District 295-4693
Libby Ranger District 293-7741
Fisher River Ranger District 293-7773
Cabinet Ranger Station 827-3533

Lewis and Clark National Forest 1.9 million acres
1101 15th Street North
P.O. Box 869
Great Falls, MT 59403
791-7700

Rocky Mountain Ranger District 466-5341
Judith Ranger District 566-2292
Musselshell Ranger District 632-4391
Kings Hill Ranger District 547-3361

Lolo National Forest   2.1 million acres
Building 24, Fort Missoula
Missoula, MT 59804
329-3750

Missoula Ranger District 329-3750
Ninemile Ranger District 626-5201
Plains/Thompson Falls Ranger District 826-3821
Seeley Lake Ranger District 677-2233
Superior Ranger District 822-4233

Bureau of Land Management

Within Montana, the Bureau of Land Management (BLM) administers more than 8,075,362 acres of federal lands, mostly in the eastern and southwestern parts of the state. That's about 8.6 percent of the land in the state.

Lands managed by the BLM extend across a varied geography, including mountains, forests, and plains, and afford extensive recreational opportunities—hunting, fishing, boating, camping, and bird watching. The bureau protects numerous archaeological and historic sites and oversees 173,000 acres of wilderness study areas and hundreds of miles of federally designated Back Country Byways and Wild and Scenic Rivers.

Montana State Office
P.O. Box 36800
222 North 32nd Street
Billings, MT 59107
255-2913

Butte District Office
P.O. Box 3388
106 North Parkmont
Butte, MT 59702
494-5059

Lewistown District Office
P.O. Box 1160
Airport Road
Lewistown, MT 59457
538-7461

Miles City District Office
P.O. Box 940
Garyowen Road
Miles City, MT 59301
232-4331

Resource Area Offices
Headwaters-Butte 494-5059
Dillon 683-2337
Garnet-Missoula 329-3914
Big Dry-Miles City 232-7000
Powder River-Miles City
 232-7000
Billings 657-6262
Judith-Lewistown 538-7461
Phillips-Malta 654-1240
Havre 265-5891
Valley-Glasgow 228-4316
Great Falls 727-0503

Wilderness Areas

Less than 150 years ago Montana was one immense wilderness. Today, there are 12 major tracts of wild land in the state, 3,372,000 acres, formally protected by the federal Wilderness Act of 1964. These wilderness areas constitute 3 percent of the land in the state. No new areas have been designated since 1983.

Approximately 9 percent of Montana is still considered roadless wild land, and is under temporary study or preservation status.

Montana wilderness areas are valuable homes for wildlife and watershed protection. They are not game preserves; hunting and fishing are permitted in accordance with state law.

Wilderness Area	Year Designated	Acres	Location
Absaroka-Beartooth	1978	920,377	Custer/Gallatin NF
Anaconda-Pintler	1964	157,874	Beaverhead-Deerlodge/ Bitterroot NF
Bob Marshall	1978	1,009,356	Flathead/Lewis & Clark NF
Cabinet Mountains	1964	94,272	Kootenai/Kaniksu NF
Gates of the Mountains	1964	28,562	Helena NF
Great Bear	1978	286,700	Flathead NF
Lee Metcalf	1983	259,000	Beaverhead-Deerlodge/ Gallatin NF
Mission Mountains	1974	73,877	Flathead NF
Rattlesnake	1980	32,976	Lolo NF
Scapegoat	1974	239,936	Helena/Lolo/ Lewis & Clark NF
Selway-Bitterroot	1964	251,441	Bitterroot/Lolo NF
Welcome Creek	1978	28,135	Lolo NF

Source: Montana Wilderness Society.

To keep Montanans informed on wilderness issues, the Montana Wilderness Society has a site on the World Wide Web at http://users.aol.com/wildmt/mwa.htm. The association is dedicated to the protection and preservation of the state's wild areas.

"The Bob"

The Bob Marshall Wilderness Area was named to honor a major advocate for wilderness preservation during the 1930s. Bob Marshall is also considered the catalyst for The Wilderness Society. While Marshall worked in and promoted wild places all over the United States, he got his start in Montana in 1925, when he went to work for a USDA Forest Service Range Experiment Station. He is remembered as a world-class hiker, often walking 40 or more miles in a day. He died of a heart condition in 1939, at the age of 38.

Answers to Up the Crick Quiz, p. 69

1. Blackfoot River
2. Little Blackfoot River
3. Clarks Fork of the Yellowstone
4. Tongue River
5. North Fork of the Flathead
6. Boulder River or East Rosebud Creek
7. Little Blackfoot River
8. Flathead River
9. Blackfoot River
10. Stillwater River

Further Reading

Alt, David D. *Profiles of Montana Geology, A Layman's Guide to the Treasure State.* Butte: Montana Bureau of Mines and Geology, 1984.

Alt, David D., and Donald W. Hyndman. *Roadside Geology of Montana.* Missoula: Mountain Press Publishing Company, 1990.

Bass, Rick. *The Ninemile Wolves.* New York: Ballantine Books, 1992.

Cunningham, Bill. *Wild Montana: A Guide to 55 Roadless Recreation Areas.* Helena: Falcon Publishing Co., 1995.

Elias, Thomas S., and Peter A. Dykeman. *A Field Guide to North American Edible Wild Plants.* New York: Outdoor Life Books, Times Mirror Magazines, Inc., 1982.

Fischer, Carol, and Hank Fischer. *Montana Wildlife Viewing Guide.* Rev. ed. Helena: Falcon Publishing Co., 1995.

Fischer, Hank. *Wolf Wars.* Helena: Falcon Publishing Co., 1995.

Hart, Jeff. *Montana Native Plants and Early Peoples.* Helena: Montana Historical Society Press, 1976.

Horner, John R., and James Gorman. *Digging Dinosaurs.* New York: Workman Publishing, 1988.

Krumm, Bob. *The Rocky Mountain Berry Book.* Helena: Falcon Publishing Co., 1994.

Magley, Beverly. *Montana Wildflowers: A Beginner's Guide to the State's Most Common Flowers.* Helena: Falcon Publishing Co., 1992.

Rocky Mountain Elk Foundation. *Majesty: Visions from the Heart of Elk Country.* Helena: Falcon Publishing Co., 1995.

Strickler, Dee. *Alpine Wildflowers.* Columbia Falls, MT: The Flower Press, 1990. *This title is an excellent guide, with color photos, covering the alpine and subalpine areas of the Rocky Mountain states. There are two other guides in Strickler's series,* **Forest Wildflowers** *and* **Prairie Wildflowers,** *both by the same publisher.*

Thompson, Larry S. *Distribution of Montana Amphibians, Reptiles and Mammals.* Helena: Montana Audubon Council, 1982.

c h a p t e r   f o u r

MONTANA'S *Past*

MONTANA WAS DESCRIBED as a "land of shining mountains" by early explorers who may have seen only the far eastern edges of the majestic Rocky Mountains. Like adventurer and storyteller Andrew Garcia, these early visitors probably thought that roaming through nineteenth-century Montana was a "tough trip through paradise." Many years later, distinguished state historian K. Ross Toole named this place "an uncommon land" and declared twentieth-century Montana to be a "state of extremes." Most recently, respected historians Michael P. Malone and Richard B. Roeder recounted the "surprisingly complex" political culture of two centuries of Montana's history—a story so rich in events and so full of colorful characters that it is almost a sacrilege to compress the saga into the few pages allotted in this book. This history is supplemented by a chronology of major events, some significant figures from the past, and a brief bibliography of excellent sources on the story of Montana and its people.

The First Montanans

It is hard to know how many early hunters and Indian tribes trekked through or made a home in this part of North America prior to the steady entry of non-Indians to the area. Archaeologists believe the first people arrived here via what is now called the Old North (or Great North) Trail along the eastern front of the Rocky Mountains. These earliest immigrants, termed Paleo-Indians, lived in the region we now know as Montana between 11,500 and 7,500 years ago and hunted large mammals such as mammoth and ancestors of the modern bison.

photo: Michael Sample

Archaeologists have found projectile points and primitive tools of these people in the south-central part of the state near Alder, Montana City, and Whitehall, and in eastern Montana near Lindsay. During a thousand-year dry period in the Great Plains that began about 5,000 B.C., the early hunting groups were forced to seek smaller animals and plant foods in the mountain valleys. The prehistoric people who lived here two thousand years ago pursued migrating buffalo as a staple of the culture. Bison could supply most items in the life of the people—clothing, tepees, tools, fuel, and food. The hunting bands often drove the buffalo herds off cliffs, or pishkuns, and perfected the use of the bow and arrow. Like earlier inhabitants, these bands of people were nomadic or semi-nomadic, moving their camps regularly to find shelter and food. Art made by these early hunters can be found on cave walls and cliffs throughout Montana—most notably at Pictograph Cave near Billings.

The ancestors of today's Montana Indians arrived in this area in the 1600s and 1700s. Some historians believe that the Kootenai (or Kutenai) may have been the first of the present-day tribes to live in Montana, arriving as long ago as the 1500s. Tribal histories and other accounts suggest that in the late 1700s the principal tribes in the Montana area included the Kalispel, Flathead, Pend d'Oreille, Shoshone, Gros Ventre, and Nez Perce. At some time in the early 1700s, the horses brought to the New World by Spanish explorers made their way into Indian culture, and life for all Plains tribes changed dramatically. The mobile tribal groups could move into new territories within the northern Great Plains.

The Blackfeet, Crow, and Assiniboine later established themselves as plains dwellers after being pushed westward ahead of the pressures of eastern settlement. The Sioux, Northern Cheyenne, Chippewa, and Cree people arrived in the 1800s. By the time of their encounter with the first Euroamerican explorers, these tribes had each established fiercely held hunting territories. Different tribes and bands had distinct traditions, beliefs, and cultures.

The tepee was the typical means of shelter used by the first Montanans (Paleo-Indians) and later Plains Indian tribes. Many "tepee rings"—circles of rocks that may have marked the outer edge of the lodges—remain in place today and are one of the most common types of archaeological sites found in Montana, mainly in the eastern part of the state.

Explorers and Fur Traders

A few parties of Spanish and British fur traders may have made their way into parts of the region as early as the mid- or late 1700s, but none left extensive documentation. Louis and François de la Verendrye, brothers exploring ever westward from eastern Canada for their father's fur trade grant, are credited with being the first white men to glimpse the land that would become Montana. They turned back from a long walk across the Dakotas after describing "shining mountains" in the distance. Historians believe they probably saw the southeastern Montana range known as the Bighorns.

In 1803, President Thomas Jefferson commissioned an exploration to trace the Missouri River to its source and find a water route to the Pacific Ocean, under the leadership of Meriwether Lewis and William Clark. These adventurous young men and their Corps of Discovery covered almost 8,000 miles from St. Louis, Missouri, to the mouth of the Columbia River, returning two years later. They journeyed westward across Montana from April 1805 to September of that year. On the return trip to St. Louis in the summer of 1806, the leaders crossed the state in two separate routes. Their extensive scientific journal entries revealed to the world the geography and many resources that were to attract the attention of those eager to capitalize on the newly opened land.

The Corps of Discovery's return coincided with the search for a source for beaver pelts—a demand made necessary by the fashion for beaver-pelt top hats. Over the next four decades of the nineteenth century, British and American fur trading companies combed the streams of Montana for precious furs, all but destroying the beaver population in the process. Many of these companies constructed posts for conducting business and for protection from the elements and Indians. Fort Benton, built on the Missouri River by the American Fur Company, became an important center for trading and shipping goods and furs. The steamboat was introduced to Missouri River traffic in 1819 and eventually replaced the keelboats and mackinaws the first traders used. Steamboats could navigate with a full load of 500 tons of freight on only 50 inches of water. This relatively inexpensive mode of travel prompted many persons with capital to make the 2,000-mile river trip from St. Louis to Fort Benton. From 1847 to the 1870s, more than six hundred steamboats arrived at what was then the world's most remote inland port.

In the mid-1800s, the beaver-skin hat fell out of fashion, but interest in leather hides for both clothing and animal tack accompanied the westward expansion. A new tanning process in the 1870s rendered bison hides suitable for much-needed leather goods. Montana's fur and hide hunters chased down bison and other prairie game almost as relentlessly as they had trapped the beaver.

The steamboat Helena near the confluence of the Marias and Missouri rivers, 1878. Montana Historical Society

notable
Montanans

Father Pierre Jean DeSmet (1801-1873)

Catholicism first came to Montana through Father DeSmet, long before gold attracted fortune hunters in the 1860s. Born in Belgium, DeSmet came from St. Louis in 1840 as the first missionary to the Flathead people. He established St. Mary's Mission in the Bitterroot Valley in 1841. His travels took him away from Montana frequently but he always returned with funds or supplies that proved instrumental to the mission, the Indians, and the region's development.

Montana Historical Society

John Bozeman (1835-1867)

At the age of 27, John Bozeman headed west with gold seekers. In 1864, he blazed a trail that led directly to Montana's mining camps, though it trespassed on Crow and Sioux territory in violation of treaties. He was killed along the Yellowstone River on April 18, 1867, a little over a month after writing to ask Acting Governor Thomas Meagher to use troops to protect settlers in the Gallatin Valley from increasingly hostile Blackfeet Indians.

Montana Historical Society

The Missionaries

Catholic priests were some of the first Europeans to be formally invited to Montana by the native inhabitants. When the few Catholic Iroquois Indians who accompanied fur companies to western Montana intermarried with the Kootenai, Salish, and Flathead Indians of the area, they were eager to have the "Blackrobes" sanctify those marriages and baptize their offspring. In the 1830s, four delegations of Flathead Indians walked the great distance to St. Louis to entice Jesuit priests to the Northwest. From this initial contact, Father Pierre Jean DeSmet came west to establish St. Mary's Mission in the Bitterroot Valley in 1841, the first permanent white settlement in Montana. Father DeSmet introduced interested tribal members to the practices of farming and irrigation. The multitalented Father Anthony Ravalli, who arrived later, brought the first European medicine and surgery to the Montana tribes and started the first sawmill and gristmill near St. Mary's Mission.

St. Labre Indian School in the Northern Cheyenne Reservation. Montana Historical Society

Wagons and Trails

In the fevered drive for westward expansion of the United States, Congress arranged for a number of wagon trail and railway surveys. An 1853 expedition led by Isaac I. Stevens, the governor of Washington Territory, recorded the most thorough descriptions of the area since Lewis and Clark. Modern-day rail lines

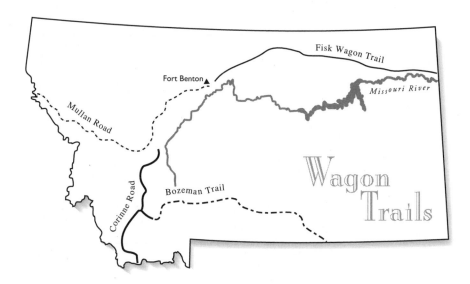

still follow much of the route. The northernmost of these surveys led to the construction of four major wagon trails for overland traffic into Montana.

The Fisk Wagon Trail, running from St. Paul, Minnesota, to Fort Benton, connected with the Mullan Road. John Mullan, veteran of the Stevens trek, had completed his namesake 624-mile route over the Continental Divide in 1862, connecting the inland west to the Pacific by means of steamboat navigation on the Columbia River near Fort Walla Walla. The Bozeman Trail pointed travelers northward off the famous Oregon Trail, providing a cutoff from Fort Laramie, Wyoming, to the mining boomtown of Virginia City, Montana. From Corinne, Utah, the Corinne Road passed through Virginia City and went as far north as Helena.

These wagon trails necessarily trespassed on the Indian territories that had been formally established by the Fort Laramie Treaty of 1851. More than a few hostile confrontations prompted the establishment of a number of military forts and outposts in an attempt to ensure safe passage on these routes. Even with several routes into Montana, the region remained isolated, with few settlers until the mid-1860s.

Gold and Its By-Products

Wagon roads proved useful when gold was discovered in the gravels along Montana streams. Although reports of gold finds in the Deer Lodge Valley had been made as early as 1858, it was the rich strike on a small tributary of the Jefferson River in southwestern Montana in 1862 that set the first big gold rush in motion. Within a year or two, thousands of miners stampeded to the major strikes at Grasshopper Creek (1862), Alder Gulch (1863), Last Chance Gulch (1864),

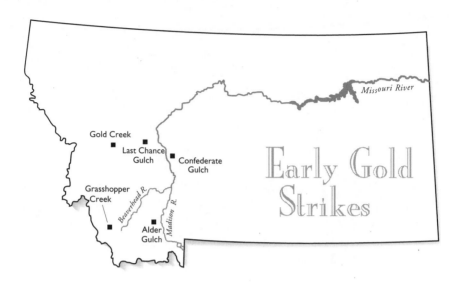

and Confederate Gulch (1864). Many came to apply themselves to the hard work of placer mining, but some came to get their gold the easy way—through robbery and trickery. Incidents ranged from minor thefts to brutal murders, resulting in the organization of the extralegal "Vigilantes." This secret society vowed to destroy the reign of terror and to establish law and order. From December 1863 to 1870, vigilantes hanged thirty-two supposed outlaws and chased off many who had reputations as road agents and criminals.

Trading and mercantile centers sprang up to serve the gold camps. Fort Benton served as an inland port for the people, machinery, and supplies destined for the gold fields. The Whoop-Up Trail led from this port on the Missouri north to isolated settlements on the Canadian prairie. More than a few enterprising pioneers saw that mining gold was not the only way to become prosperous in the boomtowns of Bannack, Virginia City, and Helena. Extensive and varied agricultural ventures developed in the southwestern mountain valleys, particularly the Gallatin Valley, to meet the needs of the placer mining boom. Several flour mills operated there by the late 1860s. Of the more than five hundred mining camps that dotted the western mountains, only a few, such as Butte and Helena, survived to become modern towns.

Cattle and Stockmen

Stockmen also made their fortunes on hungry miners and the need for horses and oxen. In 1850, Richard Grant and his sons, Johnny and James, began acquiring worn-out cattle from travelers along the Oregon Trail. After grazing and fattening them on the rich Montana grasses, they drove them back to the trail to trade one fresh animal for two weary ones. Conrad Kohrs bought the Johnny Grant ranch in the Deer Lodge Valley in 1865 and became one of Montana's leading stockmen. Dan Floweree brought a herd of cattle into Montana from Missouri in 1865. Nelson Story, another early cattle king, brought the first trail herd of Texas longhorns to Montana, settling in the Paradise and Gallatin valleys.

Panning gold in Alder Gulch, Virginia City, 1871. Montana Historical Society

notable
*M*ontanans

Mattie Castner (?-1920)

"The Mother of Belt." Enslaved until she was eight years old, Mattie came west, landed in Fort Benton, and got a job in a hotel. She and her husband, John C. Castner, built the first log cabin in Belt—it became the town's first hotel. They later opened the first store in town. Mattie also worked in the coal mine her husband developed and, above ground, grew vegetables to sell in Fort Benton, 40 miles away. Both she and her husband gave selflessly to a variety of charities and causes.

Thomas Francis Meagher (1823-1867)

This Irish revolutionary leader was convicted of treason and exiled by the British to a penal colony in Tasmania, but managed to escape and make his way to New York City. He volunteered to serve in the Civil War, and organized an Irish brigade. In 1865, he accepted a post as Montana's territorial secretary and wound up serving two stints as acting governor. Historians William L. Lang and Rex C. Myers suggest Meagher "created more problems than he solved." Others consider him a hero. He is believed to have drowned in the Missouri River after being seen drinking on a boat at Fort Benton. Whether he fell, jumped, or was pushed remains a mystery.

Montana Historical Society

Montana as a Territory

For the sixty years prior to establishment of the territory of Montana in 1864, the area had been governed from afar within numerous early divisions of the western U.S. territories. The part of Montana located east of the Continental Divide belonged, in succession, to Louisiana Territory (purchased from France in 1803), Missouri Territory (1812-1821), the so-called "Indian Country" (1821-1854), Nebraska Territory (1854-1861), and Dakota Territory (1861-1863).

The western portion was acquired from Great Britain in 1846 and belonged to the Oregon (1848-1853) and Washington (1853-1863) territories until the entire future state was included in Idaho Territory in 1863.

When gold seekers began flooding into southwestern Montana in the 1860s, newcomers and old-timers alike knew it would be wise to create a government close to the action around the gold fields near Bannack, Virginia City, and Helena. The gold strikes and improved transportation routes swelled the population to the five thousand male citizens needed to ask the U.S. government for territorial status. Bad winter weather in 1864 kept Sidney Edgerton, chief justice of the newly created Idaho Territory, from leaving Bannack to travel elsewhere in the territory. He viewed firsthand the vigilante ef-

Gold from Nelson Gulch, 1865.
Montana Historical Society

forts to control criminal activity in that raw land and volunteered to head back to Washington, D.C., in March 1864 to appeal to Congress to divide the territory. As proof of the mineral riches of the area, Edgerton carried gold ingots sewn into the lining of his coat. Congress passed the Organic Act, making Montana a territory in May 1864, and it was approved by President Abraham Lincoln.

The election of delegates to the First Territorial Legislative Assembly took place in October 1864. The body met in December in a dirt-roofed cabin in Bannack. During the next sixty days, the Assembly passed seven hundred pages of laws and chose nearby Virginia City as the first territorial capital. At the time, the Civil War raged and Montana's early politics suffered from the same strongly held allegiances as did the rest of the country. Yankees wanted to make sure that Confederate sympathizers would not gain an edge in the new Montana territory, either by law or lawlessness. Although many Montana settlers were former Southerners, the territory's population was largely pro-Union Democrats, and government lay in the hands of appointed Union Republicans.

The ink was hardly dry on the papers creating the new territory before the followers of Thomas Meagher, Democratic territorial secretary, started clamoring for statehood. When the first Republican territorial governor, Sidney Edgerton, was out of the region, Acting Governor Meagher called a constitutional convention in April 1866 on the petition of a number of citizens but without the desirable invitation of Congress. One of the greatest unsolved mysteries of Montana is just what happened to this first Montana constitution. Supposedly, a delegate lost the papers while they were in transit to St. Louis for printing. Another unsolved mystery is what happened to Meagher later that year, when he not only fell from grace with many citizens but also apparently fell from the deck of a Missouri River steamboat after a night on the town in Fort Benton. He was never seen again.

Montana

One of the hardest parts of carving out a new territory was deciding what to name the new land. Representative James Ashley of Ohio, who carried the legislation, had to convince his fellow congressmen that "Montana" was a suitable name. Others argued for the name "Shoshone," to honor Indians of the area, or "Jefferson," to honor the former president who commissioned the Lewis and Clark Expedition.

Indian Treaties

Treaties with the Montana Indian tribes in 1851 and 1855 had parceled parts of Montana into tribal reserves, giving Indians the right to approve transportation routes through them. A liberal interpretation of the 1855 treaties permitted American settlement in the mountain valleys. U.S. policy was meant to protect the miners, merchants, and settlers, confining Indians within specified boundaries. From 1866 onward, fourteen forts were established by the U.S. Army along transportation routes and near the gold fields.

The Sioux closed the extralegal Bozeman Trail in 1868 and gathered with Cheyenne and other allies in their hunting grounds along the Powder River country of eastern Montana. The army thought it could control the largest gathering of Plains Indians ever recorded. After many years of Indian wars, the result was a lose-lose situation—the U.S. Army lost the Battle of the Little Bighorn in 1876, but Indians knew they would lose the next round. Disputes over a treaty

Working on a grade along the Northern Pacific Railroad, 1881. Montana Historical Society

regarding the Wallowa Indian Reservation in Oregon resulted in an 1877 attempt by some eight hundred Nez Perce to journey across Montana Territory and head for Canada. In several encounters, the Nez Perce outwitted and outfought soldiers sent to intercept them. Poor winter weather enabled the U.S. military, under General Nelson A. Miles, to thwart this march to freedom, and the exhausted Indian survivors and their famous chief, Joseph, surrendered after the Battle of the Bears Paw Mountains.

Booms and Busts: In the Mines, On the Range, Along the Rails

In addition to conflicts between whites and Indians, the two decades preceding statehood saw the expansion of mining. By the 1870s, the great gold camps had begun to play out and with them went Montana's first boom period. Placer gold mining operations were replaced with hardrock mining for silver and copper. These potentially more profitable but technical operations required corporate organization, tremendous capital, better transportation and facilities, and legal services. This activity determined the centers of settlement and influenced Montana transportation and politics for years to come. Banks and lumber companies prospered with the silver mines. Helena became the territorial capital and a center of commerce in 1875. From 1870 to 1890, silver mining ruled the economy, but in 1893 the bottom fell out of this market. Mines closed and thousands were out of work.

New cities emerged as the Northern Pacific Railroad built westward across Montana in 1883. The railroads reduced the need for river and wagon trade and subjected Montana to more outside economic control, but also made rapid development possible. With the coming of other railroads, Montana's population again showed significant gains.

Along with the rush for the mineral treasures of Montana, a four-legged stampede ensued. Stockmen drove thousands of cattle from Texas and elsewhere to feed on the rich grasslands of central Montana. After the final Indian wars in the late 1870s, the virtual extermination of the buffalo, and the arrival of railroad transportation, the high plains opened to profitable grazing for the cattle ranchers and sheepmen. By the early 1880s, the cattle industry had claimed the public lands of central Montana as one enormous pasture and gained power and wealth within the new territory.

The boom days of the open range came to an abrupt end after the hard winter of 1886-1887, when many cattle perished. The ranching industry steadily recovered by fencing the open range and planting dependable supplies of feed. But the open-range era had introduced to Montana the colorful cowboy, whose exploits and lifestyle were romanticized in the art and literature of the day. The paintings, sketches, sculptures, and writings of Charlie Russell portrayed and perpetuated the cowboy life.

Statehood

To set the stage for statehood, a second constitutional convention was convened at Helena in January 1884, and the resulting document was ratified by the people in November of that year. But Congress failed to take any action on the subject of Montana's admission to the Union, partly because of political high jinks involved in making sure Montana (and other western territories) did not have more Democrats than Republicans at the time. The admission to the Union of other western states was stalled not only by national political tensions but also by the jockeying for positions of advantage in the Great Plains and Intermountain West by railroads and mining interests.

The Enabling Act of 1889 required Montana to create a state constitution, so a third and successful constitutional convention was called. Delegates met in Helena in July and, except for a controversy over mining taxation, worked with speed to produce the constitution in about six weeks. The 1889 constitution, patterned after constitutions of other western states, was ratified in an election held October 1, 1889. After a little more than twenty-five years as a territory, Montana was admitted into the Union as the forty-first state on November 8, 1889, by proclamation of President Benjamin Harrison.

Buried Treasures

It was no wonder that Montana came to be known as the Treasure State. The Butte area produced thousands of tons of copper annually. The refining of silver, zinc, lead ore, and by-products of copper were also important industries in Montana well into the twentieth century. Antimony was mined near Thompson Falls. Large reserves of chromium were mined in Stillwater County. Fluorspar mining was a significant commercial industry in Ravalli County. Gems such as sapphires, moss agate, amethyst, garnet, and rhodochrosite were found in scattered areas throughout Montana with varying commercial value. The coming of the transcontinental railroads (Northern Pacific, 1881-1883; Great Northern, 1887-1893; Milwaukee Road, 1907-1909) created demands for fuel from vast coal deposits in Carbon and Cascade counties and then later in Musselshell, Rosebud, and Richland counties.

As Montanans clamored for statehood, one of the most widely known chapters of Montana history was taking place in Butte—the infamous "War of the Copper Kings." The city was thought to be the "richest hill on earth." By 1887, Montana led the nation in the production of silver and copper. Proof of this economic power was a provision exempting unmined ore from taxation in the 1889 constitution. The "war" culminated in the corporate growth of the Anaconda Copper Mining Company, founded by Marcus Daly.

Daly had built a smelter at Anaconda in the early 1880s. After he enlisted the backing of some of the West's most powerful capitalists, the syndicate incorporated and, in 1895, reorganized its holdings as the Anaconda Copper Mining Company. Daly's rival, William Andrews Clark, poured his money into mines, smelters, a bank in Deer Lodge, and other businesses and properties. Fanning the flame of their intense industrial rivalry, Daly used his power to thwart Clark's bid for a U.S. Senate seat in 1889 and 1893. The Copper Kings also battled over selection of the official state capital. In that battle, Daly and the town of Anaconda lost to Clark's choice of Helena in 1894.

From the 1870s to well into the twentieth century, unions and other civic reformers tried to curb the power and excesses of the powerful copper industry. These efforts were somewhat successful in mitigating unfair working conditions and legislature tampering by the mining industry, but the greatest legacy was probably heightened citizen involvement in the affairs of the workplace and in government in general.

Homesteaders arrive at Ravalli, circa 1910-1915. Montana Historical Society

The Homesteaders

In the 1890s, farmers began to follow cattle ranchers and sheepmen onto the eastern Montana plains. The population of Montana in 1890 was more than 142,000, and by 1900 it was more than 243,000, with a large share of the increase in the plains area. By 1920, that population had doubled. The great boom in homesteading began about 1909 and lasted through World War I.

Three railroads, particularly Jim Hill's Great Northern Railway, promoted Montana farming opportunities to the world. Whereas the Northern Pacific was a land grant railroad and could sell land to build its line, the Great Northern counted on moving people and products along its northern Montana route. The Chicago, Milwaukee, St. Paul and Pacific Railroad hoped to lure settlement along its central Montana holdings. Opportunistic land speculators, the state of Montana, and dry land farming proponents also convinced thousands of hopeful homesteaders that diversified farming was possible where native shortgrass had rooted in shallow soil. Neither homesteaders nor federal officials realized how many acres were needed to support a family on the semi-arid grasslands, and this lack of foresight caused one of the most devastating periods in the state's history.

Under the Enlarged Homestead Act of 1909, the head of a family or anyone over the age of 21 could claim 320 acres of public land. A homesteader was required to build a house (a shack would do) and cultivate part of the acreage for grain production. In the years between 1909 and 1917, the homesteaders, for the most part, did well, but most were unaware that these were unusually wet years for the area. Some of the settlers were experienced farmers, but many were not. Hundreds of single women took up claims, and hired help to do the required improvement work. Some homesteaders expected to sell the land at good prices after they "proved up" on it. Towns boomed along the railroad to supply the farmers' needs. In the 10 years following 1909, the cultivated land in Montana increased from 258,000 acres to 3,417,000 acres. Some one hundred new towns had sprouted on the prairie. In 1916, farmers in one area raised 80 bushels of wheat to the acre when an average crop was 25.

Then disaster struck. In 1917, the first of the drought years hit some parts of the state, just as the U.S. government encouraged farmers to plow as much land as possible for food production during wartime. Banks were encouraged to lend money to the farmers to buy equipment, but many of the banks lost their investment. By 1919, the drought had become widespread throughout the state, and wheat lands averaged only 2.4 bushels an acre. The dry soil blew away on the unending wind. By 1925, half of Montana's farmers had lost their farms because they could not repay money they had borrowed. Half of the state banks eventually went out of business. Between 1920 and 1930, Montana was the only state in the Union to lose population, and much of this loss was from the eastern counties.

Rental Cars

For fifty dollars, a homesteader could rent an entire boxcar on the Great Northern Railway to carry his farm machinery, household goods, livestock, and lumber to eastern Montana from the railroad's origin in St. Paul. Professional "locators" charged twenty dollars for bringing newcomers west to choose their land.

The Depression, the New Deal, and World War II

Montana did not escape the drought and the Great Depression of the 1930s. Climate and economics conspired to exacerbate already tough times. Fire, winds, and insects took a toll on the plains. The price of copper dropped, leaving thousands out of work. Cattle and wheat prices also dropped dramatically.

The building of Fort Peck Dam was Montana's greatest New Deal project, but thanks to Montana's powerful Democratic congressional delegation, the federal government aided the state with hundreds of other public works projects. Federal funding made rural electrification possible, and the Civilian Conservation Corps reforestation program employed 25,600 men in 40 camps across the state. As elsewhere in the nation, the provisions of the National Labor Relations Act enabled unions to win concessions. These New Deal programs benefited Montana well beyond the years of the Great Depression.

During World War II, the weather cooperated with the need for an abundant national food supply. Copper, timber, oil, and gas output soared. There were few defense industry jobs here, so nearly ninety thousand people left the state, with forty thousand of those enlisting in the armed services. In the years after the war, Montana's population increased by 121,000. Along with returning soldiers, growth was fueled by federal defense projects—including expansion of Malmstrom Air Force Base and the housing of much of the nation's cold war nuclear missile force beneath the fields of central Montana.

Recent Change

During the 1960s, the economic power of the state shifted toward development of coal, oil, and gas resources on the eastern plains. The most important economic change in Montana in the 1970s and 1980s was the decline of the Anaconda Company. For a century, the copper giant had ruled state politics and the press, expanded into lumbering and smelting, and shared power projects with the Montana Power Company. After buying other mines in the U.S., Chile, and Mexico, the company controlled one-fourth of the world's copper. By the 1970s, fiber optic cable was replacing copper in phone lines, environmental laws were strengthened, and the Chilean properties were nationalized. Just three years after the oil giant Atlantic Richfield Company (ARCO) purchased the Anaconda Company, it closed most smelter and refinery operations, and in 1983 stopped all its mining in Butte. In 1985, Dennis Washington, a construction company owner from Missoula, purchased the copper mining interests and resumed mining activity, though at a lesser scale.

In the 1970s and 1980s, the rising influence of oil, gas, and coal interests coincided with the waning copper interests in the western half of the state. The Montana Power Company became the state's number one industrial employer but had to answer to growing environmental concerns in its corporate projects. The homegrown environmental movement that had its genesis in the 1970s continues to advocate government policies and economic growth that do not sacrifice a healthy environment and the Montana way of life. Other economic changes in the 1980s and into the 1990s include the rise of tourism and the trucking industry and the decline of labor unions and the timber industry. Also in the 1980s, most banks in the state were drawn into various regional banking networks.

Politics

For a remote and sparsely populated state, Montana has quite frequently sent representatives to Washington who have made remarkable contributions to the national political scene. Among them have been Thomas H. Carter, Thomas J. Walsh, Burton K. Wheeler, James E. Murray, Lee Metcalf, and Mike Mansfield, all powerful figures in the United States Senate. Jeannette Rankin was the first woman elected to the House of Representatives, where she served separate terms during both world wars and voted against participation in both. Also in top political ranks was Joseph M. Dixon, who gained prominence in national Republican and Progressive Party politics before returning to Montana to serve from 1921 through 1924 as a Republican governor.

The governorship was in the hands of the Democratic party from 1925 through 1940, and again from 1949 through 1952. From 1941 through 1948, and in the years from 1953 through 1968, Republicans held the governorship. Democratic governors were returned to office from 1969 through 1988. Republican Stan Stephens served as governor from 1989 through 1992, followed by Marc Racicot, also a Republican, whose second term is scheduled to end on the third day of the new millennium.

Most frequently, Montanans send liberal Democrats to Washington, D.C., but elect more conservative Democrats or Republicans to run state government. Since direct election of senators began in 1913, only Zales N. Ecton in 1946 and Conrad Burns in 1988 have won Montana's U.S. Senate seats as Republicans. It is also common in Montana for the executive branch and one or more of the legislative houses to be dominated by opposite political parties. Often, the two houses of the legislature have been evenly split between political parties. Republicans controlled both houses of the 1995 and 1997 legislative sessions.

Montana has led the nation in a number of worthy governmental reforms. The state's voters adopted the initiative and referendum process in 1906 and woman suffrage in 1914. Lawmakers passed the first worker's compensation law in 1915.

By the end of the 1960s, the original 1889 constitution contained much that was outdated. Rather than revising a document that had been amended forty-one times over the years, the people affirmed the need for a new constitution by voting in November 1970 to call a constitutional convention. One hundred elected delegates met in Helena on January 17, 1972, and by March 22 of that year had created one of the most modern state constitutions in the nation. The voters approved the new constitution on June 6, 1972, and it became effective July 1, 1973. Some progressive tenets of the 1972 constitution include the recognition of the people's right to a clean and healthy environment, an open meeting law, and liberalization of the people's right to enact legislation.

notable

Montanans

K. Ross Toole (1920-1981)

Montana Historical Society

Toole was one of Montana's favorite and most outspoken historians. He was the kind of teacher whose lectures drew rapt, standing-room-only audiences. For his students, he made history come alive. He encouraged a critical look at the state's past as prologue to the treatment of resource development of the 1970s and 1980s. He was also the first director of the Montana Historical Society and led creation of the society's museum and art galleries, founding a quarterly magazine, *Montana, The Magazine of Western History.* Toole left the state to become director of the Museum of the City of New York and directed the Museums of New Mexico before returning in 1965 to teach at The University of Montana, where he was Hammond Professor of Western History. He authored eleven books and many articles on the American West and Montana, including *Montana: An Uncommon Land* and *The Rape of the Great Plains.*

Anne McDonnell (1884-1977)

Some called her "an encyclopedia of Montana history." From 1924 until 1953, McDonnell served as a librarian at the Montana Historical Society, contributing to innumerable research efforts to unearth the region's past. Born in Minnesota and raised by her grandparents in Butte, where her father worked in the mines, she worked briefly at the Butte Public Library and also taught school before taking the job at the historical society. Though the title of "librarian" belonged to the chief administrative officer of the society, McDonnell knew the library and archives better than anyone and earned the chief post shortly before her retirement.

Montana Historical Society

Chronology:
It Happened in Montana,
1743 to 1996

1743   On a westward trek that ends near the southeast corner of modern Montana, the Verendrye brothers, French explorers, describe the "land of shining mountains" to the west.

1762   The province of Louisiana, including that part of Montana east of the Rocky Mountains, passes from French to Spanish control.

1802   Napoleon forces Spain to cede Louisiana back to France.

1803   United States purchases Louisiana from France for what amounts to three cents an acre. It becomes known as Louisiana Territory.

1805   After departing from the mouth of the Missouri in May 1804, Meriwether Lewis, William Clark, and their expeditionary Corps of Discovery cross the Montana Rockies on their way to the Pacific Ocean.

       François Larocque explores southeast Montana for the Canadian North West Company and is first to describe what is later named Pompeys Pillar, a 200-foot isolated rock on the south bank of the Yellowstone River. William Clark will name it in 1806.

1806   Lewis and Clark reach Bitterroot Valley July 1 on return trip from the Pacific. After splitting up, Lewis meets Clark at mouth of the Yellowstone River in August.

1807   American fur trade begins with Manuel Lisa's construction of the Missouri Fur Company's trading post at the confluence of the Bighorn and Yellowstone rivers.

1808   Explorer David Thompson, representing British fur interests (Northwest Company), enters Montana via "Kootenay" River and, in 1809, erects Saleesh House at present-day Thompson Falls.

       John Colter, a veteran of the Lewis and Clark Expedition, is stripped, disarmed, and forced to run for his life from a band of Blackfeet near the Three Forks of the Missouri River, escapes, and makes his way back to Fort Manuel Lisa.

1810   Andrew Henry and other Missouri Fur Company men build fort at Three Forks on Missouri River, abandoned within the year when eight men are killed by Blackfeet.

1812 Territory of Louisiana is renamed Missouri Territory. It includes the eastern two-thirds of what is now Montana.

   Ross Cox moves to Flathead Valley to work for John Jacob Astor's Pacific Fur Company.

1818 Land east of Continental Divide and south of the 49th parallel is conceded to U.S. by Great Britain; west of divide subject to joint claim by both nations.

1821 Eastern Montana becomes part of the Great Plains "Indian Country."

   Merger of North West Company and the British Hudson Bay Company strengthens latter.

1822 Andrew Henry builds a trading post on the Yellowstone River for Rocky Mountain Fur Company.

1823 Blackfeet ambush and kill Missouri Fur Company trappers (Jones-Immel party) on Yellowstone River near Billings and steal large fur cache, discouraging expansion.

1824 Intense competition between Hudson Bay Company and American Fur Company ignites when HBC parties enter Beaverhead Valley via the Snake and the Salmon rivers.

   Bureau of Indian Affairs is established within War Department.

1825 Canada's Columbia Fur Company enters bison hide trade in eastern Montana.

1827 Under the leadership of Pierre Chouteau, John Jacob Astor's American Fur Company attempts monopoly of Upper Missouri fur trade by forcing out other companies.

1828 Fort Union is founded by James Kipp near mouth of Yellowstone River.

1831 Nez Perce and Flathead delegation visits St. Louis to encourage missionaries to travel to Montana and the Northwest.

   Fort Piegan is established for American Fur Company where Marias River meets the Missouri.

   1832 Fort McKenzie is established several miles from the mouth of Marias River.

     First steamboat to navigate upper reaches of the Missouri, the *Yellowstone*, reaches Fort Union near border of Montana and Dakota, with artist George Catlin, noted portrayer of Indian culture, as a passenger.

     Fort Cass is established on the Yellowstone, near old Fort Manuel Lisa.

1834 Hudson Bay Company dominates fur trade west of Continental Divide, while American Fur Company controls the trade east of the divide.

1837 Smallpox epidemic ravages the Blackfeet and weakens their power in the area.

1840 Fur trade begins serious decline due to change in style of men's hats, no longer requiring beaver pelts.

1841 Jesuit priest Pierre Jean DeSmet establishes St. Mary's Roman Catholic Mission in the vicinity of present-day Stevensville.

1842 First crops are planted at St. Mary's Mission.

1846 Western Montana is ceded to United States by Great Britain as the international border is extended to Pacific along 49th parallel.

1848 Congress creates the Oregon Territory, which includes Montana west of the Continental Divide.

1850 St. Mary's Mission is leased by John Owen, who constructs trading post.

Fort Lewis, established on the Upper Missouri in 1845, is rebuilt as Fort Benton.

1851 Eastern Montana's Indian tribes are included in federal treaty system with first Fort Laramie Treaty.

1852 François Findlay, known as "Benetsee," finds first gold in Montana on a creek near present-day Garrison.

1853 Montana considered as site for transcontinental railroad by Isaac I. Stevens, governor of Washington Territory.

John Grant starts first cattle herd in Deer Lodge Valley.

Montana west of Continental Divide included in newly created Washington Territory.

1854 Montana east of Continental Divide included in newly created Nebraska Territory.

Roman Catholic mission is established at St. Ignatius, south of Flathead Lake.

1855 Governor Stevens, of Washington Territory, signs treaty with western Indians at Council Grove near Missoula. In Lame Bull's treaty, Blackfeet people and their allies, the Gros Ventre, accept reservation that encompasses the northern two-thirds of eastern Montana. By 1888, this huge reserve would be incrementally reduced and divided until it resembled the present-day boundaries of the Fort Peck, Fort Belknap, and Blackfeet reservations.

1858   James and Granville Stuart spread the word about their significant gold find northwest of the Deer Lodge valley on Benetsee Creek, later named Gold Creek.

1860   Steamboat *Chippewa* is first to reach Fort Benton, head of navigation on the Missouri River.

1861   Montana east of Continental Divide is included in creation of Dakota Territory.

1862   Mullan Wagon Road built between Walla Walla and Fort Benton.

James Liberty Fisk begins years of leading wagon trains over the Minnesota-Montana Road, connecting upper Midwest to Fort Benton.

Gold rush draws thousands to Grasshopper Creek diggings, later called Bannack.

First local elections are held in Missoula County, part of Washington Territory.

1863   Gold rush draws thousands to Alder Gulch. Virginia City springs up almost overnight on a tributary of Alder Creek.

Idaho Territory is organized, including all of future Montana.

1864   Montana Territory is created on May 26, with capital at Bannack. Sidney Edgerton, former chief justice of Idaho Territory, is appointed first territorial governor.

Bannack-Virginia City vigilantes hunt down and hang twenty-four members of Sheriff Henry Plummer's alleged gang of robbers and killers, including Plummer.

The "Four Georgians" find gold in Last Chance Gulch, site of future Helena.

John M. Bozeman leads first wagon train over Bozeman Trail.

First newspaper, the *Montana Post*, is published in Virginia City.

Miners rush to Confederate Gulch (Diamond City) near present-day Townsend.

1865   Virginia City becomes territorial capital, replacing Bannack.

Thomas Francis Meagher, acting governor and former Union Army general, stirs up extreme political partisanship and Civil War sentiments when he switches allegiance from Union Democrat-Republican leanings to pro-Southern Democrats.

1866   Virginia City is connected by telegraph with Salt Lake City in November. First public school is opened in Virginia City.

Fort C. F. Smith is constructed on Bighorn River to protect Bozeman Trail.

Nelson Story brings first longhorns into Gallatin Valley, traveling 1,800 miles from Texas.

1867 All acts of second and third Montana legislative sessions annulled by U.S. Congress.

Acting Governor Thomas Meagher disappears (a supposed drowning) at Fort Benton, under mysterious circumstances.

Fort Ellis erected near Bozeman, Fort Shaw on Sun River.

First band of sheep in Montana is brought to Prickly Pear Valley.

1868 U.S. cedes land east of Bighorns to Sioux and other tribes; Fort C. F. Smith burned by Indians; Bozeman Trail abandoned.

Indians are considered to be born into a foreign nation and are not included in the extension of U.S. citizenship in ratification of the Fourteenth Amendment to the U.S. Constitution.

1869 450-mile freight route links gold fields of southwestern Montana to the Union Pacific Railroad at Corinne, Utah.

Washburn-Langford expedition is first official exploration of future Yellowstone National Park area.

1870 U.S. Army troops massacre 173 non-hostile Piegan Indians, a tribe of the Blackfeet Nation.

First federal census shows 20,595 people in territory.

1871 End of treaty policy period of federal-Indian relations; reservations are created.

1872 Congressman James A. Garfield bargains with Flathead tribe for compensation and resettlement.

Salish are directed to leave Bitterroot Valley; Chief Arlee moves, but Chief Charlot refuses to sign agreement.

Yellowstone becomes the first national park.

1875 Helena becomes territorial capital, replacing Virginia City.

1876 More than two hundred men of the Seventh U.S. Cavalry, led by Lieutenant Colonel George Armstrong Custer, are killed on Little Bighorn by a combined force of Sioux and Cheyenne.

1877 Forts Missoula, Keogh, and Custer are constructed.

Nez Perce elude U.S Army, in last great Indian military success, by fleeing to Montana. Forced to surrender at Bears Paw Mountains.

1878 Butte Workingmen's Union organizes as first Montana labor group.

Northern Cheyenne Indians begin a six-week march back to Montana from exile in Oklahoma.

1879 Fort Assiniboine is constructed near Havre.

1880 Utah Northern Railroad reaches Dillon from Ogden, Utah, and is completed to Garrison in 1881.

Fort Maginnis is constructed near Lewistown.

Census lists 39,159 citizens. There are about five men to every two women.

1881 Northern Pacific Railroad stretches west to Miles City.

Slaughter of buffalo reaches peak, with fewer than two hundred left in the West.

1882 Marcus Daly's Anaconda Mine at Butte is found to contain the richest cache of copper ore in the world.

Successful sheepman Paris Gibson envisions great city on the banks of the Missouri River and files claim for townsite of Great Falls. The city incorporates in 1888.

1883 Former President Grant attends "last spike" ceremony at Gold Creek when Northern Pacific Railroad is completed from Lake Superior to the Pacific.

Montana Wool Growers Association is formed.

Compulsory school attendance is enacted.

1884 Montana denied statehood by U.S. Congress after meeting of constitutional convention in Helena.

Stockmen form vigilante group to protect cattle from rustlers in central Montana; fifteen rustlers are killed.

Anaconda Copper Mining Company builds smelter in Anaconda.

1885 Montana Stockgrowers Association is formed at peak of the cattle boom.

Refugee Métis people from Riel Rebellion in Saskatchewan flee to Montana.

1886 Open-range grazing in Montana reaches peak, with 700,000 cattle and nearly one million sheep.

1887 Severe winter blizzards kill at least half the cattle on open range.

Indians cede 17.5 million acres north of the Missouri River, with 11 million acres remaining available to them.

Federal Dawes Act requires division of Indian reservations into individual allotments for tribal members and into certain trust lands held by federal government.

1888 "War of the Copper Kings" commences as Marcus Daly fights the election of rival William A. Clark to Congress.

1889 Third constitutional convention is held in Helena on July 4. Voters ratify constitution on October 1.

Montana is admitted to Union as forty-first state on November 8, along with Washington, North Dakota, and South Dakota.

In a close election, Democrat Joseph K. Toole beats Republican Thomas C. Power to become first state governor.

First legislative session ends in disgrace with claims of election fraud, and rival Houses of Representatives are organized. Each party of each house elects a senator to send to Washington, D.C., where a Republican-controlled Senate sends the two Democrats home.

Montana is the nation's top copper-producing state; it is second in silver production.

1890 Steamboat traffic on the Missouri River declines as roads and railroads offer reliable transportation.

Census shows 142,924 Montana residents.

1891 Second legislative assembly begins constructive work on creating state government.

Chief Charlot's band of Salish is forced to move to Jocko Reservation.

1892 Fort William Henry Harrison built outside of Helena.

1893 Great Northern Railway is completed across state.

Electoral irregularities prompt Legislature to refuse to elect William A. Clark to U.S. Senate. Copper kings buy state newspapers.

Legislature establishes state university at Missoula, college at Bozeman, School of Mines at Butte, and Normal College at Dillon.

Western Federation of Miners established in Butte.

1894 Voters choose Helena as state capital in hard-fought battle with Anaconda.

Northern Pacific train is hijacked in Butte by disgruntled, jobless men hoping to join a national march on Washington, D.C. After picking up 350 men along the route east, the train is stopped by federal troops at Forsyth.

1896   Democratic-Populist coalition defeats Republicans.

Copper replaces silver as main source of Montana's mineral wealth.

1897   Bitterroot National Forest is established as first in state and one of the first in the nation.

1899   Standard Oil Company buys Anaconda Copper Mining Company and other Butte mines and creates holding company, Amalgamated Copper Company.

William A. Clark is accused of bribery in run for U.S. Senate; Senate disallows his election.

1900   Six million sheep in Montana make the state first in nation in wool growing.

In the struggle for dominance over the copper ore beneath Butte and in state politics, copper kings F. A. Heinze and William A. Clark align against Amalgamated Copper Company, Daly's former copper empire. The state judiciary is corrupted and the legislature overrun by corporate interests.

1902   State Capitol is completed in Helena.

1904   Child labor amendment is made part of Montana Constitution.

1905   Industrial Workers of the World battle other unions in Butte.

1906   Chicago, Milwaukee, St. Paul and Pacific Railroad (the Milwaukee Road) enters Montana and is completed with golden spike ceremony at Gold Creek in 1909.

Voters adopt constitutional amendment allowing initiative and referendum process.

1908   Billings Polytechnic Institute, forerunner of Rocky Mountain College, is established in Billings.

Montana enacts nation's first model law on domestic use of water.

1909   Industrial Workers of the World foments lumber strikes at Somers and Kalispell; "free-speech" strike breaks out in Missoula.

Mount St. Charles College (Carroll College) is formed in Helena.

National Bison Range is established in Mission Valley.

1910   Glacier National Park is established by an act of Congress.

Homesteading boom is in full swing, eventually resulting in over 30 million acres of public land opened to sodbusting; number of Montana farms has doubled since 1900. Agriculture replaces mining as Montana's top industry.

"The Big Blowup" forest fire burns more than three million acres of western Montana and Idaho panhandle.

1911   Socialists join forces with Industrial Workers of the World to elect socialist city government in Butte.

Excavation for the Placer Hotel on Helena's Last Chance Gulch yields enough gold to pay for the cost of construction.

1912   Ronan becomes site of first Farmers Union local.

State Capitol is expanded; two wings are added.

Theodore Roosevelt chooses Senator Joseph Dixon to manage national Bull Moose campaign.

Voters initiate and approve Progressive Era reforms to clean up politics, including direct election of U.S. senators.

County-busting craze in Montana begins, resulting in twenty-five new counties by 1920.

Cromwell Dixon makes first flight over the Continental Divide, from Helena to Blossburg.

1913   State Highway Commission is created.

Northern Montana College in Havre and Eastern Montana College of Education in Billings are established.

First Montana gas well is drilled, near Glendive.

1914   Montana grants women suffrage, five years before amendment to U.S. Constitution.

Labor violence in Butte ends recognition for the miners' unions.

The work of artist C. M. Russell is acclaimed in London exhibition.

1915   Anaconda Copper Mining Company disengages from Standard Oil and remains the world's biggest copper company.

Workmen's Compensation Act is enacted.

Oil is found in Elk Basin.

Homesteading is encouraged by record yield of 60 million bushels of wheat.

1916   Republican Jeannette Rankin is elected as first woman to serve in the U.S. Congress.

Non-Partisan League and other progressive labor and civic groups call for sweeping taxation and social reforms.

Greatest year in copper mining, with $97 million in value.

State voters approve prohibition of alcoholic beverages by overwhelming margin; state becomes "dry" at end of 1918.

Milwaukee Road completes 438 miles of electrified rail operation.

1917   The death of 164 Butte miners in Speculator Mine fire sparks strike by 15,000 workers. Federal troops intervene.

Industrial Workers of the World leader Frank Little is lynched by masked vigilantes in Butte.

Montana's U.S. Congresswoman Jeannette Rankin casts vote against entering into war with Germany.

Census miscalculation results in overdraft of Montana men for wartime service; more than forty thousand leave for duty.

First of drought years that eventually halt decade-long boom in agriculture.

1918   Wave of ultra-patriotism sweeps state; state Sedition Act is model for federal law.

Statewide influenza epidemic.

1919   Drought and low crop prices persist through 1925, leading 20 percent of Montana farms to stop production; half of all farm mortgages foreclose, and half of commercial banks fail.

1920   Census shows population increase of almost 173,000 since 1910, mainly in plains homesteading areas.

1921   First gasoline tax becomes law.

1923   Grasshopper plague destroys crops in eastern Montana.

Shelby hosts world heavyweight title fight between Jack Dempsey and Tommy Gibbons.

Kevin-Sunburst oil field is discovered.

1924   U.S. Senator Thomas J. Walsh of Montana exposes Teapot Dome scandal in Washington, D.C., and chairs National Democratic Convention.

U.S. Senator Burton K. Wheeler of Montana is vice-presidential candidate for Progressive Party.

Indian Citizenship Act extends citizenship to those Indians who had not become citizens through the allotment process.

Northern Pacific Railroad begins coal strip-mining near Colstrip.

Voters override Legislature and increase the mines tax.

1930 Census shows population of 537,606 and 10 percent fewer farms than in 1920.

1932 Going-to-the-Sun Road is completed, linking east and west sides of Glacier National Park.

1933 Senator Thomas Walsh dies on his honeymoon trip to Washington, D.C., where he was to take office as U.S. attorney general.

1934 Indian Reorganization Act (Wheeler-Howard Act) is passed, providing for tribal self-government, land and resource conservation and development, and other reforms.

James E. Murray is elected to serve in what will become the longest tenure as U.S. senator, until 1961.

1935 Helena suffers devastating earthquake that kills four people and does $3.5 million damage.

1936 More than 10,500 workers are employed in building of Fort Peck Dam.

Montana ranks second in nation per capita for federal aid during 1930s.

1937 State Welfare Commission is created.

1938 Milwaukee Road passenger train plunges into Custer Creek, killing forty and injuring eighty people.

1939 Fort Peck Dam, world's largest earth-filled dam, is completed.

1940 Jeannette Rankin is elected to Congress for a second time.

1941 Representative Rankin casts the sole vote against U.S. entry into World War II; many Montanans react bitterly.

1942 Malmstrom Air Force Base is constructed at Great Falls.

1943 First Hutterite groups arrive from Canada.

1946 Senator Burton K. Wheeler loses attempt at fifth term in primary to liberal opponent, Leif Erickson.

1949 Foundation Program Act of 1949 establishes most advanced school funding equalization mechanism in the nation.

1950 Salish and Kootenai Indians sue United States for value of lands lost by Stevens Treaty of 1855.

Great Falls surpasses Butte in population.

1951   Oil boom begins in Williston Basin, a deep and productive oil field lying beneath western North Dakota, southern Saskatchewan, and eastern Montana.

1953   Federal law transfers jurisdiction regarding law and order in Indian country to states.

1955   Columbia Falls aluminum plant opens, fueled by power from Hungry Horse Dam.

Anaconda Copper Mining Company begins digging for copper ore in what will become Butte's Berkeley Pit.

1956   Federal government and Crow Indians dispute value of lands required for Yellowtail Dam.

Butte miners reject Congress of Industrial Organization influence in favor of International Union of Mine, Mill, and Smelter Workers.

1957   State penitentiary at Deer Lodge seized by inmates; riot ends on promises of reform.

1959   Earthquake near Yellowstone National Park results in twenty-eight deaths and formation of Quake Lake.

Anaconda Company sells its Montana newspapers to Lee Newspapers, Inc.

1960   Malmstrom Air Force Base is nation's first operative Minuteman intercontinental ballistic nuclear missile site.

1962   Governor Donald Nutter and several associates are killed in airplane crash.

1964   State celebrates Territorial Centennial by sending twenty-five-car Centennial Train to World's Fair in New York City.

Congress passes Wilderness Act, establishing five major reserves in Montana.

1965   When Montana Legislature fails to act, federal district court reapportions Legislative Assembly and both congressional districts to achieve "one-person, one-vote."

1967   Montana Legislature passes Clean Air Act.

1968   Longest and costliest strike in Montana's history ends March 29; 7,200 copper workers are unemployed for 250 days, with $34 million in lost wages.

Yellowtail Dam on the Bighorn River is completed; construction begins on Libby Dam on the Kootenai River.

Timber industry peaks with 1.5 billion board feet harvested.

1969   Three major railroads—Northern Pacific, Great Northern, and Burlington—merge as Burlington Northern.

1970   First teachers' strike in state history lasts four days in Butte.

        Chet Huntley and Chrysler Corporation officials announce plans for multimil-
        lion-dollar Big Sky resort complex south of Bozeman.

1972   Voters narrowly approve a new state constitution and approve side issues allow-
        ing the Legislature or the voters, by initiative, to authorize gambling and the
        death penalty.

1973   Major Utility Siting Act, Strip Mining and Reclamation Act, and Water Use
        Act are enacted, providing strongest state environmental protection laws in the
        nation.

1974   Attorney general's investigation of state Workmen's Compensation fraud results
        in fifty-eight criminal charges.

1975   Montana adopts a coal severance tax of up to 30 percent, as the first Colstrip
        power plant is completed.

        Teachers strike in Great Falls and Billings.

1976   Senator Mike Mansfield announces his retirement after thirty-three consecu-
        tive years in Congress, including fifteen as U.S. Senate majority leader. He is
        appointed U.S. ambassador to Japan.

        Voters dedicate half of all coal severance tax funds to a constitutional trust.

1977   Oil giant Atlantic Richfield Company (ARCO) buys Anaconda Company.

1980   ARCO closes copper smelter in Anaconda and refinery in Great Falls, putting
        more than one thousand employees out of work.

        Government, schools, and many businesses close for a day as ash from the erup-
        tion of Mount St. Helens covers much of the state.

        Milwaukee Road rail service ends in four-fifths of the state.

1981   Crow Indians lose battle to control access to Bighorn River.

        Milwaukee Road declares bankruptcy.

1982   Controversy rages over placing of MX missiles with nuclear warheads in Montana.

1983   After more than 100 years of mining operations and $4 billion in mineral pro-
        duction, ARCO closes all its mines in Butte.

        Dispute rages over the web of power lines being strung through western Montana
        to the Pacific Northwest.

1984   A string of dry years results in forest fires blackening nearly a quarter million
        acres.

Montana Supreme Court rules on stream access law, opening navigable waterways for recreational purposes.

Self-styled mountain men Don and Dan Nichols kidnap and shoot Olympic biathlete Kari Swenson, and murder one of her rescuers.

1985   Drought and grasshoppers again plague Montana agriculture.

The Washington Corporation purchases Butte mining operations from ARCO, and mining resumes in 1986.

1986   Burlington Northern Railroad closes Livingston repair shops and announces it will sell its southern line through the state.

1987   A voter-approved Montana lottery begins selling tickets.

Ten people, including all members of the Montana Band, die in state's worst airplane crash, near Flathead Lake.

Two teenagers are sentenced for the killing of the parents of television star Patrick Duffy in Boulder.

1988   Helena District Court declares Montana school finance system to be unconstitutional in school funding lawsuit initiated by sixty-five underfunded districts.

Worst wildfires since 1930s sweep across Montana forests, and drought devastates crops.

1989   On a 40-degree-below-zero February night, a runaway freight train crashes and explodes near Helena's Carroll College.

Montana celebrates centennial year with cattle drives, wagon trains, and other festivities.

Bison hunt along Yellowstone National Park border sparks state and national controversy.

1990   Reapportionment of the U.S. House, based on 1990 census, reduces Montana's two seats to one.

1991   Deer Lodge prison riot results in deaths of five inmates.

1992   Two military transport planes collide over northern Montana.

1993   Debate over grazing on public lands and recreational access to state-owned school trust lands stirs intense public debate.

1994   Tax revolt flares, then fizzles as constitutional amendments defeated.

Hi-line farmers protest new free-trade Canadian grain imports. Agreement reached on limiting imports.

University system begins move to reorganize.

1995 First execution of a Montana death row inmate in fifty-two years as Duncan Peder McKenzie, Jr., is given lethal injection at Montana State Prison.

Republicans control both houses of the Legislature and the governor's office for the first time since 1958.

Montana draws worldwide attention as home to various militia and "patriot" white supremacist groups.

Wolves are reintroduced to Yellowstone National Park.

As a result of changes in federal law, Montana becomes the only state without a specific daytime speed limit.

1996 Late winter floods temporarily turn many communities into disaster areas.

Theodore Kaczynski, suspected "Unabomber" serial bomber, is arrested at his Lincoln cabin.

A Montana Rail Link train carrying chlorine gas derails near Alberton, causing evacuation of more than five hundred area residents and closing stretch of Interstate 90 for more than two weeks.

Self-designated "Freemen" and FBI face off near a Jordan-area ranch. After an 81-day standoff, Freemen surrender and are jailed.

State Senator Chet Blaylock, running for governor, suffers fatal heart attack while driving to a Missoula debate less than two weeks before the general election. His running mate, Judy Jacobson, assumes his role, appearing on ballots as the candidate for governor and lieutenant governor, but loses to Republican incumbent Marc Racicot.

MONTANANS
in War
In World War II, Montanans suffered the second highest percentage of combat deaths per capita in the nation, with the loss of 1,869 lives. More than 57,000 Montanans served their country in active military service during the war; 69,000 others left the state to take jobs in defense plants.

The Vietnam Veterans Memorial in Washington, D.C., honors the 267 Montanans who died in the Vietnam conflict. Montana has about 102,536 veterans, with nearly one-third of them Vietnam-era veterans.

Historical Museums, Archives, and Attractions

Anaconda	Copper Village Museum and Art Center, 563-2422
	Anaconda-Deer Lodge County Historical Society, 563-2220
Ashland	Cheyenne Indian Museum/St. Labre Indian School, 784-2200
Bainville	Bainville Historical Association Museum, 769-2596
Baker	O'Fallon Historical Society Museum, 778-3265
Belt	Belt Museum/Old City Jail, 277-3616
	Big Hole National Battlefield, 689-3155
Big Timber	Crazy Mountain Museum, 932-5126
Billings	Moss Mansion, 256-5100
	Oscar's Dreamland, 656-0966
	Peter Yegen, Jr. Yellowstone County Museum, 256-6811
	Western Heritage Center, 256-6809
Bozeman	Gallatin Pioneer Museum, 585-1311
	Museum of the Rockies, 994-2251
Broadus	Powder River Historical Museum-Mac's Museum, 436-2276
Browning	Museum of the Plains Indian, 338-2230
	Blackfeet Historical Site Tours, 800-215-2395
Butte	Butte-Silver Bow Public Archives, 723-8262
	Copper King Mansion, 782-7580
	World Museum of Mining and 1899 Mining Camp, 723-7211
	Mineral Museum, Montana Tech, 496-4414
	Mai Wah Historical Chinese Building, 800-735-6814
Chester	Liberty County Museum, 759-5256
Chinook	Blaine County Museum, 357-2590
Choteau	Old Trail Museum, 466-5332
Circle	McCone County Museum, 485-2414
Columbus	Museum of the Beartooths, 322-4588
Conrad	Pondera Historical Association, 278-5434
Crow Agency	Little Bighorn Battlefield National Monument, 638-2621
Cut Bank	Glacier County Historical Society Museum, 873-4904
Darby	Darby Pioneer Memorial Museum, 821-4503

Deer Lodge	Grant-Kohrs Ranch National Historic Site, 846-2070
	Frontier Montana Museum, 846-0026
	Old Montana Prison, 846-3111
	Powell County Museum, 846-3294
	Yesterday's Playthings, 846-1480
Dillon	Beaverhead County Museum, 683-5027
Ekalaka	Carter County Museum, 775-6886
Eureka	Tobacco Valley Historical Village, 296-2514
Fort Benton	Museum of the Northern Great Plains, 622-5133
	Museum of the Upper Missouri-Old Fort Park, 622-5494
Fromberg	Clarks Fork Valley Museum, 668-7650
Glasgow	Valley County Pioneer Museum, 228-8692 summer
	228-2222 winter
Glendive	Frontier Gateway Museum, 365-8168
Great Falls	Cascade County Historical Museum, 452-3462
	Mehmke's Steam Engine Museum, 452-6571
	Montana Cowboy Association Museum, 761-9299
	C. M. Russell Museum Complex, 727-8787
Hamilton	Ravalli County Museum, 363-3338
Hardin	Big Horn County Historical Museum, 665-1671
Harlowton	Upper Musselshell Historical Society Museum, 632-4301
Havre	H. Earl Clack Memorial Museum, 265-9913
Helena	Little Red School House Museum, 458-9249
	Montana Historical Society Museum & Archives, 444-2694
	Last Chance Tour Train, 442-1023
	Original Governor's Mansion, 442-4789
Huntley	Museum of Irrigated Agriculture, 967-2680
Hysham	Treasure County 89ers Museum, 342-5252
Jordan	Garfield County Museum, 557-2517
Kalispell	Conrad Mansion National Historic Site, 755-2166
Lambert	Lambert Historical Society Museum, 482-2401
Lame Deer	Northern Cheyenne Tribal Museum, 477-6284
Lewistown	Central Montana Historical Society and Museum, 538-5436
Libby	Heritage Museum, 293-7521
Livingston	Park County Museum, 222-3506
	Livingston Historical District Walking Tour, 222-0850

	Livingston Depot Center, 222-2300
Loma	Earth Science Museum, 739-4357
	House of a Thousand Dolls, 739-4338
Malta	Phillips County Museum, 654-1037
Miles City	Range Riders Museum, 232-6146
	Fort Keough
Missoula	Historical Museum at Fort Missoula, 728-3476
	Ninemile Remount Depot Historic Ranger Station, 626-5201
Pablo	The People's Center, 675-0160
Philipsburg	Granite County Museum and Cultural Center, 859-3388
Plentywood	Sheridan County Historical Society, 765-2219
Polson	Miracle of America Museum and Pioneer Village, 883-6804
	Polson Historical Museum, 883-3049
Poplar	Poplar Museum, 768-5155
	Fort Peck Assiniboine and Sioux Cultural Center and Museum, 768-5155
Red Lodge	Carbon County Historical Museum, 446-3914
	Red Lodge Historic Commercial District Walking Tour, 446-1718
Richey	Richey Historical Museum, 773-5656
Ronan	Garden of the Rockies Museum, 676-5210
Roundup	Musselshell Valley Historical Museum, 323-1403
St. Ignatius	St. Ignatius Mission, 745-2768
	Flathead Indian Museum and Trading Post, 745-2951
Scobey	Pioneer Town and Museum, 487-5965
Shelby	Marias Museum of History and Art, 434-2551
Sidney	MonDak Heritage Center, Museum, and Art Gallery, 482-3500
	Fort Union Trading Post National Historic Site, 572-9083
Stanford	Judith Basin Museum, 566-2281
	Sod Buster Museum, 423-5358
Stevensville	Fort Owen State Monument, 542-5500
	Historic St. Mary's Mission, 777-5734
	Stevensville Historical Society Museum, 777-3201
Superior	Mineral County Historical Museum, 822-4624
Terry	Prairie County Museum and Lady Cameron Museum, 637-5782
Thompson Falls	Historic Jail Museum, 827-3496

Three Forks	Headwaters Heritage Museum, 285-4778
Townsend	Broadwater County Museum and Historical Library, 266-5252
Troy	Troy Historical Museum, 295-5377
Utica	Utica Museum, 423-5208
Victor	Victor Heritage Museum, 642-3997
Virginia City/ Nevada City	Thompson-Hickman Memorial Museum, 843-5346
	Two preserved and restored mining camps, 843-5377 or 843-5331
West Glacier	Glacier National Park Museum, 888-5441
West Yellowstone	Museum of the Yellowstone, 646-7814
Whitefish	Stumptown Historical Society Museum, 862-0667
Wibaux	Wibaux County and Centennial Car Museum, 795-2427
Wolf Point	Wolf Point Area Historical Society Museum, 653-1912
	John Deere Tractor Collection and Museum, 392-5224

Selected Montana History Events

Bannack Days, Bannack State Park, Dillon, third weekend in July, 834-3413
Battle of Little Bighorn Reenactment, Hardin, third week of June, 655-1672
Big Hole National Battlefield Day, Wisdom, August, 689-3155
Black Powder Convention, Havre, May, 265-2406
Buffalo Runners Shoot, Virginia City, May, 821-3763
Burnt Hole Reenactment, West Yellowstone, August, (208) 652-7835
Central Montana Wagon Train, Lewistown, July, 538-3915
Christmas at the Daly Mansion, Hamilton, December, 755-2166
Fort Owen Day, Stevensville, July, 542-5500
Infantry Encampment, Miles City, July, 232-2182
Lewis and Clark Festival and Encampment, Giant Springs State Park, Great Falls, third week of June, 727-8314
Milk River Wagon Train, Malta, September, 654-1200
Montana Historical Society Annual Conference, October, 444-2694
Powder River Wagon Train and Cattle Drive, Broadus, August, (800) 982-0710
Red Lodge Mountain Man Rendezvous, Red Lodge, late July, 446-1718
Sandcreek Clydesdale Wagon Train, Jordan, July, 557-2865
Sun-Child Reenactment Camp, East Glacier, July, (800) 350-2882
Two Medicine Culture and Language Camp, Browning, July, 338-2882
Virginia City Heritage Days, Virginia City, August, 843-5555
Wagon Train and Trail Ride, Culbertson, September, 787-5559
Western Days, Billings, June, 652-8494 or 256-6961
Western Heritage Days, Grant-Kohrs Ranch National Historic Site, Deer Lodge, July, 846-2070

Further Reading

Though some of the following titles are out of print, most can be found in Montana's public or school libraries.

Abbott, Newton Carl. *Montana in the Making.* Billings: Gazette Printing Co., 1931.

Burlingame, Merrill C. *The Montana Frontier.* Bozeman: Big Sky Books, 1942.

Crutchfield, James A. *It Happened in Montana.* Helena: TwoDot Books/Falcon Publishing Co., 1994.

DeVoto, Bernard. *The Journals of Lewis and Clark.* Abridged. Boston: Little Brown and Co., 1953.

Dimsdale, Thomas J. *The Vigilantes of Montana, or Popular Justice in the Rocky Mountains.* Virginia City, Mont.: Montana Post, 1866.

Ewers, John C. *The Blackfeet: Raiders on the Northwestern Plains.* Norman: University of Oklahoma Press, 1958.

Fanselow, Julie. *Traveler's Guide to the Lewis and Clark Trail.* Helena: Falcon Publishing Co., 1995.

Garcia, Andrew. *Tough Trip Through Paradise, 1878-1879.* Edited by Ben Stein. Boston: Houghton, 1967.

Glasscock, Carl B. *The War of the Copper Kings: Builders of Butte and Wolves of Wall Street.* Indianapolis: Bobbs-Merrill, 1935.

Hamilton, James M. *From Wilderness to Statehood: A History of Montana, 1805-1900.* Portland: Binsford & Mort, 1957.

Hedren, Paul L., ed. *The Great Sioux War, 1876-77.* Helena: Montana Historical Society Press, 1991.

Howard, Joseph Kinsey. *Montana: High, Wide, and Handsome.* New Haven, Conn.: Yale University Press, 1943.

———. *Strange Empire: A Narrative of the Northwest.* New York: William Morrow and Co., 1952.

Johnson, Dorothy M. *The Bloody Bozeman.* New York: McGraw-Hill, 1971.

Lang, William L., and Rex C. Myers. *Montana Our Land & People.* Boulder, Co.: Pruett Publishing Company, 1979.

Langford, Nathaniel Pitt. *Vigilante Days and Ways.* (2 vols.) Boston: J. G. Cupples, 1890.

Leforge, Thomas H. *Memoirs of a White Crow Indian.* Edited by Thomas B. Marquis. New York: Century Co., 1928.

Linderman, Frank Bird. *Montana Adventure.* Edited by H.G. Merriam. Lincoln: University of Nebraska Press, 1968.

Malone, Michael P. *The Battle for Butte: Mining and Politics on the Northern Frontier, 1864-1906.* Helena: Montana Historical Society Press, 1993.

Malone, Michael P., Richard B. Roeder, and William L. Lang. *Montana, A History of Two Centuries.* Rev. ed. Seattle: University of Washington Press, 1991.

Montana Historical Society. *Not in Precious Metals Alone: A Manuscript History of Montana.* Helena: Montana Historical Society Press, 1976.

Montana Indians, Their History and Location. Helena: Office of Public Instruction, 1989.

Montana, The Magazine of Western History. Published by the Montana Historical Society, Box 201201, Helena, MT 59620. Subscriptions $29 per year (4 issues, $6.50 each).

O'Brien, Mary Barmeyer. *Jeannette Rankin: Bright Star in the Big Sky.* Helena: TwoDot Books/Falcon Publishing Co., 1995.

Petrik, Paula. *No Step Backward: Women and Family on the Rocky Mountain Mining Frontier, Helena, Montana 1865-1900.* Helena: Montana Historical Society Press, 1987.

Rankin, Charles, ed. *Legacy: New Perspectives on the Battle of the Little Bighorn.* Helena: Montana Historical Society Press, 1996.

Schultz, James Willard. *My Life As an Indian.* Boston: Houghton Mifflin, 1907.

Shirley, Gayle C. *Charlie's Trail: The Life and Art of C. M. Russell.* Helena: TwoDot Books/Falcon Publishing Co., 1996.

———. *More Than Petticoats: Remarkable Montana Women.* Helena: TwoDot Books/Falcon Publishing Co., 1995.

Small, Lawrence F., ed. *Religion in Montana: Pathways to the Present.* Vols. 1 and 2. Billings: Rocky Mountain College, 1995.

Smith, Phyllis. *Bozeman and the Gallatin Valley: A History.* Helena: TwoDot Books/Falcon Publishing Co., 1996.

Sollid, Roberta Beed. *Calamity Jane.* Helena: Montana Historical Society Press, 1995.

Stuart, Granville. *Forty Years on the Frontier: As Seen in the Journals and Reminiscences of Granville Stuart, Gold-Miner, Trader, Merchant, Rancher and Politician.* Edited by Paul C. Phillips. (2 vols.) Cleveland: Arthur J. Clark, 1925.

Swartout, Robert R., Jr., and Harry W. Fritz, eds. *The Montana Heritage: An Anthology of Historical Essays.* Helena: Montana Historical Society Press, 1992.

Toole, K. Ross. *Montana: An Uncommon Land.* Norman: University of Oklahoma Press, 1959.

———. *Twentieth Century Montana: A State of Extremes.* Norman: University of Oklahoma Press, 1972.

———. *The Rape of the Great Plains: Northwest America, Cattle and Coal.* Boston: Little, Brown and Co., 1976.

Van West, Carroll. *Traveler's Companion to Montana History.* Helena: Montana Historical Society Press, 1990.

Wilson, Gary. *Outlaw Tales of Montana.* Havre: High-Line Books, 1995.

chapter five

PEOPLE

MONTANA'S BIG SKY covers 145,556 square miles of land, but there are only about 6 people per square mile to hold up that much heaven, 6.04 to be precise. So much space may be the paramount reason so many former Montanans are moving back to the state, and so many newcomers set up homes here.

Montana's original residents were Indians. Most tribal groups arrived in the 1700s, finding the refuge and bounty they needed to survive hostile tribes in other homelands and, later, the encroachment of civilization from the east. The wave of white settlers to Montana from the 1860s to the early 1900s, though, combined with efforts of the U.S. government during that time to contain the Indians within designated boundaries, soon guaranteed that people of mainly European stock would outnumber the various tribes. Native Americans now account for just over 6 percent of the state's population, the second largest ethnic group under the Big Sky.

From the Lewis and Clark Expedition onward, many different ethnic groups have found their way to Montana. Following on the heels of the French-Canadian and British fur traders were white Americans, most of them from southern and midwestern states and other parts of the settled West. The Montana gold rush of the 1860s also attracted immigrants from Ireland, England, Scandinavia, and Germany. Chinese immigrants, who came to labor in the earliest towns and to rework the placer mines, made up the largest foreign-born population in the 1870 census. There were 1,949 Chinese counted.

The industrial copper mines brought many more diverse groups to the Butte

143

Dancer at Crow Fair. Donnie Sexton/Travel Montana

area, the largest of these ethnic groups being the Irish, the Welsh, and the Cornish, or "Cousin Jacks." After 1900, immigrants from Italy, Poland, and other European countries—mainly Greece, Austria, and Yugoslavia—added to the populations of Butte, Anaconda, and Great Falls. In the heyday of mining, you could hear as many as thirty languages on the streets of these mining and smelting towns.

In the early 1900s, tens of thousands of homesteaders were lured by the railroads' advertisements and the promise of free land along the Hi-Line, Montana's northern tier. These eager settlers were mainly from the midwestern states, Scandinavia, and Germany. Many Scandinavian Lutherans still enjoy lutefisk and lefse dinners in Montana churches and grange halls around Christmas time. The dozens of Hutterite colonies scattered across Montana represent only a portion of the state's heavy percentage of German ancestry. In the 1940s, Mexican laborers were imported to work the sugar beet fields of the Yellowstone Valley. The latest group of immigrants to Montana include Hmong refugees and other Southeast Asian peoples who came mainly to the Missoula area in the 1970s.

The population growth rate has never been as dramatic as in the years from 1870 to 1920. In the 1920s, the state lost 2 percent of its population. From 1980 to 1990, Montana's population grew by a modest 1.6 percent, less than most other states. When the 435 seats in the U.S. House of Representatives were reapportioned based on the 1990 census, Montana was just shy of the population needed to retain two representatives in that body.

The 1996 population was estimated at 879,372, making Montana forty-fourth among the fifty states in population.

Chief Charlot and Flathead Indians crossing the Clark Fork River in Missoula, October 1891.
Montana Historical Society

Modern-day Missoula, with the Madison Street Bridge in the foreground.
Donnie Sexton / Travel Montana

Montana Population Growth—1870 to 1996

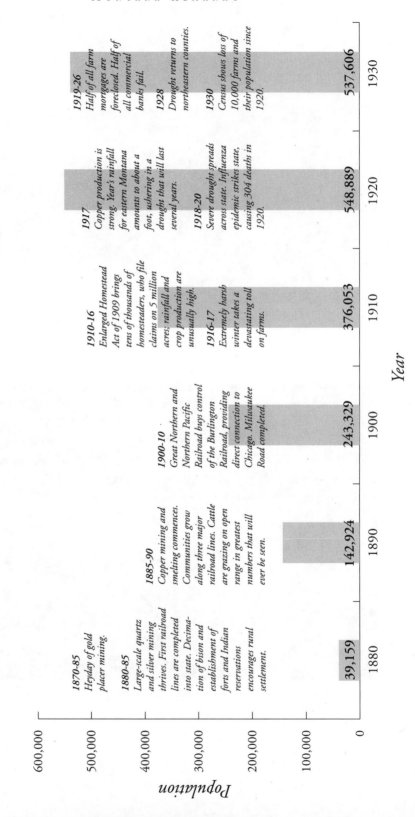

Year

Population

1870-85
Heyday of gold placer mining.

1880-85
Large-scale quartz and silver mining thrives. First railroad lines are completed into state. Decimation of bison and establishment of forts and Indian reservations encourages rural settlement.

1885-90
Copper mining and smelting commences. Communities grow along three major railroad lines. Cattle are grazing on open range in greatest numbers that will ever be seen.

1900-10
Great Northern and Northern Pacific Railroad buys control of the Burlington Railroad, providing direct connection to Chicago. Milwaukee Road completed.

1910-16
Enlarged Homestead Act of 1909 brings tens of thousands of homesteaders, who file claims on 5 million acres; rainfall and crop production are unusually high.

1916-17
Extremely harsh winter takes a devastating toll on farms.

1917
Copper production is strong. Year's rainfall for eastern Montana amounts to about a foot, ushering in a drought that will last several years.

1918-20
Severe drought spreads across state. Influenza epidemic strikes state, causing 304 deaths in 1920.

1919-26
Half of all farm mortgages are foreclosed. Half of all commercial banks fail.

1928
Drought returns to northeastern counties.

1930
Census shows loss of 10,000 farms and their population since 1920.

Year	Population
1880	39,159
1890	142,924
1900	243,329
1910	376,053
1920	548,889
1930	537,606

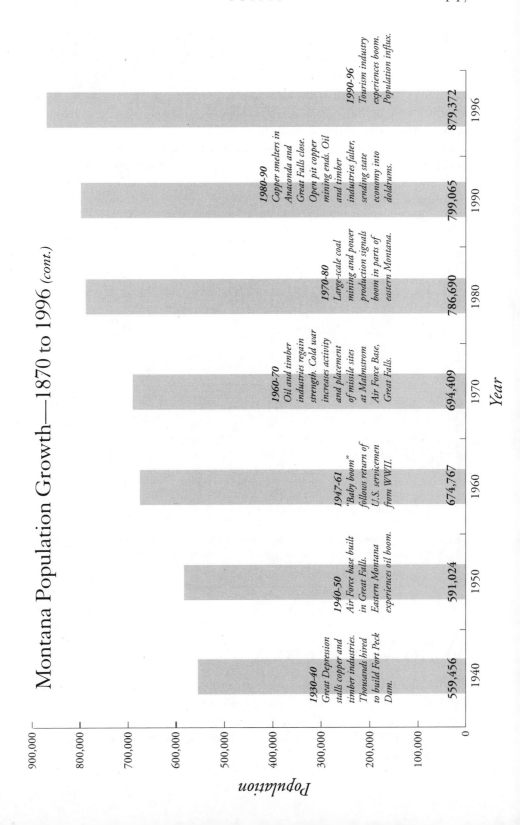

Montana Population Growth—1870 to 1996 *(cont.)*

1930-40
Great Depression stalls copper and timber industries. Thousands hired to build Fort Peck Dam.

1940-50
Air Force base built in Great Falls. Eastern Montana experiences oil boom.

1947-61
"Baby boom" follows return of U.S. servicemen from WWII.

1960-70
Oil and timber industries regain strength. Cold war increases activity and placement of missile sites at Malmstrom Air Force Base, Great Falls.

1970-80
Large-scale coal mining and power production signals boom in parts of eastern Montana.

1980-90
Copper smelters in Anaconda and Great Falls close. Open pit copper mining ends. Oil and timber industries falter, sending state economy into doldrums.

1990-96
Tourism industry experiences boom. Population influx.

Population

900,000
800,000
700,000
600,000
500,000
400,000
300,000
200,000
100,000
0

559,456   591,024   674,767   694,409   786,690   799,065   879,372

1940   1950   1960   1970   1980   1990   1996

Year

Population Density

1890   1996

1996   6.04 persons per square mile

1890   .91 persons per square mile

Montana's small population and vast size account for one of the lowest rankings for population density in the nation, historically among the bottom five states; in 1996, Montana was the forty-eighth most densely populated state. Only ten counties in the state have population densities of more than ten people per square mile. Eleven Montana counties have less than one person per square mile.

Source: U.S. Bureau of the Census, 1995 Population Estimates. Washington, D.C., 1995.

How *Crowded* is

Montana?

	population	sq. mi.*	person/sq.mi.
Alaska	603,617	570,374	1
Wyoming	480,184	97,105	5
Montana	870,281	145,556	6
Colorado	3,746,585	103,729	36
California	31,589,153	155,973	202
Los Angeles	3,489,779	469	7,441
San Francisco	728,921	47	15,509
New York City	7,311,966	309	23,663

*Square miles in land area only (i.e., excluding lakes, rivers, etc.).

Source: U.S. Bureau of the Census. State populations are 1995 estimate from Current Population Reports. City populations are 1992 estimate from County and City Data Book.

Who We Were

The Montana of 100 years ago looked quite different than it does today. The 1890 census counted only 142,924 people within the state's borders, only about a sixth of today's population. In addition to 10,765 Indians on reservations in the state in 1890, there were 89,063 U.S.-born and 43,096 foreign-born residents of Montana.

Foreign-born Population of Montana by Nationality, 1890

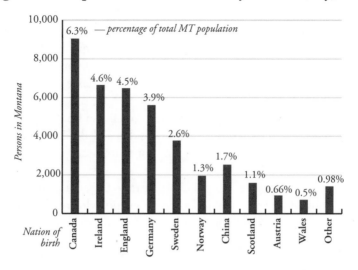

"Other" foreign-born populations in Montana in 1890 included 468 Swiss, 103 Dutch, 64 Belgians, 49 Mexicans, 13 people each from Central and South America, and 11 from Cuba and the West Indies.

Chinese merchant outside store in Chinese section of Virginia City, around 1900. Montana Historical Society

Who We Are

The 1995 census estimated a total of 870,281 people in Montana. There are not only a lot more people than 100 years ago, there are many different kinds of people here too. Today's diverse population is a reflection of the Treasure State's colorful history. If you look closely enough, you'll find descendants of Montana's first human inhabitants as well as those who can trace their roots back to early fur traders or immigrant farmers and miners. You'll also find folks from all over the world who have only recently become residents of Big Sky Country; many of these people have moved here looking for that special lifestyle that makes Montana unique.

Because of changing census policies that reflect changing attitudes toward race and ethnicity, the census breaks the population down into more specific categories of race than it did 100 years ago, making direct comparisons difficult.

Racial Makeup of Montana, 1990

Race	Number of Persons	% of Total MT Population
White	741,340	92.8%
American Indian, Eskimo, or Aleut	47,769	5.9%
Hispanic	12,167	1.5%
Asian or Pacific Islander	4,256	0.5%
Black	2,047	0.2%
Other	3,653	0.5%

Source: Data compiled by U.S. Bureau of the Census, Washington, D.C., 1990, and processed by The Census and Economic Information Center of the Montana Department of Commerce, Dec. 1992.

Montanans Born in State

Year	Percentage
1960	59.7%
1970	59.7%
1980	56.9%
1990	60.0%

Foreign-born Population of Montana by Nationality, 1990

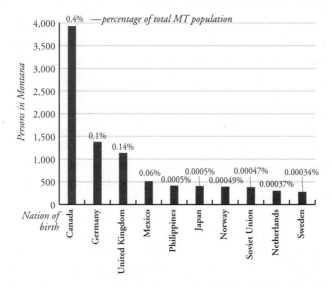

In addition to these foreign-born populations in Montana, the 1990 census counted 267 Chinese, 249 Poles, 232 Koreans, 199 Australians, 190 Vietnamese, and smaller populations from 69 other nations.

Source: U.S. Bureau of the Census. Census '90: Social and Economic Characteristics. *Washington, D.C.*

Foreign Ancestry Declared by Montanans, 1990

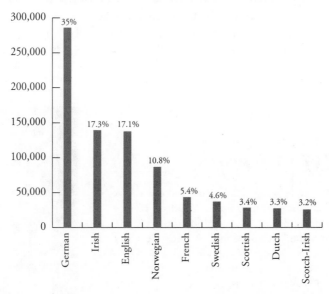

Of the 799,065 Montanans counted in the 1990 census, 736,327 specified their ancestry.

Source: U.S. Bureau of the Census. Census '90: Social and Economic Characteristics. *Washington, D.C.*

Montana's Indians

Eleven principal tribal groups of American Indians live on seven reservations in Montana. Three reservations are inhabited by more than one tribal group. Indian people are citizens of their tribe and of the United States.

The Confederated Salish and Kootenai tribe includes the Kootenai, the Salish (sometimes known as the Flathead), and the Pend d'Oreille, a Salishan-speaking tribe which includes the band once known as the Kalispel. The origin of the term "Flathead" is obscure. The tribes share the 1.5-million-acre Flathead Reservation.

The Gros Ventre and Assiniboine are separate legal entities that share the Fort Belknap Reservation. The Assiniboine were originally of Yanktonai Sioux ancestry. The name derives from the Siouan "ass-ni-pwan" or "stone Sioux," probably referring to the hot stones the people used to cook with. The Gros Ventre were of Arapaho origins. Gros Ventre derives from the French, meaning "belly" or "gut" people. The tribes own several hundred head of bison and each year offer a few licenses to hunt the once plentiful beast. Licenses are also sold to hunt on the numerous prairie dog towns within the reservation boundaries.

The Assiniboine and Sioux both reside on the Fort Peck Reservation. Both groups trace their origins to the Yanktonai Sioux. About 6,800 people live on the reservation in northeastern Montana with another approximately 3,900 members of both tribes living off the reservation.

The Blackfeet are the largest single tribal group in Montana. It is commonly thought that they acquired their name because of the characteristic black color of their moccasins, either intentionally painted or blackened with the ashes of prairie fires and campfires. The 1.5 million acres of the Blackfeet Reservation are bordered on the north by Canada and on the west by Glacier National Park.

Sharp *People*

In the Hidatsa language, the Crow tribe was called Apsalooké, which means "children of the large-beaked bird." Other Indian people called them the "sharp people" because it was thought they were crafty and alert as a bird like the raven. White people later misinterpreted the word as "crow."

The Northern Cheyenne people once farmed along the Missouri River in North Dakota but migrated to the Black Hills of South Dakota and finally settled in the Lame Deer area of Montana in the 1880s. Today the Northern Cheyenne Reservation covers 445,000 acres in southeastern Montana. It shares its western border with the Crow Reservation and is bounded on the east by the Tongue River.

The Crow also farmed after settling in the Missouri and Yellowstone river valleys, having come from North Dakota and, earlier, from Manitoba. The majority of the tribe now lives in the valleys of the Bighorn and Little Bighorn rivers. The Crow are noted for their strong ties to tribal traditions, one of which is a clan system of kinship.

The name of the Rocky Boy's Reservation in north-central Montana was derived from an attempt to honor Chief Stone Child, a leader of a band of Chippewa. The chief's name was not translated correctly from Chippewa into

notable
*M*ontanans

 ### Susan "Walking Bear" Yellowtail
(1903-1981)

After growing up a member of the Crow tribe in Pryor, "Walking Bear" went to western Massachusetts to attend a seminary, then to Boston where she trained as a nurse at Boston General Hospital. When her training ended, she was the first American Indian to become a registered nurse in the U.S. She returned to the reservation in 1929, serving her people as a nurse, midwife, and spokesperson. She worked for the Indian Health Service and served on state and federal Indian health councils. Committed to bridging cultures, she also traveled to Europe and North Africa on behalf of the U.S. State Department.

Montana Historical Society

English, and "Rocky Boy" evolved. Rocky Boy's Reservation was originally inhabited by members of the Chippewa and Cree tribes. In 1935, the Chippewa and Cree adopted a tribal constitution that officially recognized the coming together of the two tribes, through extensive intermarriage over the years, into the Chippewa-Cree tribe. Rocky Boy's Reservation is near the Canadian border, in north-central Montana. One-third is located in the beautiful Bears Paw Mountains, and the remainder is prairie land.

Montana is also home to the Little Shell Chippewa-Cree, often referred to as the "landless Indians." Members of the Little Shell band trace their origins to Pimbina Chippewa, Cree, and Métis (French-Chippewa) people. Today, tribal members live all over Montana, but Great Falls is the headquarters for the elected tribal council and an executive officer. The Little Shell are in the process of seeking federal recognition as a tribe.

According to the 1990 census, the Indian population of Montana was 47,679 persons, approximately 6 percent of the state population. While Montana's overall population increased only 1.6 percent from 1980 to 1990, the Indian population increased by 27.9 percent.

Montana ranks fifth in the nation for percentage of Indian population within the total state population. The state rank in 1980 was sixth. To recognize and celebrate the importance of Indian culture in Montana, the 1997 Legislature passed an act designating the fourth friday in September of each year "American Indian Heritage Day."

Recent State Population Trends

Reservation Populations

Names & Reservation Headquarters	Date Est.	Resident Tribes	1990 Indians on Reservation	Enrolled Tribal Members	Non-Indians on Reservation
Blackfeet Browning, MT	1851	Blackfeet	7,025	9,000	18%
Crow Crow Agency, MT	1851	Crow	4,724	7,000	16%
Flathead Pablo, MT	1855	Salish Kootenai	5,130	6,700	76%
Fort Belknap Harlem, MT	1888	Assiniboine Gros Ventre	2,508	2,800	7%
Fort Peck Poplar, MT	1888	Assiniboine Sioux	10,595	11,700	45%
Northern Cheyenne Lame Deer, MT	1884	Northern Cheyenne	3,923	5,600	10%
Rocky Boy's Box Elder, MT	1916	Chippewa-Cree	1,954	2,500	4%
Little Shell Great Falls, MT	seeking recognition	Chippewa-Cree		4,000	

Sources: The Tribal Nations of Montana, A Handbook for Legislators. *Helena: Montana Legislative Council, 1995;* Montana Indians: Their History and Location. Helena: *Office of Public Instruction, 1989, U.S. Bureau of the Census, 1990.*

In 1990, the U.S. census counted 799,065 people living in Montana, a 1.6 percent increase from the amount counted in 1980. Montana's official population estimate for July 1, 1996, was 879,372 persons, an 11.2 percent increase in only five years. Researchers attribute the state's recent population growth to three areas: more job development, higher birth to death rates, and migration into the state, or in the demographer's jargon, "in-migration."

The estimated increase has not won us a new place on the national population chart. We're still 44th, the same as in 1980 and 1990. Of the 1996 estimated U.S. population of 265,283,783 people, Montana contributes less than one percent.

Ravalli County, in the Bitterroot Valley south of Missoula, was the fastest-growing county between 1990 and 1995.

Forty counties gained population, while sixteen counties lost population since 1990. All but one of the sixteen counties reporting losses are located east of the Continental Divide, mostly in the eastern part of the state. The one exception was Deer Lodge County in southwestern Montana, which reported a 2 percent population loss. During the 1980s, thirty-nine of Montana's fifty-six counties lost population, most in eastern Montana.

Fastest Growing Counties

County	Est. Population Growth 1990-1995
1. Ravalli	28.9%
2. Gallatin	17.7%
3. Flathead	17.4%
4. Broadwater	17.1%
5. Sanders	16.4%
6. Jefferson	16.3%
Lake	16.3%
7. Stillwater	14.2%
8. Carbon	11.7%
9. Madison	11.2%
10. Lewis & Clark	11.1%

Urban Montana, Rural Montana

Montana's urban population is growing. The 1994 estimates show growth in the top twelve urban areas except Havre and Anaconda. Billings's population has grown 6.7 percent since 1990. The population of Great Falls has grown 5.6 percent since 1990. Smaller towns with significant population growth since 1994 include Polson (22 percent), Townsend (18.2 percent), and Belgrade (20.8 percent).

52.5 percent of Montana's population is urban.

47.5 percent of Montana's population is rural.

Note: The U.S. Census Bureau's complicated definatin of "urban" is simplified here to refer to places of 2,500 or more inhabitants.
Source: U.S. Bureau of the Census, 1990.

Billings. J. Wylder/Travel Montana

Percentage of Rural vs. Urban Population for Montana, U.S., Neighboring States

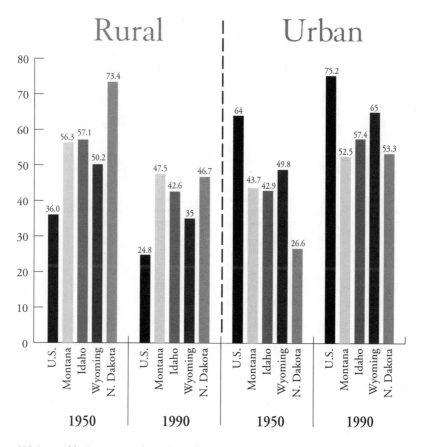

Source: U.S. Bureau of the Census, 1950 and 1990 decennial census data.

Bitterroot *Sprouts*

Among Montana towns with the fastest percentage of growth from 1990 to 1994 are three in the Bitterroot Valley:

Hamilton	24.6
Darby	23.4
Stevensville	22.4

Montana's Ten Largest Cities

City	1900 Pop.	1990 Pop.	1994 Est. Pop.	% Change 90-94
1. Billings	3,221	81,125	86,578	6.7
2. Great Falls	14,930	55,125	58,202	5.6
3. Missoula	4,366	42,918	45,364	5.7
4. Butte-Silver Bow	30,470	33,336	34,190	2.6
5. Helena	10,770	24,609	26,339	7.0
6. Bozeman	3,419	22,660	25,067	10.6
7. Kalispell	2,526	11,917	13,214	10.9
8. Anaconda-Deer Lodge	9,453	10,356	10,229	-1.2
9. Havre	1,033	10,201	10,059	-1.4
10. Miles City	1,938	8,461	8,745	3.4

*Butte-Silver Bow and Anaconda-Deer Lodge became consolidated city/county governments in the late 1970s.
Source: U.S. Bureau of the Census, Decennial Censuses of Population, Montana, 1890-1990. 1994 estimates as processed by Census and Economic Information Center, Montana Department of Commerce.

Montana's Ten Smallest Towns

Town	County	Est. 1994 Pop.
1. Ismay	Custer	20
2. Bearcreek	Carbon	41
3. Neihart	Cascade	48
4. Flaxville	Daniels	83
5. Outlook	Sheridan	108
6. Opheim	Valley	115
7. Plevna	Fallon	126
8. Virginia City	Madison	127
9. Bainville	Roosevelt	139
10. Judith Gap	Wheatland	145

Source: U.S. Bureau of the Census, compiled by Census and Economic Information Center, Montana Dept. of Commerce, Helena, Mont. for Montana 1994 Estimates of the Population (For Counties and Incorporated Places), October, 1995.

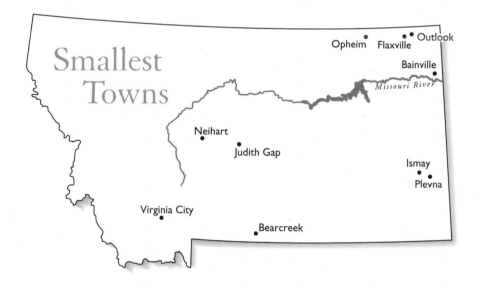

Small Populations

According to the 1990 census, Petroleum County was the state's smallest county in terms of population: 519. Of the nation's 3,141 counties, it was the seventh smallest. Garfield and Carter Counties are also among the twenty-five U.S. counties with the least people per square mile.

Montana Population by Counties

County	7/1/95 Estimate	% Change 90 to 95*	Land Area in sq. miles	People per Sq. Mile, 1995
Yellowstone	124,655	9.9%	2,635	47.3
Missoula	87,130	10.7%	2,598	33.5
Cascade	81,091	4.4%	2,698	30.1
Flathead	69,512	17.4%	5,099	13.6
Gallatin	59,406	17.7%	2,507	23.7
Lewis & Clark	52,785	11.1%	3,461	15.3
Silver Bow	34,795	2.5%	718	48.5
Ravalli	32,230	28.9%	2,394	13.5
Lake	24,479	16.3%	1,494	16.4
Lincoln	18,678	6.8%	3,613	5.2
Hill	17,668	.1%	2,896	6.1
Park	15,856	9.5%	2,656	6.0
Fergus	12,689	5.0%	4,339	2.9
Glacier	12,677	4.6%	2,995	4.2
Big Horn	12,215	7.7%	3,783	2.4
Custer	12,193	4.2%	4,995	3.2
Roosevelt	11,243	2.2%	2,356	4.8
Rosebud	10,881	3.6%	5,012	2.2
Richland	10,351	-3.4%	2,084	5.0
Deer Lodge	10,149	-2.0%	737	13.8
Sanders	10,089	16.4%	2,762	3.7
Jefferson	9,233	16.3%	2,373	5.6
Dawson	9,095	-4.3%	1,657	3.8
Carbon	9,029	11.7%	2,048	4.4
Beaverhead	9,008	6.9%	5,543	1.6
Valley	8,462	2.7%	4,921	1.7
Stillwater	7,466	14.2%	1,795	4.2
Blaine	7,032	4.5%	4,226	1.7
Powell	6,859	3.6%	2,326	2.9
Madison	6,662	11.2%	2,273	1.9
Teton	6,371	1.6%	3,587	2.8
Pondera	6,274	-2.5%	1,625	3.9
Chouteau	5,492	.7%	3,973	1.4
Phillips	5,151	-.2%	1,911	1.0
Toole	5,103	1.1%	5,140	2.7
Musselshell	4,491	9.4%	1,677	2.4
Sheridan	4,431	-6.4%	1,867	2.6
Broadwater	3,885	17.1%	1,191	3.3
Mineral	3,626	9.4%	1,220	3.0
Sweet Grass	3,374	7.0%	1,855	1.8
Fallon	3,003	-3.2%	1,620	1.9
Granite	2,619	2.8%	1,728	1.5
Wheatland	2,425	8.0%	1,423	1.7
Judith Basin	2,281	0.0%	1,870	1.2
Liberty	2,246	-2.1%	1,430	1.6
Daniels	2,140	-5.6%	1,426	1.5
McCone	2,121	-6.8%	2,643	0.8
Powder River	2,011	-3.8%	3,297	0.6

Montana Population by Counties (cont.)

County	7/1/95 Estimate	% Change 90 to 95*	Land Area in sq. miles	People per Sq. Mile, 1995
Carter	1,464	-2.6%	3,340	0.4
Garfield	1,419	-10.7%	4,668	0.3
Prairie	1,342	-3.0%	1,737	0.8
Wibaux	1,170	-1.8%	889	1.3
Golden Valley	980	7.5%	1,175	0.8
Treasure	837	-4.2%	979	0.9
Petroleum	527	1.5%	1,654	0.3
Yellowstone Nat'l Park**	54	3.8%	245	0.2

*Percent change over a period of 63 months from April 1, 1990, to July 1, 1995. Intercensal estimates were released March 8, 1996, by the U.S. Bureau of the Census. Table reflects corrected 1990 census data for Deer Lodge and Park counties. More detailed information may be obtained from the Census and Economic Information Center, Montana Department of Commerce, 1424 Ninth Ave., Helena, MT 59620; 444-2896.

**Yellowstone National Park does not constitute a Montana county but residents of the park are counted in the census. The figure above represents those that reside in the area of the park that lies in Montana.

Source: Data compiled by U.S. Bureau of the Census and processed by Mt. Dept. of Commerce, Census and Economic Information Center, March 1996.

Where the *Males* Are

Powell County — Primarily due to the population of about 1,300 male inmates at Montana State Prison, this county has 139 males to every 100 females.

In most other counties, females outnumber males. The state ratio is 98 males for every 100 females. In 1890, Montana had about half as many females (44,277) as males (87,882).*

* Native Americans were not included in the Census Bureau's 1890 population count by gender.

Source: U.S. Bureau of the Census, County and City Data Book: 1994. *Washington, D.C., 1994.*

Our Age

Montana, like most states, has an aging population. The median age in 1970 was 27; in 1980 it was 29; and in 1990, the median age was 33.8. The median age derived from the 1994 population estimates indicates a median age of 35.4.

As of July 1, 1994, there were 12,489 Montanans 85 years of age or older. According to the Montana State Office on Aging, about 141,000 Montana residents were over 60 years of age as of July 1994. This segment of the population grows by at least twenty-three every day. Currently, in 37 of Montana's counties at least 20 percent of the population is older than 60 years.

Prairie County has the greatest percentage of people 60 or older (31.25 percent), followed by Daniels (29.19 percent). The statewide average per county is 13.3 percent.

The three counties with the most youthful population—Glacier, Big Horn, and Roosevelt—all contain Indian reservations. The statewide average of population under age 17 is 27.8 percent.

Source: U.S. Bureau of the Census, Current Population Reports, National and State Population Estimates. Washington, D.C.: July, 1994.

Age and Montana's Population

Age	1994 Est. Pop.	% of Total State Pop. in 1994	% in 1990
Under 5	58,834	6.9	7.4
5 to 17	178,614	20.9	20.4
18 to 24	79,810	9.3	8.8
25 to 44	487,563	28.8	31.3
45 to 64	178,036	20.8	18.9
65 and older	113,838	13.3	13.3

Source: U.S. Bureau of the Census, Current Population Reports, National and State Population Estimates. Washington, D.C.: July, 1994.

Our Homes

Quick Housing Facts*

Owner-Occupied Houses: 205,899 (67%)

Median Value of Owner-
Occupied Housing Units: $56,600

Renter-Occupied Houses: 100,264

Median Gross Rent (monthly): $311

Houses Built Before 1939:   21.8%

Houses Built 1970-1979:   26.6%

Houses Built 1980-March 1990:   17.5%

Home Heating: Utility Gas   54.2%
                Electricity   17.9%

Owner-Occupied Mobile
Homes or Trailers: 34,497 (22,846 in rural areas)
                                 $15,800 median value

* 1990 data

Source: U.S. Bureau of the Census, County and City Data Book: 1994. *Washington, D.C., 1994. Processed by the Census and Economic Information Center, Montana Department of Commerce, June, 1995.*

Average Residential Housing Sale Prices

City/Area	1994	1993
Bozeman	$130,779	$107,953
Flathead Valley	122,700	115,000
Hamilton	115,569	101,462
Missoula	108,979	101,382
Helena	94,722	85,605
Billings	86,700	81,500
Great Falls	76,154	73,862
Havre	70,000	68,900
Libby	59,140	55,255
Lewistown	52,739	48,187
Butte	51,904	51,850
Sidney	44,398	46,322
Glendive	41,800	41,032

Source: Montana Association of Realtors. Residential Sales Prices and Closings, 1995.

Our Work

Civilian Labor Force   446,600
Unemployed   5.3%
Per Capita Income $19,047
                              — 1996 figures

Sources: Montana Dept. of Labor and Industry, U.S. Dept. of Commerce Bureau of Economic Analysis.

Median Family Income $28,044
Median Household Income $27,631
Persons Below Poverty Level   11.5%
                              — 1994 figures

Source: Census and Economic Information Center, Montana Department of Commerce. U.S. Bureau of the Census, Current Population Reports. Washington, D.C.: 1995.

Top Ten Jobs of Montanans, 1994

1. Retail Salespersons	13,638
2. General Office Clerks	8,658
3. Waiters/ Waitresses	8,191
4. General Managers, Top-level Executives	8,025
5. Bookkeeping, Accounting, Auditing Clerks	7,848
6. Cashiers	7,678
7. Secretaries (except legal and medical)	7,355
8. Elementary School Teachers	6,656
9. Janitors and Cleaners	6,646
10. Registered Nurses	6,396

Note: Below the top 10, the state's 5,883 heavy-truck drivers ranked 12th on the list. Farm and ranch workers (4,952) came in 14th. Bartenders (3,829) ranked 20th.
Montana Dept of Labor and Industry, Research and Analysis Bureau, Job Projections for Montana's Industries and Occupations, 1994-2000. Helena: 1996.

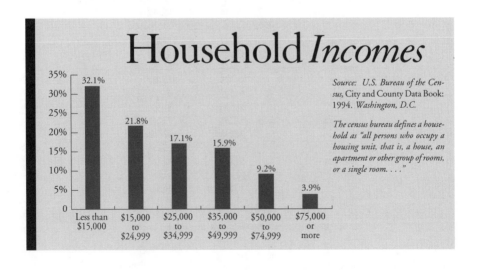

Household *Incomes*

Source: U.S. Bureau of the Census, City and County Data Book: 1994. Washington, D.C.

The census bureau defines a household as "all persons who occupy a housing unit, that is, a house, an apartment or other group of rooms, or a single room. . . ."

Less than $15,000	$15,000 to $24,999	$25,000 to $34,999	$35,000 to $49,999	$50,000 to $74,999	$75,000 or more
32.1%	21.8%	17.1%	15.9%	9.2%	3.9%

Who's Moving In

A poll conducted by The University of Montana's Bureau of Business and Economic Research in June 1995 found that many of the newcomers to Montana are actually natives returning to Montana. More than 55 percent of the migrants had at least one member of their household who had previously resided in Montana. The percentage of interstate migration into Montana in the last 5 years is approximately 15 percent of the total state population, falling in line with a national average of from 14.5 to 16.5 percent. Most first-time residents are from California and most prefer the scenic, mountainous western and southwestern part of the state and the more urban counties. Gallatin, Yellowstone, and Flathead counties saw the largest percentage of out-of-state people becoming local residents.

People moving into the state are mostly between ages 45 and 64. They tend to have more education than Montana's population as a whole, but also tend to have less declared household income. The 7 most populous counties are home to 65 percent of state newcomers.

Sources: Bureau of Business and Economic Research, University of Montana, June 1995. Bureau of the Census, 1990.

Top Ten Places New Montanans Came From, 1990-1993*

	No. of People Who Moved Into MT (90-93)	% of Total Newcomers in 1990	in 1993
1. California	18,134	14.7	14.7
2. Washington	14,824	12.1	12.0
3. Wyoming	6,161	4.9	5.0
4. Colorado	5,902	4.9	4.8
5. Idaho	5,790	4.3	4.7
6. Oregon	5,558	4.3	4.5
7. Outside the U.S.	5,546	4.4	4.5
8. Texas	4,761	3.5	3.8
9. Arizona	4,729	3.9	3.8
10. North Dakota	4,319	3.3	3.5

* These numbers may include natives returning to Montana, because IRS tax returns make no distinction between them and newcomers, that is, people moving to the state for the first time.
Source: U.S. Internal Revenue Service, 1990-1993 income tax returns statistics. Based on number of exemptions.

Top Ten Places Montanans Are Going

	No. of People Who Moved Out of MT (90-93)	% of Total Emigrants in 1990	in 1993
1. Washington	17,239	17.3	16.4
2. California	8,515	9.2	8.1
3. Idaho	7,226	6.4	6.9
4. Oregon	5,697	5.6	5.4
5. Wyoming	5,571	4.9	5.3
6. Colorado	5,386	5.2	5.1
7. Arizona	4,175	4.3	4.0
8. Outside the U.S.	3,958	4.0	3.8
9. Nevada	3,788	3.6	3.6
10. Texas	3,735	3.3	3.6

Source: U.S. Internal Revenue Service, 1990-1993 income tax returns statistics. Based on number of exemptions.

Marriages and Divorces

Matrimonial Matters

In 1993, the average age of a bride in Montana was most likely to be twenty-nine and the average age for the groom was most likely to be thirty-two. The youngest marrying age was fifteen for brides, sixteen for grooms. The oldest groom was eighty-eight. The oldest bride was ninety-two.

Source: Montana Department of Public Health and Human Services, Vital Records and Health Statistics Bureau, 1993 Montana Vital Statistics. Helena, 1996.

Marriages & Divorces in Montana, 1945-1993

Year	Marriages	Rate*	Divorces	Rate*
1945	8,147	14.2	2,380	4.1
1950	7,235	12.2	1,951	3.3
1955	6,514	10.2	1,909	3.0
1960	5,883	8.7	2,003	3.0
1965	4,688	6.6	2,002	2.8
1970	6,919	10.0	3,051	4.4
1975	7,331	9.8	4,286	5.7
1980	8,336	10.6	4,940	6.3
1985	7,178	8.7	4,258	5.2
1990	6,924	8.7	4,049	5.1
1991	6,984	8.6	4,443	5.5
1992	7,189	8.7	4,223	5.1
1993	7,041	8.4	4,311	5.1
1994	7,088	8.3	4,196	4.9
1995	6,818	7.8	4,214	4.8

*Rate per 1,000 estimated population.
Source: Montana Department of Public Health and Human Services, Operations and Technology Division, Vital Statistics Bureau, 1994 Montana Vital Statistics Tables. Helena: August, 1996.

Number of Weddings per Month, 1995

Month	No. of Marriages
January	256
February	335
March	360
April	362
May	591
June	945
July	1,100
August	966
September	697
October	389
November	345
December	472
Total	6,818

Source: Montana Department of Public Health and Human Services, Operations and Technology Division, Vital Statistics Bureau, 1994 Montana Vital Statistics Tables. Helena: August, 1996.

Age Differences Between Brides and Grooms, 1994

Groom's Age	Number of Weddings								
	Bride's Age								
	15-19	20-24	25-29	30-34	35-39	40-44	45-49	50-54	55 +
15-19	186	62	3						
20-24	427	1,106	120	9	1				
25-29	58	537	353	59	10	1	1		
30-34	8	108	148	90	22	8			
35-39		3	14	39	51	28	4	2	
40-44		2	6	6	11	13	11	1	1
45-49				1	5	2	5		
50-54			1		1	3	1	1	1
55 and over					1	3	2		

Source: Montana Department of Public Health and Human Services, Operations and Technology Division, Vital Statistics Bureau, 1994 Montana Vital Statistics Tables. Helena, August, 1996.

Familial *Facts*

The 1990 U.S. census counted 211,666 families in Montana. The average size of the families was 3.08 persons. In 1890, there were 27,501 families, whose average size was 4.81 persons.

From the Cradle

There were 11,136 babies born to Montana residents in 1995, continuing the 10-year decline in the resident birth rates since 1984, when there were 14,141 births. The 1995 rate is the lowest recorded since the state started keeping birth rate records in 1910.

- In 1995, births to mothers under age 20 accounted for 12.6 percent of all live births by Montana women.

- In 1995, 26.4 percent of the live births were to unmarried women, considerably higher than 1980 (12.5 percent) or 1970 (9.5 percent).

- More males (5,665) were born in 1995 than females (5,481).

- Medicare paid for 38 percent of the 11,062 babies born in Montana in 1994, for a total cost of $11.3 million. The average cost of delivering a baby in Montana in 1994 was $4,800, including follow-up care.

Sources: Montana Department of Public Health and Human Services; Blue Cross/Blue Shield of Montana.

UNCOVERED

Percentage of Montanans
without health insurance in 1995:   16.0%
**   in 1992:   9.4%**

Source: Montana Bureau of Business and Economic Research. Montana Business Quarterly, *Winter, 1995.* Missoula: 1995.

To the Grave

Montana's annual mortality rate in 1995 was 8.7 deaths per 1,000 estimated population.

- The tendency for women to live longer than men is reflected in Montana mortality statistics from 1989 to 1993, when the median age at death was seventy-three for males of all races and seventy-six for women of all races.

- In 1993, the median age of death for American Indians was fifteen years less than for whites of the same sex.

- For both men and women of all races, the most frequent age of death in 1993 was eighty. The most frequent age of death for American Indians and other non-white races was under one year (infancy).

- The infant mortality rate for Montana dropped in 1995 to 7.1 after holding steady at 7.4 per 1,000 live births from 1992 to 1994. The infant mortality rate for both Montana and the nation is dropping, but Montana's rate has been lower than the national average since 1990.

- There were 104 child deaths in the state in 1993.

- Sixty-three teens (ages fifteen-nineteen) suffered violent deaths in 1994. The causes included accidents (thirty-nine), homicide (three), and suicide (twelve).

Montana Births and Deaths

Year	Est. Pop.	Deaths	Rate*	Births	Rate*
1985	826,000	6,725	8.1	13,497	16.3
1990	799,065	6,835	8.6	11,602	14.5
1994	856,240	7,331	8.6	11,062	12.9
1995	870,280	7,614	8.7	11,136	12.8

*Per 1,000 estimated population.
Source: Montana Department of Public Health and Human Services, Operations and Technology Division, Vital Statistics Bureau, 1995 Montana Vital Statistics Tables. Helena: November, 1996.

Selected Causes of Death in Montana, 1910-1994 (ranked in order of prevalence in 1994)

Cause of Death	1910	1930	1950	1970	1994
	Deaths/Rate	Deaths/Rate	Deaths/Rate	Deaths/Rate	Deaths/Rate
Heart Disease	257/66.3	759/141.2	1,957/333.1	2,229/321.0	1,907/222.7
Cancer	157/41.7	424/78.9	733/124	1,059/152.5	1,740/203.2
Accidents	514/136.7	498/92.6	545/92.2	571/82.2	391/45.7
Pneumonia	282/75.0	425/79.1	157/26.6	213/30.7	276/32.2
Diabetes	38/10.1	87/16.2	49/8.3	111/16.0	215/25.1
Suicide	81/21.5	136/25.3	123/20.8	79/11.4	159/18.6
Alzheimer's			Data Not Available		93/10.9
Nephritis (Kidney Disease)	222/59.0	395/73.5	80/13.5	26/30.7	76/8.9
Homicide	37/9.8	57/10.6	24/4.1	30/4.3	34/4.0
Alcoholism	56/14.9	69/12.8	14/2.4	25/3.6	31/3.6
Influenza	24/6.4	102/19.0	23/3.9	8/1.2	15/1.8
Tuberculosis	340/90.4	337/62.7	114/19.3	12/1.7	6/0.7
Diphtheria	61/16.2	4/0.7	2/0.3	2/0.3	—
Polio	17/4.5	6/1.1	3/0.5	—	—
Rocky Mountain Spotted Fever	—	9/1.7	1/0.2	—	—
Typhoid Fever	151/40.2	16/3.0	—	—	—

Rate = deaths per 100,000 persons.
Source: Montana Department of Public Health and Human Services, Vital Statistics Bureau, 1994 Montana Vital Statistics Tables. Helena: 1996.

*M*otable *ontanans*

☞ Dr. Robert A. Cooley (1873-1964)

Born in Deerfield, Massachusetts, Cooley became interested in Rocky Mountain Spotted Fever while teaching
at Montana State College (Bozeman) at the turn of the
century. As head of the state Board of Entomology
(1913-1931), he supervised research into the disease at
laboratories in the Bitterroot Valley and became the
leading authority on RMSF. He worked tirelessly to
demonstrate that the mysterious and almost invari-
ably fatal fever was carried by infected wood ticks and

Rocky Mountain Laboratories,
National Institutes of Health

that a vaccine could be developed to treat it. Eventually, the federal government
joined the battle and a cure was found. Cooley continued to teach at Bozeman
until 1957 and authored several textbooks and journal articles. His work earned
him national recognition.

☞ George Henry Cowan (?-1924)

The son of a Bitterroot Valley farmer, Cowan never graduated from high school
but played a role in the study of Rocky Mountain Spotted Fever. From 1918 to
1924, Cowan gathered ticks and performed other duties in the field and at the

Bitterroot laboratories supervised by Dr. Cooley.
His hunting and trapping skills and his knowledge of the Valley and its animals proved invaluable to the project. In 1922, he shot a mountain
goat covered with more than 1,000 engorged ticks.
This particular bounty led Cowan and the scientists to realize the ticks needed to ingest blood from
their host before they could transmit a virulent
strain of the fever. The discovery proved key to
developing a vaccine for the disease. During its
development in the spring of 1924, Cowan was
offered a shot of the unproved vaccine but declined. Sadly, he contracted the fever a few months
later and died. He was the fourth of five men who
worked at the laboratories and died as a result of
their contact with infected ticks.

Rocky Mountain Laboratories,
National Institutes of Health

Montanans
and AIDS

From the time the state Department of Public Health and Human Services began tracking Acquired Immune Deficiency Syndrome (AIDS) in 1985 until April 30, 1997, there have been 340 cases of the disease reported in Montana. Of those people, 202 have died.

Note: Cases include 243 Montana Cases and 97 individuals diagnosed in other states who moved or returned to Montana.
Source: Montana Dept. of Public Health and Human Services, HIV/STD Section.

Traffic Deaths, 1995

In 1996, there were 198 traffic fatalities, one fatality every 44 hours, in Montana. There was one traffic-related injury every 48 minutes.

- The hour between 3 and 4 p.m. is when more accidents happened than any other time of day. Friday and January are the day and month when the most accidents occurred.

- More fatal accidents occurred between 1 and 2 p.m. than any other time of day, and in July more than any other month of the year.

- Yellowstone and Missoula Counties led the state with 16 highway deaths for 1995. Yellowstone was also the county with the most accidents from 1992 to 1996: 76 fatalities.

Traffic Fatalities & Alcohol

Year	Number of Fatalities	Alcohol-Related
1988	198	95
1989	181	95
1990	212	108
1991	200	88
1992	190	86
1993	194	91
1994	202	79
1995	215	81
Total	1,377	715

Source: Montana Highway Patrol, 1995 Annual Report. Helena: 1996.

Church Membership in Montana, 1990

Religious Organization	No. of Churches	No. of Adherents*	% of MT Population	% of MT Churchgoers
Catholic Church	233	125,799	15.7	36.9
Evangelical Lutheran Church in America	147	49,106	6.1	14.4
Church of Jesus Christ of Latter-Day Saints	106	28,620	3.6	8.4
United Methodist Church	95	19,461	2.4	5.7
Assemblies of God	77	16,235	2.0	4.8
Lutheran Missouri Synod	64	16,172	2.0	4.7
Southern Baptist Convention	77	11,776	1.5	3.5
Presbyterian Church of the USA	54	11,455	1.4	3.4
United Church of Christ	38	7,915	1.0	2.3
The Episcopal Church	47	6,644	0.8	1.9
Christian & Missionary Alliance	41	4,358	0.5	1.3
American Baptist Churches in the USA	26	4,294	0.5	1.3
International Four Square Gospel	22	4,254	0.5	1.2
Seventh-Day Adventists	41	4,140	0.5	1.2
Hutterian Brethren	40	3,307	0.4	1.0
Christian Church (Disciples of Christ)	18	3,222	0.4	0.9
Church of the Nazarene	22	2,942	0.4	0.9
Churches of Christ	52	2,909	0.4	0.9
Christian Church	23	2,812	0.4	0.8
Salvation Army	8	551	0.1	0.2
Judaism	2	310	>0.1	0.1
Other	182	14,965	1.7	4.0
TOTAL	1,415	341,247	42.7	100%

*All members, including full members, their children, and the estimated number of other regular participants who are not considered communicants, confirmed, or full members.
Source: Glenmary Research Center. Churches and Church Membership in the United States, 1990. *Atlanta, Ga.: 1992.*

Approximately forty Hutterite colonies are scattered across central Montana, where members combine their agricultural skills with a dedication to traditional Hutterite qualities of diligence and thrift. This work ethic leads to highly profitable operations.

Membership in the colonies is estimated at 3,500.

Distinguished by their Old World dress and German dialect, the Hutterites are one of three surviving Anabaptist groups in the U.S. that took root in sixteenth-century Europe during the Protestant Reformation. The other two are the Amish and the Mennonites.

Members of various Mennonite congregations live in a number of small Montana towns. Near the town of Lustre, 35 miles northwest of Wolf Point, there are three Mennonite churches and a church-sponsored school.

notable
Montanans

William Wesley Van Orsdel (1848-1919)

Better known as "Brother Van," Van Orsdel was a minister of the Methodist Episcopal Church and, like frontier judges, rode a circuit on horseback and stagecoach, spreading that old-time religion over approximately 50,000 square miles. He often had to pitch in with the chores before he could get an attentive ear. He carried "the Word" to homes, churches, and camp meetings. He also carried word of the Battle of the Big Hole to a telegraph operator of the stage line that ran from Helena to Salt Lake City. After his riding days were over, he was appointed to administrative church posts in Great Falls and Helena. He was paralyzed by a stroke in the fall of 1919 and died in December.

Montana Historical Society

Montana Historical Society

Father Anthony Ravalli (1812-1884)

An Italian Jesuit priest, Father Ravalli came to Montana in 1845, lending his considerable talents to the development of St. Mary's Mission in the Bitterroot Valley, where a county is now named for him. He spent the final thirty-nine years of his life in Montana. Missionary, woodcarver, sculptor, architect, physician, scholar: he was all these and then some. He died when he suffered a stroke after lending aid to a half-frozen miner in a blizzard.

notable $\mathcal{M}$*ontanans*

Robert Craig "Evel" Knievel (1939-)

The daredevil motorcyclist was born in Butte and became a superhero and popular culture icon for his motorcycle jump stunts. He won notice by jumping over rows of cars, then moved up to rows of school buses, shark tanks, and a fountain at Caesar's Palace in Las Vegas. His ultimate jump was his daring but failed attempt to jump Idaho's Snake River Canyon in 1974. Millions of fans and pay-TV viewers watched as his custom-built rocket bike took him out over the canyon only to crash on the rocks below when his parachute failed. He survived the crash and kept jumping (and crashing) until he put the sport aside to try his hand at painting. He is now writing an autobiography.

Self-portrait in oil.

The Rich and/or Famous

A sampling of well-known immigrants or frequent visitors:

Ted Turner and Jane Fonda, 127,000-acre ranch property near Gallatin Gateway and another property near Helena: He, the president and CEO of Turner Broadcasting and CNN, now merged with Time-Warner; also owns the Atlanta Braves baseball team. She, the two-time Oscar winning actress for *Klute* (1971) and *Coming Home* (1978); health and exercise advocate and author; former critic of the war in Vietnam.

Tom and Meredith Auld Brokaw, a ranch on the Boulder River south of Big Timber: He, the NBC news anchor; grew up in South Dakota. She, the owner of a toy store chain and author of children's books.

Huey Lewis, Bitterroot Valley: recording artist, singer, and songwriter of several contemporary hits with his band, The News.

William Hjortsberg, near Big Timber: screenwriter and novelist; his novel *Falling Angel* was made into the movie *Angel Heart* (1987).

Elizabeth Clare Prophet, Paradise Valley: founder and spiritual head of Church Universal and Triumphant, based at Corwin Springs.

Jack Nicklaus, hunting lodge near Noxon: golf great; PGA Golfer of the Year, 1967 and 1972; leading PGA money winner eight times; won every major championship, including the Masters six times.

Michael Keaton, ranch near McLeod: actor whose film credits include *Clean and Sober*, *Mr. Mom*, *Beetlejuice*, and *Batman*.

Hank Williams, Jr., ranch near Wisdom: country singer/songwriter; Grammy winner; named Entertainer of the Year, 1987 and 1988, by Country Music Association.

Peter Fonda, ranch in Paradise Valley: actor, director, producer; star of *Easy Rider*, *The Young Lovers*, and *The Wild Angels*.

Pablo Elvira, Bozeman area: baritone for the New York Metropolitan Opera.

John Frohnmayer, Bozeman: former chairman of National Endowment for the Arts; author of *Leaving Town Alive: Confessions of an Arts Warrior* and *Out of Time*.

Tim Cahill, near Livingston: editor-at-large of *Outside* magazine; the George Plimpton of the outdoor adventure world; books include *A Wolverine Is Eating My Leg* and *Road Fever.*

Jeff Bridges, Livingston area: actor whose films include *Thunderbolt and Lightfoot* and *Rancho Deluxe* (both filmed in Montana), *The Fabulous Baker Boys, Fearless,* and *Blown Away.*

Andie MacDowell, Ninemile area and Missoula: actress; starred in *Sex, Lies and Videotape; Groundhog Day; Four Weddings and a Funeral; Unstrung Heroes;* and *Michael.*

Jim Nabors, Whitefish area: actor and vocalist; star of TV's *Gomer Pyle U.S.M.C.* and co-star of *The Andy Griffith Show.*

Further Reading:

Coleman, Julie. *Golden Opportunities: A Biographical History of Montana's Jewish Communities.* Helena: SkyHouse Publishers, 1994.

Montana Legislative Council, 1995. *The Tribal Nations of Montana: A Handbook for Legislators.* Helena. **For copies, contact the council at Room 138, State Capitol, Helena, MT 59620-1706; 444-3064.**

Emmons, David M. *The Butte Irish: Class and Ethnicity in an American Mining Town, 1875-1925.* Urbana, Il.: University of Illinois Press, 1989.

Healthy Mothers, Healthy Babies—The Montana Coalition. Annual *Montana KIDS COUNT Data Book,* Helena: 1995, 1996. **For copies, contact the coalition at Box 876, Helena, MT 59624; 449-8611.**

Lang, William L., and Rex C. Myers. *Montana: Our Land & People.* Boulder, Colo.: Pruett Publishing Company, 1979.

Malone, Michael P., Richard B. Roeder, and William L. Lang. *Montana: A History of Two Centuries.* Seattle: University of Washington Press, 1991.

Merriam, H.G. "Ethnic Settlement of Montana," *Pacific Historical Review,* June 12, 1943, pp. 157-68.

Montana Business Quarterly, Montana Bureau of Business and Economic Research. Missoula: University of Montana.

Price, Esther Gaskins. *Fighting Spotted Fever in the Rockies.* Helena: Naegele Printing Co., 1948.

Travel Montana, Mont. Dept. of Commerce. *Montana Indian Reservations.* Brochure. Helena.

Montana Heritage: An Anthology of Historical Essays. Edited by Robert R. Swartout and Harry W. Fritz. Helena: Montana Historical Society Press, 1990.

Religion in Montana: Pathways to the Present. Edited by Lawrence F. Small, vols. I and II. Billings: Rocky Mountain College, 1993-1995.

GOVERNMENT

FOR THE SIXTY YEARS prior to establishment of the territory of Montana in 1864, the area's adventurers and settlers showed little interest in establishing organized government. During that time, seven different territories of the western United States governed the area that was to become Montana. After Congress made Montana a territory in May 1864, the delegates to the First Legislative Assembly gathered in December of that year in a dirt-roofed cabin in Bannack City. During the next sixty days, the assembly passed seven hundred pages of laws and chose nearby Virginia City as the new capital of Montana Territory.

Montana remained a territory for twenty-five years. It was not until the federal government passed the Enabling Act of 1889 and the voters of Montana Territory ratified a new constitution that Montana was admitted into the Union on November 8, 1889, by presidential proclamation.

State and county governments have evolved since then. By the 1960s, the original 1889 Constitution contained much that was outdated. In 1969, at the request of the Legislature, a special commission studied the Constitution, comparing it to those of other states. The council determined that 20 percent of the document needed revision; 30 percent needed outright repeal. Rather than revise a document that had been amended dozens of times over the years, Montana voters called a constitutional convention. The one hundred elected delegates who met from January to March 1972 created one of the most progressive state constitutions in the nation.

photo: Travel Montana

Throughout more than a century of Montana statehood, significant government reforms have emerged—initiated by voter-approved changes in the Constitution and the Montana code, decisions of the courts, or acts of the State Legislature. For example, a constitutional amendment gave Montana women the right to vote in 1914, five years before all U.S. women won the vote with ratification of the Nineteenth Amendment to the U.S. Constitution. Making good on a campaign promise in 1970, Governor Forrest Anderson encouraged the electorate to approve a constitutional amendment to streamline the executive branch of state government. In response to more recent calls for less-is-more government, Governor Marc Racicot's 1994 Task Force to Renew State Government recommended reorganization of several state agencies. Last but far from least, Montana's electorate frequently exercises their right to amend, reject, or create tax policy in Montana—often rejecting the merest idea of a sales tax.

The 1972 Constitution

Montana's 1972 Constitution, 25 years old in 1997, added several freedoms to the state's Declaration of Rights:

- the right to participate in governmental decision making
- the right to know about and participate in public processes
- the right of individual privacy
- the right to a clean and healthful environment

The constitution provided for county and municipal governments to review their structure every ten years and for the state to hold a referendum every twenty years to vote on a new constitutional convention.

The size of the legislature was to be decided by statute but must be between 40 and 50 senators and between 80 and 100 representatives. The constitution provided for single member districts and a five-member districting and apportionment panel. The position of state treasurer was eliminated. The terms of supreme court justices and district court judges were extended.

notable
Montanans

🐊 Jeannette Rankin (1880-1973)

Rankin, perhaps Montana's most famous woman, was born near Missoula and attended The University of Montana. She got her start in politics campaigning for woman suffrage in Washington and Montana in 1914. In 1916, she became the first woman ever to be elected to the U.S. Congress, where she served until 1919. She was reelected in 1940 and served until 1943. She saw politics as the principal avenue to needed social change and was active politically both in and out of Congress. Rankin not only fought for women's rights to vote and hold office, she also took a stand against economic injustice and in favor of civil rights. She is the only member of the U.S. Congress to oppose U.S. entry into both world wars. Her lone vote against our entry into World War II was especially controversial. "As a woman, I can't go to war, and I refuse to send anyone else," she declared as she cast it. Confronted by an angry mob in the Capitol building after the vote, she sneaked into a phone booth and called the Capitol police, who escorted her to her office and stood guard there. She was subjected to intense criticism for weeks after the vote, labelled "stupid," "ignorant," and "a disgrace to Montana." She never regretted her decision and, as an activist against the Vietnam War, she led a march on Washington in January 1968. She died in her sleep in Carmel, California.

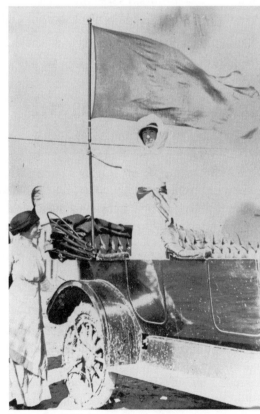

Montana Historical Society

Notable Montanans

👉 Mike Mansfield (1903-)

One of Montana's most respected politicians and highly regarded national leaders, Mansfield grew up in Great Falls and was a Butte miner and college history professor before embarking on his long political career. He was elected to serve in the U.S. House of Representatives in 1942 and the U.S. Senate in 1952. He spent sixteen years, from 1961 to 1977, as the Democratic majority leader and a member of the Senate Foreign Relations Com-

Montana Historical Society

mittee. When he retired from the Senate in 1977 at age 73, Mansfield was appointed ambassador to Japan, a post he held until 1988. Among many accomplishments, he coauthored the Twenty-sixth Amendment to the U.S. Constitution, establishing age 18 as the legal voting age. He was also a steadfast opponent to U.S. involvement in the war in Vietnam.

State Government

LEGISLATIVE BRANCH

The Montana Legislature is truly a public forum with many opportunities for citizen involvement. All activities of the Legislature, except caucuses that follow the presession election caucuses, are open to the public and press. Legislators are citizens first and lawmakers second. They are paid only for days actually engaged in legislative session activities or for committee work between sessions. Candidates must be eighteen years old, a resident of the state for one year prior to the general election, and a resident of the candidate's county, or of the legislative district, for six months.

Currently, the Senate is composed of fifty members, each elected for a four-year term from one of the fifty Senate districts in Montana. Half of the Senate membership is elected every two years. The House of Representatives is composed of one hundred members, each elected for a two-year term and each representing one of Montana's one hundred House districts. Since Montana has fifty-six counties, a county with a small population may share a Senate district with other counties.

The House of Representatives of the Eighth Legislative Assembly, meeting in Virginia City in 1874.
Montana Historical Society

    The 1972 Montana Constitution requires that the House of Representatives have no more than one hundred members and no less than eighty members. The Senate may have no more than fifty and no less than forty members. In order to mitigate the effects of party politics on the designation of legislative districts and to respond to population changes, the Constitution also establishes a five-member Districting and Apportionment Commission that can decide the number of districts and the number of citizens to be represented by each legislative district. The majority and minority leaders of the state Senate and House appoint four members. Those four appoint a fifth, who serves as chairperson.

    Both state and federal constitutions require that districts be designed for equal representation. Reapportionment occurs following each decennial U.S. census. The reapportionment following the 1990 census designed an optimum House district to represent every 7,990 persons and a Senate district to represent twice that amount, or 15,981 persons. The actual reapportionment came to within five percent larger or smaller.

The State Capitol

The Capitol is at 1301 East Sixth Avenue in Helena. The Senate and House of Representatives chambers are located on the third floor of the Capitol. A public information center is located in the lobby between the chambers. Interested parties may request a variety of useful information there concerning the current legislative session, including the committee hearing schedules and lists of the bills to be considered. The public information center also delivers phone and personal messages to legislators. Visitors have access to the balcony seating areas (the galleries) located on the fourth floor, where they can observe the business proceedings and other activities of both chambers.

Legislative Sessions

Legislative sessions occur every odd-numbered year, beginning at noon on the first Monday in January, or the first Wednesday when January 1 falls on a Monday. The length of a regular session is ninety legislative days. Sessions are occasionally extended if required to complete the work of the Legislature. In addition, under special circumstances, the Legislature may be called into special session by the governor or by written request from a majority of members to deal with a specific problem.

No later than December 1 following the general election in November of even-numbered years, the majority and minority party members of each house caucus and separately nominate officers to be elected by their entire legislative body. Nominees of the majority party are, in effect, elected without opposition. The minority party elects a floor leader and minority whip.

When both houses convene in January, joint rules of operation are adopted, along with separate rules for each house.

How a Bill Becomes Law

Each piece of legislation must go through a number of steps to become a law. A bill must be introduced by a legislator or a legislative committee. All bills containing an appropriation must be introduced in the House of Representatives. A bill may not be altered or amended in such a way that it changes the original purpose of the bill.

1. **Bill drafting and introduction**—Bills and resolutions are drafted by the Legislative Services Division of the Montana Legislative Council.

2. **First reading and committee hearing**–When the bill has been drafted and delivered to the clerk of the House of Representatives or the secretary of the Senate by the legislator who is carrying the bill, it is assigned a number and read on the floor. After this first reading, the bill is referred to a committee by the presiding officer of the house of origin. The committee studies the bill and hears testimony for and against the bill from interested citizens, lobbyists representing interest groups, and often from representatives of state agencies with some expertise in the subject. If the committee recommends a "do not pass," the bill is dead. If the committee recommends a "do pass," or a "do pass as amended," the bill is reprinted and placed on the calendar for second reading.

   A member can request that a bill that has not passed committee be printed and given a second reading. In the Senate, this requires a simple majority of the members present. In the House, such a motion requires a vote of three-fifths of the members.

3. **Second reading**–During second reading, the bill is considered and debated by the members of the entire house. If the bill passes second reading, it is reprinted and placed on the third reading calendar.

4. **Third reading**–During third reading, the bill is not debated, but simply voted up or down by the members of the body.

   When the bill has passed third reading, it goes to the other house where the same procedure is followed: first reading, committee hearing, second reading, and third reading.

5. **Transmittal to other chamber**–Often versions of the House and Senate bill will differ as a result of amendments in committees or on the floor. The house of origin can accept the amendments made in the other house or reject them and go to a conference committee. If a conference committee is needed, the presiding officers of each house will appoint three members to the committee to iron out the differences between the House and Senate. When the conference committee has completed its work, the bill is voted on again by each house for final passage.

6. **Governor's action**–Bills that pass both houses are called acts and are sent to the governor for signature. The governor then signs the bill, vetoes the bill, or amendatory vetoes the bill. If the governor does not sign or veto the bill within five days after it is delivered, the bill will become law.

SENATE
Standing Committees

The president of the senate assigns all bills to an appropriate committee from the following list:

Agriculture, Livestock and Irrigation
Bills and Journals (on call)
Business and Industry
Committee on Committees (on call)
    Meets to make appointments to committees.
Education and Cultural Resources
Ethics (on call)
Finance and Claims
Fish and Game
Highways and Transportation
Judiciary
Labor and Employment Relations
Legislative Administration (on call)
Local Government
Natural Resources
Public Health, Welfare and Safety
Rules (on call)
State Administration
Taxation

AGE *and* Service

Senator Bob Brown of Whitefish became the Dean (the longest serving member, at the time) of the Montana Senate in 1991, after having served that body for only sixteen years. At forty-two, Brown was the youngest state senate dean in the United States. He was not the longest serving member ever, though. That honor belongs to Senator Dave Manning of Hysham, who was elected with President Franklin D. Roosevelt in 1932 and served without interruption for fifty-three years. Manning was the senior state legislator in the U.S. when he left office in 1985.

Allison Conn of Kalispell was elected state representative in 1980, shortly after her nineteenth birthday. She holds the record as the youngest woman ever elected to a state legislature. Conn replaced Representative Jack Uhde, who had been elected from the same district four years earlier at the age of eighteen. No person younger than 18 has ever been elected to a state legislature.

HOUSE *Standing Committees*

The speaker of the house assigns all bills to a committee and appoints committee members.

Agriculture
Appropriations (the equivalent of the Senate Finance Committee)
Business and Labor
Education
Ethics (on call)
Fish, Wildlife and Parks
Human Services (the equivalent of the Senate Public Health
    Committee)
Judiciary
Legislative Administration (on call)
Local Government
Natural Resources
Rules (on call)
State Administration
State and Federal Relations
Taxation
Transportation

Implementation and Publication of Laws

New bills approved by both the Legislature and the governor can become laws at different times. Some bills have clauses that make them laws immediately and others contain clauses that implement the laws in later years. Most appropriation bills are implemented at the beginning of the next fiscal year, always the first of July of the year in which the Legislature has met in regular session. Revenue bills (involving a change in fees or taxes) are implemented January 1 after passage. If no effective date is specified, other bills become effective October 1 of the legislative year.

The complete texts of every bill and resolution that has been passed are published yearly by the Legislative Services Division in *The Laws of Montana*. The set is popularly called the "Session Laws." Each bill is assigned a chapter number, with Chapter One being the first bill passed and signed.

The Montana Code Annotated is the systematic arrangement of all permanent state statutes (laws) currently in force in Montana. A new edition of the "Codes" is printed every odd-numbered year with new laws added, repealed laws deleted, and amended statutes updated. This codification makes it easier to find a law.

The term "annotated" refers to the fact that the history of each statute and other pertinent legal information is included in the compilation. The Codes consist of ninety-nine titles in several volumes. Title 20, for example, deals with all the laws related to education. *The Montana Code Annotated* is also available on compact disc.

Access to the LEGISLATURE

For people who are in Helena during the regular legislative session (January through April) or a special session, daily agendas of the House and Senate as well as committee hearing schedules on bills are available free of charge at the data distribution office in Room 60 or the information office in Room 365, both in the capitol building. Bills, status reports, and other documents are also available for a nominal charge at the data distribution office.

The electronic billboards located inside the two chambers also list the daily calendar and are easily viewed from the gallery areas on the fourth floor. This information is also available on the computer system (see below).

- Write your legislator at **Capitol Station, Helena, MT 59620**.

- The **Legislative Information Office, 444-4800**, takes phone messages for legislators and provides information on the hearing schedules (between 7:30 a.m. and 5:30 p.m. Monday through Friday; 8 a.m. to 12 noon, Saturday).

- People can send a **fax** message to the Legislature, for seventy cents per minute, by calling **(900) 225-1600**.

- A telephone device for the deaf (**TDD**) can be reached by dialing **(800) 832-0283**.

By computer:

- To **track legislation**, for fifty-five cents per minute, dial **(900) 225-4300**.

- To access legislative information on **the state bulletin board** for free through your computer modem, call **444-5648** in Helena, or **(800) 962-1729**.

- **Internet access** to legislative information is available at two sites:
http://www.mt.gov/leg/branch/branch/html
http://www.metnet.mt.gov

At the Capitol, there are computers at various locations on the third floor where anyone may access on-line data concerning session activities and may read the contents of legislative bills.

The Role of Lobbying

Lobbying is a legitimate and often valuable function within the legislative process. A lobbyist or spokesperson for an interest or issue can provide information that legislators rarely have time to research on their own. In Montana, any citizen 18 years or older has the right to lobby professionally. An application for a license to lobby can be obtained from the Commissioner of Political Practices. A license is issued upon acceptance of the application and the payment of a fee of fifty dollars.

Any citizen, regardless of age, may testify before the Legislature, write to, or phone a Montana legislator. Citizens can call the legislative operator at the Capitol and ask to speak to a representative. If the legislator is not able to come to the phone, a message can be delivered to the person's desk by a legislative page.

In 1997, lobbyists reported spending $3.67 million to influence legislation.

EXECUTIVE BRANCH

The executive branch of the state of Montana includes a governor, lieutenant governor, secretary of state, attorney general, auditor, superintendent of public instruction, and five public service commissioners, all of whom are elected to four-year terms by voters at a general election. The term of office for these state leaders begins on the first Monday in January after the November general election in even-numbered years. Each elected official must keep public records of his or her office and perform other duties that are mandated in the 1972 Montana Constitution or in state law. The qualifications for candidates are as follows:

> A candidate for the office of governor, lieutenant governor, secretary of state, attorney general, auditor, and superintendent of public instruction must be twenty-five years of age or older at the time of their election. In addition, they must be a citizen of the United States who has resided in the state two years preceding their election.
>
> A candidate for the office of attorney general must also be an attorney in good standing, who is admitted to practice law in Montana and who has engaged in active practice in Montana for at least five years before election.
>
> The superintendent of public instruction is required to hold at least a bachelor's degree from any unit of the Montana university system or from an institution recognized as equivalent by the State Board of Public Education for teacher certification purposes.

- Montana Code Annotated, 20-3-301 (2)

The Governor

The governor is the chief executive officer of Montana, who must see that the laws of the state are faithfully executed. The governor is commander in chief of the militia forces of the state, except when they are in the actual service of the United States. The militia may be called out to protect life and property in natural disasters or to suppress insurrection or repel invasion, should these unlikely events occur. The governor is the official communicator between the government of the state of Montana and the government of any other state or the United States. As the ceremonial head of state, the governor receives official visitors, dedicates public buildings, and has use of the official governor's mansion as a family residence. The governor appoints, subject to confirmation by the state Senate, all officers provided for in the Constitution or by law whose appointment or election is not otherwise provided for. These appointees hold office until the governor's term ends, or until they are removed from office by the governor. The governor may grant a reprieve or pardon to a person sentenced for a crime. The governor can influence important state policies by serving as a member of the Board of Land Commissioners, the Board of Examiners, and as a nonvoting, ex-officio member of the state Board of Education, the Board of Regents, and the Board of Public Education.

Most bills passed by the Legislature are submitted to the governor for signature. If the governor does not sign or veto the bill within five days after it is delivered, the bill will become law. The governor must return vetoed bills to the Legislature with a statement of reasons for the veto. A vote of two-thirds of the Legislature is required to override a governor's veto. If the Legislature is not in session when the governor vetoes a bill approved by two-thirds of the Legislature, the secretary of state must poll the members of the Legislature by mail and must send each member a copy of the governor's veto message. Legislators must cast a vote and return it within thirty days. The secretary of state tallies the votes. If two-thirds of the legislators vote to override the veto, the bill becomes law.

In 1997, the governor's annual salary was $78,246.

> The governor's address and phone number:
> Room 204, State Capitol
> Capitol Station
> Helena, MT 59620
> 444-3111
> (800) 332-2272 (Citizens Advocate Phone)
> 444-3468 Voice or TDD (Citizens Advocate Phone)

Montana Territorial Governors

Name	Years in Office	Party Affiliation
Sidney Edgerton	1864-1866	Republican
Thomas Meagher	Acting governor 1865-1866 while Governor Edgerton was in Washington on territorial business.	Union Democrat
Green Clay Smith	1866-1869	Republican
James Monroe Ashley	1869-1870	Republican
Benjamin F. Potts	1870-1883	Republican
John Schuyler Crosby	1883-1884	Democrat
B. Platt Carpenter	1884-1885	Republican
Samuel Thomas Hauser	1885-1887	Democrat
Preston Hopkins Leslie	1887-1889	Democrat
Benjamin F. White	1889-statehood	Republican

State Governors

Name	Years in Office	Party Affiliation
Joseph K. Toole	1889-1893	Democrat
John E. Rickards	1893-1897	Republican
Robert Burns Smith	1897-1901	Democrat-Populist
Joseph K. Toole	1901-1908	Democrat
Edwin L. Norris	1908-1913	Democrat
Sam V. Stewart	1913-1921	Democrat
Joseph Moore Dixon	1921-1925	Republican
John E. Erickson	1925-1933	Democrat
Frank H. Cooney	1933-1935	Democrat
William Elmer Holt	1935-1937	Democrat
Roy Elmer Ayers	1937-1941	Democrat
Samuel C. Ford	1941-1949	Republican
John H. Bonner	1949-1953	Democrat
J. Hugo Aronson	1953-1961	Republican
Donald G. Nutter	1961-1962	Republican
Tim M. Babcock	1962-1969	Republican
Forrest H. Anderson	1969-1973	Democrat
Thomas Lee Judge	1973-1981	Democrat
Ted Schwinden	1981-1989	Democrat
Stan Stephens	1989-1993	Republican
Marc Racicot	1993-	Republican

Lieutenant Governor

Under the 1972 Montana Constitution, the governor and the lieutenant governor are required to run for office as a team. The previous constitution allowed candidates for the two offices to campaign separately and to be voted on separately. This sometimes resulted in a governor and lieutenant governor at political odds with each other.

The lieutenant governor performs duties assigned by the governor and any duties provided by law. He or she succeeds the governor in the case of a vacancy resulting from the death, resignation, or incapacity of the governor to hold the office. The lieutenant governor serves as acting governor when requested to do so in writing by the governor or if the governor has been absent from the state for more than forty-five consecutive days. The lieutenant governor may provide for the administration of an office and hire personnel for the office.

The annual salary for the lieutenant governor in 1997 was $53,407.

> The lieutenant governor's address and phone number:
> Room 207, State Capitol
> Capitol Station
> Helena, MT 59620
> 444-3111

Secretary of State

The secretary of state is the chief election officer of the state of Montana and has responsibility for the interpretation, application, and operation of election laws, except those pertaining to campaign finance. The secretary of state is the official record keeper for the state and is responsible for filing, maintaining, storing, and distributing corporate documents, agricultural lien information, official records of the executive branch, and acts of the Legislature. This office publishes the *Administrative Rules of Montana*, which are developed by state agencies at the statutory direction of the Legislature. The secretary of state administers the state agency records management function, including operation of a central microfilm unit and the state records center. The secretary of state is the official keeper of the Great Seal of the State of Montana. This officeholder serves as a member of the Board of Examiners and the Board of Land Commissioners.

The annual salary for the secretary of state in 1997 was $58,658.

> The secretary of state's address and phone number:
> Room 225, State Capitol
> Capitol Station
> Helena, MT 59620
> 444-2034
> 444-4732 (TDD)

Attorney General

The attorney general is the chief legal officer for the state and as such has the following responsibilities and duties: providing legal services and counsel to state and county agencies and officials; ensuring law enforcement and public safety; prosecuting on behalf of and defending the state, counties, or their officials in cases to which they are a party; assisting local law enforcement agencies and supervising county attorneys; issuing legal opinions when requested by state, county, or local officials; and regulating all gaming activities. The attorney general serves as a member of the Board of Examiners and the State Board of Land Commissioners and performs other duties as required by law.

The annual salary for the state attorney general in 1997 was $66,756.

The attorney general's address and phone number:
Department of Justice
215 North Sanders
Helena, MT 59620
444-2026

State Auditor

The state auditor serves as the commissioner of insurance and the commissioner of securities and is a member of the Board of Hail Insurance and Board of Land Commissioners. The auditor has the responsibility to oversee the fiscal duties of the state and to keep an account of all state warrants. The state auditor licenses and regulates insurance companies and agents within the state, adopts insurance rules, administers the Small Employer Health Insurance Availability Act, and regulates and registers securities.

The annual salary for the state auditor in 1997 was $58,658.

The state auditor's address and phone number:
Room 270, Sam W. Mitchell Building
Helena, MT 59620
444-2040
444-3246 (TDD)
(800) 332-6148

The Montana Public Service Commission

The Montana Public Service Commission (PSC) has the duty to regulate the state's public utilities, including private, investor-owned natural gas, electric, intrastate telephone, and water companies, and railroads and certain motor carriers hauling regulated commodities. The PSC does not regulate rural electric and telephone cooperatives, cable television companies, propane dealers, or municipal water and sewer services. Each of the five public service commissioners are elected by a regional district to four-year terms.

The annual salary in 1997 for a PSC member was $58,042. The chairperson was paid $58,783.

The commission's address and phone number:
Public Service Commission
1701 Prospect Avenue
P.O. Box 202601
Helena, MT 59620-2601
444-6199
444-6150 (consumer questions regarding utilities)
444-6197 (consumer questions regarding transportation)

Superintendent of Public Instruction

The superintendent of public instruction supervises the public schools and districts of the state, as provided by law. The Office of Public Instruction (OPI) provides services to Montana's school-age children and to school personnel. The staff provides technical assistance in planning, implementing, and evaluating educational programs in such areas as teacher preparation, teacher certification, school accreditation, school curriculum, school finance, and school law. The staff administers a number of federally funded programs and provides a variety of information services. The superintendent of public instruction prints school laws of the state and apportions state school funds among counties as appropriated by the Legislature. The superintendent serves as a member of the Board of Land Commissioners; an ex-officio, nonvoting member of the Board of Public Education and the Board of Regents; and performs other duties as required by law.

The annual salary for the superintendent in 1997 was $62,848.

The superintendent's address and phone number:
Room 106, State Capitol
Capitol Station
Helena, MT 59620
444-3095 (general information)
444-1812 (TDD)

JUDICIAL BRANCH

Montana has a three-tiered court structure:

I. The Montana Supreme Court

The supreme court has general supervisory control over all other courts in the state. The primary function is to hear and decide appeals on questions of the laws that come to it from the district courts. Since it is not a trial court, arguments before it are presented orally by attorneys or through written briefs.

The seven members of the supreme court—the chief justice and six associate justices—are elected to eight-year staggered terms in a statewide nonpartisan election. The supreme court may also establish rules governing appeals procedures, the practice and procedure for all other courts, admission to the bar, and the conduct of bar members. The supreme court appoints the Board of Bar Examiners to conduct licensing examinations for all who wish to practice law in Montana and several other boards and commissions.

The supreme court must hold four terms each year in Helena, commencing on the first Tuesdays of March, June, October, and December. About six hundred cases per year are filed with the Montana Supreme Court. The court issued 368 formal opinions in 1994 and 407 in 1995.

The Legislature sets the annual salaries of the supreme court justices: in 1997, $78,491 for the chief justice and $75,092 for the associate justices.

Supreme Court
Room 414, Justice Building
215 North Sanders
Helena, MT   59620
444-5490

Office of the Court Administrator
Room 315, Justice Building
215 North Sanders
Helena, MT 59620
444-5490

II. District Courts

Montana has twenty-one judicial districts with thirty-seven district court judges. These judges are elected by a districtwide nonpartisan election. District courts are Montana's trial courts, with jurisdiction, or authority, in civil cases and criminal cases amounting to a felony.

District courts also handle all civil actions against the state for monetary damage, misdemeanor cases with penalties more than $500 and more than six months in jail, divorces, annulments, and probate cases. The courts share their authority with city, municipal, and justice of the peace courts in certain misdemeanor cases and in civil cases with claims of less than $5,000.

The Montana district court system has handled an average of about thirty thousand cases a year since 1980.

Judicial Districts

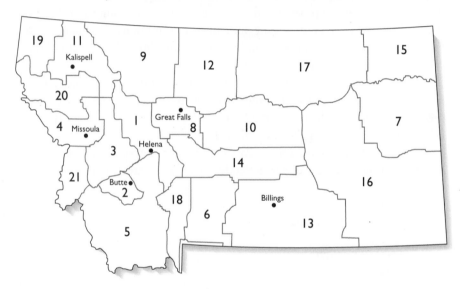

To *Judge*

To be eligible for the office of supreme court justice or district court judge, a person must be a U.S. citizen who has resided in the state two years and been admitted to practice law in Montana for five years prior to filing for office.

Youth Courts

Each judicial district must operate a youth court and must appoint one of its member district court judges as the judge of the youth court. Youths who are alleged to be delinquent, in need of intervention, or are charged with law violations appear before this court.

Provisions are made in the Montana Youth Court Act to allow the transfer of juveniles twelve or older to district court if the youth is charged with violating laws that, if committed by an adult, would constitute:

> sexual intercourse without consent
> deliberate homicide
> mitigated deliberate homicide.

A juvenile sixteen or older can be transferred to district court if he or she is charged with violating laws that, if committed by an adult, would constitute:

> negligent homicide
> arson
> aggravated or felony assault
> robbery
> burglary or aggravated burglary
> aggravated kidnapping
> possession of explosives
> criminal sale of dangerous drugs
> criminal production or manufacture of dangerous drugs.

III. Courts of Limited Jurisdiction

Justice of the Peace Courts

A Montana justice of the peace wears many hats. This judge usually handles misdemeanor cases, decides small claims cases, issues warrants in most criminal cases, shares jurisdiction in many cases with district courts, and may also act as city judge.

Justice of the peace courts generally have jurisdiction of misdemeanor criminal cases. With certain exceptions, they share jurisdiction with the district courts in civil actions involving claims of $5,000 or less, including all traffic cases.

The small claims cases include civil claims up to $3,000. Nearly any civil case that can be heard in a justice of the peace court may also be filed with the district court.

According to the Montana Constitution, each county must have at least one justice of the peace court located in the county seat. Nineteen of Montana's fifty-six counties have two justice of the peace courts. Thirty-six justice of the peace courts are also city courts.

Justices of the peace are elected in a nonpartisan countywide election during the state general election. Justices serve a four-year term. A candidate for the office must be a U.S. citizen and must have been a resident of the county for at least one year prior to the election. A justice of the peace does not have to be an attorney.

In 1995, the justice of the peace courts and city courts handled:

232,414	criminal cases
68,927	seat belt violations or daytime speeding
35,094	civil cases
2,899	small claims cases

City and Municipal Courts

Each city and incorporated town is required to provide a city court. A justice of the peace or a city judge from another city or town may act as the city judge. These courts have the same jurisdiction as justice of the peace courts but are also given exclusive jurisdiction over city ordinances. Cities with populations of four thousand or more may establish a municipal court instead of a city court. Missoula is the only city that has established a municipal court. These courts have the same jurisdiction as city courts, but a municipal judge must have the same qualifications as a district judge.

Special Courts

The legislature has created several special courts, including the following:

Workers' Compensation Court

This court was created in 1975 to provide a place for Montana employees and the insurance industry to resolve disputes arising out of work-related injuries and occupational diseases. The court is organized similarly to a district court but has exclusive jurisdiction in workers' compensation disputes.

The workers' compensation judge is appointed by the governor to a six-year term. The judge's office in Helena is attached to the Department of Labor and Industry for administrative purposes.

The final judgment of the workers' compensation court may be appealed directly to the Montana Supreme Court.

Water Court

This court was created in 1979 to expedite the adjudication of water rights existing prior to 1973 when the Water Use Act took effect. The water court has exclusive jurisdiction to interpret and determine existing water rights. It is organized into four divisions:

• Yellowstone River basin water division: those areas drained by the Yellowstone and Little Missouri rivers and any remaining areas in Carter County.

- Lower Missouri River basin water division: those areas drained by the Missouri River from below the mouth of the Marias River and any remaining areas in Glacier and Sheridan counties.

- Upper Missouri River basin water division: those areas drained by the Missouri River to below the mouth of the Marias River.

- Clark Fork River basin water division: the areas drained by the Clark Fork River, the Kootenai River, and any remaining areas in Lincoln County.

One water judge presides over each water division and is appointed to a four-year term by a committee of district judges, one from each of the judicial districts within the water division.

The supreme court has general supervisory and administrative control over the water court and appoints a chief water court judge to act as the administrative head of the water court. A water court judgment may be appealed directly to the supreme court.

Lawyers Everywhere

In 1995, there were more than three thousand attorneys licensed to practice law in Montana's courts.

City and County Governments

In 1920, there were 110 incorporated towns in Montana. Today, there are 128 incorporated cities and towns, with a variety of governmental management structures.

Town development followed the arrival of white settlers in the late 1800s and early 1900s. The location of towns was based on economic considerations like the existence of mining operations or the proximity of a railway. Most Montana towns remain small. In 1995, only seven had a population over ten thousand, forty-one had from one thousand to five thousand people, and seventy-three had a population under one thousand. Of this smallest category, nineteen had fewer than two hundred people. Ismay is the smallest, with only twenty people accounted for in 1994 population estimates.

Some of the state's most significant population growth has taken place in the unincorporated areas surrounding cities like Missoula, Billings, Bozeman, and Helena.

There is great diversity in the workings and obligations of Montana's municipalities. The larger towns are concerned with issues like zoning, public transportation, and subdivision regulation. Towns of all sizes are engaged in law enforcement, public safety, schools, and certain judicial duties. Municipalities are allowed a charter or noncharter form of government, with various types of management structures. Of the 114 noncharter governments, 108 have a ruling city commission-executive form of government, 4 have a manager form, and 2 are managed by a chairman of the city commission. Six chartered town governments have a manager form of government, and six are governed by a city commission with a chief executive. There are more than two hundred special districts, mostly fire protection or irrigation districts.

Montana has fifty-six counties. The largest county is Beaverhead with a total of 5,572 square miles, an area larger than the state of Connecticut. The smallest county is Silver Bow with 719 square miles. The average county size is 2,600 square miles, or an area 51 miles by 51 miles.

The following nine counties were either accepted or established by the first Montana Territorial Legislature—Beaverhead, Big Horn, Chouteau, Deer Lodge, Edgerton (later Lewis and Clark), Gallatin, Jefferson, Madison, and Missoula. During the twenty-five territorial years, those nine counties were further divided into sixteen. The 1889 Constitution approved those existing counties and established a method for creating new ones, along with a roster of allowable elective county offices.

The sixteen counties of 1889 had been divided into twenty-four by 1900, largely prompted by significant population growth in the period. In the 1890 census, a year after Montana became a state, the population was 142,924, an increase of 265 percent since 1880. From 1890 to 1920, Montana's population increased nearly fourfold, and the number of counties grew comparably. The number of counties grew to twenty-eight by 1910; to fifty by 1919. Five more were added by 1923. The creation of Petroleum County in 1925 gave Montana its present fifty-six counties.

The increase in population and the expansion of commerce in the distant parts of the state made county splitting seem sensible. But the good times were not destined to last. The drought years came and thousands of homesteaders left their land. Those who remained were burdened with the cost of the newly created county governments and an increased demand for welfare and farm assistance. Of Montana's fifty-six counties, twenty-nine have smaller populations today than in 1930. In 1922, the state electorate approved a constitutional amendment to allow the Legislature to create alternative forms of local government. The electors approved a 1934 constitutional amendment to permit county commissioners broad powers to consolidate elected county offices. As the Great Depression deepened, there was pressure to consolidate, but few jurisdictions responded. In fact, in 1936, Montana voters made it tougher to consolidate counties by passing a constitutional amendment that counties could not merge without approval of a majority of the affected voters.

One of the longest-standing debates in Montana is whether it makes sense economically to maintain fifty-six counties. However, in this large state, the number and location of county seats mean that Montanans are not isolated from their local governments.

Despite numerous efforts during the 1970s to allow counties to experiment with alternative forms of government, very little county reorganization has taken place in the last seventy-five years. City-county consolidation has been an available option since 1923, but today only two jurisdictions (Butte-Silver Bow and Anaconda-Deer Lodge) operate under that form.

A county is both a political and corporate body, with the power to sue and be sued. County responsibilities include elections; tax collection for local, state, and school purposes; and official recordkeeping, such as marriages, deaths, and mining claims. Counties maintain local roads and bridges and offer agricultural and rural services like county fairs, extension services, and weed and pest control. Many education services are performed by the county superintendent of schools. Other county duties include public safety and judicial administration; social services like welfare, family services, and health; and sometimes medical and emergency services.

A board of county commissioners meets to handle all county affairs either on a daily basis in the largest counties, or at various scheduled times during the month. All meetings are open to the public. Primary duties of the county commissioners include approving the county budget, levying taxes, issuing bonds, and borrowing money on behalf of the county. The fiscal powers are closely regulated by the state. The commissioners have budget control over county programs and offices. They are charged with the responsibility of appointing members to various administrative and advisory boards, such as the Board of Health, Park Board, Tax Appeal Board, Fair Board, and Weed Board. They are in charge of maintenance of all county roads and bridges.

To be eligible for a county commissioner office, a person must be a qualified elector of the county who is at least eighteen years of age, a citizen of the United States, and a resident of the commissioner district for at least two years preceding the election. Recall of elected officials can be initiated by citizen petition.

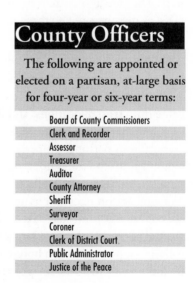

County Officers

The following are appointed or elected on a partisan, at-large basis for four-year or six-year terms:

Board of County Commissioners
Clerk and Recorder
Assessor
Treasurer
Auditor
County Attorney
Sheriff
Surveyor
Coroner
Clerk of District Court
Public Administrator
Justice of the Peace

Tribal Governments

There are nine federally recognized tribes in Montana living on seven reservations. The Little Shell tribe of Chippewa-Cree, the "landless" Indian tribe, is seeking recognition from the federal government. Reservations are areas of land "reserved" by or for an Indian band, village, or tribe to live on or use. The jurisdictions are created by treaty, congressional legislation, or by executive order.

The Indian nations of Montana are governed by tribal governments that may engage in a number of activities, including:

- regulating domestic relations of members
- levying taxes
- controlling conduct by ordinance
- administering justice
- conducting elections
- developing health and education programs
- managing tribal economic enterprises and natural resources
- maintaining intergovernmental relations with federal, state, and local authorities.

Citizenship

Each tribal government is legally empowered to determine who is a member of the tribe. All Indians born in the U.S., or born of U.S. citizens who are outside the country at the time of birth, are American citizens, with all the attendant rights and responsibilities. Indians who live in Montana are also citizens of this state. They are also citizens of the quasi-sovereign tribal nations and are recognized as members of an ethnic minority.

Taxes

Indians are subject to most of the same federal tax laws that apply to non-Indians, except for exemptions of federal compensation for takings of property, income from trust allocations, and income from gifts or land exchanges.

Montana cannot tax income earned on a tribe's reservation. Indians are also exempt from personal property taxes, such as on an automobile. The state can require, as it sometimes does, that the tribe collect a state tax. For example, the state tax on cigarettes is collected on the reservation and passed on to the state. Non-Indians on reservations and Indians not residing on their own reservation are not exempt from state taxes. The tribes can impose their own taxes on Indians and non-Indians alike. During the tourist season, the Blackfeet Tribal Council collects a 6 percent tax on hotels, motels, and campgrounds on the reservation, in addition to the state's 4 percent accommodations tax. The Blackfeet tribal government also collects taxes on alcohol, tobacco, and gasoline.

Hunting and Fishing

A tribe has the power to license hunting and fishing by non-Indians on the reservations. Indians may hunt and fish in Indian country without having to obtain a state permit. As early as 1936, the Confederated Salish and Kootenai Tribes managed fish and wildlife resources throughout the Flathead Reservation. In 1990, the tribes and the state entered into a cooperative agreement to jointly manage bird hunting and fishing on the Flathead Reservation.

notable
Montanans

 **Dolly Smith Cusker Akers
(1901-1986)**

Akers grew up in Wolf Point and became the first Assiniboine woman to lead the Fort Peck tribal governing board. In 1932, she was the first Indian to be elected to the Montana State Legislature, where she served in the House of Representatives in the 1933 session and in a special session the following year. In 1964, she was elected area vice president of the National Congress of American Indians. From 1969-1979, she served as secretary of the state Inter-Tribal Policy Board.

Montana Historical Society

Constitutional *Commitment*

Montana is the only state in the nation to have an explicit constitutional commitment to its Indian citizens. Article X, Section 1(2) of the 1972 Montana Constitution recognizes "the distinct and unique cultural heritage of the American Indians" and commits the state "in its educational goals to the preservation of their cultural integrity."

Criminal and Civil Law

Tribes do not have criminal jurisdiction over non-Indians committing a crime in Indian country. Jurisdiction over crimes on all but the Flathead Reservation resides with the federal government; on the Flathead Reservation, that jurisdiction resides with the state. In September 1994, the tribes and jurisdictions on the Flathead Reservation formally agreed that the tribes would have exclusive jurisdiction over misdemeanor crimes committed by Indians and provided for continued concurrent state-tribal jurisdiction over felony crimes committed by Indians. The other reservations do not share jurisdiction with the state.

Tribes have civil authority over the activities of non-Indians on reservations, thus requiring a non-Indian to first exhaust tribal court remedies.

Gambling

In 1988, the federal Indian Gaming Regulatory Act was enacted for the regulation of gambling in Indian country. Tribes and the National Indian Gaming Regulatory Commission share jurisdiction over games like bingo, lotto, and certain card games. If a state permits casino games, video poker, and/or horse and dog racing, the games are regulated by a compact negotiated between the state and the tribe. The compact may cover criminal and civil laws, taxation, or state assessments for regulations. All tribes have successfully concluded gaming compacts with the state.

Federal Government Activities in Montana

In 1994, Montana ranked forty-fourth in the nation for all federal funds received by states. Montana ranked forty-eighth in the nation for federal defense spending in the state. Idaho, our neighbor to the west, receives slightly more federal funds for defense and other activities than Montana does.

Federal funds distributed to the state of Montana in 1994 totaled $4.638 billion, which translates to $5,418 for each Montanan. On a per capita basis, ten states and the District of Columbia get more money back from the federal government than did Montana in 1994.

Federal grants to Montana and its local governments in 1994 totaled $906 million or about $1,058.35 per person.

Montana's Congressional Representatives

Senator Max Baucus
(Current term expires Jan. 2, 2003)
511 Hart Senate Office Building
Washington, D.C. 20510-2602
(202) 224-2651 / fax: (202) 228-3687
TDD: (202) 224-1998
e-mail: max@baucus.senate.gov

in Montana:
23 South Last Chance Gulch
Helena, MT 59601
449-5480 / fax: 449-5484

207 North Broadway
Billings, MT 59101
(800) 332-6106
657-6790
fax: 657-6793

Federal Building, Room 114
32 East Babcock
P.O. Box 1689
Bozeman, MT 59771
586-6104
fax: 587-9177

211 North Higgins #102
Missoula, MT 59802
329-3123
fax: 728-7610

Silver Bow Center
125 West Granite
Butte, MT 59701
782-8700
fax: 782-6553

18 Fifth Street South
Great Falls, MT 59401
761-1574
fax: 727-3726

220 First Avenue East
Kalispell, MT 59901
756-1150
fax: 756-1152

Senator Conrad Burns
(Current term expires Jan. 2, 2001)
187 Dirksen Senate Office Building
Washington, D.C. 20510-2603
(202) 224-2644
fax: (202) 224-8594
e-mail:
conrad_burns@burns.senate.gov
web site: www.senate.gov/burns/

in Montana:
208 North Montana Avenue
Suite 202A
Helena, MT 59601
449-5401
fax: 449-5462

2708 First Avenue North
Billings, MT 59101
252-0550
fax: 252-7768

211 Haggerty Lane
Bozeman, MT 59715
586-4450
fax: 586-7647

415 North Higgins
Missoula, MT 59802
329-3528
fax: 728-2193

Senator Conrad Burns (cont.)

324 West Towne
Glendive, MT 59330
365-2391
fax: 365-8836

575 Sunset Boulevard, Suite 101
Kalispell, MT 59901
257-3360
fax: 257-3974

321 First Avenue North
Great Falls, MT 59401
452-9585
fax: 452-9586

125 West Granite, Suite 211
Butte, MT 59701
723-3277
fax: 782-4717

Representative Rick Hill
(Current term expires Jan. 2, 1999)
1037 Longworth House Office
Building
Washington, D.C. 20515
(202) 225-3211
fax: (202) 225-5687
e-mail: rick.hill@mail.house.gov

in Montana:
33 South Last Chance Gulch
Suite 2C
Helena, MT 59601
443-7878
(800) 949-6825

27 North 27th Street
Billings, MT 59101
256-1019
fax: 256-3185

Big District

Montana's single representative to the U.S. House of Representatives is elected from the most populated congressional district in the nation.

Territorial Delegates to Congress

Years in Office	Name	Party Affiliation
1865-67	Samuel McLean, Bannack	Democrat
1867-71	James M. Cavanaugh, Helena	Democrat
1871-73	William H. Claggett, Deer Lodge	Republican
1873-85	Martin Maginnis, Helena	Democrat
1885-89	Joseph K. Toole, Helena	Democrat
Jan.-Nov. 1889	Thomas H. Carter, Helena	Republican

Congressional Representatives

Term	Senate	House of Representatives
1889-91	Thomas C. Power, Helena R Wilbur F. Sanders, Helena R	Thomas H. Carter, Helena R
1891-93	Thomas C. Power Wilbur F. Sanders	William W. Dixon, Butte D
1893-95	Thomas C. Power Lee Mantle, Butte R	Charles S. Hartman, Bozeman R
1895-97	Lee Mantle Thomas H. Carter	Charles S. Hartman
1897-99	Lee Mantle Thomas H. Carter	Charles S. Hartman
1899-1901	Thomas H. Carter William A. Clark, Butte D	Albert J. Campbell, Butte D
1901-03	William A. Clark Paris Gibson, Great Falls D	Caldwell Edwards, Bozeman D-Pop.
1903-05	William A. Clark Paris Gibson	Joseph M. Dixon, Missoula R
1905-07	William A. Clark Thomas H. Carter	Joseph M. Dixon
1907-09	Joseph M. Dixon Thomas H. Carter	Charles N. Pray, Fort Benton R
1909-11	Joseph M. Dixon Thomas H. Carter	Charles N. Pray
1911-13	Joseph M. Dixon Henry L. Myers, Hamilton D	Charles N. Pray
1913-15	Thomas J. Walsh, Helena D Henry L. Myers	John M. Evans, Missoula D Tom Stout, Lewistown D
1915-17	Thomas J. Walsh Henry L. Myers	John M. Evans Tom Stout
1917-19	Thomas J. Walsh Henry L. Myers	John M. Evans Jeannette Rankin, Missoula R
1919-21	Thomas J. Walsh Henry L. Myers	John M. Evans Carl M. Riddick, Lewistown R
1921-23	Thomas J. Walsh Henry L. Myers	John M. Evans Scott Leavitt, Great Falls R
1923-25	Thomas J. Walsh, Burton K. Wheeler, Butte D	John M. Evans Scott Leavitt
1925-27	Thomas J. Walsh Burton K. Wheeler	John M. Evans Scott Leavitt
1927-29	Thomas J. Walsh Burton K. Wheeler	John M. Evans Scott Leavitt
1929-31	Thomas J. Walsh Burton K. Wheeler	John M. Evans, Scott Leavitt
1931-33	Thomas J. Walsh Burton K. Wheeler	John M. Evans Scott Leavitt
1933-35	John E. Erickson, Kalispell D *James E. Murray, Butte D Burton K. Wheeler	Joseph P. Monaghan, Butte D Roy E. Ayers, Lewistown D
1935-37	James E. Murray Burton K. Wheeler	Joseph P. Monaghan Roy E. Ayers
1937-39	James E. Murray Burton K. Wheeler	Jerry J. O'Connell, Butte D J.F. O'Connor, Livingston D
1939-41	James E. Murray Burton K. Wheeler	Jacob Thorkelson, Butte R J.F. O'Connor
1941-43	James E. Murray Burton K. Wheeler	Jeannette Rankin J.F. O'Connor

*When Walsh died in March 1933, Erickson was appointed to succeed him and was defeated by Murray in a November 1934 election to fill out the term.

Congressional Representatives (cont.)

Term	Senate	House of Representatives
1943-45	James E. Murray Burton K. Wheeler	Mike J. Mansfield, Missoula D J.F. O'Connor
1945-47	James E. Murray Burton K. Wheeler	Mike J. Mansfield J.F. O'Connor Wesley A. D'Ewart, Wilsall R
1947-49	James E. Murray Zales N. Ecton, Manhattan R	Mike J. Mansfield Wesley A. D'Ewart
1949-51	James E. Murray Zales N. Ecton	Mike J. Mansfield Wesley A. D'Ewart
1951-53	James E. Murray Zales N. Ecton	Mike J. Mansfield Wesley A. D'Ewart
1953-55	James E. Murray Mike J. Mansfield	Lee Metcalf, Helena D Wesley A. D'Ewart
1955-57	James E. Murray Mike J. Mansfield	Lee Metcalf Orin B. Fjare, Big Timber R
1957-59	James E. Murray Mike J. Mansfield	Lee Metcalf Leroy H. Anderson, Conrad D
1959-61	James E. Murray Mike J. Mansfield	Lee Metcalf Leroy H. Anderson
1961-63	Mike J. Mansfield Lee Metcalf	Arnold Olsen, Helena D James Battin, Billings R
1963-65	Mike J. Mansfield Lee Metcalf	Arnold Olsen James Battin
1965-67	Mike J. Mansfield Lee Metcalf	Arnold Olsen James Battin
1967-69	Mike J. Mansfield Lee Metcalf	Arnold Olsen James Battin
1969-71	Mike J. Mansfield Lee Metcalf	Arnold Olsen James Battin John Melcher, Forsyth D
1971-73	Mike J. Mansfield Lee Metcalf	John Melcher Richard Shoup, Missoula R
1973-75	Mike J. Mansfield Lee Metcalf	John Melcher Richard Shoup
1975-77	Mike J. Mansfield Lee Metcalf	John Melcher Max S. Baucus, Helena D
1979-81	John Melcher Lee Metcalf	Max S. Baucus Ron Marlene, Billings R
1981-83	John Melcher Max S. Baucus	Pat Williams, Butte D Ron Marlene
1983-85	John Melcher Max S. Baucus	Pat Williams Ron Marlene
1985-87	John Melcher Max S. Baucus	Pat Williams Ron Marlene
1987-89	John Melcher Max S. Baucus	Pat Williams Ron Marlene
1989-91	Max S. Baucus Conrad Burns, Billings R	Pat Williams Ron Marlene
1991-93	Max S. Baucus Conrad Burns	Pat Williams Ron Marlene
1993-95	Max S. Baucus Conrad Burns	Pat Williams
1995-97	Max S. Baucus Conrad Burns	Pat Williams
1997-99	Max S. Baucus Conrad Burns	Rick Hill, Billings R

notable
Montanans

Thomas J. Walsh (1859-1933)

Walsh served as Democratic U.S. senator from 1913 to 1933 and was one of Montana's most distinguished and progressive politicians. He espoused various liberal causes and exposed the Teapot Dome oil scandal in 1923. He was picked by President Franklin D. Roosevelt to become U.S. attorney general but died en route to Washington, D.C. on March 2, 1933, just five days after marrying a Cuban socialite, Señora Nieves Perez Chaumont de Truffin.

Montana Historical Society

Montana Historical Society

Burton Kendall Wheeler (1882-1975)

Wheeler was Montana's controversial, progressive, Democratic U.S. senator from 1923 to 1947. He was nominated as vice president on the Progressive/Socialist ticket of Robert M. LaFollette in 1924 and nominated on the Socialist ticket in 1928. In his early career as U.S. district attorney for Montana, he was embroiled in controversies surrounding the treatment of liberal opposition to the wartime hysteria of superpatriots in Montana. He served twelve terms.

Elections

The first election in Montana was held on October 24, 1864. Approximately 6,500 people voted in this election for the territory's first legislators and a territorial delegate to Congress. In 1996, with an estimated population of 870,281, Montana counted 590,751 registered voters. Based on the census count of all U.S. citizens eligible to vote, 61 percent of Montanans turned out to vote in the November 1996 election, the second highest percentage in the nation.

Montana is an open primary state and voters do not need to declare a political party to select party nominations in a primary election. Instead, they choose one party's ballot in the privacy of the voting booth.

The voting public can approve increases in their property taxes through county, city, and school district mill levies. Electors vote on propositions to seek bonding for public buildings under each of those jurisdictions. In addition, all the voters in the state are often asked to approve statewide initiatives and referendums on various constitutional amendments and changes in state statutes concerning taxation and other issues.

Montana Election Calendar

April   first Tuesday after the first Monday; *Official school election day.* At this election, school trustees are chosen and any school mill levies or bonding propositions are offered for approval. School districts may also hold school district mill levy and bonding elections at any time before August 1 of the school fiscal year beginning on July 1.

June   first Tuesday after the first Monday; *Primary nominating election* (preceding any general election). Statewide ballot measures can be voted on at this time.

August   last Tuesday, odd-numbered years; *Primary nominating election* for certain municipal offices.

November   first Tuesday after the first Monday, even-numbered years; *General election* to select county, state, judicial, and federal offices and to vote on statewide issues offered to the voters.

first Tuesday after the first Monday, odd-numbered years; *General election* to elect certain municipal officers.

The general election for any other political subdivision, such as a fire or irrigation district, is the school election day.

Qualifications for Voting *and* Registration

Any U.S. citizen who will be at least eighteen years of age by the time of the next election and who has been a resident of Montana and of the county in which the person wishes to register for thirty days is entitled to register and to vote in Montana. A person may not vote if serving a sentence for a felony in a penal institution, or if the person is of unsound mind, as determined by a court. The elector is assigned a precinct polling location that is nearest to the elector's registration residence. A voter in Montana remains registered as long as he or she votes every four years in the presidential election.

HOW TO *Register* to Vote

A qualified individual may register with the county clerk and recorder or the designated election administrator of a county. A person may also request an official registration form from the county election office, to be returned by mail to the county of the person's residence. Voter registration forms are also available upon application for a driver's license or a hunting license. Perhaps the easiest way to register is by filling out a registration form found in many Montana phone books and mailing it to the local election administrator.

Voting by Absentee Ballot

Qualified voters are entitled to vote by absentee ballot if they expect to be out of the county or precinct on election day; if they are physically incapacitated, suffer from chronic illness or general poor health; or suffer an illness or health emergency between 5 p.m. Friday preceding the election and noon on election day.

Absentee ballots may be requested from seventy-five days prior to the primary or general election through noon on election day. They must be returned by 8 p.m. on election day. Beginning forty-five days prior to the election, absentee voters may vote in person at the county courthouse.

Political Parties in Montana

Precinct, township, county, state, and federal elections are partisan elections. District court judges and supreme court judges are elected on a nonpartisan ballot. Cities with an alderman form of government elect their officers on a partisan ballot, while those having commission or commission-manager forms of government hold nonpartisan elections for officials. School trustees and governing bodies of all special districts are also elected on a nonpartisan basis. All candidates are elected by majority vote.

The major political parties elect one committeeman and one committeewoman from each precinct in the county at the primary election. These people form the county central committee. A committeeman and committeewoman are elected from each county to be members of the state central committee.

While Montana has shown a preference for Republicans in presidential elections and Democrats in Congressional elections, the two parties are extremely competitive in the internal politics of the state. Since World War II, Republicans have won seven contests for governor, and the Democrats six. In the same period, 1946-1996, Montanans have given the Democrats the majority in the state Senate thirteen times, the Republicans eleven times, and twice elected a Senate equally divided. The Montana House in the postwar years has had thirteen Republican majorities, twelve Democratic majorities, and has been tied once.

The result of this narrow partisan balance is that neither party has known any extended period of dominance, and legislators generally don't enjoy long tenure in office. For example, Representative John Mercer of Polson became the first person in 108 years of state history to serve as speaker of the House of Representatives three times when he was reelected to that position for the 1997 legislative session.

Initiatives and Referendums

The Montana Constitution grants to the people the right to enact laws through the initiative and the referendum process. The initiative process is used to enact laws that the Legislature has failed to enact. The referendum is used to repeal laws that the Legislature has enacted. The most recent successful referendum was used to repeal an income tax increase enacted by the 1993 Legislature. This referendum resulted in a special budget cutting session being called by the governor in November 1993.

Any Montana citizen of legal voting age may seek to propose a state policy, change an existing law, or amend the Montana Constitution. The first step is to submit the written idea to the Legislative Services Division. The legal staff will put the proposal in appropriate legal terminology and review the legal concepts involved. Once completed, the proposal is given to the secretary of state's office, where the staff, along with officials from the attorney general's office, have six weeks to check it over. If the attorney general approves, supporters of the proposal have until June 21 to gather enough signatures to qualify the measure for the November ballot in a general election. It takes 40,783 signatures to get a constitutional amendment on the ballot, including at least 10 percent of the voters in at least 40 of the 100 state house districts. Initiatives to change a state law need 20,392 signatures to qualify for the ballot, including at least 5 percent of voters in 40 districts.

Highest and Lowest Turnouts

The highest percentage of votes cast by registered voters in a general election of the state was 86.3 percent turnout in 1968. The lowest percentage of votes cast by registered voters in the past twenty-five years of general elections occurred in

Montana Presidential Votes, 1948-1996

Year	State Winner	Democratic % of State Vote	Republican % of State Vote
1948	Truman (D)	53.1	43.2
1952	Eisenhower (R)	40.1	59.4
1956	Eisenhower (R)	42.9	57.1
1960	Nixon (R)	48.6	51.1
1964	Johnson (D)	59.0	40.6
1968	Nixon (R)	41.6	50.6
1972	Nixon (R)	37.9	57.9
1976	Ford (R)	45.4	52.8
1980	Reagan (R)	32.4	56.8
1984	Reagan (R)	38.2	60.5
1988	Bush (R)	47.0	53.0
1992	*Clinton (D)	37.7	35.2
1996	Dole (R)	40.2	43.1

* In the 1992 election, independent candidate Ross Perot garnered 26.2 percent of the state's presidential vote.
Sources: Office of the Montana Secretary of State; World Almanac and Book of Facts 1996, Mahwah, N.J.: Funk and Wagnalls Corporation, 1995.

1974, when only 69.7 percent of registered voters went to the polls. The highest number of registered voters participating in a primary election was the 238,215 voters who cast ballots in the 1972 vote on the new state constitution. The turnout represented 70.7 percent of those registered.

The voter turnout in the November 1996 general election was 70.6 percent, or 417,232 of the 590,751 registered voters.

White House
in the WILDERNESS

For two weeks in April 1903, the executive branch of the United States was seated not in Washington, D.C. but in the tiny town of Cinnabar, in the Paradise Valley.

On April 8, President Theodore Roosevelt arrived in town by private railroad train, with his White House staff, to dedicate the new stone arch at the entrance to Yellowstone. Cinnabar was a stop on the Northern Pacific Railroad's line, the first to reach a national park entrance. When Roosevelt visited, however, the new stretch of line from Cinnabar to the park was not yet ready for use. At the time, park visitors left the train at Cinnabar, three miles north, and traveled to the Gardiner entrance to the park by stagecoach. Roosevelt's train remained on a siding at Cinnabar for the duration of his sixteen-day stay.

Cinnabar was then a promising coal mining and tourist center, besides being a raucous gathering place for horse races and poker games. You won't find Cinnabar on the state road map. It has long since "sunk into the sagebrush," as one western history writer wrote. Like the town, the rail line has been abandoned.

notable
Montanans

Maggie Smith Hathaway (1867-1955)

Hathaway was a longtime educator in Stevensville and Helena and served several terms as the Lewis and Clark County superintendent of schools between 1894 and 1911. She spent much of her energies on social reform through the Women's Christian Temperance Movement and the suffragettes' crusade for women's voting rights, then became the first woman elected (along with Emma J. Ingalls) to the Montana Legislature in 1917. Later, she served as director of the state's Bureau of Child Welfare. She was a devoted lobbyist, pushing for passage of many social and welfare laws.

Montana Historical Society

Ella L. Knowles (1860-1911)

Knowles passed the Montana bar exam in December 1889 to become the first female lawyer in Montana. While practicing law in Butte, she was dedicated to promoting the rights of women in professions, industry, politics, and suffrage. She was the first woman political candidate for an office other than county superintendent of schools. After being defeated as a Populist candidate for the office of attorney general of the state in 1892, she was appointed assistant attorney general and held this position for four years. She had a reputation as a fine orator and was an expert in mining and land law. Knowles was the first woman to represent a state before a governmental authority in Washington, D.C.

Montana Historical Society

Women Who Run
with the
Political Wolves

Helen Piotopowaka Clarke became the first woman to hold an elected office in the territory of Montana when she was elected Lewis and Clark County superintendent of schools in 1882. She was the granddaughter of a Piegan tribal leader and daughter of Malcolm Clarke, a military man assigned to the American Fur Company in preterritorial days.

The first female legislators in Montana were: Maggie Smith Hathaway of Stevensville, Ravalli County, a Democrat; and Emma J. Ingalls of Kalispell, Flathead County, a Republican. Both were elected in the fall of 1916 and served in the 1917, 1919, and 1921 Legislatures. Since statehood, only 128 women have served in the Montana Legislature.

Two Montana women have run for governor: Dorothy Bradley of Bozeman, who ran in 1992 on the Democratic ticket with Mike Halligan as her lieutenant governor; and Judy Jacobson, the coauthor of the *Montana Almanac*, who ran a whirlwind nine-day campaign in 1996 after the sudden death of Chet Blaylock. Until his death in late October from a heart attack, Blaylock was facing an uphill battle in the race for governor against the incumbent, Marc Racicot. Jacobson was his running mate and stepped in to face Racicot. In an unusual, unprecedented occurrence, her name appeared on most ballots as the candidate for both governor and lieutenant governor.

Both Bradley, in 1992, and Jacobson, in 1996, lost to Racicot.

In the 1996 race, however, Judy Martz became the first woman to win election as lieutenant governor. She gained the office that ten other women had campaigned for.

Taxing and Spending

For state and local revenue, Montana relies on property taxes, income taxes, selected sales taxes, and natural resource taxes, including severance taxes on coal, gas, oil, and metal mining. Montana is one of only five states that have no general sales tax. In a June 1993 election, voters rejected a general sales tax for the second time in twenty-two years.

> Montana's selective sales taxes include taxes on:
> alcoholic beverages,
> cigarettes and tobacco products,
> motor fuels.

In the past, Montana has depended on the state's vast natural resources for a significant portion of its state revenue. In 1982, the $150 million in revenue from natural resource taxation made the single largest tax contribution, nearly one-fourth of the state's tax base. The fiscal year 1996 revenues from natural resource taxes declined to less than one-half of the collections a decade before. For example, the annual revenue from the coal severance tax peaked in 1985 at over $91 million. In fiscal year 1996, collections amounted to $36.2 million. Some of the contributing factors to this decline include a reduction of the coal severance tax from 30 percent to 15 percent and the lessening of the "energy crisis" of the 1970s that stimulated production of Montana's oil and gas resources.

At the same time that resource taxation resources were falling, the residential property values in Montana were increasing. The result is an increased contribution in revenue from taxation on this type of property, generally paid by homeowners. While the total state tax collections have declined since 1983, non-resource-based tax collections have actually increased. Approximately 60 percent of total revenues are derived from property taxation. Most revenue from property taxation is used for local purposes. Counties, municipalities, and school districts depend on it almost entirely.

Taxes Paid by Businesses

Businesses in Montana pay a corporate income (license) tax and property taxes. The corporate income tax rate is a flat 6.75 percent, and is calculated on net income earned in Montana. Of the 45 states with a similar tax, Montana's rate ranks 26th. The average rate among these states is 7.9 percent. Montana has eleven classes of property taxes, and businesses fall into different classes depending on the nature of their business. This is discussed under property taxes. Most of the corporate tax, about 89.5 percent, is deposited in the general fund of the state.

Corporation License Tax Revenue by Type of Industry (FY 1996)

Major Industrial Group	Revenue
Finance, Insurance, and Real Estate	$15,630,426
Transportation, Communications, and Utilities	11,785,020
Wholesale and Retail Trade	10,556,460
Manufacturing	10,080,390
Agriculture	4,061,323
Construction	2,165,142
Services	3,450,520
Mining	394,736
Other	6,385,754
Total	64,308,095

Source: Montana Department of Revenue. A Guide to Taxes. _Helena: 1997._

Total Corporate License Tax Collections, 1986-94

Fiscal Year	Total
1986	$58,584,784
1987	34,567,815
1988	46,200,103
1989	56,139,749
1990	80,340,117
1991	74,319,910
1992	57,682,673
1993	85,054,482
1994	68,871,909

Source: Montana Department of Revenue. A Guide to Taxes. _Helena: 1995._

Property Taxes

Property taxes, paid by both corporate and individual property owners, are the primary source of revenue for local governments in Montana. The state Property Assessment Division is responsible for ensuring that all property in the state is treated fairly for tax purposes. It appraises, assesses, and equalizes the value of the property in Montana.

- Only six counties in the state have elected county assessors. In those counties, the state contracts with the elected assessors for their services.

- Of all the property taxes collected in the state in 1996, 75 percent are spent locally.

- The first property reappraisal was done in 1975. Property reappraisal is required every three years. The latest revaluation was completed in December 1996. The 1997 Legislature delayed the next statewide reappraisal until 2007.

- The first half of property taxes is generally due on or before November 30 each year. The second half is due on or before the following May 31.

Property taxes were first organized into seven property tax classes (types of property) in 1919. The classifications and the rates applied to them have expanded through the years to as many as twenty classes, but recent Legislatures, by combining similar property types and tax rates, have reduced the number to eleven.

Class 1. Net proceeds
Annual net proceeds of all mines and mining claims, except coal and metal mines, is taxed at 100 percent (after deducting the expenses specified and allowed).

Class 2. Gross proceeds
Annual gross proceeds of metal mines is taxed at 3 percent.

Class 3. Agricultural land
Agricultural land is taxed at 3.86 percent of productive capacity. Nonproductive patented mining claims are taxed at 3.86 percent of productive capacity as grazing land.
Nonagricultural land 20 acres or more, but under 160 acres is taxed at 27.02 percent of productive capacity as grazing land.

Class 4. Residential real / Commercial real
Residential, commercial, and industrial land and improvements are taxed at 3.86 percent of market value. Golf courses are taxed at 1.93 percent of market value. Idle agricultural and timber processing property is taxed at 3.86 percent of market value.
Mobile homes are taxed at 3.86 percent of market value. Farmsteads and 1-acre homesites are taxed at 3.86 percent of market value.

Class 5.   Co-ops, pollution control, new industry
Air and water pollution control equipment, rural electric and telephone cooperatives, plus real and personal property of new industry and research and development firms is taxed at 3 percent of market value.

Class 6.   Livestock
Livestock, rental or lease equipment valued at less than $5,000, and equipment used in canola seed oil processing plants are all taxed at 4 percent of market value.

Class 7.   Independent telephone
Qualifying independent telephone and electric cooperatives are taxed at 8 percent of market value.

Class 8.   Business equipment
Business personal property is taxed at 5 percent of market value in 1997; 6 percent in 1998.

Class 9.   Utilities
Real and personal property of utilities, telecommunication companies, and pipelines is taxed at 12 percent of market value.

Class 10.   Timber land
Forest land is taxed at 0.79 percent of market value.

Class 12.   Railroads and airlines
Real and personal property of railroads and airlines is taxed at 6.76 percent of market value.

Class 11 has been repealed.

To Market
To Market

"Market value is the value at which property would change hands between a willing buyer and a willing seller, neither being under any compulsion to buy or sell and both having reasonable knowledge of relevant facts."

—A Guide to Taxes
Mt. Dept. of Revenue, 1995

FY97 Property Tax Base

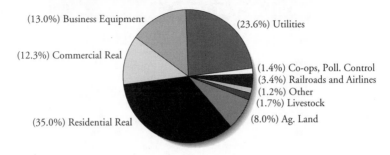

(13.0%) Business Equipment

(23.6%) Utilities

(12.3%) Commercial Real

(1.4%) Co-ops, Poll. Control
(3.4%) Railroads and Airlines
(1.2%) Other
(1.7%) Livestock

(35.0%) Residential Real

(8.0%) Ag. Land

Source: Montana Deptartment of Revenue, Guide to Taxes, 1997.

Montana's Coal Tax

The earliest taxation on coal mines began in 1921, when a license tax of 5 cents per ton was enacted into law. The most significant change in this tax occurred in 1975, when the Legislature passed legislation to create a 30 percent severance tax on coal extracted from Montana, primarily from strip mining in the southeastern part of the state. The Legislature also approved and submitted to the people a constitutional amendment to deposit a portion of the proceeds of the coal severance tax into a permanent trust fund, with the principal of the trust to remain inviolate unless three-fourths of the members of the Legislature approved a change. The remainder of the coal tax is used for a variety of purposes that have been modified through the years. The Legislature has phased down the tax rate to fifteen percent and established a lower tax rate for coal with a heating quality of less than 7,000 BTU.

Of Mills and Levies

A mill is a tenth of a cent ($0.001), so a levy of 350 mills translates to $350 per $1,000 of taxable value. The following is a sample property tax liability calculation for a home in a Montana town, using a sample mill levy:

Assessed/market value of the home	$80,000
Property tax classification (Class 4 = 3.86 percent)	x.0386
Taxable value	$3,088
District mill levy (350 mills)	x .350
Property tax liability	$1,080.80

In FY 1995, the average county mill levy was 87.7 mills, and the average municipal mill levy was 93.19 mills.

Revenue Collections from Coal Severance Tax

Fiscal Year	Total
1991	$50,457,839
1992	43,434,111
1993	38,439,386
1994	41,005,757
1995	41,701,929
1996	36,260,949

Source: Montana Department of Revenue. A Guide to Taxes. Helena: 1996.

Montana's Motor Fuels Tax

Taxes on motor fuels are levied only on fuels used to propel vehicles on public streets and highways. In 1996, the tax rate was 27 cents per gallon.

A three-fifths vote of the Legislature is required for this revenue to be used for any purpose but the following:

- construction, reconstruction, repair, operation, and maintenance of public highways, streets, roads, and bridges
- payment of county, city, and town obligations incurred for streets, roads, and bridges
- enforcement of highway safety
- driver education
- tourist promotion
- administrative collection costs

Montana's Accommodations Tax

Montana's accommodations tax was enacted in 1987. It imposes a statewide 4 percent tax on users of hotels, motels, campgrounds, and other overnight lodging facilities. The revenue is used for tourism promotion. This fund has grown considerably since enactment. Collections for tax year 1988 were just under $3.4 million. Collections for tax years 1993 through 1995 were over $8 million.

The tax proceeds are distributed as follows:

% of net

6.5	Department of Fish, Wildlife & Parks for facilities maintenance
2.5	the university system for a Montana travel research program
1	the Montana Historical Society for roadside historical signs and historic sites

balance

    75%   the Montana Department of Commerce

remaining funds

        go to regional nonprofit tourism corporations and nonprofit convention and visitors bureaus for promotion of Montana tourism and Montana locations for motion picture and TV commercial production.

Accommodations Tax Collections, 1991-1995

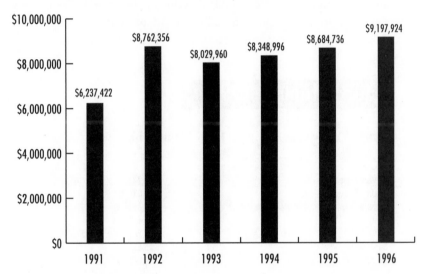

Source: *Montana Department of Revenue.* A Guide to Taxes Administered by the Montana Department of Revenue. *Helena: 1997.*

Income Tax

Individual income tax is the largest source of tax revenue for funding state government operations ($350 million in FY 1996). Of the income tax revenue, 91.3 percent goes to the state general fund and 8.7 percent is dedicated to the long-range building fund.

    Individual income is taxed at rates from 2 to 11 percent. Adjustments are made for business deductions and other allowable deductions. Montana allows a full deduction for federal income taxes, one of only seven states in the Union to grant this. Other allowable deductions in this state include some charitable contributions, some medical expenses, interest, child care expenses, and some taxes.

Montana's individual income tax is fully indexed. The tax table, personal exemption level, and standard deductions limits are adjusted annually to reflect inflation. For tax year 1995, Montana's income tax rates on taxable personal income ranged from 2 percent on taxable incomes less than $1,800 to 11 percent, less $1,845, on taxable income in excess of $64,600. The state allowed a $1,480 exemption for each dependent.

Motor Vehicle Licenses and Registration

Privately owned vehicles must be licensed each year. These license fees include local government fees, taxes, and mill levies, as well as other license fees such as a junk vehicle assessment. Automobiles and light trucks pay a 2 percent property tax on the average trade-in or wholesale value of the vehicle. County governments are permitted to impose an additional 0.5 percent tax on that value. There is a 1.5 percent sales tax on the factory list price of new vehicles.

Our Vehicles, 1995

Type of Vehicle	Number in State
Licensed Passenger Cars	429,273*
Trucks (of all weights)	208,031
Travel Trailers (campers, tent trailers, 5th wheels)	155,663
Boats	45,472
Motorcycles	18,225
Snowmobiles	15,455
Off Highway Vehicles	14,072

*Of those, 12,214 are motor homes; 59,790 are defined as rugged terrain vehicles.

Liquor Tax

Hard liquor is taxed with a 16 percent excise tax earmarked for the state general fund and a 10 percent license tax is split between state institutions (65.5 percent), cities and towns (30 percent), and counties (4.5 percent). Counties, cities, and towns must use the funds for regulation and control of liquor sale and use, and for law enforcement. Revenues from all alcoholic beverages for the past ten years have been approximately $20 million annually, with $3 million from beer sales and $1.5 million from wine sales.

Alcoholic Beverage Revenues, 1987-96

Fiscal Year	Liquor Operations Net Profit	Liquor Excise Taxes	Liquor License Taxes	Beer Taxes	Wine Taxes	Licensing Revenues	Total Revenue
1987	3,850,811	5,589,174	3,490,356	3,060,956	1,657,782	1,540,138	19,189,217
1988	3,785,922	5,322,934	3,323,773	2,997,015	1,569,140	1,610,907	18,609,691
1989	3,489,483	5,438,423	3,399,014	3,000,273	1,452,851	1,511,520	18,291,564
1990	4,162,346	5,434,746	3,396,716	3,028,991	1,403,692	1,661,818	19,088,309
1991	4,002,685	5,762,568	3,601,605	3,089,077	1,358,634	1,379,791	19,194,360
1992	4,066,047	6,122,351	3,823,659	3,470,876	1,439,696	1,552,552	20,475,181
1993	4,035,715	6,645,090	3,926,430	3,441,481	1,360,770	1,658,224	21,067,710
1994	3,717,344	6,372,756	3,930,635	3,263,346	1,289,016	1,467,686	20,040,783
1995	3,825,580	6,309,138	3,943,212	3,215,598	1,374,297	1,592,688	20,260,513
1996	5,057,401	7,304,750	4,564,287	3,329,867	1,459,901	1,569,923	23,286,130

Source: *Montana Department of Revenue,* Guide to Taxes Administered by the Department of Revenue. *Helena: 1997.*

Cigarette and Tobacco Products Tax

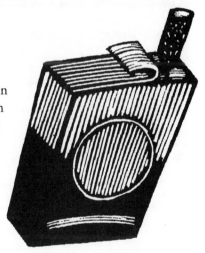

In Montana, smokers pay a tax of 18 cents on each pack of twenty cigarettes, included in the price. Other tobacco products are taxed at 12.5 percent of the price of product. Collections of $12.9 million in cigarette taxes in FY 1996 were dedicated to the state's long-range building program, with 11.11 percent going to the state veterans' nursing homes.

Tax Information

Information about state taxes may be obtained from:

State Department of Revenue
Sam W. Mitchell Building
Helena, MT 59620
444-2837

General Fund

State law defines the general fund as the one that "accounts for all financial resources except those required to be accounted for in another fund." This account is often referred to as the state's checkbook. In 1995, the general fund and the state school equalization account were combined into one account.

Total general fund appropriations for various state programs for 1994 and 1995 increased by 7.8 percent, or $135.4 million over the previous biennium. Total funds appropriated from state and federal sources increased by $432.7 million, or 11 percent.

Revenue Estimates for Montana's General Fund and School Equalization Accounts,* 1996-97

Revenue Source	Dollars in Millions	Percent of Budget
Income Taxes	$793.5	40.6
Corporation Taxes	143.0	7.3
Natural Resources	98.0	5.0
Interest	196.7	10.1
Property Taxes	413.4	21.2
Other	307.9	15.8
TOTAL	1,952.4	

*This account funds all schools, higher education, and departments of state government or parts of these that are not covered by federal, state special, and proprietary accounts.
Source: Office of the Legislative Fiscal Analyst. Legislative Fiscal Report 1997 Biennium. Helena: Montana Legislative Council, 1995.

Montana State Revenues by Source (in Thousands of Dollars)

1990	1991	1992	1993	1994	1995	1996
Licenses/Permits						
55,229	74,152	82,744	92,773	98,852	106,109	110,043
Taxes						
776,368	864,057	850,916	1,003,849	1,026,025	1,080,529	997,874
Charges for Services, Fines, Forfeits						
56,929	43,678	52,527	53,775	58,872	69,781	66,367
Investment Earnings						
37,263	31,655	24,791	20,715	19,993	29,267	28,594
Sale of Documents, Merchandise, Property						
5,548	17,146	18,091	17,055	19,905	18,987	6,776
Rentals, Leases, Royalties						
363	528	397	451	321	180	220
Contributions/Premiums						
3,199	4,113	3,355	3,466	3,617	3,773	4,165
Grants/Contracts/Donations						
8,473	7,004	3,611	3,682	7,782	8,448	9,232
Federal						
451,107	532,244	585,047	667,468	684,001	714,629	880,300
Federal IDC Recoveries						
1,790	1,823	1,738	1,817	2,334	2,602	1,685
Other Revenues						
2,078	2,367	2,792	4,503	2,301	1,135	1,552
Totals						
1,398,347	1,578,767	1,626,009	1,869,554	1,924,013	2,035,440	2,106,808

Source: Montana Department of Administration. Comprehensive Annual Financial Report, June 1996.

Crime and Punishment

Punishment for crimes on Montana's early mining frontier was swift, sure, and cheap. In the mining camps of Virginia City and Bannack, a person who committed a serious crime was often hanged from the nearest tree after a hasty trial by those who could be rounded up in a hurry. In those lawless days, some of the lawmen couldn't even be trusted, as in the case of the infamous Bannack sheriff, Henry Plummer. His outlaw gang had the nerve to call themselves the "Innocents." During their reign of terror, they were reputed to have killed as many as one hundred men on the roads to gold country. Finally, a group of citizens organized for law and order.

Tagged as part of the Plummer gang, George Ives was the first person to die for committing a violent crime in Montana. He was convicted and hanged in Nevada City on December 19, 1863, for the murder of Nicholas Thiebalt. It only took the secret society of "Vigilantes" the first month or so of 1864 to track down the other killers and thieves in the gang. The Vigilantes hanged Plummer and twenty-three others without the benefit of a trial.

Montana State Prison

Within seven years of becoming a new territory, Montana built its first prison, which consisted of thirteen cells at Deer Lodge. Upon statehood in 1889, the state instituted a private contract system for the care of prisoners. The firm of Conley and McTague won the bid to run the state prison for 74 cents a day per prisoner. Over the thirty years of Warden Frank Conley's administration, he used prison labor to build not only the new prison but also buildings at Warm Springs and Galen and miles of Montana roads.

In 1957, prisoners took over a cell block and an administration building for 15 hours, relenting when officials promised to improve conditions at the prison. During an investigation into the "bloodless riot," a respected California expert on penal institutions testified that "the old cell block is like a dungeon. Old, concrete tombs, that's what they are; no running water, the old bucket system."

Forrest H. Anderson, state attorney general at the time, said "the danger of another disturbance is not imminent." He was proved wrong two years later when the National Guard was called in to quell a far more violent riot. One of two ringleaders shot and killed a deputy warden. After a successful rescue attempt aided by bazooka and machine-gun fire freed twenty-two hostages, the same ringleader apparently murdered his partner before committing suicide.

In the early 1970s, supporters of a proposal to build a new prison included Governor Forrest Anderson. They achieved their goal and in the waning months of that decade, prisoners were moved to the new facility.

Source: Philip Kent, Montana State Prison History. *Deer Lodge: Powell County Museum and Arts Foundation, 1979.*

Montana Crime Statistics

In 1995, there were 5,484 major crimes for every 100,000 persons in Montana. That compares with a crime rate of 4,730 per 100,000 persons in 1994. The crime rate of a given area is defined as the number of the following major crimes per 100,000 people:

- willful homicide
- forcible rape
- robbery
- aggravated assault
- burglary
- larceny/theft
- motor vehicle theft

For the most part, the number of offenses has been increasing as the population increases, for an average increase in the crime rate of 1.3 percent per year over the past five years.

The 17.4 percent increase in the number of crimes reported in Montana between 1993 and 1994 was partially attributed to improvements in the way crimes are reported to the state. The large increase in reports of forcible rape may be the result of better reporting between rape crisis centers and law enforcement.

Montana still has the fifth lowest rate of violent crime in the nation. The only major offense where Montana exceeded the national average (by 20 percent) was the offense of larceny/theft, which involves such crimes as theft by

The old state prison in Deer Lodge, now a museum. Travel Montana

pickpockets, shoplifting, theft from motor vehicles, and thefts from buildings where forcible entry is not involved.

An arrest was made in 27.7 percent of all crimes in 1995, compared with a 22.2 percent arrest rate in 1994, and a 31.6 percent arrest rate in 1993. The total loss in crimes against property was $19.1 million, with $3.5 million, or 18 percent, recovered.

Prison Population

Facility	Average Daily Population November, 1996	Capacity
Montana State Prison, Deer Lodge	1,311	1,424
Swan River Correctional Center	22	63
Women's Correctional Center, Billings	67	65
County Jails, Holding Cells, and Out-of-State	134	412

*Populations rounded off to non-decimal figure.
Source: Montana Department of Corrections.

Montana Crime Rate Compared to National Crime Rate, 1994

Major Crime	Montana Crime Rate (per 100,000)	National Crime Rate (per 100,000)
Willful Homicide	3.7	9.0
Forcible Rape	33	39
Robbery	25	238
Aggravated Assault	120	430
Forcible Burglary or Attempts	622	1,042
Larceny/Theft	3,682	3,025
Motor Vehicle Theft	245	591
TOTAL	4,730	5,400

Source: Montana Board of Crime Control, Uniform Crime Report Data. Crime in Montana, 1994 Annual Report. *Statistical Analysis Center, Montana Board of Crime Control, December 1995.*

Montana Crime Clock, 1995

> **Property crime:** One every thirteen minutes, four seconds
> **Larceny:** One every sixteen minutes, two seconds
> **Burglary:** One every one hour, forty-four minutes
> **Motor vehicle theft:** One every three hours, forty minutes
> **Violent crime:** One every five hours, fifty-three minutes
> **Robbery:** One every thirty-four hours, seven minutes
> **Rape:** One every thirty-seven hours, fifty-five minutes
> **Homicide:** One every ten days, ten hours

Source: Montana Board of Crime Control, Uniform Crime Report Data. Crime in Montana, 1994 Annual Report. *Statistical Analysis Center, Montana Board of Crime Control, December 1995.*

Capital *Punishment*

On May 10, 1995, 43-year-old Duncan Peder McKenzie, Jr. was put to death by lethal injection at the Montana State Prison. He was the first inmate executed in Montana in nearly fifty-two years. McKenzie was convicted twenty years earlier for the 1974 kidnapping, torture, and murder of schoolteacher Lana Harding, near Conrad.

Prior to McKenzie's death, the last execution in Montana was on September 10, 1943, when Philip "Slim" Coleman was hanged in the Missoula County Jail for murdering a woman in Lothrup, near Missoula.

As of December 1996, there are five people on Montana's death row:

1. Terry A. Langford, convicted in 1989 for the execution-style murders of Ned and Celene Blackwood at their home near Ovando.
2. David T. Dawson, who was convicted of strangling three members of a Billings family, David and Monica Rodstein and their 11-year-old son, in 1986.
3. & 4. William Gollehon and Douglas Turner, convicted of beating another prisoner to death in 1990.
5. Ronald A. Smith, sentenced to die three times for his role in the 1982 execution-style murder of two Browning men, Harvey Mad Man and Thomas Running Rabbit.

Homicide

There were thirty homicides in Montana in 1994. In 1995 homicides increased to thirty-five, or 4.5 per 100,000 people. The national rate for 1994 was nine homicides per 100,000 people. One homicide is committed in Montana every ten days. Nationally, one homicide is committed every twenty-three minutes.

Major Crimes Reported in Montana, 1993-95

Offense	Times Reported 1993	Times Reported 1994	Percent Change	Times Reported 1995	Percent Change
Homicide	29	30	3.4	35	16.7
Rape	179	270	50.8	231	-14.4
Robbery	186	202	8.6	253	25.2
Aggravated Assault	788	986	25.1	972	-1.4
Burglary	4,943	5,099	3.2	5,060	-0.8
Larceny	26,724	30,176	12.9	32,797	8.7
Motor Vehicle Theft	1,602	2,005	25.2	2,389	19.2
Other Assaults*	6,269	8,423	34.4	8,733	3.7
Domestic Abuse	2,295	3,170	38.1	3,344	5.5
Arson	154	314	103.9	151	-51.9
Forgery	1,232	1,742	41.4	2,528	45.1
Fraud	2,703	2,738	1.3	2,358	-13.9
Embezzlement	26	47	80.8	39	-17.0
Stolen Property	169	228	34.9	225	-1.3
Vandalism	13,570	15,813	16.5	17,043	7.8
Weapons	327	487	48.9	1,198	146.0
Prostitution	32	33	3.1	22	-33.3
Sex Offenses	1,183	1,450	22.6	1,241	-14.4
Narcotics	2,191	2,893	32.0	3,633	25.6
Gambling	10	1	-90.0	6	500.0
Offenses Against Family	400	677	69.3	1,334	97.0
DUI	5,464	6,328	15.8	5,450	-13.9
TOTAL**	65,012	76,784	18.1	83,592	8.9

* Other assaults consist of assaults other than those considered aggravated. If a domestic abuse is considered aggravated, it is counted as aggravated assault and also as domestic abuse.
**Totals do not include DUIs.
Source: Montana Board of Crime Control, Uniform Crime Report Data. Crime in Montana, 1995 Annual Report. *Statistical Analysis Center, Montana Board of Crime Control, December 1995.*

Crime Rates, 1995, As Reported by Police Departments

Agency by Rank*	Rate per 100,000 Population
State Average	5,484
1. Bozeman P.D.	13,110
2. West Yellowstone P.D.	10,739
3. Hamilton P.D.	9,784
4. Great Falls P.D.	9,516
5. Billings P.D.	9,173
6. Missoula P.D.	9,153
7. Helena P.D.	8,603
8. Kalispell P.D.	8,474
9. Livingston P.D.	8,056
10. Whitefish P.D.	7,974
11. Havre P.D.	7,552
12. Harlem P.D.	6,785
13. Laurel P.D.	6,407
14. Lewistown P.D.	6,381
15. Glasgow P.D.	5,815
16. Plentywood P.D.	5,288
17. Miles City P.D.	5,266
18. Sidney P.D.	5,288
19. Libby/Lincoln County**	4,943
20. Glendive P.D.	4,687
21. Butte/Silver Bow County**	4,398
22. Belgrade P.D.	3,832
23. Fort Benton P.D.	3,586
24. Columbia Falls P.D.	3,560
25. Chinook P.D.	3,299
26. Red Lodge P.D.	3,107
27. Shelby/Toole County**	2,882
28. Anaconda/Deer Lodge County**	2,818
29. Manhattan P.D.	2,771
30. Dillon P.D.	2,522
31. Deer Lodge/Powell County**	2,187
32. Conrad P.D.	2,019
33. Boulder/Jefferson County**	1,651
34. Baker P.D.	1,399
35. Three Forks P.D.	508
36. Scobey/Daniels County S.O.**	457

* This ranking includes only those agencies that participate in reporting to the Board of Crime Control.
** The ranking is for agencies that combine data for reporting purposes or the agencies have a combined form of government. These agencies are also ranked in the county sheriffs table.
Source: Montana Board of Crime Control.

Crime Rates, 1995, As Reported by County Sheriffs

Agency by Rank*	Rate per 100,000 Population
State Average	5,484
1. Mineral County S.O.	5,255
2. Libby/Lincoln County S.O.**	4,943
3. Butte/Silver Bow County**	4,398
4. Flathead County S.O.	4,003
5. Missoula County S.O.	3,990
6. Yellowstone County S.O.	3,472
7. Hill County S.O.	3,434
8. Lewis & Clark County S.O.	3,416
9. Meagher County S.O.	3,335
10. Sanders County S.O.	3,264
11. Granite County S.O.	3,076
12. Broadwater County S.O.	2,997
13. Shelby/Toole County S.O.**	2,882
14. Musselshell County S.O.	2,848
15. Anaconda/Deer Lodge County**	2,818
16. Gallatin County S.O.	2,452
17. Cascade County S.O.	2,395
18. Valley County S.O.	2,331
19. Phillips County S.O.	2,246
20. Deer Lodge/Powell County**	2,187
21. Fergus County S.O.	1,962
22. Big Horn County S.O.	1,950
23. Rosebud County S.O.	1,793
24. Richland County S.O.	1,741
25. Chouteau County S.O.	1,720
26. Carbon County S.O.	1,684
27. Boulder/Jefferson County S.O.**	1,651
28. Custer County S.O.	1,572
29. Powder River County S.O.	1,472
30. Madison County S.O.	1,464
31. Dawson County S.O.	1,461
32. Sheridan County S.O.	1,401
33. Park County S.O.	1,398
34. Sweet Grass County S.O.	1,355
35. Beaverhead County S.O.	1,177
36. Blaine County S.O.	1,044
37. Stillwater County S.O.	981
38. Fallon County S.O.	959
39. Pondera County S.O.	863
40. Scobey/Daniels County S.O.**	457
41. Treasure County S.O.	450
42. Liberty County S.O.	308
43. Teton County S.O.	293
44. McCone County S.O.	276

* This ranking includes only those agencies that participate in reporting to the Board of Crime Control.

** The ranking is for agencies that combine data for reporting purposes or the agencies have a combined form of government. These agencies are also ranked in the police department table. *Source: Montana Board of Crime Control.*

Further Reading:

Crime in Montana. Published yearly by Montana Board of Crime Control, 303 North Roberts, Helena, MT 59620.

A Guide to Taxes Administered by the Montana Department of Revenue. Helena: Montana Department of Revenue, 1995.

Kent, Philip, *Montana State Prison History*. Deer Lodge: Powell County Museum and Arts Foundation, 1979.

Lopach, James J., Lauren S. McKinsey, Jerry W. Calvert, and Margery Brown. *We the People of Montana: The Workings of a Popular Government*. Missoula: Mountain Press Publishing Company, 1983.

Montana Code Annotated. Helena: Montana State Government Printing Office, 1995.

Montana Counties on the Move. Helena: Montana Association of Counties, 1990.

The Tribal Nations of Montana, A Handbook for Legislators. Helena: Montana Legislative Council, 1995.

Young, Douglas J. *Montana Taxation and Expenditures: Trends and Comparisons*. 1995 Update. Bozeman: MSU Department of Agricultural Economics, 1995.

chapter seven

EDUCATION

FOR 130 YEARS Montanans have demonstrated a strong commitment to providing accessible, quality educational opportunities for citizens of all ages. The outstanding educational systems that are available in Montana on the eve of the twenty-first century are a legacy of the 1972 Montana Constitution:

Article X. Section 1). It is the goal of the people to establish a system of education which will develop the full educational potential of each person. Equality of educational opportunity is guaranteed to each person of the state.

But education was a priority among Montana citizens for more than a century before passage of the 1972 Constitution. Despite the high costs of establishing and maintaining public schools and universities, Montana voters, when given the choice at the ballot box, have in most cases shown solid support for education.

That support has paid handsome dividends in the form of well-educated students and graduates. An extraordinarily high number of students from the University of Montana-Missoula are selected for Rhodes scholarships. Only seven states have higher percentages of teens completing a high school education. The state's literacy rate for adults is well above the national average.

Montana's exemplary school system includes public and private elementary and high schools, the state university system and its colleges of technology, private and tribal colleges, and community colleges. State and local governments

photo: Office of Public Instruction

also support an extensive, interconnected public library system. Nearly every large city in Montana can claim an institution of higher education, and most small towns have libraries.

In recent years, Montana's Indian tribes have developed dynamic tribal colleges, with administrators and teachers who have won renown as some of this country's leading educators. The schools strive to give their students practical knowledge to apply to life on or off the reservation and to be shared in service to the tribes.

From lessons taught amid the bustle of the mining camps and in one-room schoolhouses in the towns and on the prairies to lectures and labs on the modern campuses across the state today, Montana has put stock in its citizens and their need and desire to learn.

K-12 Education

As early as 1861, Fort Owen in the Bitterroot Valley offered schooling to area children. In 1864, the Sisters of Providence of Montreal opened the first missionary school in the Northwest for Indian children, at St. Ignatius. In the pre-territorial mining camps of Bannack, Virginia City, and Nevada City, parents could pay one or two dollars a week to send their children to the local tuition or "subscription" school.

The first territorial legislature, meeting for sixty days in Bannack in the winter of 1864-65, established a "common school system." In the same year, the federal Organic Act, creating Montana Territory, provided that when the lands of the state were surveyed, sections 16 and 36 of each township would be reserved for school purposes. It was not until many years after statehood that these lands were located and surveyed and the revenue from commercial activities on the lands could be directed to the public schools.

Virginia City organized the first public elementary school in February 1866. Other settlements were quick to follow suit. In the school year of 1867-68, Montana had fifteen public schools and 1,359 students. By the 1872-73 school year, the state was spending more than $21,000 on public education.

The pioneer schools were mainly housed in one-room buildings and were open only four or five months of the year. Schools in agricultural areas generally operated during winter, when the students were not required for farm work. In other areas, the schools set terms over the summer months to avoid heating the school buildings during severe winter weather.

Today, there are 887 separate schools scattered across Montana's urban and rural landscape. In the 1995-96 school year, Montana had approximately eighty schools that could be described as one-room or one-teacher elementary schools, with attendance ranging from one student to about twenty.

There are 173 separate high schools, with student populations ranging from twelve students in isolated rural areas to more than 2,000 in the Billings district.

Eva Deem's school in Chouteau County, 1914.
Montana Historical Society

(Flathead High School in Kalispell counts 2,289 students in its four grades, but they're not all in the same building. The ninth grade takes classes in a separate junior high school building.) Fifty-eight high schools had fewer than seventy-five students in the 1995-96 school year.

The number of school districts in Montana reached a high of 3,572 in 1930, when transportation was still a challenge in rural locations. Today, with 471 school districts, Montana has the highest number of districts in the Rocky Mountain and northwestern states.

Each school district in Montana must, by federal and state law, provide appropriate special education programs. Some offer pre-kindergarten programs. In general, school districts commence classes in the week before the Labor Day weekend and operate until the end of the first week in June. Districts are required by law to provide 180 days of pupil instruction.

Total State School Districts

Montana and Selected U.S. States, 1995-96

California	999
New York	710
New Jersey	618
Montana	471
Minnesota	364
Washington	296
North Dakota	238
Oregon	237
Colorado	176
Connecticut	176
Mississippi	153
Idaho	112
Alaska	54
Wyoming	49
Utah	40
Nevada	17

Rocky Mountain states are shaded.
Source: National Education Association. 1995-96 Estimates of School Statistics, 1996.

notable
Montanans

Lucia Darling (1839-1905)

Darling began her teaching career at the age of fourteen in Ohio. In 1863, she arrived in Bannack with her uncle, Sidney Edgerton, who was traveling to Lewistown, Idaho, to assume the post as chief justice of the new Idaho Territory. When the party decided to stay in the "tumultuous and rough" mining camp of Bannack for the winter, Lucia begged her uncle to help her start a school for the local children. Suitable accommodations were scarce and expensive, so Lucia's first school was housed in her uncle's cabin. She opened her school in October 1863, armed with few schoolbooks or materials but plenty of enthusiasm. In the following summer, local residents built a small log cabin to accommodate what Lucia's later reminiscences called "the first school in Montana." Actually, Miss Kate Dunlap's school in Nevada City near Alder Gulch opened a few months before the Bannack school. Lucia's diary, *Crossing the Plains*, tells of the tough trip to Bannack from Ohio in the summer of 1863 and her impressions of that gold camp. Her Uncle Sidney was appointed the first governor of Montana Territory.

Montana Historical Society

Though many of the schools on the approximately 40 Hutterite colonies in Montana are part of public school districts, the students meet each school day before and/or after their regular day of instruction in English to learn reading and writing in German.

School Enrollment Trends

When the baby boomer generation moved out of its high school years at the end of the 1970s, public school enrollment in Montana declined by nearly 20,000 students from the all-time high of 174,532 in 1971-72. Enrollment in the 1980s continued to decline to 151,149 students in 1989-1990, the lowest number since the 1962-1963 school year. Public school enrollment increased 9.5 percent (14,398 students) from 1989-1990 to 165,547 for the 1995-1996 school year.

The ten most sparsely populated counties have lost student enrollment, which corresponds to general population declines in those counties. Though officials expected the school age population to reach a peak of 168,000 by the year 2000, an overall decline in enrollment occurred in 1996-1997, when 164,592 students were enrolled in Montana's public schools.

Public School Enrollment

School Year	K-8	High School	Total *
1982-83	106,935	45,466	152,401
1983-84	108,268	45,378	153,646
1984-85	108,796	45,616	154,412
1985-86	107,918	45,951	153,869
1986-87	107,572	45,755	153,327
1987-88	108,030	44,177	152,207
1988-89	109,490	42,701	152,191
1989-90	109,579	41,570	151,149
1990-91	111,090	41,789	152,879
1991-92	112,743	42,779	155,522
1992-93	115,233	44,758	159,991
1993-94	116,650	46,370	163,020
1994-95	116,631	47,709	164,340
1995-96	116,337	49,210	165,547
1996-97	114,561	50,031	164,592

* Totals may include 100-200 students at three state-funded institutions: Pine Hills School, Montana School for the Deaf and Blind after 1991, Mountain View School prior to 1996.
Source: Annual OPI enrollment reports.

School Funding and Spending

In 1958, the total reported cost of operating elementary and high schools in Montana was $59 million. In the 1994-1995 school year, state and district revenue for all school budgets was $931.8 million. School general fund budgets, which include personnel salaries, materials, utilities, etc., totaled $924.4 million.

Source: OPI trustee financial summaries—1993-94.

- Montana ranks 18th for the percentage of K-12 funding from state government sources (53.4%) and ranks 11th for revenue from federal funding (9.2%).
- The state ranks 34th for revenue from state sources (41.2%).
- In 1994-95, Montana ranked 29th for per-pupil expenditures, or 93% of the national average per pupil.

Source: NEA Rankings of the States, *1995.*

Estimated Per-Pupil Expenditures for Selected States, 1995-96

State	Estimated Expenditures Per Enrolled Pupil
New Jersey	$9,786
Alaska	$9,364
Connecticut	$7,955
Minnesota	$6,928
Washington	$5,868
Wyoming	$5,808
U.S.	$5,738
Oregon	$5,736
Montana	**$5,492**
Colorado	$5,086
California	$4,927
Nevada	$4,707
North Dakota	$4,632
Idaho	$4,240
Mississippi	$4,000
Utah	$3,670

Source: U.S. Department of Education, National Center for Education Statistics.

School Organization and Governance

Superintendent of Public Instruction

The superintendent of public instruction is elected by popular vote for a four-year term. The superintendent heads the Office of Public Instruction (OPI), Montana's state education agency, and is responsible for:

- providing technical assistance to the schools
- disbursing state and federal funding
- recommending accreditation standards to the State Board of Public Education

notable
Montanans

 ## Cornelius Hedges (1831-1907)

Hedges made many contributions to the early civic life of Montana but is most remembered as the father of Montana's school system. Armed with degrees from Yale and a law degree from Harvard, he came to Alder Gulch in 1864 with other treasure hunters. But success as a miner was not in his destiny, even after he followed the gold stampede to Helena. In the mining camp that would become the capital, he applied his legal talents and education to a wide variety of professional positions. He was a federal district attorney, Helena city clerk and attorney, and writer for the *Helena Herald.* After his appointment in 1872 as territorial superintendent of public instruction, he convinced the 1872 Legislature to

strengthen the duties of the office in order to help modernize the fledgling school system. He trekked throughout the settled parts of the territory to visit each school each year of his four terms as superintendent. Hedges convinced communities to erect brick school buildings, use standardized tests, and increase attendance requirements. He established a teacher certification system administered by his office. As a delegate to the 1884 Constitutional Convention, he was largely responsible for creating the education article that was later adopted in the 1889 constitution.

Montana Historical Society

- performing accreditation reviews at various intervals
- certifying teachers
- monitoring the state's special education programs
- administering other federally funded or required programs

Superintendent of Public Instruction
Office of Public Instruction
State Capitol, Room 106
P.O. Box 202501
Helena, MT 59620-2501
444-3095

Board of Public Education

The Montana Constitution charges the Board of Public Education with the general supervision of the public school system. The board:

- adopts and enforces standards of accreditation for schools
- sets teacher certification policies
- performs various other duties

The board also serves as the governing board of the Montana School for the Deaf and Blind.

The Board of Public Education consists of seven voting members, each serving a term of seven years. Members are appointed by the governor and confirmed by the senate. A student representative is also selected annually as a nonvoting member. The governor, the superintendent of public instruction, and the commissioner of higher education serve as ex-officio, nonvoting members.

THE
Old *School*

The Trinity School at Canyon Creek in Lewis and Clark County is considered to be the oldest school building still in use in the state. Parts of the 1880s building have been modified over the years, but it has been continually used as an elementary school for over one hundred years.

The granite block Philipsburg elementary school, built in 1894, is the oldest operating two-story stone-construction school building in Montana.

Board of Public Education
2500 Broadway
Helena, MT 59620
444-6576

School District Trustees

An elected board of school trustees manages each local school district. The boards:

- select teachers, administrators, and other school personnel
- prepare and adopt budgets
- determine local curricula, in keeping with the Board of Public Education's accreditation standards
- fulfill other responsibilities assigned by the Legislature

An elementary school board may consist of from three to seven members, and a high school board may consist of up to eleven members.

A high school board consists of the trustees of the elementary school district in which the high school buildings are located, plus members elected to represent other areas of the high school district that may encompass other elementary districts.

Annual school elections are held in each district on the first Tuesday of April. Any qualified voter who is a legal resident of the district is eligible to vote or to serve as a trustee. School trustees serve without compensation for three-year overlapping terms.

County Superintendent of Schools

In each county, voters elect a county superintendent of schools on a partisan ballot for a four-year term. County commissioners may combine this office with other appropriate county offices or may combine the office with the county superintendent of schools of another county.

In the early days of the state, the county superintendent had a strong role in supervising the teachers and curricula of the many small districts. Today, work of the office has changed as the number of small, teacher-run school districts diminishes. The duties of a county school superintendent now center on assisting districts and other county officials with budgeting and taxation functions.

notable
Montanans

Helen Piotopowaka Clarke (1848-1923)

The daughter of a rancher and a Blackfeet princess, Helen Clarke won acclaim in Europe as a classical actress before returning to her home state and taking up teaching in the 1860s. She taught in Fort Benton and Helena, then won election to become the first woman county superintendent of schools—indeed, the first female elected to office in the territory. She served in Lewis and Clark County from 1882-1888. Later she worked in Indian affairs as an interpreter and mediator for the Blackfeet and for several tribal groups in Oklahoma. Clarke died at the family cattle ranch in Midvale.

Montana Historical Society

C. R. "Andy" Anderson (1901-1979)

Anderson was a school administrator in various Montana communities from 1922 to 1943. He was assistant to the superintendent of public instruction (1949-1955), the superintendent of Helena public schools (1955-1966), and a faculty

member at Western Montana College in Dillon (1966-1974). In the years surrounding his single term in the Montana House of Representatives in the 1975 Legislature, Dr. Anderson was a consultant on important education legislation of the period. His contributions include developing the state's first special education laws, major school finance legislation, and a new teacher's retirement system. In 1972, he published *Know Your Schools*, a compendium of Montana education laws and history. The C. R. Anderson Elementary School in Helena was named in his honor in 1961.

Student-Teacher Ratios in Montana and Selected States (for School Year 1995-1996)

State	Pupils per Teacher
California	24.2
Utah	23.6
Washington	21.0
Oregon	19.8
Nevada	19.4
Idaho	19.0
Colorado	18.7
Mississippi	17.5
U.S.	**17.3**
Minnesota	17.3
Alaska	16.9
Montana	**16.4**
North Dakota	15.9
New York	15.2
Wyoming	14.9
Connecticut	14.3
New Jersey	13.8

Rocky Mountain states are shaded.
Note: The figures above are either preliminary counts or estimates, by states, as of March 1996.
Source: National Center for Education Statistics. Public Elementary and Secondary Education Statistics (Estimated): School Year 1995-96. Washington: U.S. Department of Education, 1996.

Average Salaries of Public School Teachers, 1995-1996 for Montana and Selected States

Connecticut	$50,400
Alaska	$49,620 *
New York	$48,115
New Jersey	$47,910
California	$42,516 *
Oregon	$39,650
U.S. average	**$37,846**
Washington	$38,025
Minnesota	$36,937 *
Nevada	$36,167
Colorado	$35,364
Wyoming	$31,571
Idaho	$30,891
Utah	$30,452
Montana	**$29,364**
Mississippi	$27,689
North Dakota	$26,969

Rocky Mountain states are shaded.
* Data estimated by NEA
Source: National Education Association. 1995-96 Estimates of School Statistics, 1996.

To teach in the public schools of Montana, a person must complete a teacher education program, which includes a bachelor's degree, and must obtain a Montana teacher certificate or a specialist certificate. In certain circumstances, a school district may obtain from the Office of Public Instruction an emergency authorization of employment for a teacher who is not certified.

Teachers

- Montana teachers ranked 44th in the nation for average teacher salary with $28,785 in the 1994-1995 school year. This represents $8,148 less than the national average. In the 1983-1984 school year, Montana ranked twenty-fifth in the nation for average teacher salaries.

- Montana ranks seventeenth in the U.S. when the average teacher salary is compared to the annual earnings in the state's private sector employment.

- The average teacher's salary in 1883 was sixty dollars per month.

In the 1995-96 school year, there were 10,079 teachers in the public school systems of the state, 148 district superintendents and assistant superintendents, and 484 principals and assistant principals. In that year, 78 percent of elementary teachers and 42 percent of high school teachers were female. Eighty-eight percent of superintendents were male, along with 73 percent of the principals in the state.

Source: National Education Association.
Source: Montana Public School Data 1995-96. Office of Public Instruction.

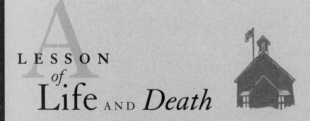

LESSON
of
Life AND *Death*

In 1914, schoolteacher Bertha Rheinhart saved her Poplar area school and her pupils from a raging prairie fire. Miss Rheinhart built a backfire, but some of the pupils ran into the path of the flames. In saving them, this heroine received burns that caused her death.

School Rules: Other State Laws Regarding Education

Compulsory Enrollment

- The parents or guardians of a child who is seven years of age or older prior to the first day of school must enroll the child in an accredited school or in a nonpublic or home school that meets certain state requirements.

- Parents or guardians must guarantee a child's school attendance until the child's sixteenth birthday or completion of the work of the eighth grade, whichever occurs later.

- A child must be six years of age by September 1 of the current school year to be enrolled in first grade.

Special Education

In accord with federal and state law, public schools provide free, appropriate education to all children with disabilities, beginning at age three. The schools are required to educate these students with other students, "to the maximum extent possible."

Approximately 11 percent of Montana's public school students receive some form of special education and related services, with the majority of these services provided in regular classes.

Nonpublic Schools

- Under Montana law, parents have the authority to instruct their children, stepchildren, or wards in a home school. They are solely responsible for the educational philosophy of the home school; the selection of instructional materials, curriculum, and textbooks; the time, place, and method of instruction; and the evaluation of the home school instruction.

- A private or home school must meet the following requirements to qualify for legal enrollment of students under Montana's compulsory attendance

Private *and* Home Schools

Approximately 6.6 percent (11,657 students) of Montana's school age population of 177,204 was enrolled in private schools or home schools in the 1995-1996 school year. Private schools enrolled 8,498 students and 3,159 children were schooled at home.

laws: maintain records on pupil attendance and disease immunization and make the records available to the county superintendent; provide at least 180 days of pupil instruction; be housed in a building that complies with applicable local health and safety regulations; and provide an organized course of study that includes instruction in the subjects required of public schools for accreditation purposes.

Montana Report Card: The Students

Over recent years, Montana students have scored well above the national average on the ACT (American College Testing) and the SAT (Scholastic Achievement Test) college entrance exams. The 1996 high school graduates who took the ACT ranked third among the twenty-eight states in which the majority of the state's students elect to take the ACT. Montana's average ACT score of 21.7 continues to be the highest in the nine-state mountains/plains region as well as 4 percent higher than the national average. About 60 percent of Montana's college-bound high school graduates took the ACT in 1996, while 20 percent took the SAT. Most higher education institutions in the middle of the nation require the ACT test, while the SAT is generally required for schools on either coast.

Montana and National Average Scores SAT

| Year | Montana | | National | |
	Verbal	Math	Verbal	Math
1992	541	542	500	501
1993	536	537	500	503
1994	540	542	499	504
1995	549	553	504	506
1996	546	547	505	508

Montana and National Average Scores ACT

Year	Montana	National
1991	21.6	20.6
1992	21.7	20.6
1993	21.6	20.7
1994	21.8	20.8
1995	21.8	20.8
1996	21.7	20.9

Source: Montana Office of Public Instruction.

The high number of students taking the tests indicates that a large majority of Montana graduates plan to continue their education. In the 1996 graduating class, 868 Montana students who took the ACT scored in the top 10 percent of all who took the test nationwide.

Montana Report Card: The School System

The accomplishments below are other examples of the long-term excellence of Montana's state and local educational systems.

- The 1990 census shows that 89 percent of the adults in Montana had high school degrees or the equivalent, compared to 82 percent nationally. About 19.8 percent of Montana's adult population earned a bachelor's degree or higher.

- For the past century, Montana's adult literacy rate has been far above the national average. The 1990 literacy rate was 93.3 percent, compared to the national rate of 88.7 percent.

- The 1990 census data show that only 7.1 percent of Montanans ages 16 through 19 were not enrolled in high school and did not have high school degrees, compared to 11.2 percent nationally. That placed Montana eighth highest in the nation for high school completion. Using the method of comparing the number of graduating seniors with the number of high school freshmen four years earlier, Montana's graduation rate has been 86 to 90 percent in recent years.

- In the 1990 National Assessment for Educational Progress (NAEP) of eighth-grade math proficiencies, Montana students scored second highest nationwide. In the 1994 NAEP fourth-grade reading assessment, Montana students placed seventh highest among the states.

- In 1994, 9,061 students graduated from public school; Montana's graduation rate is 84.8 percent, or 5th in the nation.

Colleges and Universities

More than 50 percent of Montana's yearly crop of nearly 10,000 high school graduates attend college immediately after high school. As many as 70 percent of those graduates will attend college at some point. Nearly 6,000 degrees are awarded each year by the state's university system.

Montana's University System

Montana's university system is built on a foundation set in place by acts of the U.S. Congress in 1862 and 1881. These acts dedicated sections of public land in Montana, and their potential revenue, to future institutions of higher education. The Enabling Act of 1889, which provided for the organization of the state, added another 340,000 acres of public domain for higher education funding purposes.

The constitution of 1889 established the State Board of Education, and the 1893 Legislature chartered four units of higher education:

- the **Montana College of Agriculture and Mechanics Arts** in Bozeman, which opened in the fall of 1893
- the **Montana State University** in Missoula, which first held classes in 1895
- the **Western Montana College of Education** (a "normal" school for teacher training) in Dillon, which began operating in 1897
- the **Montana School of Mines** in Butte, which opened its doors in 1900

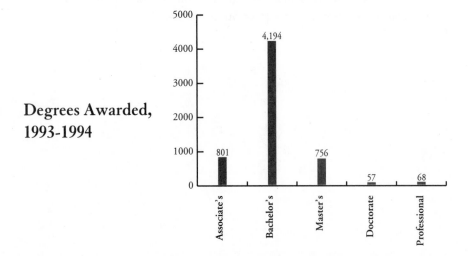

Degrees Awarded, 1993-1994

The 1913 Legislature unified these first four units into **The University of Montana** and created the position of chancellor to coordinate the work of the higher education components.

Many communities had vied for the location of either the official state capital or a college unit in their area. Paris Gibson, founder of Great Falls, even offered substantial land and money to lure a center of higher education to his growing city, but he failed to attract legislative favor for this idea.

At the end of the nineteenth century and in the first decade of the 1900s, a high school education was luxury enough for many of the state's young people, and few could dream of attending college. The four new campuses vied for students, courses of study, and scarce state finances. Lawmakers and citizens began to wonder if they could afford a multicampus system in a state of small population. However, when the state's voters had the opportunity to approve a 1914 ballot initiative to force consolidation of the higher education system, the idea was rejected. Instead, the Legislature succumbed to pressures to create two new campuses, **Eastern Montana College** in Billings in 1927 and **Northern Montana College** in Havre in 1929.

In a 1920 ballot initiative, voters approved the first statewide property tax in support of public higher education. Despite the Great Depression and severe agricultural failures, the 1930 electorate again showed strong support for public education institutions. They renewed the one and one-half mill levy on their property. Voters increased the levy to three and one-half mills in 1940. Every ten years since 1948, voters have renewed this commitment by approving a six-mill property tax levy as one source of funding for higher education. Income for the university system comes from the following sources: appropriations from the six-mill levy, state general fund, student tuition and fees, income and interest from the original land grants, campus sales and services, federal and state grants and contracts, and private gifts, grants, and contracts.

A strong federal financial commitment to vocational education encouraged the 1969 Legislature and local communities to establish vocational-technical centers in Billings, Butte, Great Falls, Helena, and Missoula. These five centers were originally part of each area high school district. The 1987 Legislature placed the centers under the control of the Board of Regents. In 1995, each center was renamed and affiliated with either The University of Montana in Missoula or Montana State University in Bozeman.

Each county with a center assesses a one and one-half mill levy to supplement appropriations of state and federal funding and student tuition.

Board of Regents of Higher Education

The 1972 Montana Constitution separated the governance of higher education from that of K-12 public education by creating both the Board of Regents of Higher Education and the Board of Public Education. The members of both these state boards meet twice a year as the State Board of Education.

The state board has responsibility for submitting to the Legislature and the people a budget for long-range planning and for coordination and evaluation of policies and programs for the state's educational systems. The governor serves as president and the superintendent of public instruction serves as secretary of the State Board of Education.

The Board of Regents of Higher Education has the full, exclusive power to govern and control the Montana university system. The governor appoints the seven members of the Board of Regents to serve the 7-year overlapping terms of office. The governor and superintendent of public instruction are ex-officio members of the Board of Regents, as is the commissioner of higher education, who is appointed by the regents.

One seat of the appointed members on the Board of Regents is reserved for membership by a student appointed by the governor. The student must be registered as a full-time student at a state unit of higher education. The length of term of the student member is determined by the governor and may range from one to four years.

Regents can be reached at the following address:

Office of the Commissioner of Higher Education
2500 Broadway
Helena, MT 59620
444-6570
444-1469 fax

Montana's Institutions of Higher Education

After a series of public and legislative studies throughout the 1980s and 1990s, the Board of Regents in 1994 restructured the six college units and the vocational-technical centers into the following affiliations of the Montana university system:

The University of Montana-Missoula
Missoula, MT 59812
243-0211
(800) 462-8636
President: George M. Dennison

Former names:
1965-94   The University of Montana
1935-65   Montana State University
1913-35   State University of Montana
1895-1913   Montana State University

The state's leading liberal arts institution comprises the College of Arts and Sciences, the Graduate School, Davidson Honors College, and seven professional schools: business administration, education, fine arts, forestry, journalism, law, and pharmacy and allied health sciences. UM-Missoula offers fifty-eight undergraduate degrees, fifty-two master's degrees, and ten doctoral degrees. In addition to its Missoula campus, UM includes four affiliated campuses.

Montana Tech of The University of Montana
Butte, MT 59701
496-4101
Chancellor: Lindsay Norman

Programs at this campus focus on the technical sciences: engineering, mineral science, energy and environmental studies, and economic development, but also include a broad range of courses in the humanities, business, and social sciences. Montana's geologic and hydrogeologic research arm, the Bureau of Mines and Geology, is also a department of the school. Montana Tech now includes the Division of Technology, offering a wide range of associate's degrees in vocational and technical areas.

Former names:
1965-94   Montana College of Mineral Science and Technology
1895-1965 Montana School of Mines

Helena College of Technology of The University of Montana
1115 N. Roberts
Helena, MT 59601
444-6800
(800) 241-4887
Dean: Alex Capdeville

This campus offers two-year programs in business, trades and industry, and technical and health occupations. Other coursework includes mathematics, communications, computer literacy, job preparation, and human relations.

Former name:
1987-94   Helena Vocational-Technical Center

Western Montana College of The University of Montana
710 S. Atlantic
Dillon, MT 59725
683-7011
(800) WMC-MONT
Chancellor: Sheila Stearns

WMC prepares students for both urban and rural teaching careers, while also offering a liberal arts education. In addition to bachelor's degree programs in elementary or secondary education or liberal studies, nine associate's degrees are offered in specialties such as business, information processing, tourism and recreation, early childhood education, and advertising design. A complete master's degree program is also available on the Dillon campus through The University of Montana-Missoula.

Former names:
1965-94   Western Montana College
1949-65   Western Montana College of Education
1893-1949   State Normal College

College of Technology of The University of Montana-Missoula
909 South Avenue West
Missoula, MT 59801
243-7811
Dean: Dennis Lerum

The college designs its programs to lead students directly into employment or to prepare them for a licensing examination in their chosen fields. Associate's degrees are offered in business management, food and beverage management, retail management, accounting, medical office technology, office administration, and computer technology. Certificate programs are offered in nursing, surgical technology, respiratory therapy, the culinary arts, business, information processing, sales and marketing, bookkeeping, and paralegal work. Associate's degrees and certificates are available in building engineering and fashion sales and marketing.

Former name:
1987-94   Missoula Vocational-Technical Center

Montana State University-Bozeman
Bozeman, MT 59717
994-0211
President: Michael Malone

Former names:
1965-94   Montana State University
1913-65   Montana State College
1893-1913   College of Agriculture and Mechanics Arts

Montana State University-Bozeman is the state's oldest public educational institution. MSU-Bozeman offers bachelor's degrees in forty-six majors (with 122 different options), master's degrees in thirty-seven fields, and doctorates in twelve fields. Disciplines include the natural sciences, social sciences, humanities, engineering, agriculture, education, the creative arts, architecture, business, nursing, medicine, and allied health fields. The Agricultural Experiment Station sponsors agricultural research across seventeen academic departments and laboratories on the campus, in addition to seven research centers located throughout the state. Other campus services to the state include KUSM-Montana Public

Television and the Museum of the Rockies. MSU-Bozeman includes four affiliated campuses.

Montana State University-Billings

1500 N. 30th Street
Billings, MT 59101
657-2011

Acting Chancellor: Ronald Sexton

This campus features programs in the liberal arts, teacher training, human services, business, and some professional areas. Bachelor's and master's programs are offered in business, teacher training, special education, and related areas. Also serving a large portion of the state is the campus-based KEMC-Montana Public Radio.

Former names:

1965-94	Eastern Montana College
1949-65	Eastern Montana College of Education
1927-49	Eastern Montana Normal College

Montana State University-Northern

P.O. Box 7751
Havre, MT 59501
265-3700

President: William Daehling

"Northern" offers degree programs in the humanities, sciences, business, nursing, technology, and teacher education. Instruction is maintained at the associate's, bachelor's, and master's levels. The school serves an area that includes four Indian reservations and functions as a cultural resource and continuing education center for north-central Montana.

Former names:

1965-94	Northern Montana College
1931-65	Northern Montana College of Education
1913-31	Northern Agricultural and Manual Training School

Montana State University College of Technology-Billings

3803 Central Ave.
Billings, MT 59102
656-4445

Dean: Robert J. Carr

MSU Billings COT offers associate's degrees for aspiring legal, medical, and executive secretaries; accountants; automotive technicians; and computer specialists. Certificate programs are available in nursing, data entry, information processing, culinary arts, and office technologies.

Former name:
1987-94   Billings Vocational-Technical Center

Montana State University College of Technology-Great Falls
2100 16th Ave. South
Great Falls, MT 59405
771-4300
Dean: Willard R. Weaver

This campus offers certificates and associate of applied science degrees in technical programs such as business, allied health, and trades/technology. The college also serves as the Montana University System Higher Education Center for Great Falls.

Former name:
1987-94   Great Falls Vocational-Technical Center

Public Community Colleges

Three public community colleges in Montana provide postsecondary education, including vocational and technical programs, adult and continuing education, and academic and associate's degree programs for students wishing to transfer to a four-year institution for a degree program. The community colleges are funded by a local property tax, state general fund money, student tuition and fees, grants, and other sources.

Dawson Community College (established 1940)
300 College Drive
Glendive, MT 59330
365-3396
President: Donald Kettner

Dawson Community College offers associate's degrees in agriculture, automotive, business and computer sciences, nurses training, human services, law enforcement, and general education. The college also offers coursework at its Sidney extension site via interactive television.

Flathead Valley Community College (established 1967)
777 Grandview Drive
Kalispell, MT 59901
756-3822
President: David N. Beyer

Flathead Valley Community College offers associate of arts and associate of sciences degrees in business administration, human services, forest technology, and surveying, as well as general studies. The campus offers community outreach educational services in Libby, Eureka, and Troy through its Libby campus and services in Whitefish, Columbia Falls, and Bigfork.

Miles Community College (established 1939)
2715 Dickinson Street
Miles City, MT 59301
232-3031
President: Frank Williams

Miles Community College offers associate's degree work in business technology, automotive, data processing, electronics, farming and ranching, nursing, secretarial, and photography. The campus coordinates with Dawson Community College via telecommunications to offer the lecture portion of a shared nursing program.

Tribally Controlled Community Colleges

Montana is the only state with a tribally controlled college located on each of its reservations. Both Indian and non-Indian students may pursue two-year associate's degrees in a number of areas. The Salish-Kootenai College recently began offering bachelor's degrees in a limited number of programs. In 1996, 2,783 students were enrolled in the seven tribal colleges.

Blackfeet Community College
P.O. Box 819
Browning, MT 59417
338-5441
President: Carol Murray

Blackfeet Community College offers associate of arts degrees in Blackfeet studies, general studies, human services, and teacher training with emphasis in Blackfeet bilingual education and Blackfeet early childhood and elementary education. Associate of science degrees are offered in business management and general studies, as well as associate of applied science degrees in construction technology, natural resources, health/wellness and counseling, and hospitality management. Some unique course offerings:

Native American Youth and Solvent Abuse
Blackfeet Drumming and Singing
Positive Indian Parenting
Blackfeet Reservation Environmental Studies
Blackfeet Philosophy

Dull Knife Memorial College
P.O. Box 98
Lame Deer, MT 59043

477-6215

President: Alonzo Spang

Dull Knife offers associate of science degrees in alcohol and drug studies, natural resource management, and office management. The college's associate of arts degree areas require credit hours in Cheyenne language, Cheyenne history, Cheyenne oral tradition, or ethnobotany. The associate of arts degree in general studies offers coursework in American Indian art and Cheyenne crafts. Distinctive course offerings include:

Plains Indian Sign Language
Foundations in Cheyenne Oral Tradition
Law and the American Indian
Cheyenne Crafts

Fort Belknap College

P.O. Box 159
Harlem, MT 59526
353-2607
President: Margaret C. Perez

The college offers associate's degrees in business management and administration, carpentry, chemical dependency counseling, human services technology, data and information processing, and natural resource management.

Fort Peck Community College

P.O. Box 398
Poplar, MT 59255
768-5551
President: James E. Shanley

This college offers associate's degrees in general studies, business administration, and education. The college also offers an associate of science degree in hazardous materials/waste technology. Other unique program areas include tribal administration, foster home parenting, industrial welding and machine shop practice, and truck driving and heavy equipment. Courses include:

Fort Peck Tribal Codes
Charlie Chaplin: The Man and His Films
Fetal Alcohol Syndrome
Waste Minimization and Recycling
Dakota Language
Truck Driving Laws

Little Big Horn Community College

P.O. Box 370
Crow Agency, MT 59022

638-2228

President: Janine Pease-Pretty On Top

Little Big Horn College offers associate of arts degrees in general science, Crow studies, business administration, mathematics, home economics, data processing, office systems, psychology, and nursing. Course offerings include:

Crow Indian Oral Literature
Economics in Indian Country
Thought and Philosophy of the Crow
Crow Socio-Familial Kinship
History of the Chiefs

Salish-Kootenai College

P.O. Box 117
Pablo, MT 59855
675-4800
President: Joseph McDonald

The first Indian college in the Northwest to earn regional accreditation (1993), Salish-Kootenai offers bachelor's degrees in human services/rehabilitation, Native American human services, and environmental sciences. Fourteen associate's degrees are offered in fields such as forestry, chemical dependency counseling, nursing, human services technology, and computer technology. Course offerings include:

Holistic Wellness
Job Seeking Skills
Critiquing Media
Nature and Cultural Tourism
Tepee Construction

Stone Child College

P.O. Box 1082, Rocky Boy Route
Box Elder, MT 59521
395-4313
President: Luanne Belcourt

This college offers associate of arts degrees in general science, Native American studies, liberal arts, mathematics, business administration, computer science, and small business management. Distinctive course offerings include:

Chippewa-Cree Art Forms
Introduction to HIV/AIDS
Story Telling
Contemporary Chippewa-Cree Music
Tribal Uses of Plants

Private Colleges

Montana's first colleges were privately endowed. In 1878, the Montana Collegiate Institute in Deer Lodge opened its rented facilities to twenty-four students, mostly for college preparatory work. The Presbyterian Church took over this struggling institution in 1883 and renamed it the College of Montana. Copper King William A. Clark helped the school establish a mining, engineering, and metallurgy program, but still the small campus struggled to attract students and find financial backing. It finally closed its doors in 1916. The Montana Wesleyan, located in the Prickly Pear Valley near Helena, was founded in 1890 by the Methodist Church. In 1923, this early college merged with the College of Montana to become the Intermountain Union College. Severe earthquake damage to this Helena campus in 1935 led to the relocation of the institution to the Billings Polytechnic Institute campus, which had been founded in 1908. After maintaining separate identities on the same campus for several years, the two institutions merged in 1947 to become Rocky Mountain College in Billings.

Montana has two Roman Catholic coeducational colleges. Mount St. Charles College, begun in 1909 by Bishop John P. Carroll as a boys' school, was renamed Carroll College in 1932. In that same year, the Diocese of Eastern Montana opened the Great Falls Junior College as a girls' school. When the school became a four-year accredited institution in 1939, the name was changed to the College of Great Falls. The name was again changed in 1994 to the University of Great Falls.

Carroll College
1601 N. Benton Ave.
Helena, MT 59625
447-4300
President: Matthew J. Quinn

former names:
1910-1932
    Mount St. Charles College
1909-1910
    Capitol Hill College

University of Great Falls
1301 20th St. S.
Great Falls, MT 59405
791-5300
President: Frederick Gilliard

Rocky Mountain College
1511 Poly Drive
Billings, MT 59102
657-1000
President: Arthur H. DeRosier, Jr.

Montana Bible College
P.O. Box 6070
Bozeman, MT 59771
586-3585

Yellowstone Baptist College
1515 Shiloh Road
Billings, MT 59106
656-9950

Mountain States Baptist College
824 3rd Avenue North
Great Falls, MT 59401
761-0308

notable
Montanans

John Carroll (1864-1925)

Born in Dubuque, Iowa, John Patrick Carroll went to St. Joseph's College there and studied for the Roman Catholic priesthood in Montreal. After being ordained, he returned to his alma mater to teach and was later named president of the college. In 1905, Pope Pius X chose him to be the first Roman Catholic bishop of the diocese of Helena after Montana was split into two dioceses. He wasted no time in establishing Catholic education in the capital city. In 1906, he set up St. Aloysius Institute, a school for boys. St. Helena Elementary School opened in 1909. Later that year, President William H. Taft helped Bishop Carroll lay the cornerstone for Mount St. Charles College, soon renamed in Carroll's

honor. Besides establishing and staffing other schools throughout the diocese, Carroll managed the building of the Cathedral of St. Helena, the largest house of worship in Montana.

While on his way to the Vatican in the fall of 1925 to report on the status of the diocese, Carroll suffered a stroke in Switzerland and died.

Montana Historical Society

Honors

Selected marks of distinction for Montana's higher education system:

✳ The University of Montana-Missoula ranks fourth in the nation for the per capita number of students selected as Rhodes Scholars over the years (twenty-eight). UM has also produced thirty-one International Fulbright Scholars and eight Truman Scholars.

✳ MSU-Bozeman is one of the top ten schools nationwide in terms of consistent student success on the National Association of State Boards of Accounting exam. Engineering graduates who take the Fundamentals of Engineering exam have a pass rate of over 94 percent. The average pass rate for nursing graduates taking the professional licensing exam has been 93 percent. Graduates of MSU's architecture program consistently score above the national average on the Architectural Registration Examination.

✳ In 1996, *U.S. News & World Report* ranked Carroll College third among regional liberal arts colleges in the West for schools that provide the best educational value for the price of tuition and fees.

✳ Montana Tech of The University of Montana, in Butte, was chosen in 1987 as the nation's best small comprehensive science and technology college by *U.S. News and World Report*. In 1992, *Money* magazine, considering educational quality and cost, included Tech among the best buys in American higher education.

✳ In a 1996 *Money* magazine survey, the University of Great Falls placed fourteenth on a list of schools in the West that provide the highest quality undergraduate education for the tuition and fees charged.

Montana College and University Students*

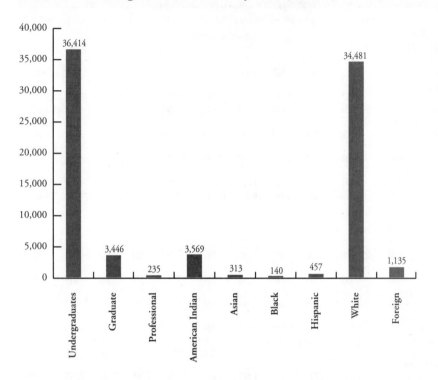

* Fall 1994 figures for state public institutions; private college statistics not available.
Source: The Chronicle of Higher Education Almanac, *September, 1996*

Learning
To Write

The University of Montana-Missoula's Master of Fine Arts creative writing program remains one of the premier graduate writing programs in the nation. When renowned author H. G. Merriam initiated the program in 1919, the only other similar program was available at Harvard University. Writers Leslie Fiedler, A. B. Guthrie, Jr., Madeline DeFrees, Walter van Tilburg Clark, Richard Hugo, Deirdre McNamer, and William Kittredge, among others, have influenced the program's fine reputation.

Enrollment of Montana University System

UNIVERSITY SYSTEM	1987-88	88-89	89-90	90-91	91-92	92-93	93-94	94-95	95-96	96-97
					Total students					
The University of Montana-Missoula	7,552	7,977	8,587	8,852	9,482	9,602	9,655	9,720	9,910	9,806
Montana State University	9,287	9,371	9,543	9,501	9,491	9,946	10,018	10,022	10,285	10,134
Montana Tech of the UM	1,582	1,546	1,499	1,612	1,694	1,728	1,763	1,660	1,679	1,673
Western Montana College of the UM	828	954	877	915	974	969	1,006	1,065	1,082	982
Montana State University-Billings	3,303	3,287	3,354	3,408	3,139	3,240	3,267	3,252	3,276	2,869
Montana State University -Northern	1,551	1,548	1,581	1,765	1,907	1,603	1,675	1,654	1,495	1,343
TOTAL UNIVERSITIES	24,103	24,683	25,441	26,053	26,687	27,088	27,384	27,373	27,727	26,807
COLLEGES OF TECHNOLOGY										
College of Technology—Billings	398	356	334	280	291	453	427	414	436	437
Division of Technology—Butte	395	354	280	248	251	313	347	320	329	345
MSU College of Technology—Great Falls	473	525	503	479	466	556	605	68	727	641
UM College of Technology—Helena	577	506	436	418	434	440	432	452	468	516
College of Technology—Missoula	487	482	446	454	435	551	573	630	629	755
Total Colleges of Technology	2,330	2,223	1,999	1,879	1,877	2,313	2,384	2,502	2,589	2,694

Note: The University System and Colleges of Technology enrollment is based on fiscal year full-time equivalent enrollment.
Source: Montana Commissioner of Higher Education

Fall 1996 Enrollment for Other Colleges

Community Colleges	Total students
Dawson Community College	457
Flathead Valley Community College	1,733
Miles Community College	600
Tribal Colleges	
Salish-Kootenai College	945
Fort Belknap College	176
Dull Knife Memorial College	460
Fort Peck Community College	439
Stone Child College	161
Blackfeet Community College	404
Little Big Horn Community College	204
Private Colleges	
Carroll College	1,316
University of Great Falls	1,291
Rocky Mountain College	841
Total enrollment	9,021

Source: Office of Commissioner of Higher Education.

Enrollment in Montana's Colleges and Universities

One-third of Montana's high school graduates go out of state for their postsecondary education, while nearly as many nonresidents come to school in Montana. Between 1988 and 1992, Montana had the second highest increase (14.5%) in the nation for college students migrating to the state. The system now has 6,300 nonresident students, with 8,200 anticipated by the year 2000. By the year 2001, the Montana university system is projected to grow by 13 percent at four-year schools and by 59 percent at two-year schools.

*M*notable *ontanans*

Joe McDonald (1933-)

McDonald was born and raised in St. Ignatius on the Flathead Reservation, a great-grandson of Catherine, a Nez Perce woman, and Angus McDonald, a Scottish Highlander. Joe McDonald earned an athletic scholarship to Western Montana College and competed in football, basketball, and track. He earned a bachelor's degree in education and a master's in health and physical education from The University of Montana. After working as a smokejumper, driving a school bus, and coaching basketball in Hamilton and at both his alma maters, McDonald returned to the reservation as a high school principal in Ronan. He left that post to work at Flathead Valley Community College, where he developed branches of the college on the Blackfeet and Flathead reservations and spearheaded the creation of Salish-Kootenai College. As the only president the college has ever had, McDonald has won acclaim and honors as a great educator. McDonald helped the creation of the American Indian Higher Education Consortium and developed the American Indian College Fund, which has raised $11 million in scholarships for the nation's thirty-one tribal colleges.

He also served two terms on the Confederated Salish and Kootenai tribal council.

Research and Development

A total of $53 million was spent in 1993-94 on research and development by the state's doctorate-granting universities.

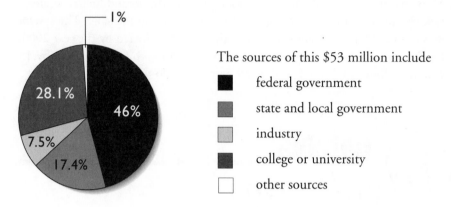

The sources of this $53 million include

- ■ federal government
- ■ state and local government
- ☐ industry
- ■ college or university
- ☐ other sources

In the 1994-1995 school year, The University of Montana attracted $22.5 million in research grants and contracts. Federal spending on college- and university-based research and development in Montana included $21,271,000 in the following selected programs:

Department of Health and Human Services	$ 3,339,000
National Science Foundation	$10,905,000
Department of Defense	$929,000
Department of Agriculture	$5,162,000
Department of Energy	$936,000

Source: The Chronicle of Higher Education Almanac, *September 1996*

Adult *Education*

In 1993 Montana State University awarded a bachelor of arts degree to its oldest graduate ever, Herbert Kirk, who, at the age of 97, walked quickly from the back of the auditorium and jogged up the steps of the stage to receive his diploma. A marathon runner in the senior division, he received a standing ovation from an audience of ten thousand, composed of other graduates and their families.

Average Salaries for Full-Time Professors at Montana Units of Higher Education, 1994-95

Institution	Average Faculty Salaries	
UM-Missoula and MSU-Bozeman	Professor	$47,208
	Associate professor	$38,688
	Assistant professor	$34,265
Other public 4-year institutions	Professor	$43,388
	Associate professor	$35,920
	Assistant professor	$30,700
Private 4-year institutions	Professor	$38,745
	Associate professor	$34,016
	Assistant professor	$29,073
Public 2-year colleges	All	$29,390
Private 2-year colleges	All	$30,943

Note: Montana ranks 48th in the nation for average faculty salaries at a public 4-year institution of higher education, ahead of only North Dakota and South Dakota.

Source: The Chronicle of Higher Education Almanac, *September, 1996.*

$\mathcal{M}$ notable ontanans

Thomas J. Dimsdale (1831-1866)

Born and educated in England, Dimsdale accomplished several Montana "firsts" toward the end of his relatively short life. He opened the first "subscription" school in Virginia City in the winter of 1863-64 and also offered singing lessons in that rough mining camp. As the Republican editor of the first newspaper in the territory, the *Montana Post,* first published in 1864, Dimsdale took on many social concerns of the day. In 1866, his series of newspaper articles on the road agents of Virginia City became the first book published in Montana, *The Vigilantes of Montana.* The same year, Governor Sidney Edgerton appointed him the first territorial superintendent of schools. Unfortunately, Dimsdale died in September of that year, serving little time in the position.

Montana Historical Society

Further Reading:

Anderson, C. R. *Know Your Schools*. Helena: State Publishing Company, 1972.

The Chronicle of Higher Education Almanac, published yearly in September.

chapter eight

COMMUNICATIONS

ON SCATTERED SLABS OF SANDSTONE and other rock in Montana, one can find ancient images painted or carved by early inhabitants. The prehistoric native people told stories and related news by applying plant resins, charcoal, animal oils, and other substances to the rock or by scraping the sandstone with sharpened implements. Some drawings are easily understandable—the hunters and the animals they pursued. Others seem abstract and unfathomable. No words accompany the images.

Eons later, Montana's news was carried by horseback, by stagecoach, and over telegraph wire. It took all three methods to bring news of the Battle of the Big Hole in 1877 to the wider world. On the first leg of this relay, the traveling Methodist minister William Wesley Van Orsdel (Brother Van), who carried the word of God to isolated homesteads and churches, carried the news on horseback to a stagecoach route east of Bannack.

Though we like to point out to guests how uncommon the Big Sky state can be, our means of communication are as modern as in most other places around the world. For over 130 years, Montana newspapers have been an essential communication tool. Montanans have access to twenty television stations and cable television connections that receive images and words from all over the earth to the Big Sky. And radio stations have been broadcasting over the Big Sky's airwaves for seventy-five years.

Since the dawn of the Information Age, Montana has remained wide awake to the possibilities the telecommunications superhighways offer: to bring citizens together in government, education, and innumerable other fields.

The education community, government agencies, and the private sector have combined to develop a telecommunications network that offers lifelong learning opportunities and public discourse across Montana.

notable
Montanans

John Tatsey (1894-1972)

Tatsey was a tribal policeman at Heart Butte on the Blackfeet Reservation, but after he began documenting humorous aspects of life on the reservation in a newspaper column during the 1950s and the 1960s, Senator Mike Mansfield called him "Montana's modern-day Will Rogers."

Tatsey was born east of Heart Butte of Blackfeet, Blood, and English descent. His Indian name was Weasel Necklace. He originally wrote his column for a Browning newspaper, the *Glacier Reporter*, but his readership increased when the column was picked up by the *Hungry Horse News*, beginning in 1956. Thanks to Mansfield, some of Tatsey's columns ended up in the pages of the *Congressional Record*. *Time* magazine also featured an article about him. Shortly after he retired from his police job, he also quit writing the column. He was getting old and getting around less, and he believed Indians did not appreciate being the subject of his humor.

Some of his more memorable columns were collected in a volume titled *The Black Moccasin*, but the book is no longer in print.

Mel Ruder collection

Tatsey's *World*

John Tatsey wrote in an unrefined style that suited readers and even editors. They ran his columns unedited. A few excerpts follow:

- Last week Paul Running Crane drove across the lopsided bridge on Big Badger when his car slid off. The front wheels hanging off. He jumped off, and left the women in the car, and now goes around the long way.

- Boy John Aims Back has not come home from potato picking. Instead, he is peeling potatoes in the county jail.

- John Tatsey, the police, made a trip to Cut Bank on business to the court house. The sheriff showed him around and the different breeds of birds he had in cages... There were two Still Smoking boys that were jailed and when they got out of the jail it was still smoking. They set fire to the mattress.

- From Lower Birch Creek a young stock man had a bull that was lousy so while it was a warm day he thought fix him up. He got the bull in the chute and gave it a stove oil rub down. the oil went down to the skin and it being a warm day he thought he'd just as well brand it. He throwed a red hot iron on the bull caught on fire. Pretty sick Bull. Hair all burned off.

- I write the news that really takes place and happens. I won't make up any lies just the truth. I'll back up anything I write.

Petroglyphs *and* Pictographs

Pictographs are images painted onto stone by ancient peoples with materials derived from plants, soils, or animal products. Petroglyphs are similar images that were etched or carved into soft rock with a sharpened tool.

You can see cave paintings at **Pictograph Cave State Monument**, southeast of Billings on the south side of the Yellowstone River. Researchers believe the members of prehistoric Indian cultures lived in these caves for about 10,000 years.

Boaters can see pictographs on steep rocks along the east side of the Missouri River, near the Gates of the Mountains, outside Helena.

*M*notable
*M*ontanans

Joseph Kinsey Howard (1906-1951)

Born in Iowa, Howard spent part of his youth in Alberta before moving with his mother to Great Falls, where he graduated from high school in 1923. He then started on a distinguished career path which won him acclaim as a journalist, regional historian, and social and political critic. Whenever "favorite Montana books" are discussed, Howard's *Montana: High, Wide, and Handsome* (1943) inevitably appears at or near the top of the list. His view of the first eighty years of Montana has endured as one of the most insightful and courageous commentaries on the state's social, economic, and political history. While the work was acclaimed by other historians, Howard's criticism of Montana's establishment was considered so shocking that the book was at first sold only "under the counter."

After high school, Howard worked as a reporter for the *Leader,* a local daily (Great Falls). He became the news editor of that paper three years later, a job he held for the next eighteen years. After publishing *High, Wide, and Handsome,* Howard worked from 1944 to 1946 on the Montana Study, a project sponsored by the Rockefeller Foundation and The University of Montana and designed to study and improve the quality of life in small-town and rural communities. As a by-product of this work, Howard edited *Montana Margins: A State Anthology* (1946), a collection of literary and historical topics on the Montana experience.

Much of Howard's later writing was done under two fellowships granted by the Guggenheim Memorial Foundation in 1947 and 1948. His articles were published in the *Saturday Evening Post, Harper's, Yale Review,* the *Nation, Esquire,* and other magazines and journals. He was Montana correspondent for *Time* and *Life.* In addition to lecturing and promoting the development of regional history and literature, Howard wrote *Strange Empire: A Narrative of the Northwest* (published posthumously in 1952), a sympathetic history of the struggles of Louis Riel and the Métis people of Canada.

Howard died of a heart attack at his summer home in Choteau. Friends rode horses up Flattop Mountain and scattered his ashes to the winds. A. B. Guthrie called him "Montana's conscience. . . the greatest Montanan of our time, perhaps of any time."

Montana Historical Society

Newspapers

Wilbur Fisk Sanders, the man who was to become one of Montana's first U.S. senators, was the editor of Montana's first news sheet, published in Virginia City in February 1864. Assisting in the venture was John A. Creighton, who later founded Creighton University in Omaha, Nebraska. By the spring of 1864, merchant Francis M. Thompson was printing commercial items and local news in his *Beaverhead News Letter* in Bannack. The *Montana Post*, Montana's first real newspaper, began publication in Virginia City on August 27, 1864. It sold for fifty cents an issue, the cost of most daily newspapers today. Under the editorial leadership of Thomas J. Dimsdale, this paper was unrelenting in its call for law and order in the rather lawless territory.

A sample of other early newspapers includes the Helena *Radiator* (1865); the first daily and staunchly Republican paper, the *Helena Daily Herald* (1867); the Deer Lodge *New North-West* (1868); Bozeman's *The Pick and Plow* (1869); the *Missoula and Cedar Creek Pioneer* (1870); the *Helena Daily Independent* (1874); the Diamond City *Rocky Mountain Husbandman* (1875—later moved to White Sulphur Springs); Fort Benton's *The Benton Record* (1875); and the Miles City *Yellowstone Journal* (1879).

In 1885, a group of editors and publishers formed the Montana Press Association. It still exists today, though the name has been changed to the Montana Newspaper Association.

The so-called War of the Copper Kings had a profound and long-lasting effect on Montana journalism. Each of the copper kings owned a newspaper with which he could incite the populace to his advantage. Marcus Daly owned the *Anaconda Standard*, and William Clark owned the *Butte Miner*. Despite its parochial interests, the *Anaconda Standard* was not only considered the best newspaper in the state, but could also be found on newsstands in major cities around the nation. The *Reveille* was owned by another copper magnate, F. Augustus Heinze, and specialized in attacking Daly and the formation of the Standard Oil-Amalgamated Copper Company (later called the Anaconda Copper Mining Company). Perhaps stirred by these attacks, that oil and copper conglomerate formed the Fairmont Company and began buying up the state's major newspapers in Montana.

Editors and publishers, one with a young boy in tow, attended the 1922 meeting of the Montana Press Association in Missoula. Montana Newspaper Association

By 1929, the Anaconda Copper Mining Company owned the *Anaconda Standard;* the *Daily Post* and *Montana Standard* in Butte; the *Daily Missoulian* and the *Sentinel* in Missoula; the *Billings Gazette;* the Helena *Independent Record;* and the Livingston *Enterprise.* These eight newspapers accounted for half the coverage in the entire state. Even the *Great Falls Tribune* was sold to Clark interests at the turn of the century but was bought back by O. S. Warden and William M. Bole in 1905.

From the early 1900s into the 1930s, the Anaconda Company papers launched seething editorial attacks on certain politicians and others who battled the mining giants. While denying any direct corporate control of the press, the newspapers in the 1930s switched from outright attacks on politicians and unions to disregard of opposing news and local views. During these years, even the *Tribune* was challenged to remain an independent daily newspaper.

In 1959, the Anaconda Copper Mining Company sold the Fairmont Company to Lee Newspapers, a midwestern chain that consolidated, professionalized, and modernized the state's press output. In 1965, the Warden family sold the *Great Falls Tribune* to the Minneapolis Star and Tribune Company. In the late 1980s, that daily Great Falls newspaper was sold to the Gannett chain.

Today, Montana has ten major daily newspapers. Many local communities rely on weekly and semiweekly newspapers for local information.

Major Daily Newspapers

Newspaper	Date Established	Circulation	
Billings Gazette* (800) 927-2345 657-1200, 657-1208 fax	1885	a.m. daily – Sunday –	54,234 59,776
Bozeman Daily Chronicle 587-4491, 587-7995 fax	1883, weekly 1911, daily	p.m. daily – Sunday –	13,545 15,992
Montana Standard (Butte) * 496-5500 496-5510 fax	1928 - merger of *Anaconda Standard* (1889) and *Butte Miner* (1876)	a.m. daily –	15,990
Great Falls Tribune 791-1444, 791-1431 fax	1884	a.m. daily – Sunday –	34,401 40,874
Havre Daily News 265-6795, 265-6798 fax	1928	p.m. daily –	4,362
Helena Independent Record* 447-4000, 447-4052 fax	1943	a.m. daily – Sunday –	14,570 15,218
The Daily Inter Lake (Kalispell) 755-7000, 752-6114 fax	1889	p.m. daily – Sunday –	15,848 17,490
Miles City Star 232-0450, 232-6687 fax	1903, weekly 1911, daily	p.m. daily –	3,673
The Missoulian* 523-5210, 532-5221 fax	1870	a.m. daily – Sunday –	30,918 37,998
Ravalli Republic (Hamilton) 363-3300, 363-1767 fax	1889	a.m. daily –	5,206

* Owned by Lee Newspapers.

Other Newspapers

Newspaper	Phone	Date Established
Anaconda Leader	563-5283	1970
(Baker) Fallon County Times	778-3344	1914
(Belgrade) High Country Independent Press	388-6762	1979
(Belt) The Eagle	277-4473	
(Big Sandy) Mountaineer	378-2176	1911
Big Sky Bugle	995-2163	
(Big Sky) Lone Peak Lookout	995-4133	
Big Timber Pioneer	932-5298	1889

An early owner, Jean P. Decker, had previously been a stagecoach guard in the Black Hills.

Bigfork Eagle	837-5131	1976
Billings Times	245-4994	1891
(Billings) Yellowstone County News	245-1624	1977
Boulder Monitor	225-3821	
(Bozeman-MSU) The Exponent	994-2611	1895

Managed independently of the university by students.

(Bridger) The Record	662-3250	1981

First office was the projection room of an old Bridger theater.

(Broadus) Powder River Examiner	436-2244	1919
(Browning) Glacier Reporter	338-2090	1930

Many readers still call it by its old name, the Browning Chief.

Cascade Courier	468-9231	1910
(Chester) Liberty County Times	759-5355	1905
Chinook Opinion	357-2680	1889

One of the oldest weeklies in the state; the oldest surviving business in Chinook.

Choteau Acantha	466-2403	late 1800s

A.B. Guthrie's father was an editor. Acantha is the name of a Greek thornbush.

Circle Banner	846-2424	1914
(Columbia Falls) Hungry Horse News	892-2151	1946

Won a Pulitzer in 1965.

(Columbus) Stillwater Country News	322-5212	
(Conrad) Independent-Observer	278-5561	1905
(Culbertson) The Searchlight	787-5821	1902

The oldest continuously published newspaper in eastern Montana.

Cut Bank Pioneer Press	873-2201	1909

An article in the first issue was "based on reliable rumour."

(Cut Bank) Western Breeze	873-4128	1953
(Deer Lodge) Silver State Post	846-2424	1889
Dillon Tribune	683-2331	1881
Ekalaka Eagle	775-6245	1909

Founded by a 21-year-old printer, Oscar Dahl, from South Dakota.

(Eureka) Tobacco Valley News	296-2514	1960
(Fairfield) Sun Times	467-2334	1941
(Forsyth) Independent-Enterprise	356-2149	1916
(Fort Benton) River Press	622-3311	1882
Glasgow Courier	228-9301	1912
(Glendive) Ranger-Review	365-3303	*1880s
(Great Falls) Montana Senior Citizen News	761-0305	
(Hardin) Big Horn County News	665-1008	
Harlem News	353-2441	circa 1908
(Harlowton) Times Clarion	632-5633	1917

Other Newspapers (cont.)

Newspaper	Phone	Date Established
(Helena) *Montana Catholic*	442-5820	
Hysham Echo	342-5508	1911
(Jordan) *Tribune*	557-2337	1913
Laurel Outlook	628-4412	1909
Lewistown News-Argus	538-3401	1883
An early editor, Tom Stout, went on to serve two terms as U.S. congressman, 1913-17.		
(Libby) *Montanian*	293-8202	
(Libby) *Western News*	293-4124	1898
Livingston Enterprise	222-2000	1883
(Malta) *Phillips County News*	654-2020	1898
Missoula Independent	543-6609	
(Missoula-UM) *Montana Kaimin*	243-6541	1909
Was a literary magazine from 1899 to 1909.		
(Pablo) *Char-Koosta News*	675-3000	
Philipsburg Mail	859-3223	1887
Originally published from a cowshed.		
(Plains) *Clark Fork Valley Press*	826-3402	
Plentywood Herald	765-1150	1908
(Polson) *Lake County Leader*	883-4343	
(Poplar) *Wowatin Wowapi Fort Peck Tribal News*	768-5387	
(Red Lodge) *Carbon County News*	446-2222	1924
Published front-page obituaries of miners for four weeks after explosion of Smith Coal Mine killed seventy-four in 1943.		
Roundup Record-Tribune & Winnett Times	323-1105	1908
Ownership has remained in one family since its founding.		
(Scobey) *Daniels County Leader*	487-5303	*1924
Seeley Swan Pathfinder	677-2022	
Shelby Promoter	434-5171	1912
Sidney Herald	482-2403	1908
(Simms) *Sun River Valley Press*	264-5555	
(Stanford) *Judith Basin Press*	566-2471	1905
(Stevensville) *Bitterroot Star*	777-3928	
(Superior) *Mineral Independent*	822-3329	1915
Terry Tribune	637-5513	1907
(Thompson Falls) *Sanders County Ledger*	827-3421	unknown
Three Forks Herald	285-3414	1908
First issue printed in a tent on Main Street when the only buildings in the town were the offices of two lumber yards. A graduating senior of The University of Montana journalism school, Lyle K. Williams, bought the paper in 1927 and ran it for forty-two years.		
Townsend Star	266-3333	1897
The second publisher was a carpenter who published the paper in his spare time.		
(Valier) *Prairie Star*	279-3722	
The Valierian	279-3719	1952
(Virginia City) *Madisonian*	682-7755	1873
Montana's oldest weekly. Presses were run by steam engine until 1911.		
West Yellowstone News	646-9719	
Whitefish Pilot	862-3505	1904
(White Sulphur Springs) *Meagher County News*	547-3831	1889
Whitehall Ledger	287-5301	1984
Wibaux Pioneer-Gazette	795-2218	1907
(Wolf Point) *Herald-News*	653-2222	1912

* Dates are approximate due to mergers, consolidations, name changes, or otherwise less-than-precise histories.

After *the* Deluge

During three days in early June of 1964, sixteen inches of rain fell in the area of Columbia Falls and Glacier National Park. Thirty-one people died in the subsequent flooding. Three homes in Columbia Falls washed away; another fifty-seven were severely damaged by the high water. Fifteen miles of Highway 2 and eleven miles of Great Northern railroad line washed out.

The weekly issue of the community paper, the *Hungry Horse News*, came out Thursday, two days after the disaster had been reported in daily newspapers. The *News* revised its coverage in special editions on Friday, Saturday, and Monday. Each edition contained gripping photos of the inundated towns, shot by the same man who established the newspaper, wrote most of the stories, and published the weekly with less than a handful of helpers.

While covering a barnyard conservation tour by a group of eighth-graders the following year, that man, Mel Ruder, learned he'd been awarded a Pulitzer Prize for local news coverage. To this day, the *Hungry Horse News* is the only Montana newspaper to be honored with the award.

Ruder gave the $1,000 that came with the honor to the Columbia Falls Library.

Mel Ruder, at his desk in the nation's only modern newsroom built of logs.
Mel Ruder collection

*M*otable
*M*ontanans

    ## Mel Ruder (1915-)

Born in North Dakota, Ruder came to
Columbia Falls in 1946 to pursue his love
of photography in nearby Glacier
National Park. With his wife, Ruth, he
founded the *Hungry Horse News* that
year. He was editor, publisher, reporter,
photographer, and more. He even
helped unload cases of liquor when ship-
ments arrived at the state liquor store,
where he rented the paper's first office.

In 1947, the *News* moved into a log
building Ruder had erected with the
help of a GI loan. He lived upstairs.
For years, the *News* was said to be the
only newspaper in the country whose
offices were housed in a "log cabin."
The copy desk was a slice of an
enormous larch tree. But in 1965, the
paper established a far greater claim
to fame.

Ruder's coverage of the disastrous floods that occurred in and around Glacier National Park the previous June won Ruder the Pulitzer Prize for local reporting. He was nominated for the award by Montana writer Dorothy M.
Johnson.

Other honors for Ruder include a National Press Award for the paper's use of
photographs, and membership in the Blackfeet tribe for his coverage of tribal
news. His Blackfeet name is Spotted Calf.

Due to his loving and diligent coverage of Glacier National Park, area residents and park personnel often refer to Glacier as "Ruder Country." Ruder School,
an elementary school building in Columbia Falls, was named for the Ruders'
longtime support of local schools. Ruder and his wife sold the newspaper and
retired in 1978.

Broadcast and Electronic Media

Montana joined the radio age when the first station, KDYS, began broadcasting in 1922 from Great Falls. The first permanent station began in Havre as KFBB in late 1922. After broadcasting for a time from the basement of a Buttrey store in Havre, the station moved to Great Falls in 1929, where it would eventually spawn present-day KFBB-TV.

By the 1930s, all of the state's larger cities supported radio stations. One of the region's first radio networks, the XL Radio Network, was established by Ed Craney of Butte.

It was Craney who also pioneered Montana's first television station in 1953, broadcasting as KXLF-TV in Butte. That same year a now-defunct station went on the air in Butte, and KOOK-TV began broadcasting from Billings. Today, eighteen commercial television stations are supplemented by extensive cable television service and by public television programming from KUSM-TV in Bozeman and KUFM-TV in Missoula.

notable
Montanans

👉 Chet Huntley (1911-1974)

For nearly fifteen years, Chester Robert Huntley, born in Cardwell, was a face familiar to millions of Americans. He joined CBS as a radio newscaster in 1939, moved to ABC in 1951, and was hired by NBC in 1955. In 1956 Huntley was teamed up with co-anchor David Brinkley for *The Huntley-Brinkley Report*, the nightly NBC television newscast. Huntley retired from NBC in 1970 to return to Montana to oversee the development of the Big Sky Inc., a ski and recreation resort in the Gallatin Canyon south of Bozeman. He died just months before Big Sky opened. Up to the time of his death, Huntley continued to broadcast radio commentaries five times weekly.

Montana Historical Society

Montana Radio Stations

City/Town	Station	On the Dial	Programming/Format	Phone
Anaconda	KANA-AM	580	oldies, talk	563-8011
	KGLM-FM	97.7 100.3 (Butte)	country	563-8011
Baker	KFLN-AM	960	country	778-3371
Belgrade	KGVW-AM	640	gospel, talk	388-4281
Billings	KBBB-FM	103.7	adult contemporary	248-7827
	KBLG-AM	910	24-hour news/talk/sports	652-8400
	KCTR-FM	102.9	contemporary country	248-7827
	KDWG-AM	970	contemporary	248-7827
	KEMC-FM	91.7	news/information/classical/ jazz	657-2941
	KGHL-AM	790	country	656-1410
	KIDX-FM	98.5	country	656-1410
	KKBR-FM	97.1	oldies	248-7827
	KRKX-FM	94.1	album-oriented rock/classic rock	656-8400
	KURL-AM	730	religious	245-3121
	KYYA-FM	93.3	adult contemporary	652-8400
	KMHK-FM	95.5, 95.1	classic rock	254-1092
	KRSQ-FM	108.3	adult contemporary/Christian	652-6102
Bozeman	KBOZ-AM	1090	full service	587-9999
	KGLT-FM	91.9 89.5 (Livingston) 98.1 (Helena)	alternative public radio	994-4492
	KMMS-FM	95.1	adult-oriented rock	586-2343
	KMMS-AM	1450	news/talk/nostalgia	586-2343
	KOBB-AM	1230	adult standards	587-9999
	KOBB-FM	93.7	oldies	587-9999
	KPKX-FM	97.5	alternative rock	587-9999
	KSCY-FM	96.7	light adult/contemporary	586-2343
	KZLO-FM	99.9	country	587-9999
Butte	KAAR-FM	92.5	modern country	494-1030
	KBOW-AM	550	country	494-7777
	KMSM-FM	106.9	rock and roll	496-4601
	KOPR-FM	94.1	adult contemporary	494-7777
	KQUY-FM	95.5	adult hit radio	494-5895
	KXTL-AM	1370	hits from 60s and 70s	494-5895
Chinook	KRYK-FM	101.3	adult contemporary	357-2296
Deer Lodge	KDRG-AM	1400	talk, news	563-8011
Dillon	KDBM-AM	1490	country	683-2800
	KDBM-FM	98.3	adult hit radio	683-2800
Glasgow	KLTZ-AM	1240	country	228-9336
	KLAN-FM	93.5	adult contemporary	228-9336
Glendive	KDZN-FM	96.5	new country	365-3377
	KGLE-AM	590	gospel	365-3331
	KXGN-AM	1400	adult contemporary	365-3377
Great Falls	KAAK-FM	98.9	contemporary hits	727-7211
	KEIN-AM	1310	oldies	761-1310
	KGFC-FM	88.9	Christian	265-5845
	KLFM-FM	92.9	oldies	761-7600
	KMON-AM	560	country	761-7600

Montana Radio Stations (cont.)

City/Town	Station	On the Dial	Programming/Format	Phone
	KMON-FM	94.5	country	761-7600
	KMSL-AM	1450	news/talk/sports	761-2800
	KQDI-FM	106.1	classic rock	761-2800
	KXGF-AM	1400	adult "middle of the road"	761-7211
Hamilton	KBMG-FM	95.9	adult contemporary	363-3010
	KLYQ-AM	1240	country	363-3010
Hardin	KHDN-AM	1230	news/talk/sports	665-2131
Havre	KOJM-AM	610	adult contemporary	265-7841
	KPQX-FM	92.5	contemporary country	265-7841
	KXEI-FM	95.1	Christian	265-5845
	KVCM-FM	103.1	Christian	265-5845
Helena	KBLL-AM	2240	news/talk/solid gold	442-6620
	KBLL-FM	99.5	country	442-6620
	KCAP-AM	1340	news/talk/sports	442-4490
	KHKR-FM	104.1	country	449-4251
	KMTX-AM	950	adult standards	442-0400
	KMTX-FM	105.3	adult contemporary	442-0400
	KROL-FM	88.5	grass roots/alternative	447-5415
	KZMT-FM	101.1	classic rock	442-4490
Kalispell	KALS-FM	97.1	Christian	752-5257
	KBBZ-FM	98.5	album-oriented rock/classic rock	755-8700
	KDBR-FM	106.3	country	755-8700
	KGEZ-AM	600	oldies	752-2600
	KOFI-AM	1180	adult contemporary	755-6690
	KOFI-FM	103.9	country	755-6690
Laurel	KBSR-AM	1490	news/sports/talk	628-8271
Lewistown	KLCM-FM	95.9	rock	538-3495
	KXLO-AM	1230	country/talk	538-3441
Libby	KLCB-AM	1230	contemporary country	293-6234
	KTNY-FM	101.7	contemporary	293-6234
Livingston	KPRK-AM	1340	country/local sports/local news	222-2841
Malta	KMMR-FM	100.1	country	654-2472
Miles City	KATL-AM	770	adult contemporary	232-7700
	KIKC-AM	1250	contemporary country	356-2711
	KIKC-FM	101.3	contemporary country	356-2711
	KMCM-FM	92.5	adult contemporary	232-5626
	KMTA-AM	1050	country	232-5626
Missoula	KGGL-FM	93.3	country	721-9300
	KGRZ-AM	1450	country	728-1450
	KGVO-AM	290	news/information/sports	721-1290
	KLCY-AM	930	entertainment/information	728-9300
	KMSO-FM	102.5	adult contemporary	542-1025
	KUFM-FM	89.1	classical/jazz/news/public radio	243-4931
	KYLT-AM	1340	oldies/sports	728-5000
	KYSS-FM	94.9	country	728-9300
	KZOQ-FM	100.1	album oriented rock	728-5000
Plentywood	KATQ-AM	1070	country	765-1480
	KATQ-FM	100.1	country	765-1480

Montana Radio Stations (cont.)

City/Town	Station	On the Dial	Programming/Format	Phone
Polson	KERR-AM	750	country	883-5255
Red Lodge	KMXE-FM	99.3	classic rock	446-1199
Ronan	KQRK-FM	92.3	adult contemporary	883-9200
Scobey	KCGM-FM	95.7	country	487-2293
Shelby	KSEN-AM	2150	full service	434-5241
	KZIN-FM	96.3	country	434-5241
Sidney	KTHC-FM	95.1	classic rock	482-5090
West Yellowstone	KWYS-AM	920	oldies/rock	646-7361
	KWWF-FM	96.5	country/rock	646-7361
Whitefish	KJJR-AM	880	news/talk	755-8700
Wolf Point	KVCK-AM	1450	country	653-1900
	KVCK-FM	92.7	country	653-1900

Montana Television Stations

City	Station	Channel	Network	Affiliation/Format	Phone
Billings	KSVI - TV	6	ABC	Big Horn Communications, Inc.	652-4743
	KTVQ - TV	2	CBS	KTVQ Communications, Inc.	252-5611
	KULR - TV	8	NBC, CNN	KULR Corporation	656-8000
	KHMT - TV	4	FOX	National Indian Media Foundation	652-7366
Bozeman	KCTZ - TV	7/20	FOX	KCTZ Communications, Inc.	586-3280
	KTVM - TV	6/42	NBC	Eagle Communications, Inc.	586-0296
	KUSM - TV	9	PBS	Montana State University	994-3437
Butte	KXLF - TV	4	CBS, MTN	KXLF - TV Communications, Inc.	782-0444
	KWYB - TV	18/28	ABC`	CTN Butte Inc.	782-7185
Glendive	KXGN - TV	5	CBS, NBC, FOX	Glendive Broadcast Corporation	365-3377
Great Falls	KFBB - TV	5	ABC	KFBB Corporation	453-4377
	KRTV - TV	3	CBS, MTN	KRTV Communications	791-5400
	KTGF - TV	16	NBC	Continental Television Network, Inc.	761-8816
Helena	KTVH -TV	12	NBC	Big Sky Broadcasting	443-5050
Kalispell	KCFW - TV	9	NBC	Eagle Communications, Inc.	755-5239
Miles City	KYUS -TV	3	FOX	KYUS Broadcasting Corp.	232-3540
Missoula	KECI - TV	13	NBC	Eagle Communications, Inc.	721-2063
	KPAX - TV	8/18	CBS, MTN	KPAX Communications, Inc.	542-4400
	KTMF - TV	23	ABC	CTN Missoula, Inc.	542-8900

Montana Online

Montana state government provides a number of telecommunications services and networks that are available to citizens free of charge.

The following description and listing of online sites and addresses was up-to-date when compiled in November 1996. However, the number of sites and addresses being added each day by schools, education agencies, and organizations in Montana and around the world makes any published list outdated the moment it is printed. This collection is intended only as a reference tool. Phone numbers are included wherever possible, so users can call for updated information.

METNET

The Department of Administration, Information Services Division, and the Office of Public Instruction jointly provide a State Electronic Bulletin Board System (BBS) that is available through the **Montana Educational Telecommunications Network (METNET)**. Individuals with a personal computer and a modem can access the METNET and the state BBS through the toll-free 800 numbers and other access points listed below.

The state government information on the BBS includes:

statewide road and weather information
legislative activities and bills
state agency reports
supreme court opinions
press releases
state agency rulemaking and bid notices
public meeting notices
board vacancies
agricultural and drought information

In addition to the state government information available on the METNET BBS, the Office of Public Instruction uses the METNET to provide educational services to school districts, libraries, and other people and organizations involved in secondary and higher education in the state. The METNET provides Montana educators and students with hundreds of places to visit "online."

Other METNET services include electronic mail for educational personnel, daily educational news, school finance and curricula information, and overnight links to the Internet national and international research and education network.

To access the METNET, call:
(800) 803-6393 within Montana
444-4851 (local and out-of-state).

To access the state BBS, call (800) 962-1729 within Montana and 444-5648 (local and out-of-state).

Other access points
http://www.metnet.mt.gov

State of Montana
http://www.mt.gov

Legislative information
ftp://161.7.114.15/Pub/or http://www.mt.gov

Office of Public Instruction
http://161.7.114.15/OPI/OPI.html

For further information, contact

Office of Public Instruction
Department of Educational Technology
444-3563

SummitNet

SummitNet, another statewide telecommunications network, links 112 cities in 12 counties, with plans to link 64 cities in all of Montana's 56 counties, including the entire university system and all 7 tribal colleges. The State Telecommunications Network (STN) provides voice, data, and video communications to state and local government, law enforcement agencies, and educational institutions throughout the state. The STN currently supports telephone communications as well as data communications for all state agencies. In addition, the STN manages two-way, interactive video communications between eight cities and supports two-way radio communications and FM radio broadcasts (KUFM).

For further information, contact

Department of Administration
Information Services Division
444-2000
fax 444-2701
http://www.mt.gov/isd.

Big Sky Telegraph

The **Big Sky Telegraph** computer bulletin board system, headquartered at Western Montana College of The University of Montana in Dillon, has promoted lifelong learning for Montana's rural citizens for the past eight years through free public access, via dial-in modems. Big Sky Telegraph has received several prestigious test grants to continue its support of community- and education-based communications networks.

The Big Sky Telegraph's World Wide Web home page is http://www.macsky.bigsky.dillon.mt.us/, from which the bulletin board system is accessible.

Telecommunication and Web Sites for Educational Institutions in Montana

The Montana university system has entered the Information Age with a number of innovative programs and telecommunications connections.

- The University of Montana-Missoula has campus-wide on-line services and public access to the Mansfield Library and other information data bases.

- As mentioned above, the Western Montana College of The University of Montana was a pioneer in distance learning for rural communities and schools, with the many services of the Big Sky Telegraph system.

- At Montana State University-Bozeman, students can register for classes through an interactive voice registration system.

Other access points
Office of Commissioner of Higher Education
http://www.montana.edu/~wwwoche

Montana State University
MSU-Billings http://www.msubillings.edu
MSU-Bozeman http://www.montana.edu
MSU-Great Falls College of Technology
http://www.montana.edu/~wwwcgf
MSU-Northern, Havre http://cis.nmclites.edu
KUSM Montana Public Television http://kusm.montana.edu

University of Montana
UM-Missoula http://www.umt.edu

UM Mansfield Library http://www.lib.umt.edu
UM-Montana Tech, Butte http://www.mtech.edu
UM-Western Montana College, Dillon http://www.wmc.edu
Flathead Valley Community College, Kalispell http://www.fvcc.cc.mt.us

Blackfeet Community College, Browning
http://www.montana.edu/~wwwai/bcc.html

Dull Knife Memorial College, Lame Deer
http://www.montana.edu/~wwwai/dkmc.html

Fort Belknap College, Harlem
http://www.montana.edu/~wwwse/fbc/fbc.html

Fort Peck Community College, Poplar http://www.rocky.edu/sta/fpcc.html

Little Big Horn College, Crow Agency http://www.lbhc.cc.mt.us

Salish-Kootenai College, Pablo http://www.skc.edu

Stone Child College, Box Elder http://www.montana.edu/~wwwai/scc.html

Carroll College, Helena http://www.carroll.edu

Rocky Mountain College, Billings http://www.rocky.edu

Education Consortiums
Big Sky Telegraph (site address above)
Mission Valley Consortium http://www.ronan.net/~mvc

Other State Telecommunications Networks and Computerized Systems

The Montana State Library provides internet access to other libraries, schools, and hospitals. The internet, a global "network of networks," provides users with access to information from millions of diverse sources such as universities, businesses, federal government, state governments, and international institutions. Multimedia kiosks in selected libraries, including the State Library, provide information on library services, community events, library holdings, etc.

State Video Conferencing Opportunities

Montanans who live hundreds of miles apart are now able to get together by video to conduct public business. The METNET Interactive Video System was developed by the Office of Public Instruction, the Office of Commissioner of Higher Education, the Department of Administration, and the telecommunications private sector for use by state agencies, schools, colleges, universities, and approved nonprofit corporations.

Two-way video conference and instruction facilities have been installed in Billings, Bozeman, Boulder, Dillon, Great Falls, Havre, Helena, Kalispell, Miles

City, Missoula, and Warm Springs. A site owned by Montana Power Company/ENTEC/TRI at Butte is also accessible to the METNET Video System. The METNET sites can also be linked with the Eastern Montana Telemedicine Network (Baker, Billings, Colstrip, Culbertson, Glasgow, Glendive, Helena, Miles City, and Sidney) and the Southwest Telepsychiatry Network (Bozeman, Butte, and Helena). The conference centers are equipped with sophisticated video and audio equipment so that participants can interact verbally and visually.

Through matching grants, schools and universities have been able to purchase satellite receivers and dishes, modems and telephone lines, video cassette recorders, and televisions to set up learning centers. As a result, there are over 250 satellite dishes located throughout Montana schools. They can receive nationally broadcast courses or "Made in Montana" courses through the university system's satellite uplink facility at Montana State University.

Newspaper Access Sites

The Missoulian
http://www.missoulian.com

Bozeman Daily Chronicle
http://www.gomontana.com

Further Reading:

Brier, Warren J., and Nathan Blumberg. *A Century of Montana Journalism.* Missoula: Mountain Press Publishing, 1971. *It may be twenty-five years old and once was used as a textbook at the University's School of Journalism, but this still makes good reading for anyone interested in newspapers in the state.*

Gilluly, Sam. *The Press Gang: A Century of Montana Newspapers, 1885-1985.* Helena: Montana Press Association, 1985.

Kennedy, Bruce M. *Community Journalism: A Way of Life.* Columbia Falls: Hungry Horse News Publishing.

chapter nine

AGRICULTURE and
Natural Resources

"Montana need not call on the outside world for a single necessity."

— from a book released in 1914
by the State Department of Agriculture and Publicity

IN THE EARLY YEARS OF STATEHOOD, it would have been fair for Montanans to think that if they were cut off from the rest of the world, they could do just fine with what was here. They would lack for nothing but a few luxuries like coffee, tea, and bananas. The same cannot be said today. As diversified and blessed with natural resources as Montana is on the eve of the new millennium, our ideas of what are essentials and what are luxuries have changed. Montanans trade their labor and resources in the global marketplace—for cars and tractors built in Japan, for fruits and vegetables grown in kinder climates, and for clothing made in countries new to the world map.

The uses of the state's bountiful natural resources have changed too. Today, the cattle grown on Montana's rich native and cultivated grasslands may end up on the table of a restaurant in Japan. The state's vast coal deposits transform into power for the cities of the Pacific Coast. Our timber is used in construction of houses across America, and Montana's gold becomes circuitry in mainframe computers and spacecraft.

photo: Michael Sample

Strip farming in a valley of the Big Snowy Mountains. Rick Jackson/Travel Montana

Agriculture

One of Montana's nicknames, the Treasure State, may bring to mind mainly extractable resources like minerals and timber, but it also celebrates the state's immeasurable wealth of natural resources like soil and water, the basis of agriculture.

Agriculture has been Montana's number one industry for almost a century, and farming and ranching have played a big role in the economy and culture of Montana—both the state and the territory. The promise of practicing agriculture has lured a great number of people to Montana over the years, especially during the homestead boom of the early part of this century. The farmers and ranchers of today practice sound land and water stewardship and tap into the global marketplace in order to remain competitive.

Agriculture replaced mining as the state's leading industry in the first decade of the 20th century, and between 1909 and 1919, tens of thousands of eager homesteaders rushed to farm the rich prairie soils. In those ten years, the land seemed as productive as promised and the rains were plentiful. Cultivated land increased from 258,000 acres to more than 3.4 million acres. At first, the drought that began in 1917 only affected parts of Montana, and farmers were encouraged to work as much land as possible for the food production needed to sustain the war effort. By 1919, the drought was widespread. By 1925, half of Montana's farmers had lost their farms because they could not repay the banks for their investments. Montanans also suffered the droughts and economic bad times of the rest of the nation in the 1930s.

Since those difficult decades, farming in Montana has seen more prosperous times. In the 1990s, agriculture has added over $2 billion in cash receipts each year to the state economy. Wheat and cattle lead Montana's agricultural economy. Wheat accounted for almost 39 percent of the cash received for agricultural commodities in 1995; cattle accounted for a little more than 36 percent.

Montana exported $465.9 million in agricultural products in 1995, an increase of $12.1 million over 1994, boosted by the export of feeds and fodder. Almost 86 percent of Montana's agricultural exports in 1995 were wheat and wheat products. Montana ranked 29th in the U.S. for export of all agricultural products in 1995. It ranked fourth for export of wheat and wheat products.

Crops accounted for 51.5 percent of total agricultural cash receipts in 1995. Livestock and livestock products accounted for 39 percent, and federal government payments accounted for the remaining 9.5 percent.

Beaverslides

The beaverslide haystacker revolutionized haying when it was invented and patented about ninety years ago by Big Hole Valley ranchers David J. Stephens and Herbert S. Armitage. The inexpensive implement caught on with haystackers in many western states and Canadian provinces because it saved stacking time and created compact, windproof haystacks.

Today it remains one of Montana's agricultural landmarks. Ranchers and farmers in the Beaverhead, Big Hole, Flint Creek, Deer Lodge, and Avon valleys of southwestern Montana still use the ingenious derrick-like beaverslide to make those tall, tidy haystacks that dot the lush hayfields of mountain valleys.

The beaverslide may look like a catapult, but it doesn't work that way. After the large haybasket is loaded, a cable and pulley system pulls the basket up the sloping arms of the slanting glide surface. At the top, the hay falls onto the stack through an opening in the frame. The side gates allow for a tall, compact pile.

Originally, horse teams moved at right angles to the beaverslide, pulling cables that muscled the hay up the slide. Today the power is more likely to come from a tractor, truck, or car axle. Some new Montana-made beaverslides are made of steel, but many hayers prefer the original type, made of lodgepole timbers and slippery spruce boards.

In 1895, this Northern Pacific Railroad car extolled the virtues of homesteading the unsettled land of the Midwest and West.

Montana Historical Society

Attracting *a* Tide

During the homestead era, the 1913 Legislature and other power-brokers of the day were so determined to "attract a tide of desirable immigration" that they created a new Department of Agriculture and Publicity. The department's 1914 "fact" book is full of the kind of "glittering generalities encompassed in superlatives" that it claimed to be dead-set against when it came to bragging about Montana's opportunities. The publication wanted to lure ". . . high class, energetic and upright men and women who, with reward assured, are not afraid of honest endeavor." The following are some samples of the dramatic boasts about the state highlighted on each page of the book.

- Literally hundreds of Montana's beautiful streams flow over beds of gold.

- Earthquakes, cyclones, tornadoes, and dangerous floods are unknown in Montana.

- Montana winters are mild.

- Heat prostrations are unknown in Montana.

- Montana is destined to be the greatest dairying state in the Union.

- God made Montana with a smile.

- Montana is a gentle and generous mistress.

- Opportunity wears brass knuckles in Montana.

- There is room for millions of prosperous, contented people in Montana.

- There is no place in Montana for the loafer.

Source: Department of Agriculture and Publicity. The Resources and Opportunities of Montana. *Helena, Mont.: Independent Publishing Company, 1914.*

Agricultural Production in Montana

The three major categories of agricultural production are range livestock, dry land agriculture, and irrigated agriculture.

• **Range livestock** uses the majority of acreage, almost two-thirds of the nearly 60 million acres of agricultural land in Montana.

• **Dry land agriculture** uses only water that falls directly on cropland in the form of rain or snow. Approximately 7.3 million acres of the state are used for dry land production of wheat, barley, and alfalfa.

• The state's 1.6 million acres of **irrigated croplands** produce a wide variety of agricultural commodities: hay, barley, sugar beets, corn, potatoes, dry beans, vegetables, and various nursery and seed crops.

Top Ten Montana Agricultural Commodities

Product	1995 Cash Receipts	% of Total Receipts for all Agricultural Commodities
1. Wheat	$714,008,000	38.7%
2. Cattle and calves	$667,838,000	36.2%
3. Barley	$127,197,000	6.9%
4. Hay	$86,372,000	4.7%
5. Sugar beets	$49,987,000	2.7%
6. Dairy products	$40,299,000	2.2%
7. Hogs and pigs	$36,044,000	2.0%
8. Sheep and lambs	$25,643,000	1.4%
9. Potatoes	$19,713,000	1.1%
10. Beeswax, bees; turkey & turkey eggs; rabbits; mink; and other products	$12,061,000	0.7%

Source: Montana Agricultural Statistics, *1996.*

Grain elevator at Whitewater, in Phillips County. Bruce Selyem

Montana's Place in U.S. Agriculture, 1995

Crops	Amount Produced	Rank in U.S.
All wheat	195,750,000 bushels	3
Barley	62,400,000 bushels	2
Oats	4,720,000 bushels	12
Dry beans	205,000 cwt.*	15
Potatoes-fall	2,940,000 cwt.	14
Sugar beets	1,193,000 tons	7
Corn-grain	1,920,000 bushels	41
Corn-silage	760,000 tons	28

Livestock		
All cattle & calves	2,750,00 head	12
All cows	1,590,000 head	9
Beef cows	1,570,000 head	6
Milk cows	20,000 head	44
Cattle on feed	105,000 head	19
Hogs & pigs	180,000 head	27
Sheep & lambs	465,000 head	6
Wool production	4,413,000 lbs.	4
All chickens	540,000 birds	41
Egg production	104,000,000 eggs	42
Honey production	8,480,000 lbs.	8

* Cwt. is abbreviation for hundredweight.
Source: Montana Agricultural Statistics, *1996.*

A Prophetic Vision

After studying the climate and geology of the arid lands of the West, John Wesley Powell, in a report to Congress in 1878, made a number of suggestions regarding the region. He warned that stockmen must have a large area to support stock. He suggested 2,560 acres or more per family for a pasture farm with as many farms as possible having waterfront on the state's rivers and streams. He concluded that homes would need to be widely scattered, and the land should not be fenced, but instead should allow for cooperative commingling of herds. He suggested legislation be enacted allowing nine or more persons to organize an irrigation district.

Though most of his recommendations were ignored, part of his report reflects the history of agriculture in Montana. The trend from 1920 to the present has been fewer and larger farms. In 1995, the average farm was 2,714 acres, just 154 acres larger than Powell's recommendation of 2,560 acres. Irrigation districts are, of course, very much a part of Montana farming and ranching. Powell's suggestion that the Homestead Act's allowance of 160 acres would be inadequate for this part of the country went unheeded. The Enlarged Homestead Act of 1909, which provided 320-acre allotments (half a section, or half a square mile) was still far smaller than Powell's recommendation.

At first, cattlemen grazed their herds unfenced and allowed them to commingle with other herds. Later, however, this gave way to fencing. Fences remain today.

In 1995, some 30,000 Montanans were employed in agricultural activities, approximately the same number as in 1985. That is nearly 200,000 fewer Montanans than those who worked the land during the heyday of homesteading. Nonetheless, the hope of owning enough acreage to raise some animals or crops is still a draw today to lifelong residents and newcomers alike. Many wealthy newcomers who have been buying up ranch properties in the state's recreational paradises in the past decade intend to keep a working ranch alive in some capacity.

Montana Farms and Farmlands, 1910-1995

Year	Number of Farms*	Land in Farms (Millions of Acres)	Average Size of All Farms (in Acres)
1910	28,800	N/A	N/A
1920	57,700	N/A	N/A
1930	55,000	N/A	N/A
1940	44,500	N/A	N/A
1950	37,200	65.0	1,747
1955	34,800	66.1	1,899
1960	31,700	66.7	2,104
1965	28,400	66.7	2,349
1970	26,400	64.2	2,432
1975	23,400	62.2	2,658
1980	23,800	61.9	2,601
1985	24,300	61.0	2,510
1990	24,700	60.5	2,449
1995	22,000	59.7	2,714
1996	22,000	59.7	2,714

N/A - Figures not available.
* The Census of Agriculture defines farms as places with annual sales of agricultural products of $1,000 or more.
Source: Montana Agricultural Statistics—State Historical Series, 1996.

Farmlands

According to the 1992 U.S. Census of Agriculture, agricultural production takes place on nearly 60 million acres of Montana's 94 million acres of land.

- Montana ranks second in the nation, behind Texas, in acres of land in farms and ranches.

- The value of wheat land keeps going up, and grain farms keep getting bigger and fewer. The larger a grain farm is, the more economical it is to operate.

- In 1994, the state's leading agricultural county in total cash receipts from crops, livestock, and livestock products was Yellowstone County, followed by Chouteau and Big Horn counties.

- The county with the most land in farms in 1992 was Big Horn County (3 million acres), followed by Rosebud County (2.59 million acres) and Blaine County (2.34 million acres).

In 1994, total farm and ranch assets (excluding farm operators' household assets and debts) amounted to $19.5 billion. The average value per farm or ranch was $867,769, with an average real estate value of $662,844. That amounts to an average value of $277 per acre for land and buildings. The average farm and ranch debt per operation was $114,836.

Farm Real Estate Values (Land and Buildings)

Year	Value in Dollars/Acre
1870	4
1880	8
1890	13
1900	5
1910	19
1920	22
1930	12
1940	8
1950	17
1960	35
1970	60
1980	235
1995	277

In the Family

In 1995, the Montana Farmers Union listed forty-two Montana farms and ranches that have been held in the same family ownership for one hundred years or more. Many of the properties are in western Montana, reflecting the contributions of farming to the state's earliest settlements.

Harvesting wheat in the 1950s. Montana Historical Society

Harvesting wheat in the 1990s. Travel Montana

Crop Production

Wheat

Montana's major grain crop is wheat, which in 1995 accounted for about 68 percent of cash receipts from crops. Montana's wheat crop in 1994 was valued at about $602 million. The 1995 wheat crop was the most valuable ever, reaching a record $897.4 million, due to unusually high prices and the second-largest volume ever. The 1995 preliminary average price per bushel for winter, spring, and durum wheat was $4.60, compared with $3.54 for 1994. Wheat prices have remained high in the 1990s due to a strong export demand. Continuation of this trend depends on production in the U.S. and the world.

Almost 86 percent of Montana's agricultural exports in 1995 were wheat and wheat products.

Wheat Production in Montana, 1880-1995

Year	Acres Harvested	Yield per Acre in Bushels	Total Bushels	Value of Production
1880	19,000	23.5	446,000	$379,000
1890	33,000	20.0	660,000	$528,000
1900	100,000	21.5	2,150,000	$1,312,000
1910	435,000	21.1	9,160,000	$8,336,000
1920	3,608,000	12.4	44,768,000	$71,629,000
1930	4,217,000	8.4	35,313,000	$20,128,000
1940	3,917,000	13.2	51,676,000	$31,522,000
1950	4,953,000	18.5	91,434,000	$173,499,000
1960	3,953,000	20.1	79,397,000	$131,805,000
1970	3,383,000	25.2	85,167,000	$111,395,000
1980	5,100,000	23.5	119,800,000	$495,624,000
1990	5,185,000	28.1	145,865,000	$384,440,000
1995	5,435,000	36.0	195,750,000	$897,378,000

Source: Montana Agricultural Statistics—State Historical Series, *1996*.

Just Dough It

In September 1995, Wheat Montana Farms & Bakery of Three Forks claimed a new world record for cutting wheat from the field, milling it, mixing a recipe, and turning it into a loaf of bread. The feat was accomplished in 8 minutes and 13 seconds by Wheat Montana employees wearing jackets that said, "Just Dough It." A loaf of the record-setting bread was shipped to President Bill Clinton.

Source: Guinness Book of World Records, *1995, Bantam Books.*

Top 10 Crop-Producing Counties, 1995

Winter Wheat

County	Bushels
1. Chouteau	13,021,000
2. Big Horn	4,792,000
3. Hill	4,422,000
4. Cascade	4,286,000
5. Fergus	4,010,000
6. Teton	3,008,000
7. Yellowstone	2,812,000
8. Judith Basin	1,724,000
9. Pondera	1,638,000
10. Stillwater	1,260,000
State Total	54,800,000

Spring Wheat (excluding durum)

County	Bushels
1. Hill	17,198,000
2. Chouteau	11,813,000
3. Liberty	9,490,000
4. Valley	8,795,000
5. Toole	8,729,000
6. Roosevelt	7,298,000
7. Pondera	6,830,000
8. Blaine	6,077,000
9. Daniels	5,950,000
10. Glacier	5,817,000
State Total	133,000,000

Durum

County	Bushels
1. Sheridan	4,877,000
2. Daniels	754,000
3. Roosevelt	439,000
4. Chouteau	280,000
5. Teton	270,000
6. Liberty	248,000
7. Pondera	199,000
8. Glacier	159,000
9. Wheatland	90,000
10. Toole	73,000
State Total	7,950,000

Top 10 Crop-Producing Counties, 1995

Alfalfa

County	Bushels
1. Gallatin	237,000
2. Fergus	197,500
3. Madison	196,500
4. Beaverhead	178,500
5. Lake	146,000
6. Cascade	141,000
7. Judith Basin	124,000
8. Blaine	121,000
9. Teton	120,000
Big Horn	120,000
10. Carbon	111,000
State Total	4,000,000

Barley

County	Bushels
1. Teton	6,955,000
2. Pondera	6,746,000
3. Chouteau	5,414,000
4. Glacier	4,840,000
5. Toole	3,374,000
6. Fergus	3,352,000
7. Cascade	3,100,000
8. Gallatin	2,866,000
9. Judith Basin	2,243,000
10. Hill	2,077,000
State Total	62,400,000

Oats

County	Bushels
1. Richland	258,000
2. Fergus	227,000
3. Roosevelt	201,000
4. Blaine	198,000
5. Hill	180,000
6. Big Horn	155,000
7. Sheridan	141,000
8. Dawson	137,000
9. Lake	137,000
10. Garfield	135,000
State Total	4,720,000

Source: Montana Agricultural Statistics—State Historical Series, *1996.*

*Grain elevator
at Waltham.*
Bruce Selyem

Exalting Elevators

Many of the old, wooden grain elevators that once stood as tall sentinels on the prairie are crumbling. In time, these elevators may be gone, replaced by their modern counterparts—monoliths of concrete or steel.

The Country Grain Elevator Historical Society has recently formed to help preserve and document these abandoned architectural landmarks of an agricultural age gone by. The society, based in Bozeman, seeks to acquire and restore an old elevator to house an archive of elevator photos and a society museum.

The photos of old elevators in this chapter were taken by Bruce Selyem of Bozeman, a founder and director of the society.

Individuals can join the society for a $20 annual fee. Corporate memberships cost $100. Further information is available from the society at P.O. Box 338, Bozeman, MT 59771, or 587-5828.

Dry Land Farming, Strip Farming, and Summer Fallowing

When you're traveling by air over Montana, you see a patchwork of strips below you, at times stretching as far as you can see. This is the landscape of strip farming, an essential part of dry land farming, where irrigating crops is impossible or impractical.

The broad strips of grain crops are green in the spring and golden at harvest time. Alternating with them are strips of summer fallow. These strips aren't planted in grain until the following year. In order to keep enough land in fallow, then, a dry land farmer needs twice as much land as the acreage he will plant and harvest in a season. Reduced tillage is the most effective way yet found to get a crop in the plains country, where the annual rainfall may be only 10 inches.

Years ago farmers burned the huge heaps of straw that remained after the grain was threshed. In central Montana's "breadbasket" country, the skies glowed at night with the light of straw fires. Now, however, they make use of the decaying leftovers. Increasingly since the early 1980s, reduced tillage practices have come to be widely accepted. Rather than turning the stubble under the soil, the stubble is left on the surface, where it helps protect the soil and preserves moisture from rain and snow. Some farmers apply chemicals to the fallow to kill weeds that sprout among the stubble.

An exhibit, the date and location of which are unknown, boasts a bounty of vegetables raised by dry land farming.
Montana Historical Society

Early Birdseye

Before his name became synonymous with frozen foods, Clarence Birdseye worked in the Bitterroot Valley as a field naturalist for the U.S. Biological Survey. He interrupted his studies at Amherst College to come west and work as a research assistant in the study of Rocky Mountain spotted fever. In 1909 alone, Birdseye shot and trapped over one thousand mammals of all sizes and species—mice, gophers, elk, bear, mountain goats—to determine which served as hosts for the tick that was known to transmit the disease. Birdseye left the area in 1912, eventually going to Labrador, where he developed the idea for frozen food.

Food Crops

Before the advent of frozen foods, imported foods, and reliable refrigerated transportation, Montana was one of the nation's largest producers of certain vegetable crops. In 1918, the Bozeman Canning Company opened to take advantage of the satisfactory climate for growing peas and green beans. It produced some 326,000 cases of vegetables in the 1920s. In the late 1930s and early 1940s, canneries operated in Billings, Red Lodge, Stevensville, and Hamilton.

Following World War II, a series of hailstorms caused crops to fail and the factories to decline. Montana's first frozen-food plant opened in Glendive in 1945. In 1947, this plant shipped five carloads of frozen corn on the cob, which represented 20 percent of the nation's production of that commodity.

Most of these canneries and plants folded by the 1950s.

Montana's sugar beet industry also got a boost during World War II. Even before those profitable years, more than 4,000 farmers were growing more than 900,000 tons of sugar beets, mainly in the Yellowstone Valley. Wartime labor shortages encouraged hundreds of migrant workers from Mexico to help bring in the sugar beet crop. In some locations, the work was done by captured German and Italian soldiers and Japanese-Americans who were interned in "relocation" camps.

Montana was also known as a primary apple-raising state. The first apple trees were planted in the Bitterroot Valley in 1866. About 1870, the Bass brothers of Stevensville planted the first commercial orchard. Once that valley could boast of irrigation, agents were sent to the Midwest to lure farmers onto 10-acre orchard tracts with promises of prosperity. In the 1910s, Montana's delicious Macintosh apple became a favorite in the "Big Apple" market of New York City, and production was high. Crops during those years sometimes yielded 900,000 bushels per year. Apples were a viable state crop through the 1930s but have gradually tapered off since that time. With the high price of farm land and Montana's unpredictable weather patterns, it became too risky to count on a crop that might be wiped out in one frosty spring night.

Cherries

Montana was once a strong producer of both sour cherries and sweet cherries. The famous Flathead cherry industry got started at the turn of the century when late-maturing Lambert cherry trees were planted. These cherries came on the market later in the season than those from other U.S. areas, affording those growers lucky enough to survive a spring frost some good prices in the nation's market basket. While growing commercial sour cherries is almost nonexistent today, Flathead sweet cherries are still a coveted summer treat both for Montanans and the national marketplace. The last good year was 1987, when some 3,800 tons plumped up for the picking. There have been some severe frost years since, requiring the replanting of many orchards.

Sweet Cherry Production and Value, 1940-1995		
Year	Total Tons	Avg. Price per Ton
1940	24	$104
1950	320	$340
1960	1,400	$500
1970	1,400	$313
1980	700	$621
1990	280	$1,670
1995	650	$1,340

State *Fair*

Helena hosted the first territorial fair in Montana in September 1870. It was sponsored by the Montana Agricultural, Mineral, and Mechanical Association and took place on the grounds of a roadhouse outside Helena. Fair buildings and a one-mile racetrack were constructed, along with an outdoor saloon. A couple of decades later, a trainload of "special dirt" from Kentucky was hauled in to enhance the track, which is still the only one-mile racetrack in the Northwest, located at the Lewis and Clark County Fairgrounds.

Other communities in Montana held successful agricultural fairs as early as the 1860s. The territorial fair became the official Montana State Fair in 1903, established by the Legislature to ". . . encourage the growth and prosperity of all agricultural, stock grazing, horticultural, mining, mechanical, artistic, and industrial pursuits in the State of Montana." Today, the city of Great Falls hosts the Montana State Fair, held from the last weekend of July through the first weekend of August.

Cowboys ride herd on a cattle drive north of York. Donnie Sexton/Travel Montana

Ranching and Livestock Production

The livestock industry accounted for about half of the nearly $2 billion annual agricultural production of the state from 1990 to 1993. In 1994, livestock products accounted for only 46.7 percent of cash receipts. In 1995, livestock cash receipts dropped to nearly 39 percent of total agricultural income.

Top 10 Counties for Cattle and Calves, 1995

County	Number of Head
1. Beaverhead	148,000
2. Big Horn	128,000
3. Yellowstone	122,000
4. Fergus	114,000
5. Madison	94,000
6. Rosebud	90,000
Cascade	90,000
7. Blaine	82,000
Custer	82,000
8. Phillips	80,000
9. Powder River	78,000
10. Teton	69,000

Source: Montana Agricultural Statistics, 1996.

Montana Cattle Inventory, 1870-1995

Year	Number of Head	Average Price per Head
1870	117,000	$26.40
1880	555,000	$19.10
1890	1,101,000	$17.40
1900	910,000	$27.70
1910	919,000	$29.00
1920	1,370,000	$47.90
1930	1,226,000	$53.80
1940	1,148,000	$45.50
1950	1,726,000	$128.00
1960	2,245,000	$141.00
1970	3,014,000	$195.00
1980	2,645,000	$510.00
1990	2,250,000	$675.00
1995	2,700,000	$675.00
1996	2,750,000	$560.00

Source: Montana Agricultural Statistics—State Historical Series, 1996.

Cowboys

It seems that lots of folks still dream of being a cowboy out in the wilds of Montana. Of course, if they knew how hard a cowboy has to work most of the year, they might stick with their nice day jobs. Movies and television may give the impression that all cowboys have to do is chase bad guys and hang around the saloon. In real life, though, the cattle business is, and always was, a serious business. For driving cattle in the late 1800s and early 1900s, a cowboy earned from $20 to $30 a week.

Stockmen raise cattle in order to sell them, and they hire cowboys to help produce good beef and get it to market. Montana still has cowboys, and some of them still work in the cowboy "kit" you might see on reruns of *Rawhide*, but in the Montana of the 1990s, someone dressed in Western gear may also be a real estate salesman or a truck driver. For the most part, cowboys still ride horses when they work with cattle. Horses can maneuver better than a Jeep, and it's easier to rope a steer from a horse than from the back of a truck.

Holy Cow!

In 1995, cattle outnumbered people in Montana by better than three to one, but the human population was nearly double the number of sheep.

Montana Horse Inventory, 1870-1960*

Year	Number	Farm Value** per Head
1870	5,000	$42.00
1880	37,000	$46.00
1890	200,000	$42.00
1900	316,000	$24.00
1910	320,000	$80.00
1920	669,000	$61.00
1930	462,000	$30.00
1940	250,000	$45.00
1950	151,000	$26.34
1960	91,000	$112.00

* Estimates discontinued after 1960
** Farm value is the estimated replacement value or current value of stock; for crops, the term usually refers to the actual cash received for a product.
Source: Montana Agricultural Statistics—State Historical Series, *1996.*

Sheep and Wool

A number of early immigrants brought small herds of sheep to the first mining areas and agricultural valleys, the Beaverhead establishing itself by 1870 as a major center. Conrad Kohrs, who was to become one of Montana's premier cattlemen, is credited with bringing 400 head of sheep to Montana in 1864. He discovered that mutton was not so popular with the miners, but they appreciated the wool for mattresses. Major C. C. Kimball brought the first sizable herd to Virginia City from Red Bluff, California, in 1865. In 1867, Jesuit missionaries of the St. Peter's Mission west of Cascade brought sheep into Montana from Oregon. They hoped to interest the Indians in the sheep business. But Indians were less interested than the coyotes who gobbled up this new, easy prey. The first permanent sheep ranch in Montana started in the Beaverhead Valley near Dillon in 1869, with 1,500 sheep brought from Oregon.

By 1880, there were 385,000 sheep in the state. Montana's peak for the sheep industry came in the first years of the twentieth century, with somewhere between 5 and 6 million head.

The industry declined as the rich grasslands were carved up and fenced by homesteaders. More damaging were predation of the sheep by coyotes, increased competition after World War II from other sheep-producing nations (Australia, New Zealand, and Argentina), and termination in the early 1990s of a federal wool incentive program initiated by President Dwight D. Eisenhower.

Montana Sheep Inventory, 1870-1996

Year	Number of Head	Avg. Price per Head
1870	11,000	$2.60
1880	385,000	2.40
1890	2,228,000	2.25
1900	4,504,000	2.85
1910	5,385,000	4.20
1920	2,420,000	10.30
1930	3,940,000	9.50
1940	3,462,000	7.70
1950	1,464,000	19.40
1960	1,767,000	18.10
1970	1,018,000	29.00
1980	574,000	91.50
1990	640,000	85.00
1995	450,000	68.00
1996	430,000	84.00

Source: Montana Agricultural Statistics—State Historical Series, *1996.*

Top 10 Counties For Sheep and Lambs, 1994

County	Number of Head
1. Garfield	67,000
2. Carter	66,000
3. Powder River	21,500
4. Wheatland	20,000
5. McCone	17,400
6. Sweet Grass	15,500
7. Beaverhead	14,800
8. Phillips	10,200
9. Cascade	9,700
10. Madison	9,500

Source: Montana Agricultural Statistics, *1996.*

notable
Montanans

Charles M. Bair (1857-1943)

Bair began ranching in 1893 after coming to Montana as a railroad conductor. By the turn of the century, Bair's sheep herd was reputed to be the largest in North America. At one time 300,000 animals belonged to him. In 1905, he filled forty-four freight cars with his wool clip. He made a fortune in the Alaskan gold rush and multiplied his assets with investments in several other interests, including cattle, coal, mines, metals, oil, banking, and irrigation projects on the Crow Reservation. He lived in a 26-room mansion in Martinsdale with his wife, Mary, and daughters Alberta and Marguerite. The home and the ranch headquarters opened as a public museum in 1996.

Montana Historical Society

Loss of Sheep and Lambs, by Selected Causes, 1984-1995

Year	Fox	Dog	Coyote	Eagle	Bobcat	Bear	Mtn Lion	Weather	Wolves	Theft
1984	6,200	2,100	38,300	2,500	200	1,400	N/A	72,800	N/A	3,200
1985	4,300	1,500	41,600	2,500	100	1,400	300	14,100	0	5,000
1986	5,100	2,900	30,500	2,000	100	1,100	400	18,000	0	3,700
1987	2,900	3,100	26,400	2,700	100	1,200	300	16,900	10	5,500
1988	4,200	3,100	31,000	2,700	300	1,300	400	15,900	0	5,900
1989	3,500	1,500	28,200	800	400	1,000	500	23,400	0	3,400
1990	4,000	1,600	29,700	2,200	*	700	600	19,100	0	2,500
1991	4,900	3,500	33,700	1,300	100	600	600	21,500	2	4,100
1992	5,000	1,800	31,100	1,900	*	800	600	11,900	0	2,900
1993	3,300	1,700	30,700	2,500	200	700	1,000	12,000	0	3,300
1994	6,000	1,000	28,500	5,300	300	600	1,000	11,800	0	2,900
1995	3,400	1,600	28,000	2,700	*	300	500	14,300	0	2,000

N/A-Data not available.
* Denotes less than 100 head.
Source: Montana Agricultural Statistics—State Historical Series, *1996.*

Wool Production, 1910-1995

Year	Sheep Shorn	Lbs. of Wool	Price per lb.
1910	5,008,000	38,061,000	$0.21
1920	2,100,000	16,800,000	$0.51
1930	3,740,000	34,034,000	$0.21
1940	3,220,000	29,624,000	$0.29
1950	1,347,000	12,796,000	$0.63
1960	1,679,000	17,041,000	$0.43
1970	933,000	9,086,000	$0.38
1980	539,000	5,358,000	$0.99
1990	627,000	6,204,000	$0.91
1995	468,000	4,413,000	$1.24

Hogs and Pigs

Montana's pork industry was one of the state's earliest agricultural industries. Many of the first permanent settlers and homesteaders here raised hogs as a reliable meat source for the family and for the essential commodity of lard for cooking and baking. Pigs proved to be adaptable to the sometimes harsh Montana climate. They could be fed grain grown on the farm, along with other family food scraps. Over the years, hog production grew from two or three sows serving the family to larger herds intended for market. From the time of earliest settlement, small local slaughter plants, or the farmers themselves, processed the hogs for butcher shops and grocery stores. One large pork packing plant in Billings bought many of the hogs raised in Montana until it went out of business in 1980.

Today, producer marketing cooperatives collect the hogs for shipment to packing plants in South Dakota, Idaho, Oregon, and California. Many farms still have a few sows or feeder pigs for home use or youth agricultural projects. For large-scale producers, hog production is now a high-technology agribusiness. Thousands of sows can be raised in confinement buildings, where temperature, cleanliness, and feed are monitored and controlled. These producers often use artificial insemination for breeding and employ strict disease control measures. In recent years, producers have bred hogs for leanness, reducing the fat and calorie content to address the concerns of health-conscious Americans. Montana's Hutterite colonies have produced over half the 350,000 market hogs raised so far in the 1990s.

Top 10 Counties for Hogs and Pigs, 1995

County	Number of Head
1. Liberty	15,700
2. Glacier	14,200
3. Cascade	13,100
4. Hill	12,100
5. Toole	11,900
Teton	11,900
6. Pondera	11,800
7. Wheatland	10,700
8. Flathead	6,900
9. Golden	6,100
10. Blaine	5,700

Source: Montana Agricultural Statistics, *1996.*

Montana Hog and Pig Inventory, 1870-1995

Year	Number of Head	Avg. Price per Head
1870	4,000	$6.40
1880	15,000	$7.40
1890	26,000	$7.10
1900	43,000	$6.60
1910	88,000	$10.40
1920	160,000	$16.30
1930	258,000	$11.30
1940	168,000	$7.90
1950	145,000	$33.90
1960	151,000	$26.70
1970	200,000	$24.50
1980	250,000	$63.50
1990	185,000	$89.00
1995	180,000	$74.00

Source: Montana Agricultural Statistics, *1996.*

Of OSTRICHES

A small number of Montanans engage in ostrich ranching. One fertile ostrich egg may sell for as much as $1,000. This African native is the world's largest, strongest bird. An ostrich can weigh up to 120 pounds. The meat from an ostrich sells for $23 a pound and tastes similar to lean beef.

Dams and Reservoirs

The building of dams for hydroelectric power and irrigation has been beneficial to both Montana and states along the great rivers that rise in the mountains here. Montana is part of the Pacific Northwest Electric Power, Conservation, and Planning Commission and other consortia that manage adequate flood control, power sources, irrigation, recreation, and habitat of the West's water resources.

The largest body of water in the state is the 134-mile-long artificial Fort Peck Lake on the Missouri River. The 379-square-mile lake is formed behind **Fort Peck Dam**. As the fifth largest manmade reservoir in the U.S., Fort Peck Lake holds 17.9 million acre-feet* of Missouri River water. The dam is a source of power and flood control for the Mississippi River downstream. Fort Peck Dam was begun in 1933 and was operational by 1940.

Libby Dam on Lake Koocanusa was built in 1973 to hold 5.8 million acre-feet of water. **Hungry Horse Dam**, 564 feet high, on the South Fork of the Flathead River, is the 10th highest dam in the nation.

For comparison, Hoover Dam in Nevada is 725 feet high and holds 28.3 million acre-feet of the Colorado River.

* The water that will cover one acre to the depth of one foot.

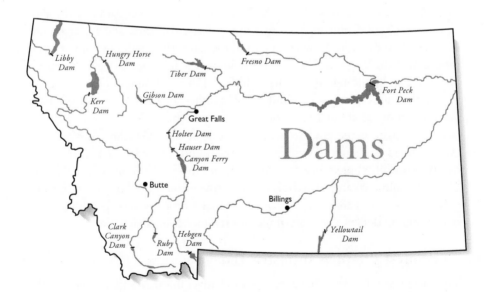

Forest Products

Twenty-four percent of Montana's land area, approximately 22.4 million acres, is forested. Some 64 percent of Montana's forests is owned by the federal government, with nearly 11.4 million acres administered by the USDA Forest Service and the remainder under the Bureau of Land Management. Some 3.4 million acres of forested land are reserved in wilderness areas, national parks, and national monuments.

The State of Montana owns 4 percent of the state's forested timberlands. The forest industry owns 8 percent (1.6 million acres), and the remaining 24 percent (4.4 million acres) is in private, nonindustrial ownership. Most nonindustrial private timberland is owned by individual farmers and ranchers. More than 600,000 acres are under the control of Indian tribes.

The estimated volume of wood on all timberlands totals almost 31.6 billion cubic feet. The two most prevalent trees of this growing stock are lodgepole pine (30 percent) and Douglas-fir (29 percent). The other major species in this growing stock are ponderosa pine, western larch, Engelmann spruce, and sub-alpine fir.

Early Days of the Timber Industry

The first sawmill of record in Montana was constructed in 1845 near St. Mary's Mission in the Bitterroot Valley by the Jesuit missionary Father Anthony Ravalli. In the early 1860s, mills opened in Virginia City, Bannack, and Helena, and dozens followed suit in the western part of the state. Two grades of lumber were produced in the Virginia City mill, sluice lumber selling for $140 per thousand board feet and building lumber that sold for $125 per thousand board feet.

Lumber mills sprang up around the gold mines. In 1869 a number of small sawmills produced about 13 million board feet of lumber. The mills were abandoned, though, as the gold strikes played out in the 1870s and 1880s. Two events turned the faltering lumber industry around. The hard rock mining industry, especially copper, began to flourish, and the Pacific Northern and Utah Northern railroads came into the state, requiring wood for rail ties, trestles, tunnels, and fuel. By 1888, the Anaconda Copper Company was spending more than a million dollars a year on timber for its smelter in Anaconda.

The Forest Products Industry Today

The past twenty-five years have seen many changes in the Montana forest products industry. In the late 1970s, there were about thirteen thousand people employed in this industry. In 1979 and the following six years, a severe drop in the housing and construction industries depressed the forest products industry. The period from 1983 to 1985 was marked by record-level consumption of wood

Logging in 1900. Montana Historical Society

products but low prices mainly due to increased Canadian imports and the high value of the U.S. dollar. The late 1980s were marked by record sales and production due mainly to high consumption and the lower value of the U.S. dollar. Employment, however, was down from the peak in the late 1970s. This was attributed to increasing mechanization and manufacturing processes that were less labor-intensive.

At the start of the 1990s, the Montana timber industry experienced a slight recession, followed by a recovery starting in 1992. Montana's 1993 timber harvest was 1 billion board feet, down 27 percent from the record harvest of 1.376 billion board feet in 1987.

In 1993 and 1994, Montana timber sales value was at a near record high with very dramatic upswings in sales. In 1995, the markets were affected by slow housing and building activity and continuing high imports of Canadian lumber. The year 1995 saw a boost from improved paper prices. While timber harvests have declined about 30 percent since the late 1980s, employment figures fell to a lesser degree. With all the ups and downs of the industry, the number of statewide employees today is not much less than in the late 1980s, when the industry employed 11,500 workers. In 1994, there were 11,100 timber-related jobs, and in 1995 the industry employed 10,900 workers.

Nine contiguous counties in western Montana account for over 80 percent of the industry's labor income in the state. In those nine counties, the timber industry contributed 41 percent of the local economic base in the early 1990s.

At its peak, in 1978, the forest products industry accounted for as much as 50 percent of the area economy.

While the industry is still centered in western Montana, eastern Montana counties have recently provided four times more than in 1981 and twenty times more than in 1976. The state's leading timber-processing county in 1993 was Flathead County, followed by Lincoln County and Missoula County.

In the 1990s, the forest products industry was the third largest basic industry sector in Montana, as measured in terms of labor income, exceeded by the federal government and agricultural activities. The forest products industry contributed just under 14 percent of the state's economic base as measured by labor income and 10 percent of the state's economic base as measured by employment.

Most of the goods Montana's forest industry produces, about 90 percent, are shipped out of state for construction or further processing. The products that remain in Montana are used by the construction industry or businesses that manufacture secondary wood products such as cabinets, prefabricated homes, mobile homes, and furniture. The mills in Montana ship throughout the world, but three-quarters of these products are shipped to the north-central and western states.

There were 192 primary forest products plants operating in Montana in 1993. These enterprises included 86 sawmills, four plywood plants, a fiberboard plant, a particleboard plant, a pulp and paper mill, 59 house-log and log home plants, 31 post-and-pole plants, two cedar products plants, a utility pole plant, five wood pellet plants, and an electric-generating facility.

Where Montana's Timber Harvest Went, 1993

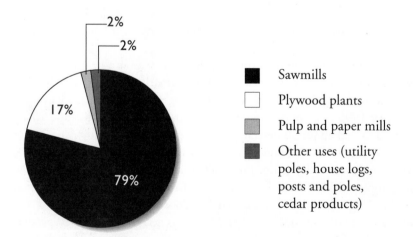

Source: Charles E.Keegan III, Roger E. Bergmeier, and Paul A. Moore, Montana's Forest Products Industry, 1969-1994. *Missoula: Bureau of Business and Economic Research, University of Montana, Dec., 1995.*

Prominent Montana Trees and Their Uses

Ponderosa pine
This tree is also referred to as yellow pine. The wood is used mainly for lumber in sashes, doors, blinds, molding, paneling, trim, and cabinets.

Lodgepole pine
Lodgepole is used for construction lumber, mine timbers, posts, poles, and railroad ties. It is also used for siding, flooring, railroad car decking, decorative veneer, log homes, rustic furniture, and to prop up orchard trees.

Douglas-fir
The wood of this tree is noted for its strength and is used mainly as lumber and plywood for building construction purposes.

Engelmann spruce
Spruce is used for dimension lumber, boards, sheathing, and framing studs. It is also good wood to use for pulp and papermaking.

Western larch
Larch is used for timbers, planks, boards, dimension lumber, glue-laminated beams, and interior paneling.

True firs
Western true firs are listed as six commercial species, two of which are found in Montana: the sub-alpine fir and the grand fir. The lumber is used for building construction, boxes, crates, planing-mill products, sashes, doors, and general mill work.

Western redcedar
Redcedar is used for exterior siding, interior paneling, greenhouse construction, boxes, crates, coffins, posts, utility poles, split-rail fencing, shakes, and shingles.

O, Tannenbaum

The 1992 Census of Agriculture reported 326 farms in 37 Montana counties with $4.25 million in gross income from Christmas trees and other forest products like huckleberries. In 1994, growers shipped as many as a half-million Christmas trees to places as far away as Taiwan.

Homemade Log Homes

Montana is one of the nation's major producers of log homes. Three types of house logs are made here—hand-hewn, sawn, and machine-lathed. Sales of log homes increased 60 percent between 1988 and 1993. Twenty percent of the log houses produced here stay in Montana. Four percent are exported to other countries.

Mining and Energy Resources

Western, central, and eastern Montana differ in the minerals they contain. The differences are related to the geology and structure of the rock formations found in each region.

The mountainous western part of the state contains numerous deposits of metallic ore. The deposits consist mostly of gold, silver, copper, lead, zinc, and tungsten. Sedimentary rocks are sources of phosphate rock, limestone, silica, crushed and dimension stone, clays, and other industrial minerals. Some bentonite has been found in beds of volcanic ash. In the southwestern part of the state, deposits of talc, corundum, iron ore, graphite, sillimanite, and kyanite are found.

Central Montana is best known for the production of petroleum and natural gas. Metallic ore deposits have been found in the Little Rocky Mountains, the Judith Mountains, the Little Belt Mountains, and other isolated ranges. Some clay in this region has been found suitable for brick and tiles.

Eastern Montana has mostly sedimentary rocks. This region contains over 90 percent of the coal reserves in the state. No metallic ore deposits have been found in this region.

In addition to the above, Montana has been mined at various times for dozens of minerals and metals.

Minerals and Metals of Montana

agate	gypsum	rare earths
antimony	indium	silica sand
arsenic	iron	sapphires
asbestos	kaolin	selenium
barite	kyanite	sodium chloride
bentonite	magnesium	sodium sulfate
bismuth	mica	sulfur
cadmium	molybdenum	thorium
calcite	phosphate	uranium
columbium	platinum	vanadium
feldspar	pumice	vermiculite
fluorspar	quartz	zircon

Mad About
Sapphires

Early prospectors sometimes cursed the sapphires that clogged the gold sluices. Even those miners willing to speculate on the sapphire's potential had a hard time rounding up local financial backing for gemstone mining during the 1860s epidemic of gold fever. However, a few decades later, far-sighted European and Eastern interests invested in the sapphire discovery areas and, for the most part, held on to many successful sites over the years. In the 1890s the rush was on to find sapphires in Quartz and Rock creeks west of Philipsburg, in Brown's Gulch and Dry Cottonwood Creek near Anaconda, and along the Missouri River north of Helena. In many of these locations, you'll still find tourists and natives alike picking through buckets of gravel at various commercial operations, with the hope of finding a valuable keepsake. The biggest bonanza occurred in 1894 at Yogo Gulch, near Utica, in the central Montana county of Judith Basin. The U.S. Geological Survey once termed the Yogo sapphire mines "America's most important gem locality."

Gold *Nugget*

When most people think of uses for gold, they think of jewelry and coinage. Actually, there are a number of other things that gold is used for. Gold crowns and fillings are probably the other most commonly known uses. Gold is also used in a drug manufactured to treat arthritis, as a coating for visors for firefighters and astronauts, and as a wire connecting microcircuit chips to mainframe computers.

The Mining Industry Today

The mining industry includes metal mining, coal and industrial mineral mining, and oil and gas extraction. Mining jobs averaged 5,400 in 1994, a substantial drop from the 7,700 mining jobs in 1984. Figures from May 1996 show a slight decrease in jobs from May 1995.

Montana ranked twenty-fourth in the nation in nonfuel mineral production in 1994. The estimated value for that year was $491 million. The mineral production in Montana accounted for about two percent of the total of U.S. production. The state was first in the production of talc and pyrophyllite and fifth in the production of copper, gold, zinc, and phosphate rock. Exploration continues in the state for gold, but there is also significant interest in exploring for sapphire-bearing material.

Of the mines producing gold in Montana, four are owned and operated by Pegasus Gold, Inc.: the Beal Mountain Mine in Silver Bow County; the Montana Tunnels Mine, a gold, lead, silver, and zinc mine in Jefferson County; the Basin Creek Mine southwest of Helena, and the Zortman Mine in Phillips County, which is the state's largest gold mine at present.

As of fall 1996, several major mining ventures are at various stages of the permitting process and may open before the year 2000. American Smelting and Refining Company (ASARCO) is proposing the Rock Creek Mine copper-silver operation in the Cabinet Mountains near Noxon. The permitting process for the McDonald Gold Project near Lincoln is also in progress. The Stillwater Mining Company plans to tap into the largest known platinum and palladium deposit in the Western Hemisphere through an underground mine in Sweet Grass County, south of Big Timber. In fall 1996, the New World Project north of Yellowstone National Park was curtailed by agreement with the federal government. The Canadian company Crown Butte Resources Ltd. had planned extensive underground mining and surface ore processing for gold, copper, and silver.

If prices go up, mining may increase. The Bull Mountain Coal Mine near

Roundup is the first full-scale underground coal mine to operate in Montana since the 1970s. Owners predict it will be the largest exporting coal mine in the nation.

In 1996, thirteen companies were permitted to mine coal on 61,063 acres in Montana. There was no uranium mining in the state. In 1995, there were 89 operating permits for hard rock mining on 37,100 acres. There were 2,082 open cut mining sites of sand, gravel, scoria, bentonite, and phosphate permitted for operation on 30,000 acres.

Source: Montana Department of State Lands Statistics, July 1, 1994 - June 30, 1995. Department of Natural Resources and Conservation.

Principal Mineral-Producing Counties

Beaverhead - talc
Broadwater - gemstones, lime plant
Fergus - gold
Flathead - aluminum plant
Gallatin - cement plant, stone and gravel
Granite - gemstones
Jefferson - cement plant, zinc, gold, silver
Judith Basin - gemstones
Lake - peat
Lewis and Clark - gold, gemstones, lead smelter
Lincoln - copper, silver, stone and gravel
Madison - talc, garnets
Meagher - iron
Missoula - barite
Park - dimension marble, gold
Petroleum - stone and gravel
Phillips - gold, silver
Ravalli - peat, stone and gravel
Rosebud - stone and gravel
Silver Bow - copper, molybdenum, stone and gravel
Stillwater - platinum group metals
Yellowstone - stone and gravel

Coal

Coal underlies 35 percent of Montana's surface area, forming the base of Montana's major mining industry. This coal is part of the Fort Union formation, probably the largest coal basin on earth. It extends under parts of Montana, Wyoming, North Dakota, and Saskatchewan. The power grid that reaps the benefits of this mother lode extends even farther. Electrical power generated at the huge coal power plants in our state's southeastern corner flows all the way to the West

Coast, where it helps to meet the high energy demands of that region.

Montana has coal reserves estimated at 120 billion tons, the largest reserve base in the nation. The Energy Information Administration estimates that as many as 1.4 billion tons of this reserve are recoverable from currently producing coal mines. If all of Montana's coal reserves were capable of being mined, and were mined at the current rate, mining of this resource could be sustained for 3,000 years.

Eastern Montana coal is both lignite and subbituminous grades. It is remarkably free from impurities and easy to extract by stripping. The overburden, the earth and rock above the coal seam, is loosened by blasting. Then the coal is loaded onto trains with huge mechanical shovels. There's nothing to cave in, so about 95 percent of the coal can be taken out.

Some 33 million tons of coal were produced in Montana in 1985. In 1995, Montana's coal production was close to 40 million tons. Coal companies predict production will remain at that level into the new century.

THE COAL SEVERANCE TAX

Montanans remembered the past economic disruptions from the ups and downs of the state's mining industry and realized coal is irreplaceable. In 1975, the Montana Legislature approved the Coal Severance Tax, meant to protect the state and its citizens from hard times in the case of a shutdown of the mines. The tax, paid by mining companies on the coal they extract, was a bitter pill for the companies to swallow but was upheld by the courts in 1981. Part of the tax proceeds are distributed in grants to towns and counties where coal has been extracted. The remainder of the proceeds is placed in a variety of state funds for highways, the arts, libraries, parks, agriculture, conservation, and more.

Oil and Natural Gas

Before the turn of the century, oil was found in and around Glacier National Park but the finds were not developed. It was not until the 1910s and 1920s, when the use of automobiles increased dramatically, that Montana's oil and natural gas industry came into being.

In 1915, the first major oil field was opened at Elk Basin, along the Wyoming-Montana border in Carbon County. Next came the Cat Creek field on the lower Musselshell River and the Devil's Basin near Roundup in 1919. The Kevin-Sunburst oil discoveries in the early 1920s made the north-central towns of Shelby and Cut Bank boomtowns. The Cut Bank and Pondera fields yielded high-quality crude oil and natural gas and convinced several large companies to get into the refinery business.

Montana's oil production remained relatively small in scale until after World War II, when national prosperity brought increased demand for petroleum. Major oil companies encouraged exploration across the state, and two refineries were built at Billings. Major discoveries in Montana's portion of the oil-rich Williston Basin sparked a leasing frenzy in eastern Montana. The basin also underlies western North Dakota and southern Saskatchewan. In the 1950s, Billings became the center of the state's petroleum industry as lucrative oil strikes were made near Wibaux, Sidney, Baker, and throughout northeastern Montana. The Yellowstone Pipeline was completed from Billings to Spokane in 1954.

Montana's oil business was somewhat quiet during the first half of the 1960s, but big oil discoveries at Bell Creek in Powder River County and a natural gas bonanza at Tiger Ridge in Blaine County sent hopes soaring again. The state's peak year for oil production was 1968, with 48 million barrels. The height of natural gas production came later, in 1973, at nearly 59 billion cubic feet. The top money year for petroleum was 1981, with $1.45 billion, largely the result of increased exploration and high prices brought on by the world energy shortage in the late 1970s. Those good times were dampened by conservation measures and overseas oil development. Many wells were capped at that time and await the next boom cycle. Only 1,400 persons were employed in oil and gas related operations in 1995, significantly less than the peak of 4,700 workers in 1980.

As of 1994, Montana's natural gas industry was experiencing healthy growth, largely due to extensive promotion of its clean-burning qualities. It is estimated that at least six trillion cubic feet of natural gas reserves remain untapped in the state.

Montana Superfund Sites

The Environmental Protection Agency's Superfund was created by Congress in 1980 to discover and clean up, if possible, areas where hazardous substances might harm human health and the environment.

Montana's Upper Clark Fork Basin is the largest Superfund area in the nation. It extends 140 miles from the headwaters of Silver Bow Creek north of Butte to the Milltown Dam near Missoula. It is the legacy of more than one hundred years of mining and smelting in the Butte-Anaconda area at the headwaters of the Columbia River Basin.

The initial investigations in this area by the EPA began in 1982. In 1983, three sites—Silver Bow Creek, the Anaconda Smelter, and the Milltown Reservoir—were put on the Superfund priority list. The Montana Pole site was added to the priority list in 1987.

The Silver Bow Creek/Butte Area

This site consists of about 450 acres of soil and water that contain heavy metals from the years of mining that took place here. The site is in Butte and Walkerville and runs from Silver Bow Creek to the Warm Springs Ponds. One of the most well-known sites of contamination is the Berkeley Pit. Water was pumped from surface and underground mines in Butte for about 100 years until 1982, when the Anaconda Minerals Company, a subsidiary of Atlantic Richfield Company (ARCO), ceased mining operations in the area and shut down the pumps. Since then, water has been filling the Berkeley Pit at about 5 million gallons a day. The water is highly acidic and contains a wide variety of heavy metals. Monitoring of the water in the Berkeley Pit began in 1990 and continues today. Treatment of the water is expected to begin after the turn of the century.

Montana Pole

This site contains about 40 acres of surface and ground water that were contaminated by wood treating operations. The site is west of Butte along Interstate 90.

The Anaconda Smelter

Operated for nearly 100 years, the Anaconda Company smelter accumulated waste materials that cover about 4,000 acres. The waste materials consist mainly of tailings and flue dust and are located in and around the city of Anaconda. The Old Works/East Anaconda Development Area contained the first copper smelting facilities built in Anaconda to process the ore being mined in Butte. The Upper Works began in 1884 and the Lower Works in 1888. A silver refinery was located between the two smelters. They operated until 1902. In 1994, the land was transferred to the County of Anaconda/Deer Lodge. Smelting wastes have been covered with limestone and topsoil, and The Old Works, a Jack Nicklaus-designed golf course, now occupies the site.

Milltown Reservoir

Located just above the Milltown Dam near Missoula, this site contains pollutants from the reservoir sediments that have seeped into the groundwater, which served as the source for Milltown's water supply.

Selected Agriculture and Resource Industry Events

Ag Days and Trade Show, Sidney; January, 482-1206.

Agri-Trade Exposition, Glendive; February, 365-6781.

American Cattle Drive, Roundup; mid-August, (800) 257-9775.

Annual Governor's Cup All Breeds Horse Show and Clinic, Lewis and Clark County Fairgrounds; July, 443-5074.

Central Montana Horse Show, Fair, and Rodeo, Lewistown; July, 538-8841.

Libby Logger Days, Libby; July, 293-4167.

Macintosh Apple Day Festival, Ravalli County Museum, Hamilton; September, 363-3338.

Montana Agricultural Industrial Exhibit, Great Falls; January, 761-7600.

Manhattan Potato Festival, Manhattan; third Sunday in August, 284-6094.

Montana Agri-Trade Exposition, Billings; February, 245-0404.

Montana Winter Fair, Bozeman, Gallatin County Fairgrounds; January, 585-1397.

Northeast Montana Exposition, Wolf Point; October, 653-2012.

Northern International Livestock Exposition and Rodeo (NILE), Billings MetraPark arena; October, 256-2495.

Northern Rockies Llama Classic, Bozeman; October, 587-8077.

Pioneer Power Day Threshing Bee, Lewistown; September, 538-5236.

"Running of the Sheep" (Sheep Drive), Reedpoint; Sunday of Labor Day weekend, 326-9911.

Threshing Bee and Antique Show, Culbertson; September, 787-5265.

Threshing Bee, Choteau; September, 446-2470.

Threshing Bee, Huntley; August, 976-6687.

Western Heritage Days, Grant-Kohrs Ranch National Historic Site, Deer Lodge; July, 846-2070.

Further Reading:

Burlingame, Merrill G. *The Montana Frontier*. Bozeman: Big Sky Books, 1980.

Federal Writers' Project. *Copper Camp, Stories of the World's Greatest Mining Town*, Butte, 1943.

Feldman, Robert. *Rockhounding Montana*. Helena: Falcon Publishing, 1985. Rev. 1996.

Fletcher, Robert H. *Free Grass to Fences: The Montana Cattle Range Story.* New York: University Publishers Incorporated, 1960.

Fritz, Harry W. *Montana: Land of Contrasts.* Woodland Hills, Calif.: Windsor Publications, Inc., 1984.

Gilles, T. J. *When Tillage Begins: A History of Agriculture in Montana.* Laurel, Mont.: UMP Publishing, 1977.

Grosskopf, Linda, with Rick Newby. *On Flatwillow Creek: The Story of Montana's N Bar Ranch.* Los Alamos, NM: Exceptional Books, Ltd., 1991.

Gustafson, Rib. *Under the Chinook Arch: Tales of a Montana Veterinarian.* Helena: SkyHouse Publishers, 1993.

_____. *Room to Roam: More Tales of a Montana Veterinarian.* Helena: SkyHouse Publishers, 1996.

Howard, Joseph Kinsey. *Montana: High, Wide, and Handsome.* Lincoln: University of Nebraska Press, 1943.

Keegan, Charles E., III, et al. *Montana's Forest Products Industry: A Descriptive Analysis, 1969-1994.* Missoula: University of Montana Bureau of Business and Economic Research, 1995.

Pukite, John. *A Field Guide to Cows.* Helena: Falcon Publishing Co., 1995.

Toole, K. Ross. *The Rape of the Great Plains.* Boston: Little, Brown, 1976.

Voynick, Stephen M. *Yogo: The Great American Sapphire.* Missoula: Mountain Press Publishing, 1985.

Sources:

Unless otherwise noted, the source for all tabular information in this chapter is *Montana Agricultural Statistics,* the 1995 and 1996 editions, compiled by Montana Agricultural Statistics Service.

chapter ten

BUSINESS

IN THE LAST DECADE of the twentieth century, agriculture* remains Montana's largest basic industry, having dethroned mining from that distinction in the first decade of the century. As we approach the first decade of the twenty-first century, though, the state is moving away from an economy built primarily on natural resource-based industries and toward a more diversified economy. Behind agriculture, which accounts for about 30 percent of economic activity in Montana, tourism and other non-goods producing businesses are growing.

Economic growth must be looked at in two ways: one, from the perspective of jobs it provides; and two, in terms of Gross State Product. Viewed from these two perspectives, the future looks very different.

The U.S. Bureau of Economic Analysis prepares annual estimates of Gross State Product, which measures Montana's contribution to the Gross Domestic Product by measuring the output or production of the state, sometimes referred to as "value added." This is a dollar figure that is equal to gross sales or receipts minus goods and services purchased.

The service industry, which includes private health and social services, business services, and hotels and other lodging, is the fastest-growing source of employment. When economists try to predict economic growth in terms of jobs, they foresee personal and business services as Montana's fastest-growing industries, followed by wholesale and retail trade.

If, however, economists consider Gross State Product data, the greatest growth

*Agriculture and natural resource industries are described in more detail in Chapter Nine.

photo: Travel Montana

is expected in agriculture and mining. These industries can contribute more to the Gross State Product with fewer employees than the service industry, mainly due to technological improvements in recent years.

In 1995, 4,444 businesses were created or changed ownership in Montana, 312 more than in 1994. Most of the new businesses were engaged in services, including government; wholesale and retail trade; and construction. Transportation, communications, and utilities were the only industries reporting fewer new and changed businesses in 1995 than in 1994.

Montana's economic markets have expanded in recent years to include increased trade relations with the Pacific Rim nations. This expansion, together with the state's close proximity to Canada and Canadian markets, have enhanced Montana's international trade opportunities. New technology and improved transportation continue to make Montana's somewhat remote location more accessible to expanded trade opportunities in the United States and abroad.

Sources: Mont. Dept. of Labor and Industry, Montana Annual Planning Information, *June, 1996;* Job Projections for Montana's Industries and Occupations,1994-2000, *Jan. 1996.* Montana Business Quarterly, *Winter 1996.*

notable
Montanans

William Andrews Clark (1839-1925)

A native of Pennsylvania and a former schoolteacher, Clark came to Bannack in 1863 with other gold seekers but moved on to Deer Lodge and became a banker. He invested in several mines in nearby "Butte City"; by 1885, he owned at least a part of forty-six mines, most producing silver or copper. The Clark-Daly feud that went down in history as "the War of the Copper Kings" boils down to petty jealousy. It is believed to have begun with a remark by Clark that slighted Daly. The conflict escalated when Clark set his sights on a seat in the U.S. Senate. He won the nomination for territorial delegate but failed to be elected for the

Montana Historical Society

seat by the Montana Legislature. When he tried again in 1899, he won election to the Senate but was never seated due to accusations, raised by Daly, that Clark bribed his way to victory. After Daly's death in 1900, Clark finally won election and served in the Senate from 1901-1907.

notable
Montanans

☞ Marcus Daly (1841-1900)

Daly immigrated to America from Ireland in 1856, and worked in New York, California, and Nevada. A mining company sent him to Montana to investigate the potential of Butte's Alice Mine. He recommended its purchase, invested $5,000 of his own money in the mine, and managed the mine for the company. In the early 1880s, he bought the Anaconda Mine, also in Butte, from the man who originally devel-

Montana Historical Society

oped the mine. After buying out neighboring mines and building a smelter, Daly amassed one of the world's most powerful monopolies. He founded the city of Anaconda and developed it into an up-to-date center of mining and processing. Bluff and genial, he remained more popular with the working miners than his rivals, William Clark and Augustus Heinze. He later established a thoroughbred ranch in the Bitterroot Valley and involved himself in irrigation projects and other development that helped settle the region.

☞ F. Augustus Heinze (1869-1914)

World Museum of Mining

Fritz Augustus Heinze, the son of German immigrants, came to Butte around 1890 as a young mining engineer. With his persuasive manner and backing from his wealthy family, Heinze soon owned mines and a smelter. After first allying himself with Daly, Heinze joined forces with Clark in a battle against the Amalgamated Copper Company, formerly Daly's Anaconda Company, which had been bought by Standard Oil.

After Daly died in 1900 and Clark had gone to Washington as a senator, Heinze continued to wage war with Amalgamated. In the *Butte Reveille*, the paper he owned, he portrayed himself as the miner's friend—the little guy out to slay the corporate giant. In the end, the giant had its way: Heinze sold out to Amalgamated in 1906. He was paid more than $10 million for his properties, on the promise that he leave Butte and stay out of the copper business. He moved to New York and to Wall Street, where he soon broke his promise and tried to corner the copper market. This bid was his last and meant his financial ruin, supposedly at the hands of his old nemesis, Standard Oil. He died at the age of forty-five.

notable
Montanans

Josephine "Chicago Joe" Hensley (1844-1899)

She was born in Ireland as Mary Welch and
immigrated to the U.S. at the age of 14. She
worked in Chicago's red-light district in her
twenties, during the Civil War. She moved
to Helena near the end of the war. On the
western frontier in the late 1800s, prostitution was the most common mode of employment for women outside the home.
Women, not male pimps, managed prostitution. Helena madams exchanged properties, borrowed money from some of the
city's reputable businessmen and merchants, and counted up their losses after
the city's devastating fires destroyed their
brothels. Hensley rose to the top of this
business class with a shrewd sense for
buying real estate and an excellent record
of repaying loans and mortgages.

Montana Historical Society

By 1880, Hensley had become
known as "Chicago Joe" and controlled most of Helena's prostitution district.
She acquired unimproved lots, a farm, a warehouse, small saloons (or "hurdy-
gurdies"), and the Coliseum, a theater where prostitutes plied their trade in the
curtained boxes. When legal, moral, and political pressures threatened to close
down her Red Star Saloon, she upgraded the venue to a vaudeville house with
great success. The same pressures, however, changed the economic face of prostitution during the 1880s and Chicago Joe met with financial ruin in the 1890s.
She died in her Helena home of pneumonia. Her death and those of the other
Helena madams who held the purse strings of the city's prostitution business
opened the way for men to take control of the business.

Employment and Labor

Recent Job Growth

Montana gained about 10,400 nonfarm jobs in 1995, for an increase of about 3.1 percent from 1994 to 1995. This gain was less than the 14,600 nonfarm jobs gained in 1994, an increase of about 4.5 percent. The largest job growth in 1995 occurred in construction, which added 8.7 percent more jobs.

Construction

The construction industry provided about 16,200 jobs in 1995. With 1,300 added jobs, that represented an 8.7 percent increase over 1994. There has been a steady increase in construction jobs, after hitting a low in 1987 of 8,600 jobs.

Predictions are that construction jobs will shift from residential and commercial business to government and industrial projects in the second half of the 1990s. This is due to rising interest rates for the private sector and the funding increases for highway repair and for several new buildings on the campuses of the Montana university system.

Manufacturing

The manufacturing sector of Montana's economy includes lumber, wood, and paper products; printing and publishing; food processing and production of food products; machinery, equipment, and instruments; primary metals processing; and miscellaneous manufacturing.

The dominant wood products industry lost about 400 jobs in 1995 but still accounted for about 31 percent of all manufacturing jobs. The loss in lumber

Job Growth, 1985-95

Employment Sector	1985	1995	Jobs Created	% Growth
Service-related jobs	60,600	96,300	35,700	58.9
Contract construction	11,500	16,200	4,700	40.8
State colleges, universities	8,700	11,400	2,700	31.0
Trade-related jobs	74,600	96,400	21,800	29.2
Local education	22,300	26,300	4,000	17.9
Finance, insurance & real estate	13,300	15,600	2,300	17.3
Manufacturing	21,800	23,300	1,500	6.9
Other local government	15,400	14,900	-500	-3.2
Federal government jobs	12,800	13,100	-300	-2.3
Other state government	10,800	11,000	200	1.8
Transportation, communications & utilities	20,700	20,800	100	0.5
Mining	6,800	5,300	-1,500	-22.1

Source: Montana Dept. of Labor and Industry, Montana Annual Labor Market Planning Information. Helena: June, 1996.

Annual Average Non-Agricultural Jobs, in Thousands

Industry	1960	1970	1980	1990	1991	1992	1993	1994	1995
Mining	7.4	6.6	8.8	6.3	5.9	5.9	5.5	5.4	5.3
Construction	11.0	11.0	14.5	10.4	11.5	12.7	13.5	14.9	16.2
Manufacturing	20.4	23.9	24.2	22.3	21.7	22.5	23.0	23.0	23.3
Transportation, Communication & Utilities	19.0	17.4	22.4	20.1	20.3	20.1	20.3	20.7	20.8
Wholesale & Retail Trade	40.5	48.1	72.3	78.9	81.7	84.5	87.5	92.6	96.4
Service	23.1	33.7	55.1	74.5	77.2	82.4	86.9	91.7	96.3
Government & Education	38.5	52.6	70.2	71.4	71.9	74.2	74.1	76.3	76.8
Total Non-Ag Jobs	166.8	201.4	280.4	297.2	303.7	316.6	325.6	340.2	350.6

Source: Montana Dept. of Labor and Industry. Montana Annual Labor Market Planning Information. Helena: June, 1996.

and wood products jobs during 1994 was offset by job gains elsewhere in the manufacturing industry, for an overall gain of three hundred manufacturing jobs since 1994.

There is concern that a number of the state's large manufacturing plants have aging infrastructure problems and other market and environmental concerns that could affect them in the future.

This industry, however, continued to show gains in 1996, up two hundred jobs between May 1995 and May 1996.

Transportation and Utilities

This sector averaged 20,800 jobs in 1995, which is about 100 jobs over the 1994 average.

Most of the increase was in trucking and warehousing. The promising sector, according to predictions, will be in railroad freight lines. Montana's transportation sector is expected to benefit from increased Canadian and North American trade.

Wholesale and Retail Trade

This sector added about 3,800 new jobs to the Montana economy in 1995. It includes general merchandise and apparel, food stores, auto dealers and service stations, building materials and garden supply stores, and eating and drinking establishments. Wholesale trade added about seven hundred jobs over the year, while retail trade added about three thousand jobs in 1995.

Retail trade is growing mostly in cities, partly due to the influx of discount stores into the state. This growth in chain discount stores could adversely affect the retail jobs in smaller towns in the state.

Finance, Insurance, and Real Estate

This segment of the economy has shown a relatively steady increase from 1990 to the present. In 1995, it averaged 15,600 jobs as compared to 1990, with 13,400 jobs. The job level in 1995 was about the same as in 1994.

The real estate markets are beginning to slow in some of the high-growth areas, probably due to higher interest rates and home prices.

Service Jobs

This is the fastest-growing component of Montana's economy. It includes employment at hotel and lodging establishments; business services; personal services; and private medical, health, and social services.

There were 96,300 jobs in this sector in 1995, compared to 60,600 jobs in 1985. The gain from 1994 to 1995 was about 4,600 jobs or 5 percent.

Government (including education)

These jobs averaged about 76,800 during 1995, an increase of 500 jobs over 1994. Most of the increases were in local government employment, with local education showing the largest increase. Federal government employment decreased by about 500 jobs from 1994. Total state government remained the same as in 1994. Overall, the largest increase in government jobs was in education.

The two largest Montana employers are public employers. The U.S. government, civilian and military, employs 23,000 people. The Montana state government employs approximately 22,000 residents.

Sources: Paul E. Polzin, "Montana's Economy: Factors and Forecasts." Montana Business Quarterly, vol. 33, no.1. Missoula: Bureau of Business and Economic Research, University of Montana, Spring, 1995. Paul E. Polzin. "What's Hot and What's Not." Economic Outlook, Winter 1995. Missoula: Bureau of Business and Economic Research, University of Montana.

Montana's Major Employers

Employer	Activity	Number of Jobs in Montana
U.S. Government (civilian & military)	Government Services	23,000
Montana Government (incl. education)	Government Services	22,000
Providence Services	Hospital Services	5,000
Montana Power Co.	Utility, Mining	2,800
Burlington Northern Santa Fe Railroad	Transportation Services	2,500
Billings School District	Education	2,200
Washington Corporations	Transportation, Mining, Construction	2,100
Buttrey Food and Drug	Retail Trade	2,000
Billings Deaconess Medical Center & Clinic	Hospital, Health Services	2,000
Great Falls School District	Education	1,700
Walmart	Retail Trade	1,600
Plum Creek Manufacturing	Timber and Wood Products, Manufacturing	1,400
Kmart	Retail Trade	1,400

Source: Data compiled by Montana Dept. of Commerce from communications with companies, local chambers of commerce, newspaper articles, Montana Dept. of Labor and Industry (for Montana state government and U.S. government, civilian), U.S. Bureau of Economic Analysis (for U.S. government, military).

Small Is Beautiful

Small businesses are a vital part of the state's business climate. About 73 percent of wage-and-salary jobs in Montana are with businesses of fewer than 100 employees. About 35 percent of Montana's small businesses employ fewer than 20 people. A random sampling follows.

Examples of Businesses with 20-50 Employees

Employer	Product or Service
Golden Ratio Woodworks Emigrant	Massage Tables
Blue Star Canvas Products Missoula	Tepees, Awnings, Tents
Western Bee Supplies, Inc. Polson	Beekeeping Equipment
Dan Bailey's Fly Shop Livingston	Fly Fishing Equipment

Examples of Businesses with 10-19 Employees

Employer	Product or Service
Wind Related, Inc. Hamilton	Windsocks, Flags
Northern Cheyenne Industries Lame Deer	Tents, Tarps, Riding Dusters, Canvas Products
Bunton Precision Machine Big Timber	Bicycle Parts, Laser Parts
Creative Sales & Manufacturing Whitefish	Knife, Scissor Sharpeners; Lawn Mower, Ax Sharpeners

Examples of Businesses with 4 or Fewer Employees

Employer	Product or Service
Gray and Gray Woodrights Bozeman	Kaleidoscopes
YETI by Molly Bigfork	Polar Fleece Footwear
Wills's Woodshed Bigfork	Cedar Pet Caskets, Pet Cremation Urns
ARBIDAR Co. Sula	Weaving Looms
Swan Bay, Inc. Bigfork	Dog Food
Speed Weld, Inc. Deer Lodge	Welding Helmets

Unemployment

In 1995, there were an average of 26,000 unemployed people in Montana, 4,000 more than in 1994. It marked a 5.9 percent increase, the first increase since 1991.

In the 20-year period from 1975 to 1995, the lowest unemployment rate, 5.1 percent, was recorded in 1979 and again in 1994. The highest rate during these same 20 years was 8.8 percent in 1983.

The state Department of Labor and Industry predicts that approximately forty thousand wage and salary jobs will be created in the state between 1994 and 2000. Most of the job growth is expected to be in service-producing industries, especially health services, social services, eating and drinking establishments, and education (both public and private). The continuing growth in population in the state is the major factor that continues to drive job growth.

A few occupations are expected to experience a decline in employment. The largest decline is predicted for general farm and ranch workers, who are expected to lose 124 jobs per year. Other occupations expected to decline at a slower rate are farm and ranch managers and operators, foresters, conservation scientists, drivers and sales workers, postal carriers, and railroad signal and track maintenance workers.

Unemployment Rates for Montana and the U.S.

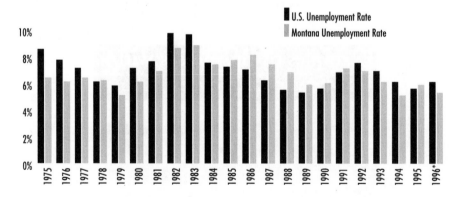

*U.S. forecast by The WEFA Group (June 1995); Montana forecast by Montana Department of Labor and Industry (June 1995).

Licensed Professionals

The following numbers indicate only the number of people granted licenses to practice the listed professions and should not be interpreted as a measure of how many are actually practicing.

Licensed Professionals	
Profession	Number Licensed
Registered Nurses	14,000
Cosmetologists	6,068
Realtors	5,521
Public Accountants	2,902
Electricians	2,896
Plumbers	2,272
Outfitting Guides	1,800
Crane Operators	1,362
Pharmacists	1,242
Architects	945
Veterinarians	943
Barbers	782
Private Investigators	779
Outfitters	750
Dentists	721
Radiological Technicians	688
Professional Counselors	530
Hygienists	415
Chiropractors	412
Social Workers	323
Optometrists	247
Morticians	239
Psychologists	203
Acupuncturists	91
Landscape Architects	74
Podiatrists	60
Naturopaths	32
Tramway Engineers	10
Midwives	9

Top Jobs, Projected to 2000 A.D.

Estimated Jobs to Be Gained Annually Due to Growth, 1994-2000

Salespersons, Retail	301
Waiters and Waitresses	274
General Managers & Top Executives	177
Cashiers	163
Registered Nurses	162
Bookkeeping/Accounting/Auditing Clerks	152
General Office Clerks	148
Carpenters	148
Food Preparation Workers	142
Fast Food Workers	131

Source: Montana Department of Labor and Industry, Research and Analysis Bureau, 1995.

Income

Montana's per capita personal income was $19,047 in 1996, a 3.3 percent increase over 1995. The nation's per capita income rose 4.5 percent to $24,231 in 1996. Montana's per capita personal income ranked 46th among the 50 states.

In the chart below, personal income includes the following:
- wage and salary income
- self-employment income
- employer contribution for benefits
- rental income
- transfer payments
- personal dividends and interest

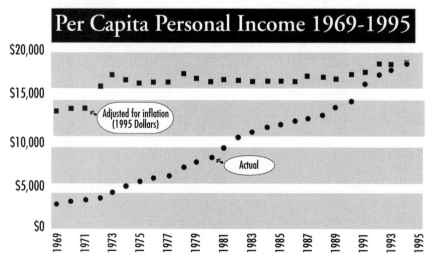

Source: U.S. Department of Commerce, Bureau of Economic Analysis, 1996.

Per Capita Income, Montana & Selected Western States

Per Capita Income*	(Dollars)			
	1995	1994	1993	1992
United States	22,788	21,696	20,812	20,147
MONTANA	18,482	17,794	17,635	16,555
Idaho	19,264	18,272	17,724	16,744
North Dakota	18,663	18,738	17,223	17,225
South Dakota	19,506	19,513	18,136	17,570
Wyoming	21,321	20,347	19,854	18,929

* Per capita personal income is the annual total personal income of residents divided by resident population July 1.
Source: U.S. Department of Commerce, Bureau of Economic Analysis, Regional Economic Information; and Bureau of the Census. 1995 preliminary income data released April 25, 1996; 1992-1994 revised data released June 4, 1996.

Total Personal Income, Montana & Selected Western States

Total Personal Income*	(Millions of Dollars)			
	1995	1994	1993	1992
United States	5,987,536	5,648,263	5,365,006	5,138,091
MONTANA	16,084	15,233	14,830	13,626
Idaho	22,409	20,703	19,503	17,853
North Dakota	11,970	11,961	10,968	10,944
South Dakota	14,221	14,121	13,001	12,466
Wyoming	10,238	9,685	9,326	8,785

* Personal income is the income received by persons from all sources—private and government wage and salary disbursements, other labor income, farm and nonfarm self-employment income, rental income of persons, personal dividend income, personal interest income and transfer payments—and is reported in current dollars.
Source: U.S. Department of Commerce, Bureau of Economic Analysis, Regional Economic Information; and Bureau of the Census. 1995 preliminary income data released April 25, 1996; 1992-1994 revised data released June 4, 1996.

notable
$\mathcal{M}$ontanans

Dennis Washington (1935-)

Chairman of Washington Corporation in Missoula, this Montana industrialist has been on the *Forbes* magazine list of the 400 richest Americans since 1989. He ranked 103rd in 1996. He heads some forty ventures that rake in revenues of an estimated $2.2 billion, according to *Forbes*.

In 1995, Washington was a recipient of the Horatio Alger Award, which is given to ten distinguished Americans who have overcome adversity to achieve success. He was bedridden with polio at age eight. Having recovered from the disease, he worked heavy construction as a young adult and managed the largest highway construction project in the state for his uncle, Bud King. In 1964, with a $30,000 loan, he started his own highway construction business and became the largest contractor in Montana before moving into dam building and mining. He bought the Anaconda Company copper mine in Butte and other holdings from Atlantic Richfield in 1986.

Washington Corporation bought Burlington Northern Railroad's southern Montana system in 1988 and revitalized it as Montana Rail Link. Besides a home in Missoula and a lodge in Canada, Washington owns trains, boats, and planes.

Lester Thurow (1938-)

Thurow, the world-renowned economist, was born in Livingston and attended school in various Montana communities. He attended Oxford University as a Rhodes Scholar and received his doctorate from Harvard in 1964. After teaching economics there, he moved across Cambridge to the Massachusetts Institute of Technology, later becoming the dean of MIT's Sloan School of Management. In 1974, *Time* magazine named him one of America's two hundred rising leaders. Thurow, who stepped down as dean in 1993, still teaches at MIT and has written eleven books and hundreds of articles on economics. His latest book is entitled *Head to Head: The Coming Economic Battle Among Japan, Europe, and America.* He describes himself as an "economics educator" and enjoys mountain climbing in his leisure time.

Tourism

Even since its earliest days, the state has attracted tourists to its many splendors and attractions. The long-standing prediction has come to pass that preserving the state's natural resources would sustain tourism and assure economic prosperity.

In 1995, tourism brought about $1.22 billion to the state from nonresident visitors. Hundreds of businesses benefited from the 7.9 million persons who visited Montana that year, more than nine times the population of the state.

While visitors to Montana have increased 36 percent since 1988, the 1 percent growth in visitors from 1994 to 1995 was the slowest since 1986. After six consecutive years of increased numbers of visitors, Glacier National Park suffered a 13.5 percent decrease from 1994 to 1995. Yellowstone National Park, though, with a 2.6 percent increase, had its best season ever: more than 3.1 million people visited.

SELECTED INDICATORS OF THE
Contributions of Tourism: 1995

- Nonresident and resident travel within the state was up 4.1 percent.
- Airport deboardings increased about 8 percent, ahead of the national percentage increase of 4.2 percent. Kalispell had the highest increase with 14.4 percent. Billings ranked second, with 8.2 percent.
- Skier visits were up 4.6 percent from the previous year. This figure has averaged a 4.7 percent increase per year over the past decade.
- Hungry Horse, Libby, and Fort Peck Dams had increases in visitors.
- The Grant-Kohrs Ranch, near Deer Lodge, had almost a 13 percent increase in visitors.
- Canada-to-Montana border crossings were down 9.6 percent from 1994.
- Each year, Montana receives about 400,000 requests for information on visiting the state.

Source: Norma Polovitz Nickerson and Neal A. Christensen, The 1996 Outlook for Travel and Tourism in Montana. *The University of Montana-Missoula: Institute for Tourism and Recreation Research, Spring, 1996.*

Growing Tourism

The following visitation figures for U.S. Department of the Interior National
Park Service sites reflect the increase in visitors Montana saw in the 1980s and
early 1990s.

Visitation at National Parks & Monuments		
	Number of Visitors	
Site	**1980**	**1992**
Yellowstone National Park	1,991,002	3,144,405
Glacier National Park	1,475,538	2,199,767
Little Bighorn National Monument	222,546	331,404
Big Hole National Battlefield	37,317	64,177
Grant-Kohrs Ranch Nat'l Historic Site	18,909	27,853

Popular Attractions

Though no definitive list exists for the most popular tourist attractions in the
state, Travel Montana, a division of the state Department of Commerce, regards
the following places as among the most popular. They are ranked according to
visitor attendance figures provided voluntarily by the sites.

Montana's Most Popular Attractions		
	Number of Visitors (May 1-Sept. 31)	
Site	**1995**	**1996**
Yellowstone National Park	2,841,147	2,750,385
Glacier National Park	1,717,747	1,598,416
Little Bighorn National Monument	353,638	318,528
Fort Peck Dam	221,412	212,321
Bighorn Canyon Nat'l. Recreation Area	272,067	189,797
National Bison Range (Moiese)	144,504	131,456
Libby Dam	164,285	129,938
Museum of the Rockies	102,859	82,207
Montana Historical Society, Helena	58,545	58,679
Lewis & Clark Caverns State Park	60,290	56,372

Tourist Regions

The Montana Department of Commerce, Travel Division, divides Montana into six tourist regions. Contact these offices for information on the various recreational activities and attractions of each area. Call (800) 847-4868 (outside MT) or 444-2654 (in MT).

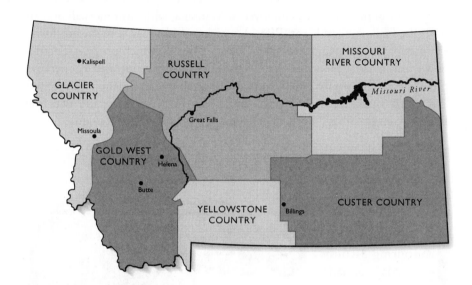

Glacier Country

1507 First Avenue West
Kalispell, MT 59901
(800) 338-5072
756-7128

Gold West Country

1155 Main Street
Deer Lodge, MT 59722
846-1943
(800) 876-1159

Russell Country

Box 3166
Great Falls, MT 59403
(800) 527-5348
761-5036

Yellowstone Country

Box 1107
Red Lodge, MT 59068
(800) 736-5276
446-1005

Missouri River Country

Box 387
Wolf Point, MT 59201
(800) 653-1319
653-1319

Custer Country

Route 1, Box 1206A
Hardin, MT 59034
665-1671
(800) 346-1876 ext. 6

Infrastructure

Utilities

Various public and private utilities provide the state with electrical and natural gas service. Private utilities include Montana Power Company (MPC), the second largest nongovernment employer in Montana, with customers all over the state; Pacific Power and Light (PP&L), which provides service to the northwestern part of the state; and Montana-Dakota Utilities, which provides electrical power and natural gas to eastern Montana. Consumer-operated cooperatives provide power to nearly 300,000 rural and small-town residences in the state. Twenty-six rural electrical co-ops, twenty-four from Montana and two from Idaho, maintain 47,000 miles of cooperative power lines in Montana.

In 1902, Big Timber's power supply was disrupted by a touring 3-ton circus elephant whose sitz bath blocked up the 3-mile ditch from the Boulder River used for power generation.

Telecommunications

The U S West company provides local telecommunication services to 70 percent of the state's population. Though it has gone by a number of names, the company was incorporated in 1881.

Montana has eighteen smaller independent telephone companies and co-operatives, listed below:

Telephone Companies and Cooperatives

Local Carrier	Year Incorporated	Counties Served	Miles of Lines	Lines per Mile*	Employees
Southern Montana Telephone Company	1904	Beaverhead, Deer Lodge, Silver Bow	631	1.27	7
Lincoln Telephone Cooperative	1921	Lewis & Clark	316	3.37	6
Project Telephone Company, Inc.	1946	Big Horn, Carbon, Stillwater, Yellowstone	1,342	1.76	16
Nemont Telephone Cooperative	1950	Daniels, McCone, Phillips, Roosevelt, Sheridan, Valley	4,909	0.56	89
Mid-Rivers Telephone Cooperative, Inc.	1952	Big Horn, Carter, Custer, Dawson, Fallon, Fergus, Garfield, Golden Valley, McCone, Musselshell, Petroleum, Phillips, Prairie, Richland, Roosevelt, Rosebud, Treasure, Wheatland, Wibaux, Yellowstone	8,762	1.12	76
Range Telephone Cooperative, Inc.	1953	Big Horn, Carter, Custer, Powder River, Rosebud, Treasure	4,872	1.09	29
3 Rivers Telephone Cooperative, Inc.	1953	Beaverhead, Cascade, Chouteau, Gallatin, Glacier, Judith Basin, Lewis & Clark, Liberty, Madison, Pondera, Silver Bow, Teton, Toole	6,317	2.29	81
Blackfoot Telephone Cooperative	1954	Granite, Lake, Missoula, Powell, Ravalli, Sanders	2,144	3.09	93
Northern Telephone Cooperative	1954	Glacier, Liberty, Toole	1,500	0.90	10
Triangle Telephone Cooperative Assn., Inc.	1954	Blaine, Chouteau, Fergus, Golden Valley, Hill, Liberty, Musselshell, Park, Phillips, Stillwater, Sweet Grass, Wheatland, Yellowstone	6,759	1.38	42
Hot Springs Telephone Co.	1955	Lake, Sanders	123	5.79	6
Interbel Telephone Cooperative, Inc.	1962	Lincoln	770	1.82	15
Ronan Telephone Co.	1971	Lake	180	17.26	23
PTI Communications	1973	Flathead, Lake, Sander	3,500	17	150
Central Montana Communications	1993	Blaine, Chouteau, Fergus, Judith Basin, Meagher, Phillips, Wheatland	3,097	2.43	27
Citizens Telecommunications of Montana	1993	Lincoln	Data not provided	Data not provided	11
Clark Fork Telecommunications	1993	Granite, Mineral, Sanders	1,057	6.52	**
Valley Telecommunications	1993	Roosevelt, Sheridan, Valley	138	46.45	14

* Refers to access lines, the lines between utility poles and buildings.
** Employees hired through Blackfoot and leased to Clark Fork.
Source: 1996 Montana Telecommunications Directory. Great Falls: Montana Telephone Association, 1996.

The Cost of INFORMATION

In 1994, Montana state government spent $46 million, or 3 percent of the state budget, for expanding information and tele-communications systems. Over six thousand state-owned computers are utilized in government agencies across the state.

There are more than 1,300 miles of fiber optic cables that connect all of the major communities in the state and some of the smaller communities. These cables allow for new interactive video and television services in these communities. They also allow for faster data transmission speeds.

The state is served by four long-distance companies that are referred to as interexchange carriers. These companies are AT&T, MCI Telecommunications Corporation, Sprint Communications Company, and Touch America.

Montana state government provides a number of telecommunications services that are available to the citizens of the state. The Information Services Division provides a central Bulletin Board Service (BBS) that provides a variety of information like road conditions, legislative information, supreme court decisions, public meeting notices, and board vacancies. There is also METNET, the Montana Educational Telecommunications Network, which is managed cooperatively by the Department of Administration and the Office of Public Instruction.

To access the METNET, call (800) 803-6393 within Montana or 444-4851 (local and out-of-state).

To access the state BBS, call (800) 962-1729 within Montana and 444-5648 (local and out-of-state).

Several state agencies provide additional information technology to citizens of Montana. The Department of Commerce has a Superhost Program that provides visitor information centers in Culbertson, Dillon, Hardin, and West Yellowstone with computerized information on lodging facilities, campgrounds, chambers of commerce, car rental agencies, museums, restaurants, and churches. It also includes information about road conditions, ski reports, weather reports, fire conditions, and recreational area closures.

The Department of Revenue has two electronic tax reporting systems. One allows employers to file and to pay state income tax withholding and liability tax electronically. Another electronic filing system allows individuals to file state income taxes electronically.

Railroads

Railroads were vital in the development of mining, agriculture, tourism, and other commerce in Montana. Farmers and ranchers needed the railroads to enable them to reach their markets. Mining corporations utilized the railroads to transport heavy equipment to their operations in Montana, to move their ore to smelters, and to export metal products to the world.

The Utah and Northern, a branch of the Union Pacific Railroad, came north from Ogden, Utah, to the site of Dillon in 1880, and marched on to the promising mining town of Butte by December of 1881. In September of 1883, the Northern Pacific celebrated the connection of its east-west, transcontinental route with a "golden spike" ceremony near Gold Creek (between present-day Garrison and Drummond).

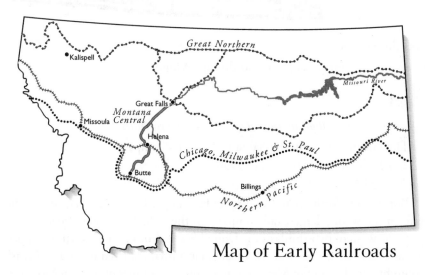

Map of Early Railroads

In 1887, James J. Hill made railroad history when his crew of 9,000 men finished the 550-mile line of the St. Paul, Minneapolis, & Manitoba Railroad from Minot, North Dakota, to Great Falls in less than eight months. Helena's Col. Charles Broadwater completed Hill's Montana Central line from Great Falls to Butte, via Helena, in 1889. This hard-won route provided Hill and the copper kings with a direct shipping route to the Great Lakes.

That same year, Hill and his associates consolidated their holdings to form the Great Northern Railway Company. This company expanded westward from Havre over Marias Pass through Columbia Falls and Kalispell and into Idaho. It reached Seattle in 1893. The well-managed Great Northern Railway Company not only survived the nationwide depression of 1893-94, but Hill and associates acquired controlling shares of the troubled Northern Pacific. The Great Northern and Northern Pacific were known as the "Hill Lines," and Hill was crowned the "Empire Builder."

The Chicago, Burlington & Quincy Railroad reached the Montana site of Huntley in 1894, with an agreement to use Northern Pacific track into Billings. In 1901 Hill and the other owners of Great Northern and Northern Pacific purchased control of the Burlington, which had a direct connection to Chicago. In 1969 these holdings became the Burlington Northern. The Chicago, Milwaukee and St. Paul Railway Company, "the Milwaukee Road," completed a line through central Montana and along the Clark Fork River to Seattle in 1909. This railroad was the last main line construction in Montana but made history as the first long-distance electrified rail span in America.

Freight Trains

Seven rail lines carry freight in and through Montana:

Class I

more than $250 million in annual gross operating revenues

> The Burlington Northern Santa Fe Railway Company
> 235 Main Street, Havre, MT 59501
> 265-0416

Burlington Northern and The Santa Fe Railway Company merged in 1996 to form the second largest rail company in the U.S. The new railroad system spans the western two-thirds of the United States, from Pacific Northwest ports to the Great Lakes and from two Canadian provinces (Manitoba and British Columbia) to the Gulf of Mexico. It operates 2,244 miles of track in Montana, about 66 percent of Montana's rail system. Two of its twenty-two operating divisions are located in the state—the Montana Division, based in Havre, and the Yellowstone Division, based in Glendive. Coal, wheat and other farm products, lumber, container freight, automotive goods, and general merchandise are the main commodities that it carries. Approximately thirty-five trains move across the northern line in a day; about twenty across the southern route.

> Union Pacific (UP)
> 1416 Dodge Street,
> Omaha, NE 68179
> (402) 271-5000

This railroad operates 125.8 miles of track from Butte south through Dillon into the state of Idaho, and accounts for 3.7 percent of the rail in the state. It provides access to the Pacific Northwest, the Southwest, and California. The primary products it carries are grain, talc, stone, lumber, wood, and chemicals.

Class II

$20 million - $250 million in annual gross revenues

Montana Rail Link (MRL)
101 International Way
P.O. Box 8779, Missoula, MT 59807-1500
523-1500

MRL extends from Huntley, Montana, to Sandpoint, Idaho, to serve southwest Montana. It operates 808.5 miles in Montana, 24 percent of the rail system in the state. This is the second largest railroad operating in the state. Grain, coal, lumber, and wood products are the main goods it carries.

Class III

less than $20 million in annual gross revenues. These lines deliver loaded rail cars to the Class I and II railroads:

Montana Western (MW)
700-1/2 Railroad Avenue Butte, MT 59701
782-1249

This line has 58.1 miles of track. It provides a connection between Montana Rail Link at Garrison and the Union Pacific and RARUS railroads at Silver Bow. This is considered essentially a "bridge" carrier, which is a railroad that primarily handles traffic between two other railroads and has little or no originating and terminating traffic. It also carries talc, fertilizer, lumber, grain, and other commodities to and from the Port of Montana in Butte.

RARUS (RARW)
300 West Commercial, P.O. Box 1070
Anaconda, MT 59711-1070
563-7121

This is a segment of the old Butte, Anaconda and Pacific Railroad that was donated to the State of Montana in 1985 by ARCO, which operated the Butte copper mines. This short line was formed and leased from the state in 1985 and operates 25.29 miles or 0.8 percent of the Montana rail, between Butte and Anaconda. It transports copper residue, slag, and scrap.

Central Montana Rail (CMR)
P.O. Box 868
Denton, MT 59430-0868
567-2223

CMR operates 84.2 miles of track out of the Lewistown area. This line was formed in 1984 from a branch that was abandoned by the Burlington Northern Railroad, obtained by the state, and turned over to a nonprofit corporation to manage in order to preserve service on this short line. Its main products are grain and fertilizer.

Dakota, Missouri Valley and Western (DMVW)
2101 East Broadway
Bismarck, ND 58501
(701) 223-9282

This railroad leases 56.6 miles of rail line in the northeast corner of the state.

notable Montanans

Thomas C. Power (1839-1923)

Born in Dubuque, Iowa, Power rode up the Missouri to Fort Benton on a riverboat in 1867 with a shipment of dry goods. He stored the goods in a large tent, which was loaned to him from his soon-to-be rival, I. G. Baker. By the following year, Power and his brother John had entered the freighting business, transshipping goods from Fort Benton by wagons and teams of draft animals. Power invested his fortune in scores of businesses. Evidence suggests he founded or had interest in almost one hundred firms, most of them involved with cattle, sheep, mining, and freight. He formed several stagecoach lines and was a founding partner of the Judith Cattle Company in the late 1870s. He moved to Helena in 1878, where he had established a store and where he would enter politics. In 1889, he lost the new state's first election for governor by a slim margin but was chosen by Republicans for a seat in the U.S. Senate later that year.

Montana Historical Society

Freight Service and Parcel Delivery

Of the 7,000 motor carriers operating in Montana, about 650 operate just within the state's borders, with the rest providing service to the entire United States, Mexico, and Canada. The Montana Public Service Commission has jurisdiction over the intrastate carriers, and the Interstate Commerce Commission regulates the interstate carriers.

Several courier and freight express services are available in Montana, providing delivery to most places in the U.S. and many international locations. The U.S. Postal Service has more than four hundred facilities in Montana.

notable
Montanans

Isaac Gilbert Baker (1819-1904)

Montana Historical Society

Baker, a native of Connecticut, came by riverboat to Fort Benton several times in the 1860s, trading with Indians and supplying the fort's trading post. On one trip he brought 400 tons of goods. Though he served as chief clerk for fur trader Pierre Chouteau, Jr., at the fort, by the mid-1860s, he had broken off to form a trading company with his brother George. Like Power, Baker stocked the shelves of his Fort Benton stores and warehouses with everything from agricultural implements and mining equipment to fine wines, cigars, and silks. Later he expanded his interests into mining, banking, freighting, and other businesses. By 1874, he had moved downriver to St. Louis and supervised his empire from there.

Before the Royal Canadian Mounted Police put a stop to illegal trade and transport of whiskey, Baker's and Power's companies were known to engage in both illegal practices along the Whoop-Up Trail, a freight route from Fort Benton to Fort Whoop-Up in Alberta.

The Gambling Industry

The gaming industry, especially video gaming machines, plays a significant part in Montana's economy. In 1988, there were about 8,000 video gaming machines in Montana, producing about $70 million in income reported for tax purposes and earning the state $10.5 million in tax revenue. By 1995, $208 million in income on about 15,000 machines was reported with a tax revenue of $31 million. This $31 million is split, with a third going to the state and the other two-thirds going to local governments.

Video gaming machines were legalized in 1985. There are three types of video games: poker, keno, and bingo.

In 1996, live horse racing was held at seven sites in the state from mid-May to the third week in September. There were ten establishments around the state offering simulcast horse racing.

The following pie chart shows that of the six forms of legalized gambling in Montana, video machines rate as the overwhelming favorite.

Percentage of Gambling Activity, 1994

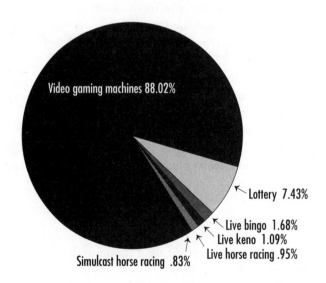

Video gaming machines 88.02%

Lottery 7.43%

Live bingo 1.68%
Live keno 1.09%
Live horse racing .95%

Simulcast horse racing .83%

Amount Wagered on Selected Gambling Activities*

Activity	1992	1993	1994
Video Gambling Machines+	$358.8	$397.0	$444.5
Lottery	28.0	36.8	37.5
Commercial Live Bingo	11.1	9.4	8.5
Commercial Live Keno	6.1	5.7	5.5
Live Horse Racing **	5.2	5.8	4.8
Simulcast Racing ***	3.7	5.4	4.2
Totals	$412.9	$460.1	$505.0

* Dollar amounts given in millions.

** Live season covers May through September of each year.

*** Covers winter season (October-May).

\+ Figures for amounts wagered on video gaming machines include credits played and may not translate to cash paid out to players.

Source: Mont. Dept. of Justice, Gambling Control Division. Biennial Report (FY 1993 and 1994). Gaming Advisory Council, Helena: May 1995.

Distribution of Gambling Revenues (FY 1994)

Revenue Source	Total Distributed	Local Gov't	Gambling Control Account	General Fund
Video Gambling Machine Tax	$30,052,587	$20,020,455	$0	$10,032,132
Bingo/Keno Tax	$30,728	$30,728	$0	$0
Sports Tab Tax	$2,304	$0	$2,304	$0
Video Gambling Machines Permit Fees	3,082,750	$1,541,375	$1,541,375	$0
Bingo/Keno Permit Fees	$21,375	$0	$21,375	$0
Card Table Permit Fees	$79,500	$53,200	$26,300	$0
Casino Night Permit Fees	$350	$0	$350	$0
Antique Slot Dealer	$150	$0	$150	$0
Operator License Fees	$108,546	$0	$108,546	$0
Card Dealer License Fees	$19,125	$0	$19,125	$0
Card Room Contractor Fees	$3,450	$0	$3,450	$0
Manufacturer License Fees *	$189,739	$0	$189,739	$0
TOTALS	$33,590,604	$21,645,758	$1,912,714	$10,032,132

* Includes fees from the following licenses: manufacturer, distributor, route operator, manufacturer of illegal gambling devices, sports tab card manufacturer, and manufacturer of electronic live bingo and keno equipment.

Source: Montana Department of Justice, Gambling Control Division. Biennial Report, (Fiscal Years 1994 and 1995). Helena: 1996.

Lotteries

The 1985 Legislature approved a referendum to allow for a state lottery. The referendum was sent to the voters on the November 1986 ballot and won approval by almost 70 percent of the voters. The first scratch or "instant win" game was "Pot of Gold," which went on sale in June 1987. These games are changed frequently; a new game is introduced every six weeks.

Montana Cash was established in May 1991 with a minimum jackpot of $20,000. The odds of winning are 1 in 217,949.

Powerball is a twenty-state drawing partnership that was established in April of 1992 with nine prize levels. This replaced the Lotto America game, which had five Montana jackpot winners during its lifetime. The odds are 1 in 54 million for winning the jackpot and 1 in 35 of winning some prize.

Tri-West Lotto was established in February 1994 and is available in Montana, Idaho, and South Dakota. There are four prize levels with overall odds of 1 in 32. The odds for winning the jackpot are 1 in 1,107,568. Drawings for Powerball, Tri-West, and Montana Cash are held on Wednesday and Saturday nights.

The Montana Lottery is governed by a five-member commission, appointed by the governor, which sets policies and oversees the operation of the lottery. The governor also appoints the lottery director, who supervises the security, operations, and marketing divisions. The lottery is administratively affiliated with the state Department of Commerce.

Lotteries Montanans Play

Name of Game	Cost of Chance	Potential Jackpot	Odds
Montana Cash	$0.50	$20,000 - Up	1 in 217,949
Powerball	$1.00	$5,000,000 - Up	1 in 55,000,000
Tri-West	$1.00	$150,000 - Up	1 in 1,107, 568

BIG Winners

In March 1996, two waitresses at Helena's House of Wong won $1,437,007, the largest Montana Tri-West Lotto prize ever. One woman had worked there for thirty years, the other for twenty-six. The two friends bought a ticket together every Wednesday since the game began in February 1994.

Where the Lottery Money Goes

Until July 1, 1995, most of the net lottery revenue (90.9 percent of net) was dedicated to the State Equalization Aid Account, a source of funding for Montana's elementary and secondary public schools. To that date, the lottery transferred over $49 million to Montana's public schools. In July 1991, the Board of Crime Control began receiving a small portion of the lottery's net revenue to help fund the operation of juvenile detention centers. The Board of Crime Control received $89,325 the first year (1.6 percent of revenue) and 9.1 percent of the net after that (not to exceed $1 million per fiscal year) for a total of more than $2.6 million.

Beginning July 1, 1995, the Legislature redirected all lottery net revenue to the State General Fund.

Lottery Revenues, Expenditures and Transfers**

	Fiscal Years							
	87-88	88-89	89-90	90-91	91-92	92-93	93-94	94-95*
Revenue from ticket sales, license fees, investment earnings	$25.6	$11.6	$21.5	$23.9	$28.0	$36.9	$37.6	$32.8
Prizes (minimum of 45% of sales)	11.5	5.3	10.2	11.7	13.6	17.7	18.1	16.1
Commissions and bonuses to retailers	1.4	0.7	1.3	1.3	1.6	2.1	2.1	1.8
Ticket Costs	0.9	0.6	2.9+	4.0	4.2	5.2	4.9	3.5
Operations	3.6	2.1	2.9	2.7	3.0	3.0	3.1	2.8
Proceeds to State Equalization Account	8.3	2.8	4.2	4.2	5.5	8.1	8.5	7.8
Proceeds to Board of Crime Control	N/A	N/A	N/A	N/A	0.1	0.8	0.9	0.8

*Unaudited.
** Amounts in millions of dollars.
+ Increase in ticket costs due to introduction of on-line games in November 1989.
Source: Department of Commerce. Montana Lottery Annual Report, Helena: July 1995.

Problems with Gambling

In a study funded by the state, a random 1,020 Montanans answered questionnaires by telephone. Researchers concluded:

- An estimated 8,000 to 18,600 Montana residents have been problem gamblers at some time in their lives. Another 3,500 to 11,500 Montanans may have been pathological gamblers at some time in their lives.

- Montana is believed to have a higher percentage of female problem and pathological gamblers than other states studied (South Dakota, Iowa, California, New York, New Jersey, Maryland, and Massachusetts).

Of respondents determined to be problem and pathological gamblers:

31 percent wanted to stop gambling but could not.

20 percent admitted to have claimed winning when they in fact lost.

89 percent spent more time or money than they intended.

58 percent felt guilty about the way they gambled.

42 percent spent household money on gambling.

47 percent borrowed money from a spouse.

22 percent cashed bad checks.

11 percent sold personal or family property.

6 percent borrowed money from loan sharks.

3 percent cashed stocks or bonds for gambling money.

At the time of the study (1992), "a minimum of 5,500 adults in Montana (were) experiencing moderate to severe problems related to their involvement in gambling."

Source: Gemini Research, Gambling Involvement and Problem Gambling in Montana. Albany, N.Y.: 1992.

Further Reading:

Larson, Paul. *The Montana Entrepreneur's Handbook.* 2nd ed. N.p.: Montana Business Development Council, 1995.

Montana Business Directory. Published by American Directory Publishing Company. *A list compiled from statewide telephone yellow pages, white pages, chambers of commerce, state and federal government records.*

Montana Business Quarterly. Published by the Bureau of Business and Economic Research, The University of Montana, Missoula.

Montana Labor Employment and Labor Force Trends. Published periodically by the Montana Department of Labor and Industry.

chapter eleven

SPORTS

MANY MONTANANS ARE ACTIVE sports participants. Some compete in amateur leagues. Others either make an appearance or lend a hand at their favorite annual events. The list of activities is long. It includes sports and events you'd find almost anywhere in the U.S.—fast- and slow-pitch softball, baseball, basketball, football, soccer, volleyball, tennis, golf, track and field, sailing, ice and roller hockey, bowling, fishing, motocross races, figure skating, equestrian events, swimming, distance running, and road and mountain biking races. Other popular pastimes and passions pursued here include archery, target and clay shooting, snowmobiling, downhill and cross-country skiing, snowboarding, and dog sledding.

A hearty few of us are called to participate in rodeo; thousands more of us choose to stay glued to our seats in the stands, content to just watch.

Almost each week during the school year, tens of thousands of fans gather in gymnasiums and beside playing fields to cheer on Montana's high school and college teams. Even the smallest high schools field teams for basketball, football, volleyball, and track and field. At the other end of the scale, The University of Montana's Washington-Grizzly Stadium can accommodate 18,800 fans and all the noise they can muster.

Montana has a rich history of professional baseball and today the "national pastime" continues to draw fans to ball parks in Billings, Butte, Great Falls, and Helena to watch minor league games. A junior hockey league operating teams in five Montana cities has begun to develop a similar following. These leagues may

photo: Montana State University

not be the majors but Montanans get the chance to watch contests in comparably intimate settings and pay a fraction of the cost to sit in a cavernous big league stadium.

Under the Big Sky, competitors strive for big wins and grand achievements. In the following pages, we recognize some of their feats.

notable
Montanans

Dave McNally (1942-)

He pitched his way from Billings, where he played brilliantly in American Legion ball, to the World Series, where, playing for the Baltimore Orioles in the 1970 series, he hit a grand slam in the third game. The homer helped the Orioles beat Cincinnati, 9-3, and they went on to win the series, 4-1. McNally helped the team to 184 victories during the 1960s and 1970s. From 1968-71, he recorded at least twenty wins each year. His 21-5 record in 1971 amounted to a .808 winning percentage, the best in the American League that season. He currently lives in Billings, where he owns a car dealership.

 Alice Greenough Orr (1902-1995)

She was born in Red Lodge into the Greenough family of rodeo performers and was one of five siblings known as the Riding Greenoughs. Later in her life, the rodeo world crowned her "Queen of the Bronc Riders." She won four world saddle bronc championships in the 1930s and 1940s, had tea with the Queen of England, and rubbed shoulders with the likes of Will Rogers and Ernest Hemingway. She

Montana Historical Society

thrilled crowds around the world as a performer in Wild West shows and international rodeos. In 1975, she was the first inductee into the Cowgirl Hall of Fame and was named to the National Cowboy Hall of Fame in 1983. She died in her sleep in Tucson, Arizona, at the age of 93.

Montana Sports Trivia Quiz

What's your Montana sports IQ? Here are the questions.
The answers are at the end of the chapter on p. 388,
but no peeking.

1. She was a two-time world champion bull rider (in 1986 and 1988), a model, and a movie stunt consultant, and was named a CNN woman of the '80s. Who is she and where is she from?

2. What three high schools have each won three state volleyball championships?

3. He played center and offensive tackle for The University of Montana Grizzlies (1976 to 1979), the New York Jets, and the Atlanta Falcons. He retired from professional play and now lives in Missoula. Who is he?

4. What high school has won fourteen state wrestling championships?

5. His skiing career started in Whitefish and reached its zenith in Albertville, France, in 1994 when he won the Olympic gold medal in downhill skiing. Who is he?

6. Name the five Montana teams that compete in the American Frontier Pro Hockey League.

7. He played as a defensive tackle for The University of Montana Grizzlies in 1963 and 1964, then went on to an eleven-year pro career with the Chicago Bears, Minnesota Vikings, New Orleans Saints, Houston Oilers, and Atlanta Falcons. He now lives in Chinook. Who is he?

8. The total distance of the passes Dave Dickenson completed at The University of Montana would clear the summit of which of the following mountains:
    a.) Mount Jumbo
    b.) Granite Peak
    c.) Big Rock Candy Mountain
    d.) Mount Everest (highest mountain in the world)
    e.) each of the above

9. He was born in Norway and came to Montana State University on a skiing scholarship. He joined the football team in his junior year as placekicker, and in 1966 established the NCAA record for the most points in a season for a kicker. The next thing we knew, he was kicking field goals for the Kansas City Chiefs (1967-79), the Green Bay Packers (1980-83), and the Minnesota Vikings (1984-85). He kicked his way into the Pro Football

Hall of Fame in 1991. Who is he?

10. What year did the Montana State University Bobcats win the NCAA Division I-AA football championship?

11. Besides being the state's first woman lieutenant governor, Judi Martz was also one of the two first women Olympians from Montana. In what sport did she compete and at what Olympiad?

12. What winter Olympic event was Kari Swenson training for when she was kidnapped, held in the mountains, and shot?

13. Rachel Myllymaki, from Arlee, is a four-time champion on the Montana Circuit and the youngest rider ever to qualify for the National Finals Rodeo. She placed ninth in her event there in 1994. a.) What event is she known for and b.) how old was she when she qualified?

14. What high school's boys' cross-country team has won a record 17 state championships, including 11 straight from 1974 to 1984?

15. He threw the discus for Montana State University where he achieved All-American status in 1984 but had even greater success after college in the hammer throw. At the 1996 Atlanta Olympics, he earned the U.S. its first medal, a silver, in the hammer since 1956. Who is he?

Ring of
Gold

Montana's first professional sports event, a boxing match between Virginia City saloonkeeper Con Orem and local miner Hugh O'Neil, was staged outdoors on January 2, 1865. The fight ended in a draw, with each fighter receiving $1,000 and various sacks of gold tossed into the ring by enthusiastic fans.

High School Sports

The Teams and Their Mascots

You learned your ABCs a long time ago, but do you know your As, double As, Bs, and Cs? Montana's twelve largest high schools compete as Class AA schools. There are 20 Class A high school teams, 42 Class B teams, and 101 Class C teams. Nine teams from nonpublic high schools also compete with the public school teams.

You also may know your Dolphins from your Marlins and your Pirates from your Buccaneers, but Montana's high school team names or mascots cover a wide variety of species. There are:

9 Bulldogs	Brady, Broadwater, Butte, Carter County, Choteau, Hardin, Moore, St. Ignatius, and Whitefish high schools.
9 Panthers	Alberton, Belgrade, Jefferson, Park City, Roundup, Peerless, Saco, Sheridan, and Valier.
8 Eagles	Blue Sky, Fairfield, Manhattan Christian, Missoula Big Sky, Northern Cheyenne, Sidney, Two Eagle River, and Valley Christian.

Understandably, we have Cowboys (at Conrad, Culbertson, and Custer County), Wranglers (at Geyser and Rosebud), Rustlers (at Great Falls C.M. Russell), Horsemen (at Plains), Herders (at Sweet Grass County), and, to accompany those, Dogies (at Forsyth), Broncs (at Billings Senior, Frenchtown, Hamilton, Melstone, and Willow Creek), Mustangs (at Ennis, Garfield County, the Montana School for the Deaf and Blind, Malta, and Shepherd), Colts (at Colstrip), and Longhorns (at Fort Benton).

Harder to figure in this landlocked state are our seven Pirates (at Broadview, Hysham, Polson, Power, Reedpoint, Roy, and Victor) and the Vikings (at Charlo and Opheim). We have no Vigilantes.

We do have Bats (in our Belfry), Penguins (at Whitewater), Copperheads (in the former smelting center of Anaconda), Locomotives (at Laurel), Engineers (at Harlowton), Miners (at Centerville), Wardens (at Deer Lodge, the town with the state prison), and Refiners (in Sunburst, where oil was discovered in 1923).

We have Red Devils (at Dawson County, Noxon, and Huntley Project), Blue Devils (at Corvallis), Red Raiders (at Winifred), Bluejays (at Outlook), Blue Ponies (at Havre), Bluehawks (at Thompson Falls), Blackhawks (at Seeley-Swan), Golden Bears (at Billings West), Golden Eagles (at Fergus), and Yellowjackets (at Stevensville).

There are Rockets (at Rapelje and Roberts) and the Morning Stars (girls) and Northern Stars (boys), at Rocky Boy.

We run the gamut from Demons (at Ryegate) and Savages (at Hot Springs) to Royals (at Richey). Perhaps the team that has garnered us the most attention, though, is the Sugar Beeters of Chinook High School, recognized nationwide on *Late Night with David Letterman* for having the strangest mascot that could be found.

For the Record Books (as of 1995)

Football

- Most state championships: 14 by Butte (1924, 27, 29, 30, 31, 35, 37, 40, 41, 67, 68, 77, 81, 91).
- Most all-time wins: 427 by Great Falls (since 1918).
- Most undefeated seasons: 6 by Dawson (Glendive) and Charlo.
- Most game points scored by one team: 144 by Dawson (Glendive) against Custer (Miles City) (1919).
- Most career touchdowns: 78 by Ryan Herman, Terry (1989-92).
- Most offensive career yards: 5,980 by Dave Dickenson, Great Falls CMR (1989-90).
- Most yards in a season: 3,331 by Dave Dickenson, Great Falls CMR (1990).
- Most yards averaged per game, season: 277.6 by Dave Dickenson, Great Falls CMR (1990).
- Most career passing yards: 5,104 by Dave Dickenson, Great Falls CMR (1989-1990).
- Best career pass completion percentage: 64.0% by Dave Dickenson, Great Falls CMR (1989-90).
- Longest punt return: 85 yards by Charles Hood, Custer (Miles City) (1956).
- Most field goals in a career: 25 by Tim Klinger, Great Falls (1987-89).
- Winningest coach: Bob Cleverley, Ennis, 199 wins (1964-92).
- Coach with most state championships: Jack Johnson, 10 titles for Great Falls CMR (1975, 76, 80, 82, 84, 85, 86, 89, 90, 92).

Boys Cross-Country

- Most state championships: 17 by Browning (1971, 74-84, 86, 87, 89, 90, 91)
- Most consecutive wins: 11 by Browning (1974-84).
- Four-time individual state champion: Fernandel Omeasoo, Browning (1977-80).
- Winningest coaches: Sam Samson, Jefferson (Boulder), 10 between 1978 and 1992; Randy Shapiro/Browning, 10 between 1980 and 1991.

Girls Cross-Country

- Most state championships: 11 by Flathead (Kalispell) (1971, 72, 80, 86, 87, 88, 89, 91, 93, 94, 96).

- Most consecutive state championships: 8 by Glasgow (1973-80).

- Four-time individual state champions: Kathy Jarvis, Havre (1982-85); Ruby Yellowtail, Lodge Grass (1989-92).

- Coach with most state championships: Paul Jorgensen, Flathead (Kalispell), 9 championships (1980, 86, 87, 88, 89, 91, 93, 94, 96).

CROSS-COUNTRY'S
Low Point

The team with the lowest score wins in cross-country (the first runner gets one point; if a team's first finisher comes in sixth, the team gets six points). The first five runners for each team are combined for the team total.

A team can score no fewer than fifteen points, which happens when a team captures the first five places—a "shutout." Though a strong team can easily earn a shutout in a dual meet with a weak team, it's extremely rare to shut out the field in a championship race. It's been done once in the history of Montana high school cross-country, when the girls from Hot Springs took the first five places in the 1971 Class C race. Two boys' teams have come close to a championship shutout, scoring 16 points: Browning in the 1975 Class A race, and Jefferson (Boulder) in the 1987 Class B race.

Girls Basketball

- Most state championships: 4 by Great Falls (1974, 80, 81, 82) and Billings Central (1985, 86, 87, 90).

- Most consecutive state championships: 3 by Great Falls (1980-82).

- Most consecutive wins: 72 by Great Falls (1980-83).

- Most game points scored by two teams: 172 (Flathead defeats Columbia Falls, 87 to 85, in 1983).

- Most game points scored by one team: 126 by Big Sandy (1986).

- Most career points scored: 2,508 by Carla Beattie, Granite (Philipsburg) (1987-90).

- Most points in one game: 58 by Marietta Bahnmiller, Big Sandy (1985).

- Winningest coach: Delmar Fried, Brady and Malta, 426-155 (1972-1997).

Boys Basketball

- Most state championships: 10 by Butte High (1917, 24, 25, 28, 32, 33, 41, 57, 58, 84), Helena High (1914, 15, 16, 19, 45, 53, 54, 55, 71, 91), and Missoula Sentinel (1922, 46, 47, 49, 59, 61, 64, 72, 73, 86).

- Most consecutive state championships: 4 by Sidney (1957, 58, 59, 60).

- Most consecutive wins: 56 by Missoula Sentinel (1962-65).

- Most game points scored by two teams: 224 (Belt defeats Augusta, 127 to 97, in 1993).

- Most game points scored by one team: 152 by Missoula Loyola (1991).

- Most career points scored: 2,763 by Reece Gliko, Highwood (1990-93).

- Winningest coach: Don Peterson, Laurel and Bigfork (546-238).

Soccer

- Most state championships, most consecutive state championships: Missoula Sentinel (1991, 92, 93).

- Most wins in a season: 12 by Missoula Sentinel (1992).

- Most wins in consecutive seasons: 21 by Missoula Sentinel (1991-92).

- Longest winning streak: 8 by Missoula Sentinel (1992).

- Most shutouts in a season: 5 by Missoula Sentinel (1992).

- Most minutes played in a career: 3,290 by Dave Driscoll, Helena Capital (1991-94).

- Most minutes played in a season: 1,245 by Cory Chenoweth, Helena Capital (1994).

- Most goals scored in a career: 23 by Jeremy Stern, Missoula Sentinel (1991-92).

- Most goals scored in a season: 16 by Jeremy Stern, Missoula Sentinel (1992).

- Most assists in a career: 14 by Dave Driscoll, Helena Capital (1991-94).

- Most assists in a season: 8 by Ryan Grinsteiner, Missoula Sentinel (1994).

- Most saves by a goalie in a season: 120 by Paul Clark, Helena Capital (1993).

- Most saves by a goalie in a game: 13 by Paul Clark, Helena Capital (1993).

- Most shutouts by a goalie in a career: 9 by Land Towney, Missoula Sentinel (1991-92).

- Ravi DeSilva, coach at Missoula Sentinel, holds records for: most consecutive wins (8 in 1991-92); most career wins (39 in 1991 and 92); and state championships, the three consecutive titles he led Sentinel to in 1991, 92, and 93. His career record is 55-18-8.

Wrestling

- Longest winning streak (dual meets): 112 by Butte (1981-89).

- Most takedowns by a team in a season (all meets): 1,045 by Billings West (1994).

- Most consecutive wins, individual: 94 by Cody Bryant, Missoula Hellgate (1982-84).

Fastest Falls, by Weight Class

Weight Class	Time	Record Holder	Home Town	Year
98 lbs.	:11	Jerome Faulhaber	Shelby	1990
103 lbs.	:14	Todd Huffman	Missoula	1981
	:14	Brandy Pulver	Valier	1987-88
105 lbs.	:08	Forrest Anderson	Helena	1990
112 lbs.	:06	Larry Detienne	Plentywood	1977
119 lbs.	:08	Mark Mogan	Laurel	1978-79
125 lbs.	:08	Jason Gaskill	Laurel	1988-89
126 lbs.	:12	Pat Mullen	Shelby	1981
130 lbs.	:08	A. J. Welch	Laurel	1987-88
135 lbs.	:07	Shane Nicholas	Shepherd	1993
140 lbs.	:08	Clint Milliron	Laurel	1988-89
	:08	Chilo Perez	Choteau	1989-90
	:08	Ryan Wehding	Baker	1989
145 lbs.	:14	Robert Azure	Harlem	1989-90
152 lbs.	:09	A. J. Bigby	Harlem	1993
	:09	Paul Niederegger	Harlem	1989-90
160 lbs.	:06	Shane Burbank	Huntley Project	1990
171 lbs.	:05	Justin Schwartz	Glendive	1991
185 lbs.	:05	Eugi Wood	Fairfield Chouteau Classic	1983-84
189 lbs.	:08	Weldon Knight	Harlem	1989-90
Unlimited	:04	Jeff Stewart	Fergus	

Fast-Pitch Softball

- Most consecutive wins: 27 by Libby (1992-93).

- Most runs scored in an inning: 19 by Libby, vs. Bigfork (1992).

- Most hits in a season: 335 by Libby (1992).

- Most runs scored in a career: 127 by Kristy Hays, Missoula Hellgate (1992-95).

- Most home runs in a career: 13 by Lindsay Jordan, Billings Senior (1993-95).

- Most home runs in a game: 3 by Kate Hall, Billings Senior (vs. Billings Skyview, 1994).

- Highest season batting average: .629 by Robin Jones, Libby (1993).

Boys Swimming, Fastest Times

Event	Record Holder	Record	Year
50-yd Freestyle	Thad Michalson, Helena Capital	:21.35	1992
100-yd Freestyle	Trent Hartl, Billings West	:46.89	1993
200-yd Freestyle	Trent Hartl, Billings West	1:43.12	1994
500-yd Freestyle	Tom Knapton, Helena Capital	4:54.66	1988
100-yd Backstroke	Jim Kohl, Bozeman	:53.32	1993
100-yd Breaststroke	Scott Newell, Billings Skyview	:59.11	1991
100-yd Butterfly	Scott Smid, Missoula Big Sky	:51.57	1988
200-yd Individual Medley	Barry Flightner, Missoula Sentinel	1:59.44	1991
200-yd Medley Relay	Billings Senior	1:40.93	1993
200-yd Freestyle Relay	Billings West	1:30.07	1994
400-yd Freestyle Relay	Bozeman	3:16.85	1992

Girls Swimming, Fastest Times

Event	Record Holder	Record	Year
50-yd Freestyle	Sarah Robson, Bozeman	:24.29	1987
100-yd Freestyle	Sarah Robson, Bozeman	:52.05	1987
500-yd Freestyle	Jill Rutledge, Bozeman	5:17.68	1986
100-yd Backstroke	Mandy Cuff, Billings Senior	1:01.05	1995
100-yd Breaststroke	Lee Frye, Bozeman	1:08.81	1995
100-yd Butterfly	Jill Rutledge, Bozeman	:59.07	1984
200-yd Individual Medley	Marion Warner, Havre	2:12.87	1984
200-yd Freestyle Relay	Missoula Hellgate	1:57.93	1990

Volleyball

• Most match wins: 77 by Park (Livingston) (1988-91).

• Most service aces by a team in one season: 391 by Billings West (1992).

• Winningest coach: Rich Ramondelli, Troy, 324-95 (1984-95).

Track and Field

• Most Boys State Championships: 24 by Missoula County High School.

• Most Girls State Championships: 14 by Flathead (Kalispell).

• Boys: 70 schools have won at least one state championship.

• Girls: 43 schools have won at least one state championship.

- Boys: 4 Montana high school students have been four-time state champions in their events:

Athlete	School	Event	Years
Bob Hawke	Butte	discus	1962-65
Roy Robinson	Glasgow	100-yard dash	1963-66
Craig Stiles	Malta	javelin	1968-71
Gordon Ruttenbur	Powell	1600 meter run	1979-82

- Roy Robinson also holds the most state championships for an individual, with fifteen—four in the 100-yard dash, three in the 220-yard dash, three in the low hurdles, two in the high hurdles, and three in the 880-yard relay.

- Girls: Eight Montana high school students have been four-time state champions in their events:

Athlete	School	Event	Years
Debbie Hileman	Whitefish	100-yard dash	1970-73
Judith Wildey	Hamilton	440-yard dash	1976-79
Janie Glenny	Harlowton	shot put	1976-79
Terri Holzworth	Richey	400-meter dash	1979-82
Penny Pagett	Seeley-Swan	100-meter hh*	1981-84
Tanya Tesar	Columbia Falls	300-meter lh**	1987-90
Tanya Tesar	Columbia Falls	long jump	1987-90
Katie Rued	Froid	javelin	1987-90
Emily Nay	Helena Capital	1600-meter run	1992-95
Emily Nay	Helena Capital	3200-meter run	1992-95

*hh = high hurdles
**lh = low hurdles

Christy Otte holds the girls title of most individual state championships with thirteen—three in the 200-meter dash, three in the 400-meter dash, three in the 1600-meter relay, two in the 100-meter dash, and two in the 400-meter relay.

Boys Tennis

- Most state championships: 14, Billings West (1971, 75, 76, 78, 79, 80, 81, 82, 83, 84, 86, 87, 88, 89).

- Most consecutive state championships: 7, Billings West (1978-84).

- Roger Mergerth won the state singles championships four times for Missoula Sentinel (1951-54). There are no three-time or four-time winners in the state boys' doubles championships.

- Mergerth is also the winningest coach, holding the record for coaching Billings West to the most state championships and most consecutive titles, as detailed above.

High School Track and Field

Event	Record Holder	Individual Record
100-Meter Dash	Boys: Craig Galle, Flathead (Kalispell) Girls: Pala Good, Fort Benton	:10.81 (1994) :12.14 (1982)
200-Meter Dash	Boys: Dan Hanley, Butte Girls: Vicky Sturn, Billings West	:21.51 (1981) :24.64 (1975)
400-Meter Dash	Boys: Hal Anderson, Billings Senior Mike Guon, Great Falls Girls: Denise Pidcock, Great Falls CMR	:48.04 (1973) :48.04 (1976) :56.44 (1980)
800-Meter Run	Boys: Stacey Smiedala, Billings West Girls: Julie Brown, Billings Senior	1:51.84 (1986) 2:11.14 (1973)
1600-Meter Run	Boys: Dereck Stordahl, Great Falls Girls: Kathy Jarvis, Havre	4:14.94 (1986) 4:58.44 (1984)
3200-Meter Run	Boys: Branch Brady, Great Falls Girls: Emily Nay, Helena Capital	9:10.34 (1965) 10:38.4 (1995)
Intermediate Hurdles	Boys: Jason Brockel, Billings West Girls: Paula Payne, Great Falls CMR	:37.74 (1985) :43.54 (1981)
High Hurdles	Boys: Jamison Banna, Flathead (Kalispell) Girls: Claudine Robinson, Missoula Hellgate	:14.11 (1988) :14.34 (1990)
Pole Vault	Boys: Todd Foster, Helena Bill Halverson, Great Falls Girls: Laura Daniel, Absarokee Shannon Agee, Helena, Suzanne Krings, Helena Capital	15'9" (1988) 15'9" (1976) 10'6" (1995) 10'6" (1996) 10'6" (1996)
High Jump	Boys: Mark Reed, Great Falls Girls: Pam Spencer, Great Falls	7'2" (1983) 5'11" (1975)
Long Jump	Boys: Harry Clark, Cascade Girls: Janice Anderson, Malta	23'10" (1984) 19'3¾" (1978)
Triple Jump	Boys: Mark Reed, Great Falls Girls: Kim Tivey, Missoula Big Sky	48'10¼" (1983) 38'3" (1985)
Shot Put	Boys: Dennis Black, Great Falls Girls: Meg Jones, Helena Capital	70'7" (1991) 47'6" (1983)
Discus	Boys: Dennis Black, Great Falls Girls: Meg Jones, Helena Capital	205'10" (1991) 149'8" (1983)
Javelin	Boys: Chad McKinney, Missoula Big Sky Girls: Mary Osborne, Billings West	249'7" (1989) 175'6" (1979)
400-Meter Relay	Boys: Billings West Jason Brockel, Slade Foster, Tim Wolff, Pat Dringman Girls: Great Falls CMR Judy Chesterfield, Paula Payne, Denise Pidcock, Suzanne Robitrille	:42.27 (1985) :48.44 (1979)
1600-Meter Relay	Boys: Billings West Noel Kulbeck, Brad Welbes, Jim Anderson, Jon Ueland Girls: Great Falls CMR Paula Payne, Mary Korsmoe, Sara Robitaille, Denise Pidcock	3:19.26 (1995) 3:56.17 (1981)

Girls Tennis

• Most state championships, most consecutive state championships: 10, Bigfork (1986-95).

• Carol Ferguson and Sara Roberts from Billings West teamed up to win the state doubles championship three times: 1990, 91, and 93.

Boys Golf

- Most state championships: 12, Missoula Sentinel (1957, 59, 64, 65, 67, 68, 69, 70, 72, 75, 79, 88).

- Most consecutive state championships: 4, Billings West (1990-93).

- Gerry Gelner holds records for coaching Billings West to the championships mentioned above.

- Three golfers have won the state championship three times each: Rudy Merhar of Butte (1929, 31, 32), Mike Barnett of Missoula Sentinel (1967, 69, 70), and Shane Langstaff of Columbus (1992, 93, 94).

Girls Golf

- Most consecutive state championships: 7, Whitefish (1981, 82, 86, 87, 88, 89, 90).

- Most consecutive match victories: 28, Whitefish (1987-90).

- Two girls have won the state championship four times: Joanne Dixon of Missoula Sentinel (1960-63) and Jane Farnum of Polson (1956-59). The state's two-time winners are Edean Anderson of Helena (1946-48) and Tina Jovanovich of Fort Benton (1985-88).

Those CHAMPIONSHIP *Seasons*

The 1931 Mount St. Charles (now Carroll College) football team was named Montana State Collegiate Football Champs when, against all odds, they shut out all six opponents from much larger schools and one private team of miners and professional players.

In the 1995 championship season, University of Montana coach Don Read was named Division I-AA coach of the year by *American Football Quarterly*. Read is the winningest coach in UM history with a 75-35 record. He retired in April 1996.

The 1995 University of Montana-Boise State football game had the highest attendance (18,505) of any Montana sporting event since the Jack Dempsey-Tommy Gibbons fight in Shelby in 1923.

The Montana State University Bobcats won the NCAA Division I-AA championship in 1984 against Louisiana Tech (19-6) in Charleston, South Carolina.

College Sports

The rivalry between the Montana State University Bobcats and The University of Montana Grizzlies began in 1897 and is one of the longest-running competitions west of the Mississippi. In the early years, the annual football game was held in Butte, with enthusiastic fans arriving from Missoula and Bozeman in railroad cars for the statewide party of the year. Today, the annual football and basketball contests between the two teams still draw sellout crowds of students and alumni from across the state.

Generally, the sports accomplishments of the smaller public and private colleges in Montana are overshadowed by MSU and UM team events, but it was a different story in 1931 when the Mount St. Charles (now Helena's Carroll College) football team became the Montana State Collegiate Football Champs.

Montanans

 Dave Dickenson (1973-)

This Great Falls native has been called the greatest quarterback in University of Montana history. He broke thirteen school records and led the Grizzlies to the 1995 NCAA Division I-AA football championship over the Marshall University Thundering Herd, from West Virginia.

Dickenson was given the 1995 Walter Peyton Award for being the best player in Division I-AA. He was also named to the Associated Press I-AA All-American first team that year. His accomplishments include the following single season records:

most touchdowns rushing	14, 1993	most total offense	4,209, 1995
most pass completions	309, 1995	most points scored	84, 1993
most passing yards	4,176, 1995	most touchdown passes	38, 1995
highest completion rate	68.2%, 1994	most passing yards per game	379.6, 1995

Other records set by Dickenson include longest touchdown pass (90 yards, 1995), highest career completion percentage (67.3 percent), and most career passing yards (11,080).

Dickenson is now a member of the Calgary Stampeders of the Canadian Football League.

Grizzlies vs. Bobcats—Men's Football

	the Grizzlies	vs.	the Bobcats
Victories in Rivalry	58	5 ties	32
Overall Record	370-421-23		360-378-33
Big Sky Conference Championships	5 (1969, 70, 82, 93, 95)		7 (1964, 66, 77, 72, 76, 79, 84)
Longest Field Goal	52 Yards Eby Dobson, 1985		59 Yards Jan Stenerud, 1965
Most Yards Gained in a Game	574 Dave Dickenson, 1995		298 Don Hass, 1967
Most Yards Rushing in a Career	2,228 Rocky Klever, 1977-81		2,997 Steve Keecher/Delmar Jones
Most Yards Passing in a Career	11,080 Dave Dickenson, 1992-95		8,152 Kelly Bradley, 1983-86
Best Completion % in a Career	67.3% Dave Dickenson		N/A

Dave Dickenson / Todd Goodrich   *Kelly Bradley*

Grizzlies vs. Bobcats—Men's Basketball

	the Grizzlies	vs.	the Bobcats
Victories in Rivalry	120		115
Overall Record	1,057-958		1,331-945
Big Sky Conference Championships	5 (1974-75, 77-78, 90-91, 91-92, 94-95*)		4 (1963-64, 66-67,** 86-87, 95-96)
Most Points Scored in a Career	2,017 Larry Krystkowiak, 1982-86		2,034 Larry Chaney, 1956-60
Highest Scoring Average (per game in a season)	24.2 Michael Ray Richardson, 1977-78		23.6 Larry Chaney, 1959-60 Tom Storm, 1965-66
Most Rebounds in a Career	1,105 Larry Krystkowiak, 1982-86		1,011 Jack Gillespie, 1966-69
Highest Rebound Average	15.1 Ray Howard, 1954-55		15.3 Jack Gillespie, 1968-69
Most Assists in a Career	435 Travis DeCuire 1991-94		608 Scott Hatler, 1992-96

Shared title with Weber State.
**Shared title with Gonzaga.*

notable
Montanans

Robin Selvig (1952-)

Todd Goodrich

One of eight children born into an Outlook family, Selvig went to The University of Montana and played freshman and varsity basketball. In his senior year, 1973-74, he was the top defensive player on the team, an all-conference guard, and won the Grizzly Cup, recognizing him as the top athlete on campus. He has far surpassed his achievements as a player, though, in the years since he stepped off the court to coach the Lady Grizzly basketball team.

He took over the team in 1978 and eked out a 13-13 season. The following season, the team went 19-10 and earned a berth in its first national tournament. In 1980-81, he guided the team to 22 wins and the Lady Griz have not won fewer than 20 games a season since then.

In regular season games, Selvig's teams have dominated their Big Sky Conference opponents, 189-15. They have established a 25-3 record in Big Sky tournaments. At the end of the 1996-97 season, the team made its 12th NCAA Championship appearance.

Selvig's other achievements are too numerous to mention here, but two cannot be left out:

When Selvig started with the team, it drew just over 200 fans per game. In 1994-95, the team ranked 10th in the nation among women's basketball teams in attendance, with an average of 5,235 fans per game.

Selvig has won 84 percent of the games he has coached at the university.

He lives in Missoula with his wife Janie, originally from Redstone, and two sons.

Grizzlies vs. Bobcats—Women's

	the Grizzlies	vs.	the Bobcats
Victories in Rivalry	40		5
Overall Record	444-113		296-261
Most Points Scored in a Career	2,172 Shannon Cate, 1988-93		1,176 Kathleen McLaughlin, 1982-86
Highest Scoring Average	23.3 Shannon Cate, 1991-92		18.4 Lynne Andrew, 1987-88
Most Rebounds in a Career	886 Ann Lake, 1990-94		990 Kathleen McLaughlin, 1982-86
Highest Rebound Average	10.6 Jill Greenfield, 1980-81		9.4 Kathleen McLaughlin, 1985-86
Most Assists in a Career	511 Margaret Williams, 1982-87		443 Vicki Heebner, 1980-84

Lynne Andrew, Brian Dewey

Baseball

Baseball has been a popular sport here since the earliest days of the Montana Territory. Historical records tell us that games took place in the mining camps of Virginia City in 1866 and Helena in 1867. In 1892, a statewide league was established. In 1948, a Great Falls team, the Selectrics, and the Billings Mustangs joined the fledgling Pioneer Baseball League, with teams from Utah, Idaho, and Canada. The Helena Phillies and the Butte Copper Kings joined in 1978. The Missoula Mavericks played in the Pioneer League from 1956 to 1960.

Teams of the 1996 Pioneer League

Team	Box office numbers
Helena Brewers	449-7616
Butte Copper Kings	723-8206
Great Falls Dodgers	452-5311
Billings Mustangs	252-1241
Ogden Raptors	(801) 393-2400
Lethbridge Black Diamonds	(403) 327-7975
Medicine Hat Blue Jays	(403) 526-0404
Idaho Falls Braves	(208) 522-8363

Montana's Pioneer League teams, which play at the Rookie Advanced level, have sent many talented players on to major league teams over the years. George Brett, who played for Billings in 1971, went on to the Kansas City Royals, where he won the American League's batting championship in 1976 (.333) and 1990 (.329). George Bell, who played in Helena in 1978, was the American League's Most Valuable Player in 1987 as a member of the Toronto Blue Jays.

LEGION LEGENDS

The Billings American Legion baseball team has won twenty-four state championships and played in four American Legion World Series playoffs.

The Name Game

What's in a name? In minor league baseball, it usually has to do with an affiliation. Minor league teams constitute the farm system of major league teams, though the major league organizations change their affiliations with minor league teams fairly regularly.

• Great Falls team: the **Selectrics**, the **Electrics**, the **Giants**, the **Dodgers**

Someone thought to combine "Select," a beer produced by the Great Falls Brewery, and "Electric," the nickname of the city, to give the team its original name. The brewery, which owned the team, sold it to the Great Falls Baseball Club in the late 1950s and the "S" was dropped, making the team the Electrics. The team has also called itself the Giants (affiliated with San Francisco's NL team) and the Dodgers (the NL's Los Angeles team).

• Helena team: the **Phillies**, the **Gold Sox**, the **Brewers**

The team started out as an affiliate of the Philadelphia Phillies and spent a year independent of the major leagues in 1984 as the Helena Gold Sox. The team allied itself with the Milwaukee Brewers in 1985. To this day, it shares the American League team's name.

• The Billings **Mustangs** have been affiliated with the NL Cincinnati Reds since 1974.

Hockey

In the world of ice hockey, Montana is still part of the American Frontier. That's the name of the league in which six Montana cities field teams. The AFHL league is a junior league which develops 17- to 20-year-olds to play in the NCAA or National Hockey League.

Helena Ice Pirates. Donnie Sexton/Travel Montana

Teams of the 1996-97 American Frontier Hockey League

Team	Box office numbers
Helena Ice Pirates	443-4574/443-1442
Great Falls Americans	452-8911
Billings Bulls	256-2456
Butte Fighting Irish	782-7311
Bozeman Ice Dogs	586-4588
Central Wyoming Outlaws	(307) 577-4809
Bismarck Bobcats	(701) 222-3300

World-class Athletes & Olympians from Montana

Jim Barrier went from Kalispell in 1960 to the Winter Olympics at Squaw Valley, California, to race in the slalom and giant slalom competitions. He now lives in Southern California.

Terry Casey of Great Falls was named captain of the 1968 U.S. Olympic hockey team but was killed in an automobile accident in July 1967 before he was to report to training. The Great Falls Hockey Association named an annual tournament in his honor. The Terry Casey Memorial Cup tournament is held in late winter.

Gene Davis, a four-time state wrestling champion from Missoula County High School, won four national freestyle championships and a bronze medal in the 1976 Montreal Olympics. He also coached the U.S. team in the 1988 Olympics in Seoul, South Korea.

Scott Davis of Great Falls represented the U.S. at the World Figure Skating Championships from 1992 to 1995. He finished seventh in 1994 and 1995 and sixth in 1993. Davis took fourth place at the 1996 U.S. Figure Skating Championships, just out of contention to skate in the world championships. He was a U.S. champion in 1993 and 1994, and a runner-up in 1995. At the 1996 Centennial on Ice, a world-class competition in St. Petersburg, Russia, celebrating the 100th anniversary of the world championships, he placed fourth, the top effort by an American.

Todd Foster of Great Falls represented the U.S. as a boxer at the 1988 Olympics in Seoul, South Korea. He won the National Golden Gloves championship and the National Olympic Festival championship in 1987. When he turned professional in 1989, he was a contender for the World Lightweight Boxing Championship. By September 1996, Foster had recorded thirty-six victories in forty professional fights, including thirty-two knock-outs.

John Misha Petkevich, a Great Falls native, won both the National and the North American Figure Skating Championships in 1971. He finished fifth at the 1972 Sapporo Olympics. After a successful career in skating, he earned a doctorate in cellular biology from Oxford as a Rhodes Scholar. He then went on to study music, becoming a composer in residence at Harvard in 1980. He is author of *The Skater's Handbook*, a respected reference work for figure skaters.

David Silk, a Butte native, won the 5,000-meter World Cup Speed Skating Championship in 1986 and competed on the 1984 U.S. Olympic speed skating team.

Lones Wigger, Jr., a native of Carter, has won more Olympic medals than any other Montanan. At the 1964 Tokyo Olympics, he won a gold medal in the three-position small-bore shooting event and a silver in the standing small-bore event. At Munich in 1972, he won the gold medal in the three-position free-rifle event. In addition, he has won over 80 national championships, held 29 world records and 32 U.S. records, and has managed U.S. Olympic shooting teams.

Big Man
ON THE
Ski Slopes

Dr. A. R. "Bud" Little of Helena is a member of the United States Ski Association's Ski Hall of Fame. Little was a top administrator of ski events for the USSA and the International Ski Federation. His travels—to Europe, Russia, Japan, South and Central America, Taiwan, Australia, the Canary Islands, North Africa, and other countries—brought him into contact not only with the best alpine skiers in the world, but also with kings, queens, prime ministers and the Pope. He officiated at events, managed the U.S. ski team (1960-68), and attended the Winter Olympics in 1960, 64, 68, 72, 76, and 80.

THE U.S.
High Altitude Sports Center, Butte

The speed skating oval at the sports center (elevation: 5,528 feet) is the highest in the world and, among skaters who compete there, is known for its fast surface. Besides having hosted a world championship, World Cup meets, and national and Canadian-American championships, it is a national training site for the U.S. speed skating team.

In keeping with Butte's history of a varied ethnic mix, flags of many nations fly during world competitions at the oval. In March 1997, the center hosted the World Junior Speed Skating Championships. Skaters came from the Netherlands, Russia, Italy, Sweden, Japan, South Korea, and other countries for the event.

For Montana residents who don't feel ready to skate in international competitions, the oval is occasionally open to the public. The Montana Amateur Speed Skating Association supervises a "Learn to Skate" program at the center.

Call 723-8005 for information.

Rodeo and Horse Events

Rodeo is truly the definitive Western sport. Some say it is the roughest of all sports. The rodeo events you see today derived from the activities of the day-to-day work of early cowboys, who held informal contests and wagers to see who was the best hand.

Early public exhibitions of bronc riding, steer roping and wrestling, and bull riding grew in popularity as an athletic event and spectator sport across the West. Here in Montana, they qualify strongly as both. Each summer, in addition to over fifty sanctioned National Rodeo Association and Pro National Rodeo Association events across the state, there are dozens of ranch rodeos, old-timer rodeos, youth rodeos, and team roping contests. Most participants are no longer working cowboys, but are trained professional athletes who get their start on the high school and college rodeo circuit.

In addition to the exhilarating and often dangerous contests between man and beast, rodeos often feature novelty events like greased pig chases, children's "Little Britches" events, and wild-cow milking contests. Rodeo clowns are not there for laughs alone, but to help keep cowboys, cowgirls, and the rodeo stock out of danger.

A cowgirl leans her horse into the turn during a barrel race.
G. Wunderwald/Travel Montana

Selected Rodeo Terms

coasting - when a cowboy fails to spur his horse.

dudine or dudette - a young lady who comes west to marry a cowboy.

high roller - a horse that leaps high in the air when bucking.

hoolihan - an illegal fall, when a steer somersaults while running.

pigging string - a short piece of soft rope that a roper uses to tie the feet of a roped calf or steer.

pick-up man - a mounted cowboy who helps the rider off a bronc when the ride is complete and then removes the flank strap from the bronc and leads it out of the arena.

pulling leather - when a bronc rider holds onto the horn or any part of the saddle, he is pulling leather. This disqualifies a rider if his ride is not complete.

"put 'em east and west, boy" - an expression shouted by judges to cowboys. It means for the rider to spur the horse's shoulders with toes pointing outward.

scratch - spurring the horse back and forth.

screwing down or tight legging - when a rider comes out of the chute with knees clamped tightly to the saddle and both spurs digging in.

snubbing - the work of a pick-up man, astride a horse, leading a bronc out of a chute.

waddie - any cowhand.

Source: Don McCarthy, Afternoons in Montana. *Aberdeen, So. Dak.: Northern Plains Press, 1971.*

BATTLE CRY

One of the world's most recognizable slogans during World War I, the battle cry "Powder River, let 'er buck!" originated in the Powder River country of southeastern Montana. The yell greets a bronc rider as he comes out of the chute on some fishtailing horseflesh. You can still hear this challenging, sometimes admiring, term from the stands at rodeos and other Montana sporting events today.

Donnie Sexton/Travel Montana

Montana Women Honored at the National Cowgirl Hall of Fame & Western Heritage Center, Fort Worth, Texas

Name/Hometown	Year Inducted	Accomplishments
Alice Greenough Orr, Red Lodge (1902-1995)	1975	Very first cowgirl honoree Four-time World Champion Bronc Rider
Margie Greenough Hensen, Red Lodge (1908-)	1978	Another of the "Riding Greenoughs" Bronc rider in King's Wild West Show of 1930s
Fanny Sperry Steele, Helena (1887-1983)	1978	1912 World Champion Bronc Rider
Lynn "Jonnie" Jonckowski, Billings (1956-)	1991	1986 and 1988 World Champion Bull Rider

Other Notable Montana Riders and Rodeoers

Nancy Dear: In 1995, this Simms horsewoman won a Heritage Award from the National Cowboy Hall of Fame for her lifelong dedication to the raising of quarter horses. She helped organize the Montana Quarter Horse Association.

Deb Greenough: Born in Red Lodge into the famous Greenough rodeo family, he won the bareback riding title at the 1993 National Rodeo Finals.

Dan Mortensen: This Manhattan cowboy won three straight saddle bronc championships at the National Rodeo Finals—1993-1995.

Lloyd Ketchum: From Miles City, Ketchum was the 1991 National Finals World Champion bull rider.

Colin Murnion: This Jordan cowboy qualified for the National Rodeo Finals each year from 1987 to 1990 and was the 1986 and 1989 Montana Pro Rodeo Bareback Champion.

Billy Stockton: At the age of 51, this Wise River outfitter was the 1995 Senior Pro Rodeo All-Around World Champion Cowboy.

Montanans Honored at the National Cowboy Hall of Fame in Oklahoma City, Oklahoma

Name/Hometown	Year Inducted	Accomplishments
Bob Askin, Ismay (1900-1973)	1978	1925 World Champion Bronc Rider
Turk Greenough, Red Lodge (1905-1995)	1983	1928 World Champion Saddle Bronc Rider
Margie Greenough Hensen, Red Lodge (1908-)	1983	Bronc rider in the wild west shows in the 1930s
Alice Greenough Orr, Red Lodge(1902-1995)	1983	Four-time World Champion Bronc Rider in the 1920s and 1930s
Bill Linderman, Red Lodge (1920-1965)	1966	1953 All-Around Cowboy, 1950 and 1943 World Champion Bareback Rider, 1945 World Champion Saddle Bronc Rider
Bud Linderman, Red Lodge (1922-1961)	1987	1945 World Champion Bareback Rider
Benny Reynolds, Melrose (1936-)	1961	1961 All-Around Cowboy
Paddy Ryan, Ismay (1896-1980)	1978	1924 World Champion Bronc Rider
Fanny Sperry Steele, Helena (1887-1983)	1975	1912 World Champion Bronc Rider
Oral Zumwalt, Missoula (1903-1962)	1963	Bronc rider and rodeo stock producer who died in the arena

Horse Racing

Copper King Marcus Daly started his Bitterroot Stock Farm in 1887 near Hamilton because he believed that a mountain climate would produce horses with a greater lung capacity and superiority over horses from England or the East Coast. After building barns for six hundred harness and thoroughbred horses, Daly erected the brick show barn called Tammany Castle to house his famous stallions. He also built a three-quarter-mile covered track and a covered straight-away three-eighths of a mile long. The farm's tree-lined lanes made it the equine showplace of the West, and Daly's copper-and-green racing colors became familiar around the world as the winnings poured in from his most famous horses: Tammany, Ogden, Hamburg, Sysonby, and Prodigal. These horses and the direct offspring of their bloodlines resulted in four Kentucky Derby winners: Regret, Paul Jones, Zev, and Flying Ebony.

Another Montana horse, Spokane, owned by Noah D. Armstrong of the Alaska Ranch at Twin Bridges, won the 1889 Kentucky Derby at 6-to-1 odds.

Today, Montana's racing season begins in May in Miles City. There is horse racing at the Flathead County Fair and Race Meet in August, at MetraPark in

Two of Marcus Daly's prized horses, Tammany, left, and Hamburg, outside their opulent home. Montana Historical Society

Billings throughout the summer, and at Missoula's Western Montana Fair in mid-August.

M notable *ontanans*

Montana Historical Society

Tammany

In the 1890s, Marcus Daly's horse farm turned out big winners on racetracks around the country—Bathhampton, Scottish Chieftain, Montana, and others. Only one, however, was memorialized on the floor of the Montana Hotel in Anaconda. It was there, after Tammany's death, that Daly would remove his hat and pause in reverence over a replica of his beloved horse's head, carved from colored hardwoods and inlaid on the floor.

Tammany won many of the great races of the day, becoming a legend among the people of Butte and Anaconda. The horse's stable at the farm was said to contain carpeted floors, brass rails, and modern plumbing. After he'd won the Withers, Lorillard, Lawrence Realization, and the Jerome stakes, Tammany was beaten by Charade in the Tidal Stakes at Coney Island. His trainer devoted the next month to eliminating whatever weakness caused the defeat. In their next meeting, four weeks after the Coney Island race, Tammany beat Charade by three lengths.

The horse died after that season.

Sled Dog Racing

The men and women who compete in the intrepid sport of sled dog racing must be tough and shrewd to end up the winners, but they are, in truth, only the "coaches" in this event. The true athletes are the sled dogs.

Among the most successful Montana mushers are Doug Swingley and his brother Greg, of Simms; Dave Armstrong of Helena, who started mushing dog teams in 1936 and was still racing in 1995 at the age of 74; and Terry Adkins of Sand Coulee, who has run Alaska's Iditarod Trail Sled Dog Race twenty times, more than any other Montanan.

Race to the Sky

From 1986 to 1996, a 500-mile test of endurance, speed, and survival teamed men or women ("mushers") with dogs and pitted them against other such teams in the February cold along the west slope of Montana's Continental Divide. The

A musher urges his dogs on during the Race to the Sky.
Margaret Harlin

Race to the Sky was the longest sled dog race in the lower 48 states.

In 1997, organizers shortened the race to 350 miles to eliminate parts of the course where the snow cover was often insufficient, consolidating the 500-miler with a shorter race that has shared the bill since 1991.

Until 1996, the 500-miler began and ended close to Helena. That year, it was extended in the direction of Missoula. A ceremonial, commemorative leg of the race now begins at Camp Rimini, running on original Camp Rimini trails over MacDonald Pass to Elliston. The official start of the race is at the Seven-Up Ranch near Lincoln. The finish line is near Gold Creek, north of the Rattlesnake National Recreation Area.

The youngest musher ever to win the Race to the Sky is Jessie Royer of Philipsburg and Gallatin Gateway, who was 17 when she won the 1994 race, beating eleven other mushers to the finish after five days on the course. She was also the first woman to win the race.

Jessie Royer shows her appreciation to a member of her team.
Margaret Harlin

Race to the Sky Winners

500-miler		
	1986	Linwood Fiedler, Helena
	1987	Mark Nordman, Grand Marais, Minn.
	1988	Linwood Fiedler
	1989	Greg Swingley, Simms
	1990	Dean Osmar, Clam Gulch, Alaska
	1991	Doug Swingley, Simms
	1992	Greg Swingley, Simms
	1993	Robin Jacobson, Squaw Lake, Minn.
	1994	Jessie Royer, Philipsburg
	1995	Maria Hayashida, Jackson, Wyo.
	1996	Cliff Roberson, Seattle, Wash.
Short race	1991	Kenny Hess, Gallatin Gateway (250 miles)
	1992	Ray Gordon, Rock Springs, Wyo. (250 miles)
	1993*	Frank Teasley, Jackson, Wyo.
	1994	Frank Teasley
	1995	Rusty Rise, Leavenworth, Wash.
	1996	Butch Parr, Whitefish
	1997**	Cliff Roberson

* In 1993, the shorter race was extended to 300 miles.

** In 1997, the two races were consolidated to one 350-mile race.

notable
*M*ontanans

 Doug Swingley

Margaret Harlin

In 23 years, no one except Alaskans had won the famed 1,161-mile Iditarod Trail Sled Dog Race from Anchorage to Nome, Alaska. Swingley, a former mink farmer from Simms, west of Great Falls, was the first non-Alaskan in the winner's circle. He came home from Nome $52,500 richer, driving a new pickup truck (another race prize), after his 1995 victory. He took an early lead, before the halfway point of the grueling race, and never relinquished it. Other major victories for Swingley include Montana's own Race to the Sky in 1991 and Minnesota's John Beargrease Sled Dog Marathon in 1994, both 500-mile events.

Answers to Montana Sports Trivia Quiz:

1. Lynn "Jonnie" Jonckowski, from Billings
2. Bridger, Hardin, and Choteau
3. Guy Bingham
4. Butte High School
5. Tommy Moe
6. The Helena Ice Pirates, Billings Bulls, Bozeman Ice Dogs, Butte Fighting Irish, and Great Falls Americans
7. Mike Tilleman
8. e.) Dickenson's total would clear the summits of each of the above mountains (though not if the mountains were all heaped on top of one another). Dickenson passed for 11,080 yards, or 33,240 feet in his University of Montana career. Mount Everest is 29,028 feet high, plus or minus ten feet because of snow, so Dickenson's total would clear the summit by 4,172 feet, more than three-quarters of a mile above the top of the world.
9. Jan Stenerud
10. 1984, against Louisiana Tech in Charleston, South Carolina
11. Martz finished 15th in the 1,500-meter speed skating event at the 1964 Winter Olympics in Innsbruck, Austria. At the time, it was the best finish ever by a U.S. woman in the event.
12. the biathlon, which combines cross-country skiing and riflery
13. a.) barrel racing　　　b.) eleven years old
14. Browning High School
15. Lance Deal

Scores, Please

If you answered all 15 questions correctly, you're a genius and deserve a Rhodes Scholarship.

If you answered 10-14 questions correctly, you're a sports expert and deserve a job as an on-air personality for ESPN.

If you answered 6-9 questions correctly, you're a knowledgeable Montana sports fan and deserve six months' worth of free ESPN credited to your cable bill.

If you answered 2-4 questions correctly, you know a thing or four and deserve a stool at the Missoula Club and a handful of peanuts.

If you couldn't answer any of these questions, don't feel bad. You're probably too busy to know such trivia, an out-of-stater, or just not into sports. Make up your own excuse.

Further Reading:

"The Bobcats and the Grizzlies," *The New Yorker,* Dec. 13, 1969, pp. 152-167.

Two good sources for information (and trivia) on high school sports are:

Montana High School Sports Record Book. Helena: Montana High School Association, 1995.

Moran, Keith L. *The Roll of Champions: A Record of Montana High School State Basketball Tournaments from 1911 to 1996.* Livingston: Keith L. Moran, 1996.

c h a p t e r   t w e l v e

TRAVEL

DECADES AGO THE FOLLOWING WORDS were etched onto large wooden signs posted at the state line on all arterial highways leading into Montana:

> You are coming into the heart of the West where you will cut a lot of mighty interesting old time trails. Just turn your fancy loose to range the coulees, gulches, prairie and mountains and if your imagination isn't hobbled you can people them with picturesque phantoms of the past.
>
> We have marked and explained many of the most interesting historical and scenic spots along the highways. Watch for them and help us to preserve these markers.
>
> Here is wishing you lots of luck and many pleasant miles in Montana.

More recently, these border greetings have been replaced with modern signs whose message of welcome is far briefer. Montana roads and roadsides have changed a lot since visitors read the old signs. Automobiles are faster. Travelers seem in more of a hurry to get someplace. The wood of the signs may have turned to splinters and dust by now, but its message is still very true and scores of wooden signs still point out interesting parts of the state's history, geography, and people. Despite all that has changed, Montana still offers incomparable opportunities to the traveler, the explorer, the student of regional and local histories.

On the following pages, we offer "roadside assistance," help in getting around. Make plans. Pack provisions. Hit the road.

photo: Michael Sample

Our Roadways

Many parts of Montana's modern highway system follow the travel routes used by Indian tribes and the migrating bison. These trails were most often the best way through the lowest mountain passes and around rivers and other obstacles, while providing good trailside grazing and protection from the elements. The Mullan Road, a military supply route, was the first engineered road in the Northwest. With the completion of the Mullan Road from Fort Walla Walla in the Oregon Territory to Fort Benton in 1862, Montana was linked to a natural highway from the Pacific to the Atlantic.

Today, Montana's highway system consists of over 11,000 miles of interstate highways, primary highways, and secondary roads.

road type	miles
• Interstate	1,200
• Primary highways	5,450
• Secondary roads (county, state, and frontage)	4,760 *(including about 1,760 miles unpaved)*

Montana's portion of the nation's interstate system was completed in 1988. The system includes Interstate I-90, I-94, and I-15. It cost over $1.2 billion to create Montana's interstates, a sum paid mainly by the federal government with a $100 million investment by the state.

Source: Montana Business Quarterly, *Summer 1995.*

Montana Mileage Chart

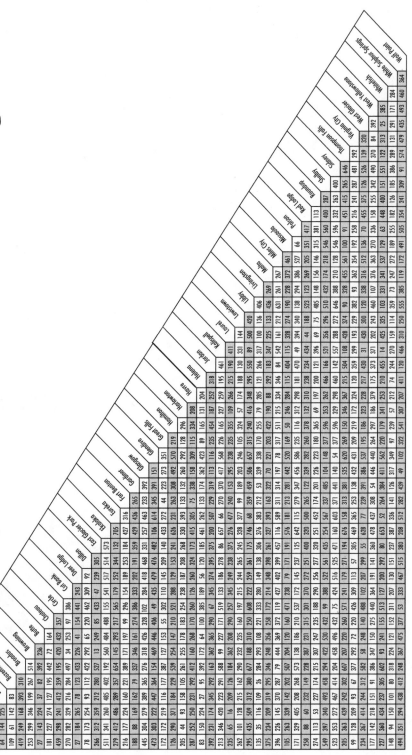

The
MONTANA
License Plate
Numbering
System

1. Silver Bow
2. Cascade
3. Yellowstone
4. Missoula
5. Lewis and Clark
6. Gallatin
7. Flathead
8. Fergus
9. Powder River
10. Carbon
11. Phillips
12. Hill
13. Ravalli
14. Custer
15. Lake
16. Dawson
17. Roosevelt
18. Beaverhead
19. Chouteau
20. Valley
21. Toole
22. Big Horn
23. Musselshell
24. Blaine
25. Madison
26. Pondera
27. Richland
28. Powell

29. Rosebud
30. Deer Lodge
31. Teton
32. Stillwater
33. Treasure
34. Sheridan
35. Sanders
36. Judith Basin
37. Daniels
38. Glacier
39. Fallon

40. Sweet Grass
41. McCone
42. Carter
43. Broadwater
44. Wheatland
45. Prairie
46. Granite
47. Meagher
48. Liberty
49. Park
50. Garfield
51. Jefferson
52. Wibaux
53. Golden Valley
54. Mineral
55. Petroleum
56. Lincoln

On Our Plates

There were only six thousand "horseless carriages" in Montana in 1913, the year the state first required registration of motor vehicles. The rationale for the system of assigning each county a prefix number for license plates remains one of Montana's unsolved mysteries.

The legislated numbering system was purportedly based on a county census in 1930—though politics and local pride also may have played a role in number assignments. Silver Bow County, home of Butte and the most powerful politicians of the day, was awarded the number "1," even though several other counties had larger populations. Every once in a while, the Montana Legislature considers matching the prevailing county population to a new numbering system, but rarely does such a radical idea get off the ground.

As part of the World War II war effort, in 1944 Montana's steel license plates were replaced by a tag made of soybean composition fiberboard. It wasn't unusual to have the corners nibbled off by the family goat.

Volunteers *Hit the Road*

Montana's roadsides are cleaner as a result of the "Adopt a Highway" volunteer litter cleanup program begun on Earth Day, April 22, 1992. As of 1995, 1,750 individuals or groups have adopted more than 3,500 miles of the state's highways.
Source: Montana Dept. of Transportation.

Memorial Highways

The following routes are noted for their scenic and historic interest and are designated memorial highways.

1. Veterans Memorial Highway   Interstate 15 from the Montana-Idaho border at Monida Pass to the international boundary at Sweetgrass.

2. Maureen and Mike Mansfield Heritage Route   Interstate 15 between Butte and Great Falls.

3. Charles M. Russell Trail   U.S. Highway 87/Montana 200 between Great Falls and Lewistown and continuing to Jordan and the portion of County 543 connecting US 87/MT 200 to the Charles M. Russell National Wildlife Refuge.

4. Lewis and Clark Highway   U.S. Highway 12 from Idaho state line west of Lolo Hot Springs to the junction with U.S. Highway 93 at Lolo; north from Lolo to Missoula; east on Interstate 90 to Garrison; east from Garrison on U.S. 12 through Forsyth and Baker to the North Dakota state line.

5. Donald J. Ruhl Medal of Honor Highway   Montana 73 from Columbus through Absarokee and Roscoe to Red Lodge, named for Pfc. Donald Jack Ruhl, a U.S. Marine killed on Iwo Jima in 1945. He rescued a wounded comrade under heavy enemy fire and died after smothering a hand grenade in an effort to protect his fellow troops. He received the Medal of Honor for his sacrifice.

Gateway Visitor Information Centers

At gateways to Montana, these community-based visitor centers are open seven days a week, May through September, except for the Hardin and West Yellowstone centers, which are open year-round. In addition to these centers, there are locally operated information centers in other communities throughout the state.

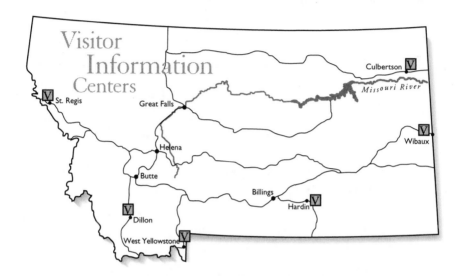

Culbertson Visitor Information Center
1 mile east of Culbertson on U.S. Highway 2
787-6320

Dillon Visitor Information Center
125 S. Montana, in Dillon
683-5511

Hardin Visitor Information Center
0.5 mile east of Hardin off Interstate 90
665-1671

St. Regis Visitor Information Center
Exit 33 on Interstate 90
649-2290

West Yellowstone Visitor Information Center
100 Yellowstone Avenue in West Yellowstone
646-7701

Wibaux Visitor Information Center
End of E. Orgain Street in Wibaux
795-2253 or 795-2481

Scenic and Back Country Byways

The USDA Forest Service and the Bureau of Land Management have given official designation to certain routes in the U.S., both paved and unpaved, for their outstanding scenic value. Three routes in Montana have earned the Scenic Byway designation from the USDA Forest Service. An equal number carry the BLM's title of Back Country Byway.

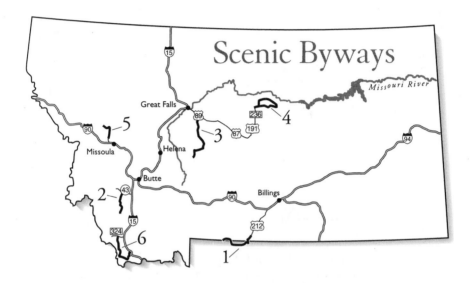

Scenic Byways

1. Beartooth Highway

60 miles over alpine plateaus, past lakes, magnificent vistas, and access points to rugged expanses of wilderness. Open Memorial Day to about mid-October, depending on the weather. The road, U.S. Highway 212, climbs to 10,946 feet and features 10 campgrounds and travel services at Cooke City and Red Lodge. Be prepared for high altitude and variable weather.

Michael Sample

2. Pioneer Mountains Scenic Byway

27 miles bisecting the East and West Pioneer Mountains southwest of Butte; paved and gravel. Open from mid-May through Thanksgiving; then closed by winter snows between Elkhorn Hot Springs and Sheep Creek. Features of the route include six campgrounds, limited travel services in Wise River, lodging at Elkhorn Hot Springs, hiking, trout streams, and rockhounding.

3. Kings Hill Scenic Byway

70 miles of road among the coulees, buttes, ranchland, limestone canyons and wooded peaks of the Little Belt Mountains in central Montana; route follows U.S. Highway 89; four campgrounds in Lewis and Clark National Forest. Attractions include historic mines and buildings, fishing, hunting, camping, and downhill and cross-country skiing. Traveler services in White Sulphur Springs.

Back Country Byways

Note: Because of the primitive nature of these roads, travelers should not attempt to drive them without first contacting BLM offices for information on essential vehicles and equipment and seasonal conditions of the roadways.

4. Missouri Breaks

73 miles of central Montana landscape that contains farms, ranches, and badlands; part of this byway follows the southern rim of the Upper Missouri River. Spur roads lead to the river bottom, overlooks, the north edge of the Missouri Breaks, and more.

5. Garnet Range

12 miles of winter recreation byway near Missoula, maintained for snowmobiling and ski touring; leads to the well-preserved ghost town of Garnet. Deer, elk, and moose winter in the area.

6. Big Sheep Creek

50 miles of gravel road through remote country near the Idaho border; generally passable from May through October, but some stretches can pose problems during wet periods. Attractions include camping, hiking, fishing, and scenic views.

Ports of Entry

There are fifteen ports of entry on the border between Montana and three Canadian provinces, including two on the edges of Glacier National Park that are open during the summer only. The border crossings at Roosville (on U.S. Highway 93 north of Eureka), Sweetgrass (Interstate 15 north of Shelby), and Raymond (Montana 16 north of Plentywood) are open 24 hours a day. U.S. citizens need to show a driver's license or proof of citizenship to cross back and forth over the international border. Citizens of other nations should be prepared to show a passport or the appropriate visas.

The port of entry north of Scobey on Montana 13 became the world's first voice-activated port of entry in 1996. Carefully screened local residents on both sides of the border are able to open the border barrier by punching in an identification number and speaking a predetermined phrase. If the computer recognizes all three—number, voice, and phrase—the barricade opens.

There are twenty-two highway ports of entry on the Montana borders where highways cross from Wyoming, Idaho, and the Dakotas. There are numerous unnumbered or unpaved local or logging roads that enter the state along these borders.

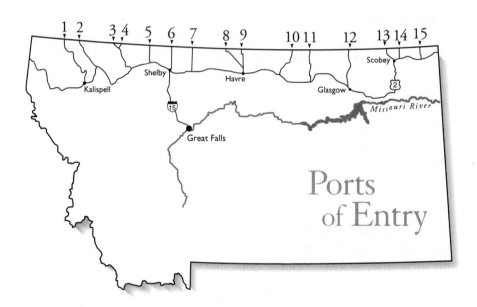

Travel Information

Travel Montana is the state's travel and tour information bureau. It can provide maps and vacation guides to help plan a trip in any season. Call Travel Montana at (800) 847-4868 or 444-2654. The bureau's TDD number is 444-2978. Montana visitor information is available on the World Wide Web at http://travel.mt.gov.

International Border Crossings

Port of	Location	Season	Hours of Operation*
1. Roosville 889-3865	MT 93, north of Eureka	all year	24 hours a day
2. Trail Creek (radio contact only)	northwest corner of Glacier Nat'l. Park	June 1–Oct 31	9:00am–5:00pm
3. Chief Mountain (403) 557-5256	MT 17, northeast of Glacier Nat'l. Park	May 20–31 June 1–third Sunday in Sept.	9:00am–6:00pm 7:00am–10:00pm
4. Piegan 732-5572	MT 89, 16 miles north of Babb	all year	7:00am–11:00pm
5. Del Bonita 336-2130	Hwy 213, northwest of Cut Bank	Sept 16–May 31 June 1–Sept 15	9:00am–6:00pm 8:00am–9:00pm
6. Sweetgrass 335-2434	I-15, north of Shelby	all year	24 hours a day
7. Whitlash 432-5522	northwest of Chester	all year	9:00am–5:00pm
8. Wild Horse 394-2371	Hwy 232, northwest of Havre	Oct 1–May 14 May 15–Sept 30	8:00am–5:00pm 8:00am–9:00pm
9. Willow Creek 398-5512	north of Havre	all year	9:00am–5:00pm
10. Turner 379-2651	Hwy 241, northeast of Harlem	Sept 16–May 31 June 1–Sept 15	9:00am–6:00pm 8:00am–9:00pm
11. Morgan 674-5248	Hwy 242, north of Malta	Sept 16–May 31 June 1–Sept 15	9:00am–6:00pm 8:00am–9:00pm
12. Opheim 724-3212	MT 24, north of Glasgow	Sept 16–May 31 June 1–Sept 15	9:00am–6:00pm 8:00am–9:00pm
13. Scobey 783-5372	Hwy 13, north of Scobey	Sept 16–May 31 June 1–Sept 15	9:00am–6:00pm 8:00am–9:00pm
14. Whitetail 779-3531	Hwy 511, northeast of Scobey	Sept 16–May 31 June 1–Sept 15	9:00am–6:00pm 8:00am–9:00pm
15. Raymond 895-2664	Hwy 16, north of Plentywood	all year	24 hours a day

*Note: These seasons and hours of operation were in effect in 1996. Call number listed to assure they haven't changed.

Ferries 'cross the Missouri

Three ferries cross the Missouri River in north-central Montana. They are open from various dates from spring through October, depending on river conditions, to vehicles weighing not more than 30,000 pounds. Call ahead to schedule a ride at times other than listed. The crossings are indicated on the map below.

Carter Ferry   14 miles west of Fort Benton and 20 miles northeast of Great Falls off U.S. Highway 87, then a 5-mile drive on gravel road from Carter to the ferry; 734-5335. Open March-October, Mon-Sat, 7 a.m.-7 p.m.; Sunday, 9 a.m.-5 p.m. Free. A toll is charged for unscheduled crossings.

Virgelle Ferry   30 miles northeast of Fort Benton off U.S. Highway 87, then 8 miles on gravel road from highway to the ferry; 378-3194. Open May-October, Mon-Sat, 7 a.m.-7 p.m.; Sun 9 a.m.-5 p.m. Free. A toll is charged for unscheduled crossings.

McClelland Ferry   At mouth of Missouri River's White Cliff area, 50 miles north of Lewistown; 462-5513. Open April-October, 7 a.m.-7 p.m. Free.

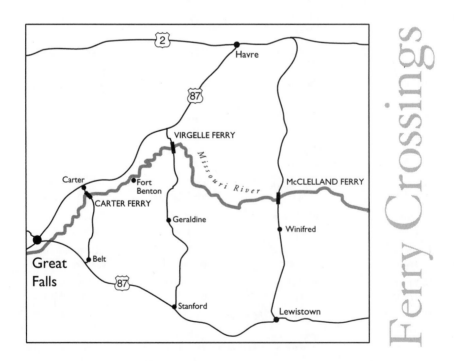

Ferry Crossings

Road Conditions

Due to the wide-ranging and quick-changing weather conditions of the Big Sky, it's always advisable to check on travel conditions before hitting the road. If the wind is picking up or the sky is darkening, pick up the phone before getting behind the wheel.

Statewide	(800) 226-ROAD (7623)
	444-6339
	444-7696 TDD or (800) 335-7592
Billings	252-2806
Bozeman	586-1313
Butte	494-3666
Glendive	365-2314
Great Falls	453-1605
Havre	265-1416
Kalispell	755-4949
Lewistown	538-7445
Miles City	232-2099
Missoula	728-8553
Wolf Point	653-1692

Road and weather conditions are also available on the State Electronic Bulletin Board System through METNET. To access METNET by modem, dial (800) 962-1729 or 444-5648. Internet access: www.mdt.mt.gov.

Roadside History Lessons

Since 1935, Montanans and tourists have enjoyed reading the state's colorful history on historical markers along the state's highways. These history lessons were the first such markers in the country. The now-famous signs were created by Bob Fletcher, a traffic engineer for the Montana Highway Department. His survey work around the state had brought him into contact with many of the people who participated in or collected stories about Montana's early years. Fletcher's charming, colloquial renditions of Montana history tell much about local landmarks and events across Montana. Unfortunately, many of the markers along the state's main routes had to be removed because of rules governing interstate signboards, but 150 still remain along roads and at various rest areas.

Source: Glenda Clay Bradshaw, ed. Montana's Historical Highway Markers. *Helena: Montana Historical Society, 1989.*

*M*notable
*M*ontanans

Robert H. Fletcher (1885-1972)

Born in Iowa, Fletcher traveled all over Montana as a surveyor before going to work for the state Highway Department in Helena. He managed promotional campaigns that urged tourists to visit, then authored the highway markers that cause so many travelers to pause along the roadway and learn some Montana history. He also wrote a historical account of Montana's cattle industry, "From Free Grass to Fences," and poetry. His best-known verse became the basis of the Cole Porter song, "Don't Fence Me In."

Montana Historical Society

Motor Vehicle Laws

Montana earned national attention in December 1995 for not having a specific daytime speed limit to replace the standard 55 or 65 mph when the government lifted speed limit mandates. Even when the federal limits were in place, though, the state had a certain fame for issuing tickets as low as $5 for "the offense of unnecessary waste of a resource." The $5 speeding violation was not recorded on a person's driving record.

Contrary to recent notoriety, Montana does have reasonable laws in place regarding proper speeds on the roads of the state. Even during the years of the federal speed limits, Montana had a concurrent law often referred to as the "basic rule" or careless driving law. This law requires vehicles to be driven in a "careful and prudent manner and at a rate of speed that is no greater than is reasonable and proper under the conditions." A violation of the basic rule is applied to a person's driving record and may result in higher insurance rates.

After the sun goes down, the basic rule is superseded by nighttime speed limits—65 mph on interstates and 55 mph on other state highways.

Visions of the state's highways turning into the "Montanabahn" haven't materialized. When the federal speed limit was in place, studies show that 85 percent of drivers cruised at 72 mph or less on the interstates. Since suspension of the law, the rate has crept up to 74 mph. Average speeds on primary highways went from 62 mph to 64 mph. The rate of traffic fatalities, though, has dropped slightly. In 1996, 198 people were killed on Montana's roads, compared to 218 in 1995.

On a July day in 1996, a convoy of fifteen cars driven by test drivers for the German automaker Mercedes-Benz was pulled over on Interstate 90 near Park City and ticketed for speeding. The Montana Highway Patrol fined each driver $70 for failing to drive "at a speed no greater than is reasonable and proper" under existing conditions, according to state law. A newspaper account said the cars were clocked "at a speed in excess of 95 mph."

- Newcomers to the state must apply for a Montana driver's license within ninety days of residence and must register their motor vehicles immediately upon establishment of residence, acceptance of employment, or placement of children in public school.

- The fee for a driver's license, valid for four years, is $4 per year. The state charges an additional fifty cents per year for a motorcycle endorsement. Licenses expire on the licensee's birthday. A vision test is required to renew licenses. Applicants may be required to take a road test. A valid out-of-state driver's license may be exchanged for a Montana driver's license without written or road testing.

- The minimum driving age is 16, or age 15 if the applicant has passed an approved driver's education course.

- Annual registration of motor vehicles is required. Registration and license plate fees are based on the weight of the vehicle: automobiles weighing 2,850 lbs. or less, $10.25; and automobiles weighing over 2,850 lbs. and all trucks, $15.25. Property tax assessed for the current year is payable at the time of registration. Proof of ownership is required. The fee for certificate of title is $5. A copy of registration must be carried in all vehicles.

- A driver's license is required to operate a motorcycle. Title registration is $7.25.

- Safety helmets are required for motorcycle riders 18 years of age or younger. Motorcycles must have one rearview mirror. Lights must be on at all times. Riding between lanes is prohibited.

- All occupants of a vehicle must wear a safety belt; children under two years of age must wear a child safety restraint.

- Littering upon or near a highway is prohibited, and is punishable by fine, imprisonment, or both.

- The maximum blood-alcohol concentration level for drivers is 0.10. A person with blood alcohol level between 0.05 and 0.10 may also be charged with driving under the influence, depending on the circumstances. The maximum blood-alcohol level for drivers under 21 years of age is 0.02.

- It is unlawful for anyone to operate a motor vehicle (excluding motorcycles) in Montana without a valid policy of liability insurance. Owners must sign a statement stating that they have liability insurance when registering a motor vehicle.

For further information about vehicle registration, contact the County Treasurer in the county of residence or:

Montana Department of Justice
Motor Vehicle Division
303 North Roberts
Helena, MT 59620-1419
444-1772

Montana Department of Justice
Title and Registration Bureau, Motor Vehicle Division
1032 Buckskin Drive
Deer Lodge, MT 59722
846-6000

The Montana Highway Patrol

In 1933 and 1934, Montana led the nation with a 74 percent increase in highway fatalities. In the year following the creation of the Montana Highway Patrol in 1935, traffic fatalities decreased 25 percent.

In addition to enforcing the highway safety laws of the state, the approximately 212 highway patrol officers enforce state drunken driving laws, assist in drug interdiction, and perform various records management duties.

In 1979, women joined the force for the first time. The patrol added four female officers. In 1996, there were as many as eighteen female patrol officers.

Since 1935, four Montana Highway Patrol officers have died in the line of duty.

On duty, 1995

answered calls for service	66,100
(assistance, complaints, queries, etc.)	
made "driving under the influence" arrests	2,457
issued seat belt citations	11,182
issued seat belt warning	9,355
accidents investigated	9,341

Flying the Big Sky

If you think airfare is expensive, remember that in 1868, Wells, Fargo, and Company charged passengers $120 to ride a stagecoach from Helena to Salt Lake City and $25 to ride from Helena to Virginia City or Fort Benton. Here are Montana's air carriers, today's fastest transportation providers:

Big Sky	(800) 237-7788
Delta and The Delta Connection	(800) 221-1212
Horizon Air	(800) 547-9308
Northwest Airlines	(800) 225-2525
Skywest	(800) 453-9417
United Airlines	(800) 241-6522

Montana's Commercial Airports

Airport/ Location	Carriers	Parking Rates	
Gallatin Field Bozeman/Belgrade, MT 388-6632	Delta, Horizon, Northwest, Skywest, Continental	Hour Day Week	$1.25 $4.00 $20.00
Logan International Airport Billings, MT 59101 657-8495	Delta, Horizon, Big Sky, Northwest, Skywest, United, Continental	Hour Day Week	$1.40 $4.50 $31.50
Bert Mooney Airport 101 Airport Road Butte, MT 59701 494-3771	Horizon, Skywest	Hour Day Week	$1.00 $4.00 $20.00
Great Falls International Airport 2800 Terminal Drive Great Falls, MT 59404 727-3404	Delta, Horizon, Big Sky, Northwest	Hour Day Week	$1.50 $4.24 $20.00
Helena Regional Airport 2850 Skyway Drive Helena, MT 59601 442-2821	Delta, Horizon, Skywest	Hour Day Week	$0.25 $1.00 $5.00
Glacier Park International Airport 4170 Highway 2 East Kalispell, MT 59901 257-5994	Delta, Horizon, Northwest, Skywest	Hour Day Week	$1.25 $4.00 $20.00
Missoula County Airport 5225 Highway 10 West Missoula, MT 59801 728-4381	Delta, Horizon, Northwest, Skywest, Continental	Hour Day Week	$0.75 $6.00 $21.25

Montana's Smaller Airports

Airport/Location	Telephone
Glasgow International Airport	228-4023
Dawson Community Airport/Glendive	359-2054/Mobile 365-5528
Havre City County Airport	265-4671
Lewistown Airport	538-3264
Frank Wiley Field/Miles City	232-1296
Sidney-Richland Airport	482-2415
Wolf Point Airport	653-1740
West Yellowstone Airport*	646-7631/Winter 444-2506

*West Yellowstone provides commericial service on a seasonal basis. This airport is open from June 1 to September 30. The airport is owned by the State of Montana.

On the Bus

Because passenger trains cover little more than the northern tier of the state, Montanans depend on buses to get them to other points.

Greyhound Lines
(800) 231-2222

Serves the following cities and towns along Interstate 90: St. Regis, Superior, Alberton, Missoula, Drummond, Deer Lodge, Warm Springs, Butte, Whitehall, Three Forks, Manhattan, Belgrade, Bozeman, Livingston, Big Timber, Columbus, Park City, Laurel, Billings, Worden, Custer, Hysham, Forsyth, Miles City, Terry, Glendive, and Wibaux.

Rimrock Trailways
(800) 255-7655

Serves over 60 Montana communities, including Butte, Great Falls, Missoula, Billings, Havre, Whitefish, Big Timber, St. Ignatius, Simms, Belt, Moccasin, and Big Sandy. Also connects to points served by Greyhound.

Powder River Trailways
(800) 442-3682

Serves Billings, Laurel, Bridger, and Hardin; also travels south to Gillette, Wyo., and Denver.

City Bus

Bus Line	Areas Served	Phone Number
Great Falls Transit	Great Falls and Black Eagle	727-0328
MET Transit	Billings	657-8218
Mountain Line Transit	Missoula	721-3333
The Bus	Butte	723-8262
Eagle Transit*	Kalispell	758-5728

*Limited out-of-town service is available.

Call-A-Ride*

Bus Line	Areas Served	Phone Number
Blackfeet Transit	Browning*	338-5604
Fergus County Council on Aging	Lewistown*	538-7486
Fort Peck Transportation System	Poplar*	768-5155
Helena Dial-A-Ride	Helena	447-1580
Powder River County Transportation System	Broadus*	436-2635
Valley County Council on Aging	Glasgow*	228-8225

*Limited out-of-town service is available.

Most cities, including Billings, Butte, Great Falls, Helena, and Missoula, provide mass transit services. Local transportation services can also be found in Fergus, Flathead, Garfield, Liberty, McCone, Powder River, and Valley counties and on the Fort Peck and Blackfeet Indian Reservations.

Call-A-Ride services are available in several communities—mostly small, rural ones. The services do not follow a designated route. Most require passengers to call 24 hours ahead to arrange to be picked up and delivered to the destination of their choice.

Riding the Rails

The National Railroad Passenger Service (AMTRAK) provides east and west passenger service across northern Montana, making stops in Libby, Whitefish, West Glacier, Essex, Browning, Cut Bank, Shelby, Havre, Malta, Glasgow, and Wolf Point. The train services Chicago and Minneapolis/St. Paul to the east; Portland and Seattle to the west. This train, known as the "Empire Builder," has both coach and sleeper accommodations. Most boardings and deboardings occur in Whitefish. AMTRAK also provides delivery services of everything from cut flowers to medical supplies along its route. This service is vital to the northern part of the state, especially in severe weather when other modes of transportation may be halted.

Tourist rail trips through western Montana are offered by Montana Rockies Rail Tours, (503) 274-4290 or (800) 519-7245.

The Montana Daylight, a comfortable touring train, offers three tours during July and August.

- The Rockies Tour is a two-day tour that begins in Billings with a bus transfer to Laurel, stops overnight in Missoula, and continues to Sandpoint, Idaho, with a bus transfer to Spokane.

- The Yellowstone Tour is a six-day, five-night tour that begins with a bus transfer from Spokane to Sandpoint. It has overnight stops in Missoula, Livingston, Yellowstone National Park, and Billings. Passengers are then flown back to Spokane.

- The Continental Divide Tour is a four-day, three-night tour from Spokane to Billings or Livingston to Spokane.

Both the Rockies Tour and the Yellowstone Tour begin in either Billings or Spokane. The fares include the bus transfers, meals, and overnight accommodations. Hotels visited on the tour offer special rates to passengers who want to spend additional nights before or after the tour. The train travels only during the daylight hours.

AMTRAK
Washington Union Station
60 Massachusetts Avenue
Washington, D.C. 20022
(800) 872-7245

Montana Rockies Rail Tours
218 Cedar Street
Sandpoint, ID 83864
(800) 519-7245

Sources: Montana Department of Transportation, Guide to Public Transportation in Montana. *Helena.*
Montana Aeronautics Division, 1996 Montana Aeronautics Rates and Charges Survey. Helena.
Montana Aeronautics Division, Air Carrier/Commuter Flights and Passengers. Helena: 1996.
Department of Commerce, Montana, A Sizable Advantage. Helena.

notable
*M*ontanans

 ## Shep (?-1942)

"SHEP, ED SHIELDS AND A.V. SCHANCHE
Montana Historical Society

Epitome of the faithful dog, Shep was a half-breed collie who had followed the body of his now-unknown sheep-herder master to where it was placed on a train at Fort Benton in 1936. From then up to January 1942, Shep lived at the depot and went out to meet every incoming train to see if his master had returned, until the morning that he slipped crossing the tracks and was crushed by the train he had come to meet. A booklet celebrating Shep was sold to Great Northern passengers and helped raise funds for the Montana School for the Deaf and Blind. Shep's story made it into a *Ripley's Believe It or Not* strip, into a Gold Medal paperback story for children, and into the periodicals *Farm Journal* and *Reader's Digest*.

Further Reading:

Alt, David, and Donald W. Hyndman. *Roadside Geology of Montana.* Missoula: Mountain Press Publishing Company, 1986.

Bradshaw, Glenda Clay. *Montana's Historical Highway Markers.* Helena: Montana Historical Society, 1989.

Fanselow, Julie. *Traveler's Guide to the Lewis and Clark Trail.* Helena: Falcon Publishing Co., 1995.

Federal Writers' Project of the Work Projects Administration. *Montana: A State Guide Book.* New York: Hastings House, 1949. *A paperback edition has recently been published, making this wonderful traveling companion available again. The reissue includes a foreword by Missoula writer William Kittredge.*

Green, Stewart. *Back Country Byways.* Helena: Falcon Publishing, 1991.

James, H. L. *The Beartooth Highway.* Butte: Montana Bureau of Mines and Geology, 1995.

_____. *Scenic Driving the Beartooth Highway.* Helena: Falcon Publishing, 1997.

McRae, W. C., and Judy Jewell. *Montana Handbook.* Third edition. Chico, Ca.: Moon Publications, Inc., 1996.

Magley, Beverly. *National Forest Scenic Byways.* Helena: Falcon Publishing, 1990.

_____. *National Forest Scenic Byways, Vol. II.* Helena: Falcon Publishing, 1992.

Montana: The Last Best Place. Helena: Falcon Publishing, 1993.

Montana Atlas and Gazetteer. Freeport, Maine: DeLorme Mapping Co., 1994. ***Indispensable for finding your way under the Big Sky.***

Raup, Omer B., Robert L. Earhart, James W. Whipple, and Paul E. Carrara. *Geology Along Going-to-the-Sun Road, Glacier National Park, Montana.* West Glacier, Mont.: Glacier Natural History Association, 1983.

Snyder, S. A. *Scenic Driving Montana.* Helena: Falcon Publishing, 1996. ***From the Anaconda-Pintler Scenic Route to Yaak River country, here are twenty-four drives along some of the state's most cherished roadways.***

Terell, Norma. *Montana.* Oakland: Compass American Guides, Inc., 1991. ***A thoughtful description of Montana culture and places.***

Van West, Carroll. *Traveler's Companion to Montana History.* Helena: Montana Historical Society Press, 1990.

Wyss, Marilyn. *Road to Romance: The Origins and Development of the Road and Trail System in Montana.* Helena: Montana Department of Transportation, 1992.

chapter thirteen

OUTDOOR *Recreation*

MONTANA IS A FOUR-SEASON outdoor recreation playground, with 30 million acres of public lands including more than 6 million acres of state forests, parks, and fishing access sites. The state contains more than 3 million acres of designated wilderness areas and more than 4,000 miles of trails—plenty of space and soul-satisfying solitude for hikers, campers, skiers, bikers, rock climbers, rockhounds, water skiers, boaters, snowmobilers, and more. Hunting and fishing are part of the traditional Montana lifestyle; both began as a way to survive on the frontier. Today, hundreds of thousands of hunters and anglers carry on that way of life through the recreational pursuit of Montana's varied and plentiful game and fish.

One of the best things about living in Montana is the possibility of being at a favorite trout stream, ski slope, hiking trail, or other outdoor adventure within a few minutes of leaving home or work. On sunny summer days, it's easy to find a restful campsite, an inviting body of water, or a trail with a view of heaven. Even on a starry winter night, you can be skiing or ice fishing close to home.

The abundance and variety of Montana's outdoor recreation opportunities attract a large number of visitors each year; those visitors pump millions of dollars into local economies. And many Montana residents choose to live here in large part for the chance to get outdoors and have fun. Today, there are more people on Montana's hiking trails, fishing streams, ski slopes, and snowmobile routes than ever. So it has become more important than ever to use our natural resources for recreation wisely and share those resources courteously with other users. After all, there are plenty of outdoor treasures in the Treasure State to go around.

Hiking and Backpacking

Backpacking and hiking opportunities in Montana are nearly unlimited. A 1994 trail inventory by Montana Fish, Wildlife & Parks identified 14,633 miles of hiking trails within the state. Many of these trails meander along rivers and streams, touch the shores of alpine lakes full of trout, and scale lofty summits with endless views. Eighteen trails are listed as National Recreation or Scenic Trails, including more than 900 miles of the Continental Divide National Scenic Trail within Montana.

Many sections of state and national trails are accessible to persons with disabilities. For example, in the Sheepshead Recreation Area near Butte, there is a 5-mile paved trail around Maney Lake. For the urban hiker, many Montana towns provide maps of walking tours through designated historic districts and nature areas  within the city limits. A brief sampling includes: Mount Helena City Park and historic district; the river walks in Missoula, Great Falls, Billings, and Fort Benton; the historic district walks in Livingston, Butte, Deer Lodge, and Philipsburg; and the Pattee Canyon Recreation Area and Rattlesnake Wilderness Area walks just a few miles outside Missoula.

National Recreation Trails

National Recreation Trail	Distance	National Forest	Trailhead
Basin Lakes	4.8 miles	Custer	FR 71
Big Hole Battlefield	3.8 miles	Bitterroot	Indian Trees Campground
Crystal Lake Shoreline	1.7-mile loop	Lewis and Clark	Crystal Lake Campground
Danny On Memorial	6.4-mile network	Flathead	Big Mountain Ski Resort
Hanging Valley	6 miles	Helena	Vigilante Campground
Holland Falls	1.5 miles	Flathead	end of FR 44, Holland Lake
Louise Lake	1.75 miles	Deerlodge	FR 107
Morrell Falls	2.3 miles	Lolo	FR 4364, near Seeley Lake
Mortimer Gulch	5 miles	Lewis and Clark	Mortimer Gulch Campground
Palisade Falls	0.6 miles	Gallatin	East Fork Road
Pioneer Loop	35-mile loop	Beaverhead-Deerlodge	Lacy Creek Road
Skyline	13-mile loop	Kootenai	end of FR 399
Stateline-CC Divide	5.5 miles	Lolo	FR 7 at state border

Camping

Even in Montana's busy summer tourist season, you can generally find a campsite. Camping opportunities range from campgrounds with swimming pools and stores to primitive areas with limited facilities. There are about 120 campgrounds on lakes that are accessible by car and some 170 campsites along the rivers and

Camping at Upper Granite Lake in the Beartooths. Bill Schneider

streams of the state. There are also many hundreds of locations in the backcountry where camping is allowed, but the facilities may be primitive. Campers are required to pack their garbage out of most areas.

Most state parks and forest service campsites are available on a first-come, first-served basis. Some forest service campgrounds require reservations. While services vary among individual parks, most sites have a picnic table, a fire ring or grill, and parking for one vehicle and a recreational vehicle. For those requiring camping with more creature comforts, there are more than 120 private campgrounds along the byways and highways. Fees for private campgrounds vary widely depending on the area and services. Some locations offer hot water soaks and plunges, like Fairmont Resort near Anaconda, Quinn's near St. Regis, and Beartrap Hot Springs near Norris.

USDA Forest Service reservations: (800) 280-CAMP

For information on private campgrounds, contact Montana Campground Owners Association, 3695 Tina Avenue Missoula, MT 59802; 549-0881.

Cabin Rentals

The USDA Forest Service offers rustic cabins and fire lookouts for rent on a first-come, first-served basis at 48 locations within the state's nine national forests. Some of the cabins can even be rented in the winter months. Cabins are furnished with the bare basics, like table, chairs, a wood stove, and bunks. Cooking utensils, electricity, and indoor plumbing may also be available but not at all rental cabins. For rates ranging from $15 to $35, you can enjoy scenic splendors and the life of early rangers for up to five consecutive nights. Most of these cabins were built in the 1920s and 1930s to house forest rangers and their crews. Most of the rentable former fire lookouts are in the northwestern corner of the state. For more information, contact local ranger stations. For a directory of all cabin rentals, write Regional Office of the USDA Forest Service, Federal Building, P.O. Box 7669, Missoula, MT 59807; 329-3511.

Montana Fish, Wildlife & Parks also rents rustic cabins at Lewis and Clark Caverns State Park.

Bicycling

The advent of the mountain bike has tremendously increased the number of people pedaling wherever the pavement, dirt roads, and single-track trails will take them. Mountain bike races, often with several amateur categories open to the public, are held in the mountains near Missoula, Helena,

Kalispell, and Bozeman. Check with area bicycle shops for dates and details. Mountain bike guidebooks from Falcon Publishing offer detailed information on local rides around Bozeman and Helena.

Road races, sanctioned by the United States Cycling Federation, are held throughout spring and summer near Missoula, Helena, and Billings. The annual Tour of the Swan River Valley offers "roadies" two days and more than 200 miles of scenic pedaling between Missoula and Bigfork. Each fall the Double Divide Ride draws hardy cyclists to Helena for a two-day 170-mile loop that twice climbs over the Continental Divide at 6,320-foot MacDonald Pass and 6,131-foot Flesher Pass.

The Adventure Cycling Association has additional information on road routes and bike trails throughout western Montana.

> Adventure Cycling Association
> Box 8308
> Missoula, MT 59807
> 721-1776   721-8754 fax

Climbing

The Rocky Mountains have special meaning to Montana's technical climbers and mountaineers. Numerous world-class mountaineers and rock climbers have trained here. The exposed cliffs of steep, compact rock along with dramatic glacier-carved mountains are a geologic wonderland and a climber's paradise. Moreover, Montana's easily accessible climbing areas are relatively uncrowded and unknown, while the remote backcountry still holds first-ascent adventures for the intrepid.

Often tucked away in idyllic settings, the sweeping expanses of granite and gneiss, craggy limestone fins and faces, and steep quartzite cliffs are gymnastic playgrounds for the vertically inclined. The high peaks of Glacier National Park, and the Mission, Bitterroot, Madison, Absaroka, and Beartooth mountains tantalize those with a desire to visit high and remote summits.

Scaling "Second Thoughts," a climb on Sheep Mountain, near Clancy. Randall Green

Prospecting & Rockhounding

Folks have been hunting for gold for at least 140 years in Montana, and there is still some left for those who know where to look (and those who just get lucky). Montana also offers numerous opportunities to hunt for agates, quartz crystals, and semiprecious stones like sapphires. Sapphire mines offer the opportunity to dig for this sought-after stone or to buy buckets of dirt for sorting through. At a sapphire mine in Philipsburg, you can sift through your bucket of treasures indoors in a comfortable setting. You can hunt for gold in Confederate Gulch, sapphires in French Gulch near Helena, quartz crystals at Crystal Park in the Pioneer Mountains, and moss agates along the Yellowstone River near Forsyth. If fossils are the treasure you seek, you can volunteer to help with the Museum of the Rockies dinosaur digs at Egg Mountain near Choteau.

The best spot to find the Montana agate is in alluvial gravels along the lower 200 miles of the Yellowstone River, from Custer, 50 miles east of Billings, to the Missouri River. Petrified wood, colored jasper, and fossils are also common in the area. It takes a trained eye to find top grade rough Montana agate, but if you do, it may be worth as much as $40 a pound. The low water times of early spring and late fall are best for hunting along the bars and banks where virgin gravel has been exposed. To help overcome the challenges of hunting for agates on a river of unpredictable waters and limited access, Montana Agate Adventures in Glendive offers the combination of a guided float trip on the Yellowstone and an agate hunt. Glendive hosts an annual rock and gem show in June, featuring rough gems and jewelry.

Water Sports

Montana has over 120 lakes and dozens of rivers that are accessible by motor vehicle so you can launch a boat, personal watercraft, raft, or canoe. Montana Fish, Wildlife & Parks maintains dozens of boat launching sites at various state parks and fishing access sites. High-powered motorboats are not allowed on all lakes and rivers. Some waters, like Flathead Lake, Georgetown Lake, Lake Mary Ronan, or Fort Peck Reservoir, are many miles long, offering hours of scenic cruising and sailing.

One of Montana's favorite tourist attractions is the boat trips through the Gates of the Mountains in the Holter Lake Recreation Area of the Missouri River. This area was named by Lewis and Clark for its magnificent cliffs that seem to open and close like a gate as one floats upriver. The boat ride can include a picnic at the Meriwether Campground or a hike through the Gates of the Mountains Wilderness Area. The boat rides are available from Memorial Day to the middle of September. (Contact Gates of the Mountains Boat Club, 458-5241). The boat ride cruises by the entrance to Mann Gulch, where a devastating forest fire killed thirteen men in 1957. The fire is immortalized in Norman Maclean's book, *Young Men and Fire.* More than 31,000 visitors enjoyed the Gates of the Mountains tour boats in 1996.

For those seeking nonmotorized water adventures, the choices include rafting, canoeing, or kayaking on Montana's many lakes and rivers. More than twenty-five of Montana's wildlife viewing areas can be enjoyed from canoes or rafts. The Blackfoot River corridor and the Clearwater River Canoe Trail are two newly developed river access areas.

If you're crazy enough to want to float some of the whitewater sections of Montana's rivers, you can go it alone or engage the services of dozens of whitewater rafting outfitters. There are great whitewater floats on the Sun River, the Dearborn River, the Beartrap Canyon of the Madison River in the Lee Metcalf Wilderness Area, the Yankee Jim Canyon of the Yellowstone River, and the Flathead National Wild and Scenic River. For a lazy and lovely float, try the 149-mile Wild and Scenic portion of the Missouri River, from Fort Benton to the Fred Robinson Bridge.

Kayaking the Gallatin River. Travel Montana

Hot Springs

There are thirteen commercial hot springs in Montana, ranging from the completely low-key and funky to full-scale resorts. There are also numerous noncommercial hot springs around Montana, but you usually have to bribe someone to tell you where they are.

Hot Springs

Area Name	Location	For Information	Description
Lost Trail Hot Springs	6 mi south of Lost Trail Pass	821-3574	Outdoor hot swimming pool, indoor soaking pool, sauna, lodging, RV park, picnic ground, restaurant.
Hot Springs, Montana			The springs in this town are noted for their exceptionally high mineral content.
Camp Aqua	East of Hwy 28, 2.5 mi north of Hot Springs	741-3480	Indoor hot pools, steam baths, saunas, lodging, RV park, picnic ground.
Quinn's Hot Springs	At the junction of Hwys 200 and 135	826-3150	Outdoor swimming pool and soaking pool, lodging, RV park, picnic ground, restaurant, bar.
White Sulphur Springs	202 W Main, White Sulphur Springs	547-3366	The town grew up around this natural hot spring. Two pools are open yea- round to the public.
Bozeman Hot Springs	81123 Gallatin Road, Bozeman	586-6492	Indoor hot swimming pool, four soaking pools, cold pool, campground, RV park, picnic ground, grocery store.
Chico Hot Springs	South of Livingston off US 89	333-4933	Indoor and outdoor hot swimming and soaking pools, massage, lodging, restaurant, bar.
Sleeping Buffalo Hot Springs	10 mi west of Saco	527-3370	Two indoor pools and one outdoor pool. Bar, cafe, steakhouse, casino, lodging, golf course, rodeo grounds, RV campground, waterslide, hunting, fishing.
Elkhorn Hot Springs	North of Polaris on Pioneer Mountains Scenic Drive	834-3434	Surrounded by Beaverhead National Forest at 7,500 feet in elevation. Outdoor soaking pool, indoor wet saunas, rustic cabins, restaurant, camping, cross-country skiing.
Jackson Hot Springs	in Jackson	834-3151	Indoor-outdoor swimming pool free of chemicals or sulphur odor. RV park, camping, cabins, restaurant.
Boulder Hot Springs	1 mi south of Boulder on MT 69	225-4339	Separate men's and women's indoor soaking pools and steam baths, outdoor heated pool. Lodging, restaurant.
Beartrap Hot Springs	Just east of Norris on Hwy 84	685-3303	A wooden frame pool built by early homesteaders as a public bath sits directly on top of the springs. A half-million gallons of clear, odorless, hot water flow through the pool each day. Campground, picnic area, RV park.
Fairmont Hot Springs	1500 Fairmont Rd. Anaconda	797-3241	4 hot spring pools, golf course, waterslide, lodging restaurant.

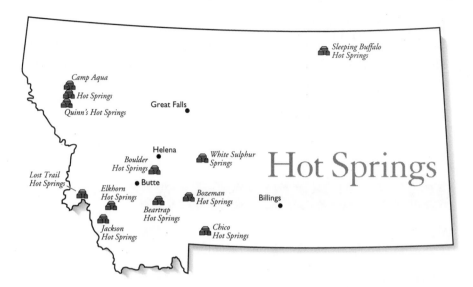

Hot Springs

Downhill Skiing

It may not have as many ski resorts as Colorado and Utah, or the angle of repose of other western slopes, but Montana has several resorts with "major league" skiing and much shorter lift lines than you'll find at Vail, Park City, and other famous slopes.

Skiing has been a popular family sport in Montana since the 1930s. Local ski clubs cleared promising hillsides and started volunteer-run ski hills in Anaconda, Helena, Butte, Bozeman, Townsend, Whitefish, and a few other towns and ranching communities. In the late 1940s, the sport really took off. Big Mountain opened in 1947, complete with a T-bar. In 1967, Snowbowl was the site of the U.S. National Alpine Championships. In 1995, Big Sky Resort completed a $3 million project to expand the lifts and runs. Big Sky now has the most vertical feet of skiing (4,180 feet) in the nation.

In addition, Montana's big skies drop snow on about a dozen smaller ski areas.

Contact Travel Montana, the state tourism office, for a *Montana Winter Guide*, which provides further details on Montana's ski opportunities: (800) 847-4868 ext. 6 for out-of-state callers; in Montana, call 444-2654.

For Skiers with Special Needs

Several Montana ski areas make it possible for skiers with disabilities or special needs to make use of the slopes. The **Dream Ski** program at Big Mountain offers individualized one-on-one ski instruction and free use of adaptive ski equipment from December 1 through March.

Eagle Ski Montana is a similar program available at Bridger Bowl, Red Lodge Mountain, and Showdown. At each of these areas, downhill and cross-country skiing are taught to skiers with special needs.

Montana Downhill Ski Areas

Ski Area	Map No.	1996-1997 Vertical Drop (in Feet)	Single-day Adult Lift Ticket Price	Description
Bear Paw Ski Bowl Havre 265-8404	1	900	$15	Day-use area 29 miles S of Havre, along Amtrak route on Rocky Boy's Indian Reservation; full services in Havre
Big Mountain Whitefish 862-1900	2	2,300	$38	Full service destination resort in NW Montana, on Amtrak route & served by Delta, Northwest, and Horizon airlines; near Glacier National Park
Big Sky Big Sky (800) 548-4486	3	4,180	$46	Full service destination & conference resort between Bozeman & Yellowstone National Park; open summer & winter
Bridger Bowl Bozeman (800) 223-9609	4	2,000	$28	Destination area with plenty of skiing & full services in Bozeman
Discovery Basin Anaconda 563-2184	5	1,300	$22	Day-use area near Anaconda; cafeteria, lounge, sales, rentals, and cross-country trails; Fairmont Hot Springs Resort 30 miles east
Great Divide Marysville 449-3746	6	1,510	$20	Day-use area about 20 miles NW of Helena; cafeteria, bar, restaurant, night skiing, groomed cross-country skiing; full services in Helena
Lost Trail Powder Mt. Connor 821-3211	7	1,200	$17	Day-use area S of Missoula on the Montana-Idaho border; lodging nearby; 6 miles to Lost Trail Hot Springs
Marshall Mountain Missoula 258-6000	8	1,500	$17	Day-use area outside of Missoula; lessons, rentals, snack bar, pub, night skiing; full services in Missoula
Maverick Mountain Dillon 834-3454	9	2,120	$18	Day-use area W of Dillon; open Thurs.-Sun.; half-price lift tickets Thurs. & Fri.; nursery available/reservations required
Montana Snowbowl Missoula 549-9777	10	2,600	$25	Day-use area outside of Missoula; expert slopes attract extreme skiers, but there's plenty of terrain for other skill levels
Red Lodge Mountain Red Lodge 446-2610	11	2,350	$29	Destination area with plenty of skiing & full services in Red Lodge
Rocky Mountain Hi Fairfield 467-3664	12	1,000	$20	Day-use area on the Rocky Mountain Front; rentals, lessons, lounge, and concessions; services in Choteau
Showdown Ski Area Neihart 236-5522	13	1,400	$24	Day-use area S of Great Falls; cross-country & snowmobile trails nearby; services in Neihart, Monarch, White Sulphur Springs, and Great Falls
Turner Mountain Libby 293-4317	14	2,110	$16	Day-use area 22 miles N of Libby in Montana's NW corner; warming hut and snack bar; services in Libby

Note: *Map numbers are referenced to tables on pages 421 and 423.*

Skiing for SPAM

West Yellowstone can almost always be counted on for plentiful snow weeks before the first day of winter. Recreational and competitive skiers alike converge on the town for the Thanksgiving holiday, when U.S. Olympic cross-country skiers are hitting the trails and working on speed and form. Recreational skiers who visit around Thanksgiving can learn the latest techniques during multi-day clinics and a week-long camp. The instructors are experts, some of them world-class.

Races are also part of the community's winter scene. Hundreds of competitors have taken part in the Rendezvous Ski Race (usually held in early March), and a "Spam Cup" citizens' race is held each month, with a can of the legendary meat going to the winner.

For information on cross-country skiing in West Yellowstone, call 464-7701.

Cross-Country Skiing

Wherever there is adequate snowfall to cover rocks and roots, the hardy species of cross-country skier can practice the sport as it was meant to be—by simply heading out and making fresh tracks. Many Montanans choose to telemark off-trail on public lands—in times of low avalanche danger.

Montana has twenty-seven designated cross-country ski areas at various locations within six national forests. The designated cross-country ski trails are marked by signs with a skier. Some are groomed and some require skiers to break their own trails on accessible public lands and logging roads throughout the state. Sixteen wildlife viewing areas offer cross-country skiing trails. The Mount Haggin Nordic Ski Area, off Highway 274 between Anaconda and Wise River, is within a state wildlife management area. The trails of this area lead skiers along the remnants of an 18-mile-long flume that once carried logs along a zigzag route over creeks and the Continental Divide to provide timber and boiler fuel for the Anaconda Smelter.

Many Montana towns allow cross-country skiing on local golf courses or river walks.

Cross-Country Ski Resorts

Name Address	Map No.	Location	Trail Distance	Amenities
Izaak Walton Inn Box 653 Essex, MT 59916 888-5700	15	Halfway between West and East Glacier, Hwy 2	30 km + w/ set track, and skating lane	guided ski tours, rentals, sauna, lessons
Lone Mtn. Ranch Box 160069 Big Sky, MT 59716 (800) 514-4644 995-4644	16	Hwy 64, Big Sky Road, between village and Big Sky ski resort	65 km groomed w/ set track and skating lane	7-night stays include backcountry ski tours of Yellowstone N.P., sleigh ride, dinners, trail fees
Bohart Ranch 16621 Brider Canyon Rd. Bozeman, MT 59714 586-9070	17	Hwy 86 in Bridger Canyon	25 km groomed w/ set track and skating lane	biathlon range, rentals, lessons, warming cabin
Mountain Timbers Wilderness Lodge Box 94 W. Glacier, MT 59936 (800) 841-3835 387-5830	18	Rabe Rd., between N. Fork Rd. and U.S. 2	15 km of groomed trails	secluded lodge w/ library, pool table, views, hot tub, country breakfasts
Wade Lake Resort Box 107 Cameron, MT 59720 682-7560	19	40 miles south of Ennis; west of Hebgen Lake in Beaverhead N.F.	25 km track-set trails	Wade Lake is a wildlife viewing area; ski in or ride a shuttle from Hwy 287; hot tub

Source: *Travel Montana*, Montana Winter Guide, *1996-97. Helena: Montana Department of Commerce, 1996.*

Snowmobiling

Montana boasts 4,100 miles of groomed snowmobile trails and nearly 20 million acres of public lands accessible to snow machines. In the snowiest parts of Montana the snowmobile season can be as long as six months, running from as early as the end of October to as late as May.

No wonder, then, that during the winter of 1995-96 nearly 20,030 residents registered snowmobiles for use on public lands within Montana (and an untold number of unregistered snowmobilers use their machines only on private land). Twenty-nine local snowmobile associations throughout the state promote the sport, hold competitions, and groom trails. During the winter of 1994-95 snowmobiling directly contributed $103 million to the state's economy.

Source: Montana Department of Fish, Wildlife & Parks, Montana Snowmobile Association.

Montana Snowmobiling Areas

Area Name	Location	Miles Groomed	Contacts
Cut Bank	Between Cut Bank and Kalispell on U.S. 2	45	Cut Bank Chamber of Commerce, 873-4041; Lewis & Clark National Forest, 791-7700; Rocky Mountain Ranger District, 466-5341
The Flathead	Columbia Falls, Whitefish, Big Fork, and Kalispell	220	Flathead Convention & Visitor Assoc., (800) 543-3105; Flathead Snowmobile Assoc., 756-6139; South Fork Snowmobile Assoc.,387-9090; Flathead National Forest, 755-5401
Haugan/ Thompson Falls	On the Montana-Idaho border in Northwest Montana	150	Montana Nightriders Snowmobile Club, 687-4242; Superior Ranger District, 822-4233; Thompson Falls Chamber of Commerce, 827-4930
Libby/Ten Lakes Scenic Area/Yaak	Northwest Montana	153	Libby Ranger District, 293-7773; Three Rivers Ranger District, 295-4693; Libby Chamber of Commerce, 293-4167; Lincoln County Sno-Kats Snowmobile Club, 295-5858; Ten Lakes Snowmobile Club, 882-4474
Lolo Pass	On U.S. 12 at the Montana-Idaho border	250	Missoula Ranger District, 329-3750; Powell Ranger District, 942-3113; Missoula Snowgoers, 543-4558; Missoula Convention & Visitors Bureau, 526-3465
Mission Mountains	Between Missoula and Kalispell on U.S. 93	45	Mission Mountain Snowmobile Club, 676-5000
Seeley Lake	15 miles north of the junction of MT 83 and 200 in western Montana	230	Seeley Lake Ranger District, 677-2233; Seeley Lake Area Chamber of Commerce, 677-2880
Skalkaho	15 miles east of Hamilton on Skalkaho Hwy. 38	56	Bitterroot National Forest, 363-3131; Darby Ranger District, 821-3913; Bitterroot Chamber of Commerce, 363-2400; Bitterroot Ridge Runners Snowmobile Club, 363-4689

Montana Snowmobiling Areas, (cont.)

Area Name	Location	Miles Groomed	Contacts
Deer Lodge	80 miles east of Missoula & 40 miles west of Butte	40	Deerlodge Ranger District, 846-1770
Dillon/Polaris	33 miles northwest of Dillon	200	Dillon Ranger District, 683-3900; Beaverhead Sno-Riders, 683-6333/683-2205
Garnet	30 miles east of Missoula	100	Garnet Resource Area, BLM, 329-3914; Garnet Preservation Assoc., 329-1031; Missoula Convention & Visitors Bureau, 543-6623/(800) 526-3465
Georgetown Lake	MT 1 between Drummond and Anaconda	90	Philipsburg Ranger District, 859-3211; Anaconda Snowmobile Club, 563-7945
Helena	At the junction of I-15, U.S. 12, and U.S. 287	245	Helena Ranger District, 449-5490; Helena Snowdrifters, 449-2685; Helena Chamber of Commerce, 442-4120
Lincoln	Between Great Falls and Missoula on MT 200	250	Lincoln Ranger District, 362-4265; Ponderosa Snow Warriors, 362-4078/362-4335; Lincoln Valley Chamber of Commerce, 362-4949
Virginia City/Ennis	In southwest Montana along U.S. 287	130	Madison Ranger District, 682-4253; Madison Valley Snow Snokes, 682-7152; Outback & Beyond Trail Club, 682-7335; Vigilante Snowmobilers, 843-5484/683-7755
Wisdom/Jackson	Junction of MT 43 and 287 in southwest Montana	150	Wisdom Ranger District, 689-3243; Big Hole Snowmobile Club, 689-3400
Wise River	12 miles west of I-15, between Butte and Dillon	150	Wise River Ranger District, 832-3178; Wise River Jackpine Savages, 832-3258
Big Timber	I-90 between Bozeman and Billings	34	Big Timber Ranger District, 932-5155; Sweet Grass County Recreation Assoc., 932-5319
Bozeman/Big Sky	I-90 between Billings and Butte	200	Bozeman Ranger District, 587-6920; Gallatin Valley Snowmobile Association, 586-3437; Bozeman Area Chamber of Commerce, 586-5421
Cooke City/ Silver Gate	South-central Montana on U.S. 212	60	Gardiner Ranger District, 848-7375; Yellowstone National Park, 307-344-7381 ext. 2206; Upper Yellowstone Snowmobile Club, 838-2246
Livingston	Junction of I-90 and U.S. 89 in southwest Montana	84	Livingston Ranger District, 222-1892; Big Sky Snowriders, 222-1863 or 222-2676; Livingston Chamber of Commerce, 222-0850
West Yellowstone/ Gardiner	West and north entrances to Yellowstone National Park	600	West Yellowstone Chamber of Commerce, 646-7701; Hebgen Lake Ranger District, 646-7369; Yellowstone National Park, 307-344-7381 ext. 2206
Kings Hill/Little Belts	U.S. 89 between Great Falls and White Sulphur Springs	225	Kings Hill Ranger District, 547-3361

Source: Travel Montana, Montana Winter Guide, 1996-97. Helena: Montana Department of Commerce, 1996.

A Great Ride

At 450 miles, the TransMontana Ride from Eureka to West Yellowstone is the state's longest snowmobile riding event. Although participants must trailer their machines over some sections, they ride much of the distance on groomed trails.

Avalanche DANGER

In the 1993-1994 winter season, twelve snowmobile riders were involved in six different avalanches, resulting in six deaths. Avalanches may occur at any time during the winter. Advice on avalanche conditions is available at local USDA Forest Service offices. The following are avalanche advisory numbers in your area.

Northwest Montana (800) 526-5329
Cooke City 838-2341
Southwest Montana 587-6981
West Yellowstone 646-7912
Lolo and Bitterroot national forests 549-4488 or (800) 281-1030

Snowmobile Contacts

Montana Snowmobile
Association
Box 3202
Great Falls, MT 59403

Montana Department of Fish, Wildlife & Parks
Attention: Snowmobile Program Coordinator
1420 East 6th Avenue
Helena, MT 59620
444-4585

State Parks

Montana's natural, cultural, and recreational resources are greatly enhanced by its fine state park system. In turn, at least one of the state's natural resources helps support the system. The interest on 1.27 percent of the state's coal severance tax is dedicated to a trust fund for the acquisition and maintenance of park sites. Each year, the state park system has over 4 million visitors.

In 1936, Lewis and Clark Caverns became Montana's first state park when the site was transferred to the state from the federal government. Makoshika State Park in southeastern Montana is the largest state park, with 8,834 acres of land, much of it containing unique geologic formations.

State parks and other state recreational lands offer a variety of landscapes, natural features, historical significance, and recreational opportunities in areas all across Montana. Some parks feature a wide range of visitor facilities such as camping, boat launch sites, and concessions. Other sites are less developed but, depending on rules established for each park, visitors may still camp, picnic, observe wildlife, and enjoy other recreational activities.

All of Montana's state parks are open for day use. Many offer camping facilities. Others prohibit overnight stays. When camping is allowed, fees vary according to the services provided. Some parks close some or all of their facilities during the winter months. With the purchase of an annual State Parks Passport ($15 in 1996), visitors can enter any park in the system without paying day use fees.

A self-registration system is in use at most state parks. Recreation use fees are also charged for designated group use of facilities, guided tours, and other services. (In 1996, the day-use fee was $3 at twenty-eight of the state parks.)

Under the Montana Primitive Parks Act of 1993, certain Montana state parks are to retain the unique, primarily undeveloped character for which they were originally acquired in order to provide a variety of recreational opportunities for Montanans. The only development allowed for the parks are those necessary to meet minimum public health standards regarding sanitation and safe public access; establishment of new hiking trails or improvement of existing hiking trails; and installation of minimal signage. Visitors to primitive designated parks must pack out their own trash.

For more information contact Montana Fish, Wildlife & Parks, 1420 East 6th Avenue, Helena MT 59620, 444-3750.

Hunting

Hunting is very much a part of Montana's past. The early Indian tribes depended on the bison herds and other game animals for food, shelter, and clothing. The early fur trappers were lured to Montana by the abundance of fur-bearing animals. The early prospectors and homesteaders depended on wild game to supplement their diets.

Today hunting in Montana offers a large selection of big game, waterfowl, and game birds in a wide variety of habitats. Upland game birds include sharp-tailed grouse, sage grouse, Hungarian partridge, chukar partridge, ruffed grouse, blue grouse, spruce (or Franklin's) grouse, ring-necked pheasants, and Merriam's turkeys. Willow ptarmigans also occur in some parts of Montana, but they cannot be legally hunted. Waterfowl that may be hunted include geese, ducks, swans, cranes, mourning doves, coots, and snipes. Whooping cranes are protected by law and may not be hunted.

Montana is known to have the best big game selection in the lower 48 states including mule deer, white-tailed deer, elk, antelope, bighorn sheep, mountain goats, Shiras moose, black bears, mountain lions, and bison. Many big game populations have been increasing since the 1930s and are now at record levels.

But management problems persist as civilization encroaches on plains and low-lands where game species like to feed. This has required the development of some winter ranges for big game.

Nearly half the adult males and 20 percent of the adult females in the state purchase Montana hunting licenses. Though out-of-state hunters may take home some of our wildlife, they generally spend over $50 million every year on outfitter services and equipment.

In 1995, 482,233 total big game licenses were issued, and 6,641 hunters, along with 2,358 young bowhunters, received their Montana Hunter Education Certificates.

The week beginning on the third Monday in September is an official week of observance in Montana to commemorate this state's valued heritage of hunting.

TIP-MONT *Program*

TIP-MONT, Montana Fish, Wildlife & Parks's toll-free "Turn in Poachers, Montana" hot line, allows hunters and other citizens to report incidents of poaching. An average of 500-600 calls a year, most made by sportsmen, has led to the arrest and conviction of deer, bear, elk, moose, and upland game bird poachers. Callers may remain anonymous and do not have to testify in court. The rewards are substantial. To report suspected poaching activities, call (800) TIP-MONT or (800) 847-6668.

Hunter Harvests (1994)

Game	Number of Licenses Issued	Total Harvest
Deer	280,892	161,773
Elk	138,567	32,433
Moose	748	655
Antelope	51,937	37,858
Bighorn Sheep	651	328
Mountain Goat	275	211
Black Bear	9,163	386

Source: Montana Department of Fish, Wildlife & Parks.

Fishing

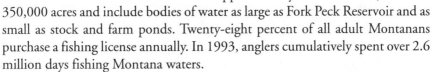

Montanans love to fish, and the state boasts an impressive number of places for anglers to go—4 million acres of cold-water lakes, 15,000 miles of cold-water streams, and 6,100 miles of warm-water rivers and streams. Warm-water lakes cover approximately 350,000 acres and include bodies of water as large as Fork Peck Reservoir and as small as stock and farm ponds. Twenty-eight percent of all adult Montanans purchase a fishing license annually. In 1993, anglers cumulatively spent over 2.6 million days fishing Montana waters.

Montana's climate and geography, along with a strong commitment to natural resources conservation and fisheries management, contribute to the state's reputation as a fishing paradise. As early as 1963, the state enacted the nation's first stream preservation legislation. In the 1970s, the state curtailed the stocking of hatchery trout in the rivers and streams of the state to increase populations of wild trout. Hatchery trout are still stocked in many lakes and reservoirs. In 1996, nearly 45 million fish, including rainbow trout, kokanee salmon, walleye, and largemouth bass, were stocked in waters throughout Montana.

Fishing at Mollman Lakes in the Mission Mountains. Russ Schneider

Fishing Facts

• The net economic value of cold-water fishing in Montana is estimated in excess of $200 million a year, plus another $18 million spent on fishing for warm-water species.

• In 1993, the rivers receiving the heaviest fishing pressure were the Madison River above Ennis, the Clark Fork, and the Bighorn below Afterbay Dam. Those lakes receiving the heaviest fishing pressure in 1993 were Canyon Ferry Reservoir, Hauser Reservoir, and Holter Lake.

• It is illegal to transplant or introduce live fish into Montana waters. Use of live fish for bait is also prohibited in many waters. These activities can result in the introduction of parasites and disease, which can radically alter the kinds and quantity of fish in a lake or stream. A desirable fish in one body of water can become a pest in another.

Montana's Record Fish (as of 1995)

Fish	Record Weight	Year	Area
Arctic grayling	3.21 lb.	1994	Handkerchief Lake
Bigmouth buffalo	57.75 lb.	1994	Nelson Reservoir
Brook trout	9.06 lb.	1940	Lower Two Medicine Lake
Brown trout	29.00 lb.	1966	Wade Lake
Bull trout	25.63 lb.	1916	Unknown
Chinook (king salmon)	31.13 lb.	1991	Fort Peck Reservoir
Cutthroat trout	16.00 lb.	1955	Red Eagle Lake
Golden trout	4.90 lb.	1993	Lightning Lake
Lake trout	42.00 lb.	1979	Flathead Lake
Largemouth bass	8.16 lb.	1984	Milnor Lake
Mountain whitefish	5.09 lb.	1987	Kootenai River
Northern pike	37.50 lb.	1972	Tongue River Reservoir
Paddlefish	142.50 lb.	1973	Missouri River
Rainbow trout	29.02 lb.	1991	Kootenai River
Smallmouth bass	6.09 lb.	1990	Fort Peck Reservoir
Walleye	16.29 lb.	1995	Fort Peck Reservoir

Blue-Ribbon Streams

The following bodies of water, totaling 541 miles, are classified as "Blue-Ribbon Streams" because of their productivity, number of game fish present, use by anglers, accessibility, and aesthetics.

Beaverhead River
Big Hole River
Bighorn River
Blackfoot River
Flathead River (main stem)
Flathead River (North Fork)
Gallatin River

Kootenai River below Libby Dam
Madison River
Missouri River from Holter Dam
   to Cascade
Rock Creek
Yellowstone River

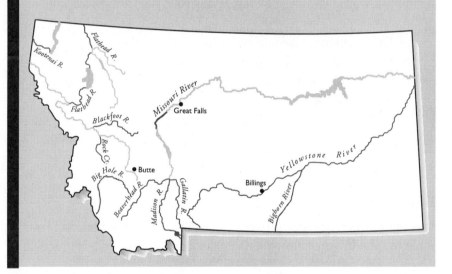

SELECTED Fishing Events

- Federation of Fly Fishers International Fly Fishing Show, Livingston, August, 585-7592
- Governors Cup Walleye Tournament, Glasgow, July, 228-2222
- Hell Creek/Jordan Walleye Tournament, Hell Creek State Park, July, 232-4365
- Montana Walleye Unlimited Fall Classic, Glasgow, August, 265-3411

Whirling Disease

In only the past few years, Montana's rainbow trout populations have been locally decimated by whirling disease, a waterborne infection that disturbs the equilibrium of these fish. The Madison River near Ennis is the epicenter of whirling disease in Montana.

The following tips may help you prevent the spread of whirling disease to your own favorite stream:

- Remove all mud and aquatic plants from your vehicle, boat, anchor, trailer and axles, waders, boots, and fishing gear before departing the fishing access site or boat dock.

- Drain all water from your boat and equipment—including coolers, buckets, and live wells—before departing the fishing access site or boat dock.

- Dry your boat and equipment between river trips.

- Don't transport fish from one body of water to another.

- Don't dispose of fish entrails, skeletal parts, or other by-products in any body of water.

- Don't collect sculpins (also known as bullheads) or use sculpins as bait.

Further Reading:

Cunningham, Bill. *Wild Montana.* Helena: Falcon Publishing, 1995. *A guide to 55 roadless recreation areas.*

The Elk Hunter's Cookbook. Missoula: Rocky Mountain Elk Foundation, 1995.

Feldman, Robert. *The Rockhound's Guide to Montana.* Helena: Falcon Publishing, 1985.

Green, Randall, ed. *Rock Climber's Guide to Montana.* Helena: Falcon Publishing, 1995.

Harmon, Will. *Fat/Trax Bozeman.* Helena: Falcon Publishing Co., 1996.

Montana Hunting Almanac. Annual publication of *The Missoulian,* P.O. Box 8029, Missoula, MT 59807.

Montana Outdoors. The official bi-monthly publication of the Montana Department of Fish, Wildlife & Parks, 1420 East 6th Avenue, Helena, MT 59620.

Posewitz, Jim. *Beyond Fair Chase: The Ethic and Tradition of Hunting.* Helena: Falcon Publishing, 1995.

Sample, Michael S. *Fishing Montana.* Helena: Falcon Publishing Co., 1997.

Outfitters & Guides

Montana has excellent outfitters and guides available for a half-day hunting or fishing trip or an entire vacation. For more information, contact:

Fishing Outfitters Association of Montana (FOAM)
Box 67
Gallatin Gateway, MT 59730
763-5436

**Montana Outfitters and
Guides Association**
Box 1248
Helena, MT 59624
449-3578
443-2439 fax

Montana Board of Outfitters
111 North Jackson
Helena, MT 59620
444-3738
444-1667 fax

Schneider, Bill. *Bear Aware: Hiking and Camping in Bear Country.* Helena: Falcon Publishing, 1996.

_____. *Hiking Montana.* Helena: Falcon Publishing Co., 1995.

Thompson, Curt. *Floating and Recreation on Montana Rivers.* Lakeside, MT: 1993. ***Available from Curt Thompson, Box 392, Lakeside, MT 59922. Also distributed by Falcon.***

Call (800) 582-2665 and ask for a free catalog listing all of Falcon's outdoor recreation titles.

chapter   fourteen

ARTS *& Culture*

MONTANANS CHERISH A ROBUST tradition of public and private support for the arts of all kinds. This nurturing atmosphere has produced an astonishing number of successful folk artists and craftspersons, visual artists, writers, and performers—many of whom are just plain folks with day jobs and remarkable talents.

Folk and traditional arts have long been part of the picture. Across the state, most towns have at least one annual community event celebrating local heritage and folklife, including such varied arts as chainsaw sculpture, quilting, cowboy poetry, and old-time fiddle music. Woven, sculpted, or somehow blended into these traditional arts are pieces of Montana's many heritages. The colorful decorative arts of the state's many Plains Indian tribes are but one example.

Montanans love to explore art in all its forms. Visit a few of our more than 150 galleries, museum shops, and arts markets, and you will see for yourself that our state continues to inspire and nurture artists whose works tell of their love of this special place. Painters, photographers, sculptors, ceramists, and fiber artists create unique visions of our surrounding landscapes—and the landscapes of the mind.

For a state of small population, Montana boasts an impressive number of museum collections, community art centers, and art auctions that have gained widespread fame: the Montana Historical Society Museum in Helena, the Yellowstone Art Center in Billings, and the Museum of the Rockies in Bozeman, to name a few. The tremendous attendance at the world-famous C. M. Russell

photo: Blanton Owen/ Montana Arts Council

Art Auction in Great Falls each spring indicates continued interest in the realistic style of contemporary artists who portray the wildlife, landscapes, native peoples, and historical life of the region.

Perhaps our area is best known as a literary haven. Writers are an abundant species in Montana, and most have something interesting to say. Some of our homegrown novelists, poets, and essayists write about life here in the Big Sky state; others write of distant frontiers, older cities and civilizations, or theoretical realities.

Montana's performing arts shine equally as bright. Theater and dance companies entertain us regularly and garner grants and awards in the process. Hundreds of musicians meet weekly to play music together and to share their gifts with their neighbors. Nine cities support symphony orchestras, many of which have been active for a half-century or more. Local jazz scenes bubble up with sound, just another instance of the artistic ferment around us.

And, as most folks around the nation know, Montana is one of the last, best places for making films—both homegrown filmmakers and major industry productions have used the state as either set or inspiration.

The arts have not only intrinsic value to Montanans but also important economic benefits for the state. Montana's arts advocacy groups, the Montana Arts Council, and the state tourism office work hand in hand with local governments, businesses, and individuals to create vibrant cultural offerings that stimulate Montana commerce as well as the creativity of its citizens and visitors.

Arts Festivals

Event	Location, Date, or Season	For Information
Bigfork Festival of the Arts	Bigfork, August	881-4636
Artist and Craftsmen of the Flathead	Kalispell	881-4288
Kaleidoscope Festival of the Arts	Helena, August	442-0400
Daly Days	Hamilton	Valley Arts Council P.O. Box 744, Hamilton 59840
Festival of Nations	Red Lodge, August	446-1718
Montana Cowboy Poetry Gathering	Lewistown, 3rd weekend in August	538-5436
Sunrise Festival of the Arts	Sidney, July	482-1916
Cowboy Poetry Gathering	Sidney, June	483-1916
Sweet Pea Festival of the Arts	Bozeman, 1st weekend in August	P.O. Box 717, Bozeman 59715
Whitefish Annual Arts Festival	Whitefish, July	862-5875
Outdoor Art Fair	Polson, August	883-5956
Hi Line Art Festival	Plentywood, April	Chamber of Commerce Plentywood 59254 765-1607
Virginia City Arts Festival	August	843-5345

Traditional and Folk Arts

Folk artists are people working in traditional forms that are passed from generation to generation through the family, ethnic, or occupational group. Their work serves to give identity to the groups from which they arise. Folk arts might be divided into three major categories:

• Occupational arts, such as folk architecture, basketmaking, leather working, whittling, blacksmithing, or weaving. Montana is home to many quilters, furniture makers, and other craftspersons who use traditional methods or elaborations on these to create beautiful and functional objects.

• Ethnic arts, such as decorative work, music, dance, or costume. Montana's many Indian tribes continue to pass on their cultural legacy to younger generations by means of native arts. Other Montana ethnic groups, such as those celebrated in Red Lodge's Festival of Nations, also share their heritage through song, dance, artwork, and other creations.

• Verbal and musical arts, such as stories, poetry, legend, song, humor, or family narratives. Among Montana's treasures are its oral and aural traditions, including folk music and cowboy poetry. From singers to storytellers, Montana is an earful. Montana old-time fiddlers, such as the Krieger Family Fiddlers, gather at annual festivals and contests to maintain the state's musical lineage.

RED LODGE
Festival of Nations

For nine days in early August, a visit to Red Lodge is a trip around the world as this small Montana town, once a mining center, celebrates the many ethnic groups who migrated to it. The town's kaleidoscopic heritage includes Scottish, Finnish, German, Italian, Irish, English, Welsh, Scandinavian, and Slavic cultures. Each day of the festival is dedicated to a different ethnic heritage and culminates with the All Nations Parade on the final Sunday.

The festival, held since 1950, attracts more than 15,000 visitors each year. Events include arts and crafts exhibits, ethnic foods, music, and dancing.

Culture and Heritage Calendar

Event	Location	For Information
Billings Hispanic Fiesta	Billings, August	259-0191 or 248-8492
Canadian Days Festival	Kalispell	1640 Lake Butte Rd., Kalispell 59901
Festival of Cultures	Billings, June 9	657-1105
Festival of Nations	Red Lodge, August	446-1718
Heritage Day	Anaconda, August	563-2400
Heritage Days	Columbia Falls, June	892-PLAY
Heritage Festival	Butte, September	782-1859 or 782-0742
Indian Fair	Harlem	P.O. Box 631, Harlem 59526
International Festivals	Glendive	Chamber of Commerce P.O. Box 930, Glendive 59330
Libby Nordicfest	Libby, September	293-4167
Native American Days	Browning	
Herbsfest	Laurel	628-8306

notable

Montanans

John L. Clarke (1881-1970)

This beloved Montana sculptor, painter, and carver was also known as Cutapuis (Man-Who-Talks-Not), his Blackfeet name. He was born in Highwood and as a toddler, he became deaf from scarlet fever. Clarke studied the wild animals of his home region near Glacier National Park and made figures of them in clay, later turning to carving. He attended the Montana and North Dakota Schools for the Deaf and studied woodcarving at the St. Francis Academy in Milwaukee. He later had his own shop in the northwest corner of East Glacier, where John D. Rockefeller was one of his customers. His carvings of the wild-

Montana Historical Society

life and paintings of the landscapes of the Glacier region gained him national recognition. He was included in the recently published *Deaf Heritage: A Narrative History of Deaf America*, released by the National Association of the Deaf. The Museum of the Plains Indian at Browning and the School for the Deaf and Blind in Great Falls display Clarke's large-scale murals of Blackfeet life.

Folk Arts Organizations

Event	Address, Phone
Alpine Weavers & Spinners Guild	125 Birch Drive Whitefish 59937 862-6507
Blackfeet Cultural Program	P.O. Box 2038 Browning 59417 338-3535
Center for Native American Studies	Montana State University, P.O. Box 172340-38812 179 Wilson Hall Bozeman 59717-2340 994-0211
Crow Culture Committee	Box 721, Crow Agency 59022
Dillon Fiddlers Association	4275 Bloody Dick Road, Dillon 59725
Dillon Junior Fiddlers	324 S. Washington, Dillon 59725
Folklife Programs, Montana Arts Council	P.O. Box 202201, Helena 59620-2201 444-6430
Old Timer's Concert	218 South Main Street, Sheridan 59749 842-5431
Dull Knife Memorial College Cultural Committee	P.O. Box 98, Lame Deer 59043 477-6215
Salish Culture Committee	P.O. Box 418 St. Ignatius 59865 745-4572
Helena Folklore Society	526 Clarke St. Helena 59601
Helena Indian Alliance	436 North Jackson Helena 59601 442-9244
Helena Weavers and Spinners Guild	SR Box 165 Clancy 59634
Indian Development/Education Alliance	P.O. Box 726, Miles City 59301
Indian Fair	P.O. Box 631 Harlem 59526
Intertribal Indian Club	MSU-Billings, Box 123 59101 657-2561
Kootenai Culture Committee	P.O. Box 155 Elmo 59915 849-5541
Loud Thunder International, Inc.	P.O. Box 601 Great Falls 59403
Métis Cultural Recovery Trust	P.O. Box 181 Choteau 59422
Montana Indigenous People's Committee	127 N. Higgins, Missoula 59802 543-3550
Montana United Indian Association	P.O. Box 6043 Helena 59604 443-5350
Native American Center	700 10th St. S. Great Falls 59405 761-3165
Native American Cultural Institution	Box 531, MSU-Billings 1500 N 30th St. Billings 59101 657-2011
North American Indian Alliance	100 E. Galena Butte 59701 782-0461
Northern Plains Folklife	502 Chaucer Helena 59601 443-7651
Piegan Institute	P.O. Box 909 Browning 59417
Rocky Boy Cultural Committee	Stone Child College RR1, Box 1082, Box Elder 59521 395-4334
Spirit Talk	P.O. Drawer V Browning 59417 338-2882
Sundance Training Center	9230 Pryor Road Billings 59101 259-6342
Two Medicine Lake Society	Box 1509 Browning 59417
Western Heritage Center	2822 Montana Ave. Billings 59101 256-6809

Crow Fair

On the third weekend of every August, Crow Agency is host to the Crow Fair and Rodeo Celebration, billed as the "tepee capital of the world" and the biggest all-Indian rodeo in the state. Indians from all over the western states and Canada converge to camp along the Little Bighorn

Crow Fair, in August. Donnie Sexton/Travel Montana

River and to participate in competitive Indian dancing, pari-mutuel horse racing and betting, wild horse races, and other Indian games. Each morning visitors wake to camp criers on horseback and Crow language wake-up calls on the loudspeaker, followed by a spectacular parade to herald the day's colorful events. There are Giveaways and Specials, in which family, friends, lost loved ones, and other deserving persons are honored with gifts like blankets or branches tied with dollar bills.

Over 40,000 tickets were sold for the 78th Crow Fair in August 1996. Considered one of the premier powwows of the Plains Indians, Crow Fair is part family reunion, part party, part sporting event, part tourist attraction, and a cornucopia of visual delights, tasty foods, hypnotic music—a spiritual and intercultural renewal for all.

Authentically Indian

The Indian Arts and Crafts Act of 1990 requires a registered trademark or a label to authenticate the Indian origin of any arts or craft item sold in the state. It is a misdemeanor crime to sell unauthenticated items that claim to be American Indian art.

My Favorite Parts
of Montana's Arts

by George Heavy Runner, Browning

George Heavy Runner is a member of the Blackfeet tribe and a Democratic representative in the Montana Legislature. He works as a resource person for Blackfeet Community College in Browning.

1. The beat of the drum and the songs of the native people who first inhabited this place during the summer powwows . . . brings back memories of what used to be when buffalo roamed.

2. **Jack Gladstone**, a unique artist who blends his songs with ancestral threads of the Blackfeet in a reflection of yesterday and today.

3. *Winter in the Blood*, the novel by James Welch—one of the earlier works by this Native American author who can write with the best of them.

4. **Museum of the Upper Missouri**, Old Fort Park, in Fort Benton, a must-see place to stop and get a feel of the site that was, for many Montanans, where their dreams and hardships began.

5. **The Helena Jazz Festival**, a great time to visit the capital city and enrich yourself in the "blues."

6. Local fishing on the Blackfeet Reservation: for the fly fisher who'd like to pit his flies against the local boys at Mittens or Hidden Lake, recognizable by their coolers, colored marshmallows, and oil-sprayed night crawlers, come see the art of local fishing at its best.

7. *Suzanna of the Mounties*, the movie starring Shirley Temple, a great opportunity to see scenes of Glacier National Park and members of the Blackfeet tribe who served as extras and could still remember days of hunting the buffalo in the Prickly Pear Valley.

8. Golfing, an art that allows you to create a masterpiece one day and have nightmares the next, due to too many strokes of the putter. Experience those moments at the beautiful **East Glacier Golf Course**, which is my home away from home.

9. *Backroads of Montana*, a video produced by The University of Montana. If you're not from Montana and want some insights into our culture, here's your chance.

10. The videos of historian **K. Ross Toole**'s work are noteworthy and frank about Montana's illustrious history.

Powwow Calendar

Event	Location, Date, or Season	For Information
Arlee Powwow	Arlee, July	883-3313
Badlands Indian Celebration	Brockton, June	768-5151
Bitterroot Good Nations Powwow	Hamilton	P.O. Box 1421 Hamilton 59840 363-6390
Christmas Powwow	Busby, December	477-6284
Crow Fair	Crow Agency, August	638-2601
North American Indian Days	Browning, July	338-2230
North American Indian Alliance Powwow	Butte, September	728-0461
Northern Cheyenne New Year's Powwow	Lame Deer, January	477-6284
Red Sky Powwow and Art Fest	Vaughn, June	965-3322
Rocky Boy's Powwow	Havre, August	395-4478
Standing Arrow Powwow	Elmo, July	849-5541
United Peoples Powwow	Missoula	P.O. Box 7218, Missoula 59807
Valley of the Chiefs Powwow and Rodeo	Lodge Grass, July	638-2601
White River Cheyenne Powwow	Busby, August	477-6284

notable
Montanans

William D'Arcy McNickle (1904-1977)

Born in St. Ignatius to a Métis mother and an Anglo father, McNickle became an honored novelist and writer-editor on American Indian cultural heritage. He graduated from The University of Montana in 1925 and went on to study at Oxford University (1925-26) and the University of Grenoble (1931). Following his degree work, McNickle wrote for the Federal Writers' Project in Washington, D.C. and was the director of tribal relations for the Bureau of Indian Affairs.

McNickle's three novels were released over a period of some four decades. The first, *The Surrounded* (1936), was inspired by his own Montana background. The second, *Runner in the Sun*, was released in 1954. His third, the highly acclaimed *Wind from an Enemy Sky*, was published following his death in 1977. McNickle wrote or edited numerous histories of Indian culture in America.

In later life, he taught anthropology at the University of Saskatchewan and became program director of the Center for American Indian History at The Newberry Library in Chicago, later renamed the D'Arcy McNickle Center for the History of the American Indian in his honor.

notable
Montanans

☞ A. B. Guthrie, Jr. (1901-1991)

His richly detailed novels of life in Montana and the Old West won him wide acclaim, including the Pulitzer Prize for *The Way West* in 1950, and made him one of the state's most beloved writers. Alfred Bertram Guthrie, Jr. was born in 1901 in Indiana, but grew up in Chinook and Great Falls and graduated from The University of Montana in 1923. He worked as a writing teacher, a journalist, and an editor in Kentucky before turning to writing novels. From his home near Choteau, he wrote stories that matched the scope of the land around him and the sky above him.

Montana Historical Society

He wrote of Indians, fur trappers, mountain men, and other inhabitants of Montana and of their relationship to the land, the waters. Later in his life, in lectures and essays, he spoke just as eloquently, but more directly, for the defense and stewardship of that land, those waters. In addition to the Pulitzer winner, his books include *The Big Sky, These Thousand Hills, The Last Valley*, and an autobiography called *The Blue Hen's Chick*.

☞ James Welch (1940-)

Born in Browning to a Blackfeet father and Gros Ventre mother, Welch went to schools on the Blackfeet and Fort Belknap Reservations. After studying under Richard Hugo at The University of Montana in the 1960s, Welch began telling the world about life on the Hi Line. His books have been translated and published in France, Italy, Sweden, Japan, Germany, and other countries. They have been widely read here in the U.S.

Welch's first book was published in 1971, the beginning of an impressive body of poetry and fiction. His novels include *Winter in the Blood* (1974), *The Death of Jim Loney* (1979), *The Indian Lawyer* (1990), and *Fools Crow* (1986), for which Welch won an American Book Award and the Los Angeles *Times* Book Prize.

Among his most prized honors is the Lifetime Achievement Award from the Native Writers' Circle of the Americas. In 1995, Welch, who lives in Missoula, was knighted by the French government for his contribution to arts and letters.

Visual Arts

Talented artists, with a sensitive eye focused on the amazing natural canvases and the diverse faces of our Big Sky, were part of the stream of people who followed the first explorers or accompanied the early settlers to Montana.

A century and a half later, Montana continues to be an inspirational working environment for hundreds of visual artists of all mediums. The Archie Bray Foundation for the Ceramic Arts in Helena, for example, attracts renowned potters from the world over.

Montana photographers and painters work on the advance edge of their chosen fields. Contemporary artists enjoy free range here—Rudy Autio, the Finnish-American painter and ceramist from Missoula known for his colorful, swirling designs with human and animal figures; Floyd Tennison DeWitt, who sculpts bronze horses and historical scenes with a nod to the European tradition; David Shaner, the Bigfork potter who also sculpts highly textured works in metal; Deborah Butterfield, the Bozeman-based sculptor, perhaps the best-known Montana artist on the national contemporary art scene, noted for her horses made of bronze and other materials; John Smart, who captures the lay of the land and the telling interiors of Montana bars in his black-and-white photographs.

From early modernists to the many Montana artists who represent the state of the arts today, our state sustains those who actively seek new visions.

Visual Artists

In 1832, the painter George Catlin (1796-1872) rode up the Missouri River on the steamboat *Yellowstone* and spent a summer soaking up details of the Indian culture of Montana and the Upper Missouri country. The paintings inspired by his time here contributed to our historical understanding of this land.

Karl Bodmer, a young Swiss artist who had been studying in Paris, came up the river on the same steamboat the following year, accompanying a wealthy Prussian prince who was collecting specimens of the area's natural history. Bodmer gave us some of the first drawings and paintings of the river and its valley. They show us what the land looked like before settlements sprang up.

Later, resident artists gave us their renditions of our landscape and people. Among them was Charlie Russell. Russell may not have expected his illustrated letters to friends near and far to bring him fame, but Montana has come to claim the man whose later oil paintings and watercolors captured its essence as its own painter king. His canvases of the Montana sky may appear romantic or impressionistic, but anyone who spends a few days here knows he got it right.

Other artists include Olaf C. Seltzer (1878-1957), who immigrated from Denmark, befriended Russell, and became known for portraits of early Montanans; Edgar S. Paxson (1852-1919), whose murals can still be seen today in the

Missoula County Courthouse; and Winold Reiss (1888-1953), noted for depicting the art and costumes of the Blackfeet.

Western and landscape art is still one of Montana's favorite representations. Gary Carter, a painter and sculptor from West Yellowstone, specializes in mountain men and Indian scenes from the nineteenth century. Russell Chatham is a cultural guru and Renaissance man of the Paradise Valley. He produces fine oils and lithographs of impressionistic landscapes, particularly of the Paradise. He owns galleries, an art center, and a restaurant. He has also delved into publishing as the owner of Clark City Press. Jessica Zemsky, a watercolor and pastel artist from Big Timber, is

Charlie Russell, left, and O. C. Seltzer. Montana Historical Society

known for her pictures of western children, especially Indian children, and nineteenth-century homestead scenes. Dale Livesey of Helena paints impressionistic landscapes, bolder in color than Chatham's hazy or snowy scenes. The images of Jay R. Rummell, Missoula ceramist, painter, print-maker provide insight on Montana's past, present, and future.

Much current art shows a sense of humor, too. Monte Dolack, Nancy Erickson, and Parks Reece, with their pun-intended animal prints, are just a few of the many artists here who keep us looking and laughing. Many homes and businesses display at least one of Dolack's engaging, often humorous, poster depictions of the West and its animal icons.

Sold!

Each March, Great Falls hosts the C. M. Russell Art Auction, a four-day western art show remembering western artist Charlie Russell. The annual auction has raised more than $7 million since 1969. Over the years, more than $2.4 million in auction proceeds have been donated to the C. M. Russell Museum by the Great Falls Advertising Federation.

notable
Montanans

E. McKnight Kauffer (1890-1954)

Kauffer was born in Great Falls. His father, an itinerant fiddler, abandoned the family when the boy was three. After eight years of school, Kauffer was forced to work odd jobs to supplement the family's income. He went to San Francisco at age sixteen, took a job in a bookstore, took art classes at night, and spent his weekends painting. In 1912, he studied for several months at the Art Institute of Chicago, then moved to New York.

While in Chicago, he'd seen the famous Armory Show, America's first taste of modern art, and it affected him dramatically. He moved to Europe, seeking mentors in the powerful new styles. He lived in Munich and Paris, moving to London as World War I began. There, he began a distinguished career in art and design. He employed color, Cubism, futurism, and other elements to create striking designs, among them a series of posters for the London Underground and the cover of the Vintage edition of James Joyce's *Ulysses*. After World War II, he returned to the United States and continued to work until his death.

Monte Dolack (1950-)

Dolack was born in Great Falls, where he worked for a short time in the refinery of the Anaconda Copper Company and played in local rock bands. The money he earned at these jobs helped him get started in the study of art, first at Montana State University, later at the university in Missoula and at the California College of Arts and Crafts. Along the way, Dolack developed the whimsical style he brings to the making of his posters and prints. He borrowed traditional watercolor methods for use in his acrylic painting, also using an airbrush. His work, especially the posters that comment slyly on the coexistence of humanity and nature, is seen in galleries and museums, but perhaps most pervasively in Montana's living rooms, kitchens, bedrooms, and bathrooms. After gaining some fame and some fortune for his posters, he has honed his talent in the creation of handmade lithographs. His gallery is on West Front Street in Missoula.

A Few of My Favorite Parts
of Montana's Arts

by Monte Dolack

1. The Montana arts community, which I'm lucky enough to be a part of. It is especially strong in Missoula, where I live. I don't just exist, I "live" here because of the strong community feeling.

2. Our Montana writers have helped us figure out our place in the unfolding history of the West. Especially important have been the influence of **Bill Kittredge** and **Annick Smith**, **James Welch**, and the late voices of **Bud Guthrie**, **Norman Maclean**, **Dorothy Johnson**, and **Richard Hugo**.

3. **James Lee Burke**, **Jon Jackson**, and **Jim Crumley**, our leading Montana mystery writers.

4. **Russell Chatham** — His subtle and beautifully moody paintings and lithographs help me understand the mysterious, quiet, and powerful beauty of the Montana landscape.

5. **Rudy** and **Lela Autio**, **Dana Boussard**, **Nancy Erickson** — They find a contemporary pictorial voice that I hear loud and strong. Also, the symbolism of **John Buck** and graceful strength of **Deborah Butterfield's** sculpture.

6. **The Montana Arts Council** and the arts advocates who contribute constantly to help move our cultural ideas and artists forward. The arts need all the help they can get.

7. Montana visionaries, storytellers, and poets like **Jay Rummel**, **Ernie Pepion**, **Paul Zarzyski**, **Dave Thomas**, and **Wally McRae**.

8. The untiring heart and music of **Rob Quist** and the legacy of the **Mission Mountain Wood Band**. The **Montana Rep** and the **Missoula Children's Theatre**, and my public radio station, **KUFM**.

9. **The Montana Committee for the Humanities** and the past work of **Margaret Kingsland**, which helped me to know more about our first people—the Native Americans and their wealth of craft, myth, and culture.

10. The visionaries, artists, and storytellers who came before our time, like **Charlie Russell**, **Evelyn Cameron**, **Karl Bodmer**, and **Chief Joseph**.

A popular image by Monte Dolack, Leave It to Beavers

Art Shows and Auctions

Event	Town or City/ Date or Season	For Information
C. M. Russell Auction of Original Western Art	Great Falls/March	P.O. Box 631 Great Falls 59403 761-6453
Jaycees Western Art Roundup	Miles City/3rd week of May	232-2890
JK Ralston Western Art Show and Auction	Billings/October	254-0959
Chinook Art Fair and Auction	Chinook	P.O. Box 157, Chinook 59523
Harbor Art Fair	Polson	P.O. Box 1656, Polson 59860
Harvest Festival Art Display	Plentywood	223 W. Laurel Ave., Plentywood 59254
Havre Art Show	Havre	1248 Cleveland Ave., Havre 59501
Missoula Art Auction	Missoula	
Sidewalk Art Show	Helena	1812 6th Ave. , Helena 59601
Spring Art Show and Sale	Libby	52 Cross Roadway, Libby 59923
Whitefish Art Walk	Whitefish/February	862-7544
Whitefish Annual Arts Festival	July	862-5875
Yellowstone Art Auction	Billings	256-6804

Photographers

Montana's open spaces have inspired photographers, too. F. J. Haynes rode the rails of the Northern Pacific, shooting the landscapes he passed through and the people he met. He processed and printed some of his work in a customized railroad car. Haynes was also an early documenter of the wonders of Yellowstone National Park. Many of his works can be seen in an exhibit at the Montana Historical Society Museum. L. A. Huffman of Miles City captured cowboys and the Plains Indians in his photographs.

In the early years of this century, Lady Evelyn Cameron, an Englishwoman who came to the U.S. with her husband in 1889, worked her ranch in Terry while creating some of the most poignant pictures of eastern Montana's dry land settlers. Later photographers saw some of the same beauty in sparse country. On the contemporary scene, Joann Berghold, based in Wilsall, shoots landscapes and still lifes in black and white. Many of her photographs are marked by glossy, shiny surfaces—wet roads and such. John Smart is a Helena photographer noted for landscapes that showcase our wide skies and open range, often in a horizontal format. His work is featured in the book *Montana Spaces*.

notable
$\mathcal{M}$ontanans

Montana Historical Society

Evelyn Cameron (1868-1928)

She was born in England and came to eastern Montana as a 21-year-old bride in 1889. She and her husband Ewen S. Cameron, the son of Lord Cameron, fell in love with eastern Montana after their honeymoon hunting trip and returned to establish a ranch near Terry. They later moved to the Marsh area, between Miles City and Wibaux.

Evelyn bought her first camera in 1894 and began to document frontier life in rich, black-and-white detail. Her camera captured people of all economic and ethnic classes at work and at play, recorded the lonesome landscapes on which she ranged, and above all, reflected her own intelligence and wit. In the accompanying photo, she poses with a kestrel, gaining its attention with a grasshopper.

Her diaries add to the legacy she left. Cameron's extensive photographic gift was nearly lost to posterity. Her photographs sat in a friend's cellar for half a century before being rediscovered by writer Donna Lucey, who compiled Cameron's work in *Photographing Montana, 1894-1928*.

Lady Cameron managed the ranch for thirteen years after her husband died, until her own death in 1928.

My Favorite Parts
of Montana's Arts

by Governor Marc Racicot

Republican Marc Racicot has served as Montana's governor since 1992.

1. Favorite authors: **Michael Malone** and **Ivan Doig.** Both are so insightful describing our state's unique heritage and flavor.

2. Favorite scenic artist: **the Good Lord**, for causing the phenomenon that resulted in the creation of Montana.

3. Favorite actor: **Gary Cooper.**

4. Favorite singer: **Anne Racicot**, my daughter. No one puts more heart and effort into a song.

5. Favorite storyteller: my father because his stories got better and more colorful every time he told them.

6. Favorite movie: **A River Runs Through It.**

7. Favorite photographer: **John Warner**, for capturing the Northern Cheyenne and Crow people in a way that conveys the dignity, beauty, and strength of our first citizens.

8. Favorite cowboy poet: **Mike Logan**. His images and words speak to lasting values that hold us together.

9. Favorite culinary artist: my grandfather, **Harry**, who made the best and largest raised donuts I ever saw or ate.

10. Favorite moviemaker: **Mike Gurnett**, of the state Department of Fish, Wildlife & Parks. The stars of his film stories are always the people, the creatures, and the magnificent land of Montana.

Governor Racicot, left, enjoys a laugh with Tex Pate, a Helena auctioneer, in the cafe at the Helena airport.
John Warner

Public Art Museums and Community Galleries

City or Town	Museum/Gallery	Address/Phone
Anaconda	Copper Village Museum & Art Center	563-2422
Bigfork	Bigfork Art Center	837-6927
Big Timber	Crazy Mountain Museum	932-5126
Billings	Northcutt Steele Gallery of Art	MSU-Billings/657-2980
	Sundance Gallery	2137 Beloit Dr. 256-9225
	Whole in the Wall Gallery	MSU-Billings/659-2980
	Yellowstone Art Center	256-6804
Blaine	Blaine County Museum	P.O. Box 927, Chinook 59523
Bozeman	Beall Park Art Center	586-3970
	Emerson Cultural Center	587-9797
	Exit Gallery	MSU-Bozeman/994-1828
	Hayne's Fine Arts Gallery	School of Art MT State U 994-2562
	Museum of the Rockies	994-DINO
Browning	Museum of the Plains Indian	338-2230
Butte	Arts Chateau	321 W. Broadway/723-7600
Deer Lodge	Powell County Museum	846-3294
Dillon	Western Montana College Gallery	710 S. Atlantic
Great Falls	Art Gallery	Art Dept. University of Great Falls
	C. M. Russell Museum Complex	400 13th N. /727-8787
	Galerie Trinitas	University of Great Falls/791-5295
	Paris Gibson Square Museum of Art	727-8255
Hamilton	Ravalli County Museum	363-3338
Helena	Archie Bray Foundation for the Ceramic Arts	443-3502
	Holter Museum of Art	12 E. Lawrence/442-6400
	Montana Historical Society Museum	444-2694
	Myrna Loy Center	443-0287
Kalispell	Hockaday Center for the Arts	755-5268
Lame Deer	Northern Cheyenne Tribal Museum	477-6284
Lewistown	Lewistown Art Center	801 Broadway/528-8278
Livingston	Danforth Gallery/Park County Friends of the Arts	222-6510
	Livingston Depot Center	222-2300
Malta	Phillips County Museum	654-1037
Miles City	Custer County Art Center	232-0635
	Mineral County Museum	302 2nd Ave. E./822-4078
Missoula	Art Museum of Missoula	335 N. Pattee/728-0447
	Gallery of Visual Arts	Art Dept. U of M/243-2019
	UM School of Fine Arts Paxson Gallery	243-4970
	University Center Gallery	243-6661
Philipsburg	Granite County Museum & Cultural Center	859-3388
Poplar	Fort Peck Assiniboine & Sioux Cultural Center & Museum	768-5155
Pryor	Chief Plenty Coups Museum	Chief Plenty Coups State Park
		P.O. Box 100 252-1289
Red Lodge	Carbon County Museum	P.O. Box 881/446-2858
St. Ignatius	Flathead Indian Museum	745-5501
Shelby	Marias Museum of History & Art	434-2551
Sidney	MonDak Heritage Center, Museum, & Art Gallery	P.O. Box 50/482-3500
Terry	Prairie County Museum & Cameron Photo Gallery	637-5782
Three Forks	Headwaters Heritage Museum	202 S. Main/285-4778
West Yellowstone	Museum of the Yellowstone	646-7814

notable
Montanans

Frank Bird Linderman (1869-1938)

The Indians called him "Sign-Talker with a Straight
Tongue." He lived several lives—trapper, cow hand,
miner, woodsman, newspaper editor, merchant, and
politician—but we remember him best for his
books on Indians and Montana.

   He moved to the Flathead Valley at the age of
sixteen from Cleveland, Ohio. In 1917, he moved
to the west shore of Flathead Lake and assumed
the life of a writer, publishing five volumes on traditional Indian lore, two novels, a book of poetry,
and more. His books were the end-product of ex-

Linderman Collection/K. Ross Toole Archives

haustive, meticulous research. He interviewed In-
dian elders, confirming his interpreter's translation with his thorough knowledge of sign language. His efforts to get the facts straight may have been part of
the reason he was adopted into the Blackfeet, Cree, and Crow tribes. His best
known works are *Indian Why Stories; The American,* a biography of Chief Plenty
Coups; *Pretty Shield;* and *Old Man Coyote.* After Linderman finished *The American,* Plenty Coups said "I am glad I have told you these things, Sign-Talker. You
have felt my heart, and I have felt yours."

 Grace Stone Coates (1881-1976)

Coates gained national fame in the 1920s and 1930s for
poetry and her critically acclaimed first novel, *Black Cherries.* Coates's work appeared in the *Christian Science
Monitor, New York Times,* and other publications. She
lived and wrote in Martinsdale, where she also served as
Meagher County Superintendent of Schools from 1918
to 1921. In the early 1960s, neighbors managed to have
Coates, who was losing her memory, committed to a nursing home. A book dealer got Coates's collection of books, and many of
her journals and papers were destroyed. She died in the nursing home.

   The life of Grace Coates is told in *Honey Wine and Hunger Root,* by
Martinsdale writer Lee Rostad.

Literary Arts

In an attempt to capture the pageant of life here, numerous Montana writers have made significant contributions to the literary wealth of America. The number and quality of contributions to *The Last Best Place: A Montana Anthology*, compiled in the mid-1980s by William Kittredge, Annick Smith, and a distinguished editorial board, speak volumes on this point.

The book's 1,160 pages encompass the state's literary traditions: myths and stories, handed down orally and in great writing, by Native Americans; observations taken from journals of early explorers; writings by pioneers and Indians; stories inspired by life on the farm and ranch; poems, stories, and recollections

*M*notable *ontanans*

Norman Maclean (1902- 1990)

Maclean was born in Iowa but grew up in Missoula. When he was seventy years old, he began writing about his beloved Montana. He made a significant contribution to the state's literature with only two books—his memoir, *A River Runs Through It and Other Stories* (1976) and *Young Men and Fire* (1992), an account of the 1949 Mann Gulch fire and its aftermath. As revealed in *A River Runs Through It*, he attended Dartmouth College, accepted a job with the University of Chicago's English Department, and earned a doctorate there. Though most of his life was spent in a rigorous academic environment, his writing reflects his upbringing as the son of a Presbyterian minister, his work as an adolescent for the Forest Service, and his love of Montana, especially its rivers and wild land. His family owned a place on Seeley Lake and, as his much-loved memoir showed, he spent innumerable hours fishing the Blackfoot River.

of Butte; modern literature; and contemporary poetry and fiction.

Before Indian writers had gained a wide audience, non-Indians such as James Willard Schultz and Frank Bird Linderman portrayed with respectful voices the lives and legends of the first Montanans.

In the intervening years, the voices have risen and grown, producing novels and short stories out of our cities, small towns, and wilderness. We have heard from an abundance of fiction writers—B. M. Bower, Dan Cushman, Dorothy Johnson, A. B. Guthrie (Montana's only Pulitzer Prize winner, in 1950, for *The Way West*), and Norman Maclean, as members of earlier generations; Thomas McGuane, Ivan Doig, Mary Clearman Blew, William Kittredge, Pete Fromm, David Long, Deirdre McNamer, William Hjortsberg, and Lise McClendon, among others today.

Poetry lives here, too, in new work produced by writers such as Sheryl Noethe, Dave Thomas, Lowell Jaeger, Sandra Alcosser, Ed Lahey, Wilbur Wood, Roger Dunsmore, and others, and in a cult of nearly mythic proportions—a "dead poets society" of sorts—around such disparate late poets as Richard Hugo and Richard Brautigan.

Cowboy poets address a wide range of subjects, some traditional, some modern, with free-spirited voices. Wally McRae, Paul Zarzyski, and Gwen Petersen are a few that ride our literary fence line.

Montana continues to serve as a grounding point for an impressive number of modern essayists and magazine writers who portray Montana and the West—or American culture in general—with fresh observations. The works of David Quammen, Tim Cahill, and Peter Stark first came to us through *Outside* magazine. Between them, these men have since published a number of books. Before finding a niche at *Outside*, Cahill was a top-flight journalist for *Rolling Stone*, the magazine that spawned *Outside*.

Ellen Meloy, Gary Ferguson, and Annick Smith are others who have won acclaim with their essays and articles.

Montana is also blessed with a number of publishing houses committed to promoting Montana to a world that can't seem to get enough of it.

The Best Montana Books

With all that has been written about Montana or by Montanans, who can say which authors or books are the best? Everyone has a favorite or a list of favorites.

Steve Shirley, an editor for the *Great Falls Tribune*, made a stab at naming the best Montana books by surveying *Tribune* readers in December 1996. Approximately eighty readers responded. Since readers listed their favorites in a general fashion, Shirley did not rank the books. He did say that **This House of Sky** by Ivan Doig was the most frequently listed favorite. Others on the list:

A River Runs Through It and Other Stories / Norman Maclean

The Big Sky / A. B. Guthrie, Jr.

We Pointed Them North / Edward "Teddy Blue" Abbott and Helena Huntington Smith

The Vigilantes of Montana, or Popular Justice in the Rocky Mountains / Thomas J. Dimsdale *The first book published in Montana.*

Montana: A History of Two Centuries / Michael Malone, Richard Roeder, and William Lang

Montana: High, Wide, and Handsome / Joseph Kinsey Howard *A 1982 survey of readers of* Montana, The Magazine of Western History, *declared this to be the best book ever written about Montana.*

Montana: An Uncommon Land / K. Ross Toole *Essays examining recurring themes in Montana's development.*

Winter Wheat / Mildred Walker

The Last Best Place: A Montana Anthology / edited by William Kittredge and Annick Smith

Undaunted Courage: Meriwether Lewis, Thomas Jefferson and the Opening of the American West / Stephen E. Ambrose

A Bride Goes West / Nannie T. Alderson and Helena Huntington Smith *A memoir of the cattle ranching days of the late 1880s and harsh life on the prairie.*

Stay Away, Joe / Dan Cushman *A humorous tale that became an Elvis Presley movie.*

Journals of Lewis and Clark / edited by Bernard DeVoto

Rock Springs / Richard Ford *Short stories set in Montana, written by an author who lives part-time in Chinook and won the Pulitzer Prize in 1996 for* Independence Day.

Tough Trip Through Paradise, 1878-1879 / Andrew Garcia, edited by Bennett H. Stein

Trails Plowed Under / Charlie Russell *The acclaimed artist could tell stories with the best of 'em.*

Wolf Willow / Wallace Stegner *A combination of history, fiction, and memories of frontier days in the region where Montana and Saskatchewan meet.*

Forty Years on the Frontier: As Seen in the Journals and Reminiscences of Granville Stuart, Gold Miner, Trader, Merchant, Rancher and Politician / edited by Paul Phillips

Fools Crow / James Welch

Finally, Shirley added to the list a recent release, published too late to get many votes from his readers, but one he feels will be on future lists: **Bad Land: An American Romance** by Jonathan Raban. *The travails of eastern Montana homesteaders in the early 1900s.*

notable
Montanans

 ### Mary MacLane (1881-1929)

MacLane came to Butte from Winnipeg as a 10-year-old with her family. Nine years later she wrote a book that became a national sensation overnight. In *The Story of Mary MacLane*, the teenager detailed her life in Butte, her longings, her reverence for the Devil, and her "good odd philosophy." Her candor shocked the average reader. After her early success, she left Butte, living in bohemian New York and later in Chicago. She wrote two other autobiographical books and the script for a silent film, *Men Who Have Made Love to Me*, which she also starred in, but never regained the attention she had when she was 19. She died in a Chicago rooming house at the age of 48.

Montana Historical Society

My Favorite Parts
of Montana's Arts

by Gwen Petersen

Gwen Petersen, who lives in Big Timber, describes herself thusly:

> A writer of ranch-woman verse,
> Some funny, some poignant, some terse
> Intends to keep ranching
> And laughing and dancing
> 'Til taken away in a hearse.

1. *Montana: High, Wide, and Handsome* by Joseph Kinsey Howard. If you want to read authentic Montana, this book says it all. First published in 1943, the wisdom and truth and grit of those special people who became Montanans vibrates off the pages.

2. *Montana Margins*, an anthology of Montana prose and poetry, edited by Joseph Kinsey Howard. This book, as well as *High, Wide, and Handsome*, should be on every shelf in Montana and mandatory reading for all who seek to put down roots in this state.

3. **Dorothy Johnson.** The brilliance of her work will live on. Her wisdom and wry wit can be found in her autobiography, *A Pocket Full of Wry,* published shortly before her death.

4. **Gary Svee**. For current-day Montana writers, you can't beat Svee. His books tell the stories of Montanans with wit and insight and nostalgia.

5. **Greg Keeler**, poet, professor of English at Montana State University. Keeler jabs into bloated sacred cows with a blade so sharp, the cows have to shake their heads to know they've been decapitated.

6. **Bill Koch**, a genius in the art of bringing entertainment to the Montana stage. He is the driving energy behind The Firehouse 5, a small playhouse in Livingston. Open year-round, Firehouse features summertime melodrama and vaudeville. In winter, more serious plays are offered.

7. **The enormous statue of the Virgin Mary**, mounted high on a peak overlooking and blessing the town of Butte. While it was being erected, all sorts of controversy roiled the atmosphere. Now that it's a beacon of white, shining down on the ethnic and religious mixture that is Butte, there's still controversy, but as usual in Butte, "you can do anything you want if you think you're big enough to do it." The statue remains. It's now fondly referred to as "East Jesus" by local wits.

8. **Butte, Montana, anytime**, but especially on St. Patrick's Day. Butte has art, literature, colleges, mining—name it: you'll find it in Butte. And some of the greatest eating establishments in the state; maybe the world. It has history that writers have only begun to tap. Its people are tough and sentimental, rough and tender, raucous and kind. You cannot be bored with Butte.

9. **Vigilante Players**, Bozeman. Traveling in the summers, traveling in the winters, this group of players represents Montana as does no other theater troupe.

10. **The Ringling Five**, of Clyde Park and Wilsall—seven ranchers who pick guitar and sing original, outrageous songs lampooning themselves and lambasting foolishness. They perform for banquets, 4-H benefits, etc.

11. **Terri Mimnaugh**—Montana painter and sculptor who created the Jeannette Rankin statue that stands in Washington, D.C.

notable
$\mathcal{M}$ontanans

 Thomas McGuane (1939-)

McGuane's books, which include novels, short stories, and essays, have been translated into ten languages and a number of Hollywood movies. Born in Michigan, he attended Michigan State University, earned an MFA at the Yale School of Drama, and was a Wallace Stegner Fellow at Stanford University. He began to divide his time, for both work and pleasure, between Montana and the Florida Keys in the early 1970s. McGuane's early works include *The Sporting Club* (1969), *The Bushwhacked Piano* (1971), for which he was honored by the American Academy of Arts and Letters, and *Ninety-Two in the Shade* (1973), which was nominated for a National Book Award. He later directed the screen version. His books set in Montana include *Nobody's Angel* (1982), *Keep the Change* (1989), and *Nothing But Blue Skies* (1992). His screenplays include *Rancho Deluxe, Tom Horn,* and *Missouri Breaks.* He is a contributor to *Sports Illustrated.* McGuane is also a strong conservationist and on the board of several environmental organizations.

He was married briefly to actress Margot Kidder and married Laurie Buffett, the sister of singer Jimmy Buffett, in 1977. They live on a ranch near McLeod, where McGuane raises Angus cattle and cutting horses.

Writers' Organizations

Organization	Address/Phone
Authors of the Flathead	3201 Hwy 40 West, Columbia Falls 59912 892-1960
Bitter Root Writers	P.O. Box 1100, Hamilton 59840 363-7680
Bozeman Authors	6413 Cattle Dr., Bozeman 59715
Great Falls Writers' Group	P.O. Box 6608, Great Falls 59406 453-0256
Hellgate Writers, Inc.	P.O. Box 7131, Missoula 59807 721-3620
Montana Authors Coalition	P.O. Box 1872, Bozeman 59771 586-3027
Montana Center for the Book	Lewis and Clark Library 120 S. Last Chance Gulch, Helena 59601 447-1690
Montana Cowboy Poetry Gathering	Lewistown Chamber of Commerce P.O. Box 818, Lewistown 59457
Montana Sagebrush Writers Workshops	Box 1255, Big Timber 59011 932-4227
Montana Sagebrush Writers / Dillon Authors	c/o The Bookstore 26 North Idaho, Dillon 59725 683-6807
The Writer's Voice	Billings Family YMCA 402 N. 32nd St., Billings 59102 248-1685
Yellow Bay Writers' Workshop	Center for Continuing Education The University of Montana, Missoula 59812 243-2094

notable
Montanans

William Kittredge (1932-)

Kittredge grew up on a ranch in southeastern Oregon, but a love for books led him to the prestigious University of Iowa Writers' Workshop. After earning an MFA there, he came to Missoula to teach in the creative writing program at the university. His works include a memoir, *Hole in the Sky* (1992); the short story collections *We Are Not in This Together* (1984) and *The Van Gogh Field* (1978); and a collection of autobiographical essays, *Owning It All* (1987). He also contributes short stories and essays to periodicals such as *Harper's* and *Outside* magazine.

He has also made significant contributions to Montana literature as an editor. With his partner, Annick Smith, he edited (and is credited with naming) the massive anthology of the state's literature, *The Last Best Place*. He also edited a book of essays, *Montana Spaces*, with contributions by Thomas McGuane, Wallace Stegner, Gretel Ehrlich, and Tim Cahill, among others.

Richard Hugo (1923-1982)

Dick Hugo was born in Seattle, served in the Army, Air Corps as a bombardier, and received a master's degree from the University of Washington, where he studied under the poet Theodore Roethke. After working as a technical writer for the Boeing Company, Hugo accepted a job with The University of Montana's English department, where he would direct and cultivate the creative writing program. His poetry is the most beloved form he left, but he also wrote autobiographical essays, a book about writing, and one detective novel set in western Montana, *Death and the Good Life*.

Hugo was a member of a literary family. Works by his wife, poet Ripley Schemm; his mother-in-law, novelist Mildred Walker Schemm; and his stepson, Matthew Hansen, appear in the anthology of Montana literature, *The Last Best Place*.

notable
Montanans

Deirdre McNamer (1951-)

McNamer grew up in Conrad and Cut Bank. She studied creative writing during a fellowship at the University of Michigan, taken after she had worked as a journalist for *The Missoulian* and the Associated Press. She returned to reporting and taught at The University of Montana's School of Journalism. She crafted her first novel, *Rima in the Weeds* (1992), in the basement office of her Missoula home. It is set in Madrid, a fictional town along the Hi Line in central Montana. Her second novel, *One Sweet Quarrel,* was released in 1994.

Performing Arts

Music

Montana is home to several classical music organizations, including large symphony orchestras with regular seasons. The Missoula Civic Symphony began in 1903. The Great Falls Symphony came into being in 1947. Butte, Billings, Helena, and the Flathead Valley initiated symphony orchestras in the 1950s, and Bozeman followed in 1986. The Miles City Symphony and the Scobey-based Prairie Symphonette are music to the ears of eastern Montanans.

Many of the musicians receive their training in the fine musical programs supported by the community through the public schools and the institutions of higher education in the state. Some young people become accomplished members of a local orchestra well before they can vote.

Symphony performances are often accompanied by outstanding local choral groups or are presented in conjunction with the state's several ballet and dance companies.

In summer, the Montana hills are alive with the sound of music, from bluegrass and jazz festivals to week-long music festivals at Red Lodge, Kalispell, Bigfork, and Big Sky, which feature a vast array of musical offerings.

Many talented musicians often return from national recording and performing schedules to play for appreciative audiences in the state they once called home. George Winston, the pianist who records for the Windham Hill record label, grew up in Miles City and Billings. He has described his compositions as "rural folk piano" pieces. Winston also exposes audiences to the legacy of older blues and jazz pianists.

Other musicians with roots in Montana include Philip Aaberg, who played with rhythm-and-blues artist Elvin Bishop before following a route that led to a more refined style blending jazz and classical nuances; Christopher Parkening, the noted classical guitarist; and soprano Judith Blegan, who grew up in Missoula and has performed at the Metropolitan Opera, Carnegie Hall, and with the major opera companies of San Francisco, Nuremberg, Vienna, and other cities.

Montanans are jazzed up, too. Jazz in its traditional forms—Dixieland, ragtime, and big band/swing—collects audiences from all over the country and Canada in Helena in the third week of June, in Great Falls on the Labor Day weekend, and in Kalispell in October. Perhaps this present-day enthusiasm for jazz festivals hearkens back to the ragtime music of the mining camp hurdy-gurdies and saloons of the 1890s, or to the dozens of dance bands in the 1920s to 1950s that had folks "dancin' 'til after milking time" in the urban clubs and rural roadhouses of the state.

Here in the 1990s, the Big Sky still has plenty of homegrown talent and plenty of clubs and roadhouses. On any Saturday night, you can dance to "reggae in the Rockies" by Helena's Jah Provide; swing your "podna" to the western tunes of Pollo Loco from Great Falls; bump and grind to rhythm and blues by Helena's Little Elmo and the Mambo Kings, Missoula's Andre Floyd and Mood Iguana, or Kalispell's Big Daddy and the Blue Notes; or bop 'til you drop with Missoula's Bop-a-Dips. The list, of course, goes on. We've got plenty of home-grown musical talent to fit your mood or preferences.

Other groups that appear statewide to lively up our musical life include: Bob Wire and the Fence Menders, Diamond City, Thrill Hill, Big Sky Mudflaps, and the Tropical Montana Marimba Ensemble. Rob Quist and his Great Northern band perform throughout the West and even venture eastward with old and new Montana favorites like "In Without Knockin'" and "Take a Whiff." Quist originally performed with the Montana Band, whose national fame ended in 1987 when ten people, including band members, died in the state's worst air disaster near Flathead Lake.

A Billings songwriter who goes by only one name, Kostas, left Montana to find fame as a key Nashville songwriter. Kostas has written dozens of songs that have made the country and western charts. He appeared with Jimmy Buffett playing "Livingston Saturday Night" in the movie *Rancho Deluxe*. That song is among several of Buffett's Montana-based tunes, which also include "Come Monday Morning," and "Ringling, Ringling."

Those who don't require a dance floor can often find a venue with a ballad-eer like Browning's Jack Gladstone, troubadours like Bozeman's Greg Keeler, jazz groups like the Chuck Florence Jazz Quartet or Three Form, a bluegrass ensemble like Helena's Parlor Pickers, or a music and humor troupe like the Ringling Five or the Montana Logging and Ballet Company. Some acts are harder to define. The Drum Brothers, from Arlee, beat out ancient and New Age rhythms. Walkin' Jim Stoltz treks hundreds of miles through Montana wilderness, then hits the road for a few months with his guitar, slide shows, and songs.

Ms. Merrill's source: a misspent youth and mid-life in Montana bars.

notable
Montanans

Jean Wrobel (1920-)

As a teen-ager in the Bitterroot Valley, Wrobel listened to the latest 78 rpm records and discovered the music of Willie "The Lion" Smith, Earl "Fatha" Hines, and other great jazz musicians. Before graduating from Hamilton High, she was playing piano professionally in a dance band. She went to Portland, Oregon, to study with a teacher who exposed her to the music of Fats Waller, Count Basie, and a pianist who would figure in her future—Teddy Wilson.

She returned to the valley and after two and a half years of saving the money she made in jobs at a Hamilton drugstore and the Rocky Mountain Laboratories, she got on a train for New York, determined to find Wilson, whose style she envied.

Soon her goal was achieved. Wilson gave Wrobel lessons in his Harlem home and would often drive her back to her apartment in Greenwich Village on his way to gigs at the Village Vanguard, Cafe Society, and other legendary nightclubs.

"They were all right in my neighborhood. The club featured jam sessions in those days, and that's where you got to know other musicians. I heard so many great players, and got to look right over their shoulders sometimes—Fats Waller, Art Tatum, Willie 'The Lion' Smith, all my heroes."

In the 1940s, Wrobel signed with the William Morris Agency and adopted the stage name of Jean Hamilton, in honor of her hometown. Billed as the "young, boogie-woogie sensation," she worked clubs in the East and as far west as Detroit. She once shared a dressing room with a legend: Billie Holiday.

Wrobel also was hired to play a network radio show called "Onstage Everybody." With the rest of the show's cast, she was sent to Hollywood and appeared in a movie of the same name with Jack Oakie and Julie London. Then, the cast of the movie toured the country, performing a week of stage shows, six or seven a day, on a bill with the movie. She met a theater manager in St. Paul whom she married in 1946 and by 1953 had moved back to Hamilton with her husband and two children.

Since then she has played bars and lounges of western Montana, treating Montanans to a rare gift: jazz piano handed down to a young woman from the Bitterroot by some early masters of the form.

Nina Russell (1911 -)

She's played jazz and blues at nightclubs in Las Vegas, Chicago, and Los Angeles, where she entertained Judy Garland, Lana Turner, John Wayne, and other Hollywood stars. Al Capone's brother threatened to burn her family's house down if she didn't play at his Chicago nightclub, but she showed him the error of his ways. Now she plays in a piano bar on the west shore of Flathead Lake, and in a Bigfork bookstore on Sunday afternoons, passing out song sheets so her audience can sing along. Well into her eighties, Nina Russell hasn't slowed down much.

Russell was born in South Carolina to a "buffalo soldier," a member of the 25th Infantry under Colonel Nelson Miles, with a heritage which includes Cherokee Indian, Jewish, Irish, Scot, and "Negro" bloodlines. (She prefers this term.)

Her early musical training was in the church, and at her first nightclub performance, intimidated by the surroundings, she kept her eyes closed. Later, filling in for a friend at Capone's club, she impressed listeners so much that Capone wanted her to stay and issued his threat in a phone call to Russell's mother. But Russell had promised another club owner she'd return to her regular job at his club. She asked Capone how Capone would feel if she gave him her word, then broke her promise. Capone relented.

At a date in Las Vegas, Judy Garland was in the audience and sent word she'd like to join Russell for a song. When the message was delivered, Russell said, "You tell Miss Garland my name is Ethel Waters, and I do the singing around here."

Russell heard her father's stories of Montana and came here to fish on vacations. She and her husband bought property in Hungry Horse in 1950. Russell moved there in 1971, after her husband died. She played organ at a church in Coram for seventeen and a half years. She's also played the Alibi Club in Shelby, the Hi-Line Club in Havre, and at dozens of restaurants and bars in the Flathead. She loves to fish and to paint. She now lives in Kalispell.

notable
Montanans

Eden Atwood (1969 -)

A gifted young jazz singer, Atwood hails from a family long respected for its patronage of and contributions to the arts in Montana. She was born in Memphis but moved to Montana at the age of five with her mother, Gus Guthrie Miller of Butte. Miller is a longtime advocate of the arts and the daughter of A.B. Guthrie Jr. Eden's father, Hub Atwood, was a well-known composer and arranger who worked for Frank Sinatra and Harry James.

Concord Jazz, Inc.

On a 1996 CD, *A Night in the Life,* Eden dedicates her rendition of Kurt Weill's "Lost in the Stars" to "my mother, who gave me the love of words," and "So Many Stars," by Alan and Marilyn Bergman, to "my father, who gave me the love of music."

Both her parents encouraged Atwood's talents as a pianist and singer, and throughout her youth, she visited her father's Memphis musical world for training and inspiration. She studied drama and musical theater at the University of Montana, and performed with a Missoula jazz combo, but left Montana at the age of 19 for Chicago's lively jazz scene. She headlined at the Gold Star Sardine Bar there.

For a brief time, Atwood was a television actress in New York and a model in Paris, but she returned to music, performing at New York's Algonquin Hotel and other top jazz venues. She has released four CDs of jazz standards, ballads, and her own compositions on the Concord jazz label and toured Japan in 1996. She lives in Chicago.

"I'm from Montana and I want to go back," Atwood has said. "It for sure won't become the jazz mecca of the universe, but I'm not a big-city girl. Maybe I can open my own club there and travel around to sing with my idols."

Jazz Men

Some outstanding jazz musicians got their start playing jazz and western country swing in Montana. Drummer **Monte Mountjoy**, born in Roundup in 1912, became a member of a hot Dixieland band in the 1950s, the Firehouse 5 + 2. **Burton "Burt" Bales**, born in Stevensville in 1916, was a great traditional jazz piano player and played with many famous bands and trios from the 1930s to the 1950s.

My Favorite Parts
of Montana's Arts

by Carol R. Brenden, Scobey

Carol R. Brenden has taught music in elementary and secondary schools and currently has a private piano and voice studio in her home on an eastern Montana wheat farm. She is active statewide in music education and choral conducting. She is also a member of the Montana Arts Council.

1. **Basin Creek School**, in the shadow of the Crazy Mountains—It was typical of the many one-room schools throughout the state before rural populations dwindled and consolidations forced closure of the schools. Creativity blossomed here. The Christmas program was the culmination of writing the play and then producing it for the surrounding neighborhood. The first taste of the theater and the appreciative applause led to a graduate degree in theater.

2. **The Virginia City Players**—I remember my first taste of professional theater: traveling the thirty-five miles from our ranch to Big Timber, where the Players performed *Rip Van Winkle*. This led to many a trip to Virginia City to be entertained by this group. Long may they live!

3. The weavings of **Laurie Gano**—I first saw them hanging in the lobby of the Northern Hotel in Billings, awesome in their beauty. She now lives near Melville and has done striking representations of the Crazy Mountains and the prairies to the east.

4. The photographs of **Barbara Van Cleve** tug at my heartstrings as I

think of the West of yesteryear. She has a gift of bringing it to life, even for those who have not experienced it.

5. **The Custer County Art Center** in Miles City. Imagine the daring and creative drive of the person who first dreamed of putting an art gallery in old water storage tanks. It's a must-see for any visual art buff in the state.

6. Hats off to all the wonderful teachers of art, music, speech, and drama in our public and private schools. Guest conductors coming from out of state are immensely impressed by the talent of our students. I firmly believe our wide open spaces and Big Sky provide the perfect environment for developing innate artistic talent. From Flaxville to Frenchtown, from Ekalaka to Eureka, I have heard some amazing musical talent at district and state music festivals.

7. **The International Choral Festival**—We are privileged to be able to share in the thrill of this event, held biennially in Missoula, thanks to the work and organization of Dr. Don Carey.

8. **The C. M. Russell Art Museum** and the **C. M. Russell Art Auction** in Great Falls—I'll never forget my first Russell Auction and it's since become an annual must-do if at all possible. What better place to acquaint oneself with the western artists of Montana?

9. **Don Greytek**—He has visually presented a humorous reminder of happenings at the farm or ranch which were NOT funny at the time, but become hilarious when reproduced in his artistry.

10. **Scobey**—Remote, small, and full of people interested in creating their own culture; home of the nationally televised **Prairie Symphonette**, a forty-piece string and wind ensemble, and the **Daniels County Museum**, which produces the annual "Dirty Shame Show." All volunteers, these people entertain thousands in a professional way.

CULTURAL *Mix*

The Chief Cliff Singers, of the Confederated Salish and Kootenai Tribes, collaborated with jazz pianist Don Pullen's African-Brazilian Connection to create *Sacred Common Ground*, a highly acclaimed recording released by Blue Note in 1995. The project, initiated by Helena Presents, spanned three years of cross-cultural sharing, learning, performing, and celebrating Indian and jazz song and dance traditions.

notable
Montanans

Taylor Gordon (1893-1971)

From his hometown of White Sulphur Springs to Harlem in its heyday, this black concert singer trod the vaudeville stages of the U.S., later touring European concert halls. He even appeared in a number of motion pictures in the 1930s. Gordon's singing talents were first encouraged in 1915 while he was working on the private railway car of financier and circus impresario John Ringling. Ringling had befriended the young black man on a visit to the White Sulphur Springs area, where Ringling owned property.

In 1915, Gordon, who worked as Ringling's chauffeur, cook, and attendant, was singing along with an Enrico Caruso recording in the railroad car when a passerby complimented him on his voice and gave him the name of a New York voice teacher. Thus Gordon began a long, sometimes frustrating effort to sing professionally. He did not meet with success until the mid-1920s. Gordon's autobiography, *Born to Be* (1929), tells of his life in Montana and features some impressions of the Harlem Renaissance he was a part of in the 1920s. In the winter of 1935-36, Gordon returned to Montana to write a utopian novel, *Doanda*. He met with bitter disappointment when he was unable to find a publisher for the book, but he did find modest success with a mechanical toy he had invented during his 1935 retreat to a cabin near his hometown. After several hospitalizations for mental illness in New York, he returned to White Sulphur Springs in 1959 where he found solace and a respected place in the community.

Montana Historical Society

Music Organizations

Organization	Address/Phone
American Guild of Organists Yellowstone Chapter	1427 Colton Blvd., Billings 59102
Anaconda Community Concerts	Box 1406, Bozeman 59771
Big Sky Chorus	2165 Beloit Dr., Billings 59102 248-1990
Billings Banjo Band	417 Wyoming Ave., Billings 59101
Billings Symphony Orchestra and Chorale	P.O. Box 7055, Billings 59103 252-3610
Bitterroot Community Band	524 N. 4th, Hamilton 59840 363-2021
Bitterroot Valley Chorus	P.O. Box 567, Hamilton 59840
Bozeman Chord Rustlers	329 Lindley Pl., Bozeman 59715
Bozeman Symphony Association	P.O. Box 1174, Bozeman 59771 585-9774
Intermountain Opera	P.O. Box 1174, Bozeman 59771 585-9774
Bozeman Symphonic Choir	P.O. Box 1174, Bozeman 59771 585-9774
Butte Symphony Association	P.O. Box 725, Butte 59706 723-5590
Conrad Community Chorus	Lewis Building Conrad Jr. High School Conrad 59425 278-3875
Chinook Winds	P.O. Box 1078, Great Falls 59403 453-4102
Ennis Community Choir	P.O. Box 397, Ennis 59729
Flathead Valley Aires	111 West Reserve, Kalispell 59901
Flathead Valley Community Band	492 Conrad Dr., Kalispell 59901
Flathead Valley Jazz Society	P.O. Box 2627, Kalispell 59901
Forsyth Community Choir	Box 745, Forsyth 59327
Glendive Community Chorus	210 South Highland Park, Glendive 59330
Great Falls Symphonic Choir	P.O. Box 1078, Great Falls 59403 453-4102
Great Falls Symphony Association	P.O. Box 1078, Great Falls 59403 453-4102
Cascade Quartet	P.O. Box 1078, Great Falls 59403 453-4102
Havre Community Concert Association	44 Saddle Butte Drive, Havre 59501 265-5254
Montana Chorale	P.O. Box 6083, Great Falls 59403 771-7110
Montana Association of Symphony Orchestras	717 5th Ave., Helena 59601 449-7159
Montana Music Institute	P.O. Box 20783, Billings 59103 259-0701, 656-5334
Montana String Teachers Association	Billings Public Schools, Billings 59102
Montana Percussive Arts Society	Roundup 59072
Montana Band Masters	500 32nd Ave. NE, Great Falls 59404
Helena Symphony Society	P.O. Box 1073, Helena 59601 442-1860
Helena Presents/Myrna Loy Center	15 N. Ewing, Helena 59601 443-0287
Glacier Orchestra & Chorale	P.O. Box 2491, Kalispell 59903 257-3241
Livingston Community Chorus	Box 370, Livingston 59047 222-3304
Miles City Community Orchestra	52 Balsam Drive, Miles City 59301 232-6889
Missoula Civic Symphony Chorale	300 Keith, Missoula 59801
International Choral Festival	11 Greenbrier Drive, Missoula 59802 549-8438
Missoula Symphony Association	131 S. Higgins, Missoula 59802 721-3194
String Orchestra of the Rockies	P.O. Box 8265, Missoula 59807 549-7814
Old Time Fiddlers Association	District 1–26184 East Shore Route, Bigfork 59911 District 2–P.O. Box 53, Darby 59829 District 3–1429 Warren Ave., Butte 59701 District 5–P.O. Box 104, Raymond 59256 District 6–P.O. Box 73 ,Choteau 59422
Prairie Symphonette	P.O. Box 126, Scobey 59263 487-5542
Sidney Community Band	P.O. Box 42, Sidney 59270
Ruby Valley Chorale	P.O. Box S, Twin Bridges 59754 684-5465

Music Festivals of Note

Event	Town/Season	Information
Bitterroot Valley Bluegrass Festival	Hamilton/July	
Country Music Campout	Troy/July	295-4358
Dixieland Jazz Festival	Great Falls/August	(800) 851-9980
Fiddler's Champion Contest	Jordan	
Flathead Music Festival	Whitefish/mid-July to mid-August	257-0787
Glacier Jazz Stampede	Kalispell/October	755-0592
Helena Traditional Jazz Festival	Helena/June	(800) 851-9980
High School Festival of Chamber Music	Missoula/July	Music Department, MSU Bozeman 59717
International Choral Festival	Missoula/July	542-3481
Lincoln Fiddlers Contest	Lincoln/August	362-9200
Montana State Old-Time Fiddlers Contest	Polson/July	323-1198
Montana Traditional Jazz Festival	Helena/June	(800) 851-9980
Music in Montana Summer Festival	Missoula	P.O. Box 3704, Missoula 59806
Musician's Rendezvous	Laurel	1010 6th Ave., Laurel 59044
Red Lodge Music Festival	Red Lodge/June	446-1905
Sweet Pea Festival	Bozeman/August	587-9169

My Favorite Parts
of Montana's Arts

by R. W. "Rib" Gustafson, Conrad

Rib Gustafson is a veterinarian who dabbles in music and poetry and has written two books of memoirs, Under the Chinook Arch *and* Room to Roam, *both available from Falcon Publishing.*

• Best living artist: **Bob Scriver**—If you don't believe me, visit his House of Bronze in Browning.

• Favorite place: **Glacier National Park**—You can feast your eyes with a never-tiring vision. You ain't seen nothin' until you've looked.

• Favorite reading: Excerpts from *The Journals of Lewis and Clark.*

• Other nominees: **the history of Montana**, from the beaver days to the sodbuster. Forget the present-day "sons of the soil."

• **My ranch**, part of a never-ending love story of land, livestock, and contentment, the blankets of snows and the hiss of skis in powder, the cheers of a (rodeo) crowd and the feel of a good horse between your legs; and watching my family come to prominence—Wylie and "Fingers Ray," with their musical talents; Sid and Barr, with their love of animals and never-ending quest for knowledge; Kristen, and her integrity in the practice of law; their progeny as they grow and become lovers of a land under the chinook arch where there is room to roam; and my wife, Pat—mother, artist, cook, and homemaker.

Dance

Dancers find Montana's open spaces just right for choreography. Dance programs at both The University of Montana and Montana State University have gained acclaim for their teachers, alumni, and the works they produce. Local ballet and dance corps pull in younger Montana students. With our share of touring dance companies and dance arts cooperative projects, we are a state in motion.

Dance Companies and Organizations

Organization	Address/Phone
Butte International Folk Dance Group	641 Sampson St., Butte 59701
Dance Works	Front Street Dance Center 229 East Front, Missoula 59802
Department of Dance	MSU Billings 1500 N 30th Street, Billings 59101
Department of Drama/Dance	University of Montana, Missoula 59812 243-4481
Garden City Ballet Company/ Front Street Dance Theatre	229 East Front St., Missoula 59802 721-3675
Kalispell Dance Company	1112 2nd Ave. West, Kalispell 59901
MSU Dance Company	HPER Department Montana State University, Bozeman 59717
Missoula Square and Round Dance	705 North 3rd, Missoula 59802
Montana Ballet Company	P.O. Box 6021 221 East Main St., Bozeman 59771 587-7192
Montana Dance Arts Association	P.O. 1872, Bozeman 59771 585-9551
Montana Transport Company (MOTRANS)	Department of Drama/Dance University of Montana, Missoula 59812 243-2875
Pine Cone Squares	Ekalaka 59324
Two Medicine Lake Society	Box 1509, Browning 59417
Yellowstone Ballet	109 South B Street, Livingston 59047 222-0430
Yellowstone Square Dance	P.O. Box 20141, Billings 59101

Theater

A summer without theater in Montana is like a winter without snow. Each summer season, Montanans and visitors enjoy theatrical offerings in communities across the state, including offerings by the Port Polson Players, the Badland Players in Havre, the Fort Peck Summer Theater, and the Bigfork Summer Playhouse, celebrating its thirty-sixth season in 1996. The oldest theatrical company in Montana, the Virginia City Players, has played to packed audiences since it first offered melodramas in 1949. Folks all across the state mark their calendars to catch the summer tour of the Shakespeare in the Parks troupe, celebrating twenty-five years of bringing to dozens of Montana communities some creative interpretations of the works of Shakespeare and his contemporaries.

Dozens of theater groups in the state also have winter performance seasons, the mainstays of the Montana stage. The Montana Repertory Theatre, the Vigilante Theater Company, and Missoula Children's Theatre are a few of the professional theater organizations in the state. Some of the most vibrant shows are presented by college students or talented local children and adults, including the shows at the Grandstreet Theater in Helena, Montana's oldest year-round community playhouse.

Theater Companies & Organizations

Organization	Address/Phone
Bigfork Community Players	P.O. Box 786, Bigfork 59911 752-4483
Bigfork Summer Playhouse	P.O. Box 456, Bigfork 59911 837-4886
Billings Studio Theatre	1500 Rimrock, Billings 59101 248-1141
Alberta Bair Theater	P.O. 1556, Billings 59103 256-8915
Red Lodge Community Theatre	1373 Hardrock Lane, Billings 59105 252-2474
Birney Shakespeare Club	P.O. Box 518, Birney 59102 984-6281
Shakespeare in the Parks	Dept. of Theatre Arts, MSU-Bozeman 59717 994-3901
Theatre of Silence	Speech/Communication, MSU Bozeman 59717
Vigilante Theatre Company	111 S. Grand Ave., Bozeman 59715 586-3897
Montana Theatreworks	P.O. Box 3672, Bozeman 59772 586-5597
Butte Community Theater	1924 Carolina, Butte 59701
Redwater Company of Theatre & Art	341 Road 422, Circle 59215
Pondera Players	103 S. Kansas, Conrad 59425
Deer Lodge Community Theatre	710 Kentucky, Deer Lodge 59722
Tobacco Valley Community Theatre	P.O. Box 162, Eureka 59917
Hamilton Players	143 Wyant Lane, Hamilton 59840
Jawbone Players	P.O. Box 206, Harlowton 59036
Montana Actors Theatre	2755 Bullhook Road, Havre 59501 265-6315
Montana Logging & Ballet Co.	1515 Winne, Helena 59601 443-1960
Grand Street Theatre	P.O. Box 1258, Helena 59624 442-4270
Helena Presents/Myrna Loy Center	15 N. Ewing, Helena 59601 443-0287
Big Dry Players	P.O. Box 145, Jordan 59337 557-2896
Paper Moon Theatre Company	81 Trails End Drive, Kalispell 59901 755-5332
Firehouse 5 Playhouse	P.O. Box 1264, Livingston 59047 (800) SLAPSTICK
Missoula Children's Theatre	200 North Adams, Missoula 59802 728-1911
Montana Players, Inc.	P.O. Box 4771, Missoula 59806 721-9568
Montana Repertory Theatre	University of Montana, Missoula 59812 243-5288
Granite Repertory Theatre	P.O. Box 731, Philipsburg 59858 859-3601
Plentywood Theater	310 Highland Ave., Plentywood 59254
Port Polson Players	P.O. Box 1152, Polson 59860 883-4691
Old Jail Museum Players	1147 Blue Slide Road, Thompson Falls 59873
Virginia City Players	305 West Wallace, Virginia City 59755
Playmill Theatre	29 Madison Ave., West Yellowstone 59758
Whitefish Theatre Company	P.O. Box 1463, Whitefish 59937 862-5371

The World's a Stage

In 1995, more than 36,000 children in as many as 600 towns from Hiroshima, Japan, to Augusta, Maine, performed in—or simply enjoyed—presentations by the Missoula Children's Theatre.

My Favorite Parts
of Montana's Arts

by Stephen Ambrose

Stephen Ambrose is a historian and author. He wrote Undaunted Courage: Meriwether Lewis, Thomas Jefferson, and the Opening of the American West, *a best-selling account of the Lewis and Clark Expedition. He divides his time between homes in Bay St. Louis, Mississippi, and Helena.*

1. **Charlie Russell**, the painter, "for obvious reasons."

2. **K. Ross Toole**, "a great historian and storyteller."

3. **A. B. Guthrie**, the author of *The Big Sky* and *The Way West*, who was "made for Montana."

4. **Bev Doolittle**.

5. **Monte Dolack**.

6. **Thomas McGuane**, the author of *Ninety-Two in the Shade* and other novels and screenplays.

7. **Carroll O'Connor**, the Emmy-award-winning actor who played Archie Bunker on the long-running TV comedy *All in the Family* and starred in *In the Heat of the Night*. O'Connor earned his Masters of Fine Arts from The University of Montana in 1956.

8. **Ivan Doig**, the writer.

9. **Harry Fritz**, the historian and University of Montana professor whose lectures "are the best of the art form of oratory."

Media Arts

Montana filmmakers, such as Swain Wolfe, Annick Smith, Bruce Weide, and others, remind us that film and video art is more than documentation—it is a way of looking at the world. Watching homegrown films is a favorite pastime of Montanans, who flock to such events as the Helena Film and Video Festival. The International Wildlife Film Festival, held each spring in Missoula, is said to be the largest, longest-running festival of its kind in the world. The festival draws top-notch films from around the globe. Entrants into the festival's juried competition range from student-amateurs to the internationally renowned BBC and National Geographic organizations. The scope of the festival extends far beyond wildlife; film categories include ecological and environmental concerns, children, animation, and native and indigenous peoples. In addition to the films, wildlife and conservation organizations man booths to educate and inform audiences about local efforts to protect and preserve wildlife and habitat in Montana.

Film work also attracts students to the film and television program at Montana State University in Bozeman. Its alumni work for major Hollywood studios, special effects companies, and independent producers.

The source of scripts and ideas runs deep here. Like Smith and Beth Ferris, whose 1979 film *Heartland* won critical praise, other Montana writers have inspired unforgettable movies based on their presentations of Montana and the West. *Rancho Deluxe* and *Thunderbolt and Lightfoot* made Montanans and others long for an extended road trip through stunning scenery. In recent years, *A River Runs Through It* has brought new legions of fly fishers to our streams; Ruth Ann Lum McCunn's *A Thousand Pieces of Gold* told our history as it was.

In 1995, four feature films, nineteen commercials, eight documentaries, and twenty television shows were shot in the state. The Montana Film Office was created in 1974 as a central information source for filmmakers who seek locations in Montana. It is part of the Travel Montana office of the Department of Commerce and is funded entirely by the state's 4 percent tax on accommodations. The primary role of the Montana Film Office is to bring productions (feature films, commercials, television, still shoots, and documentaries) into Montana for the overall economic benefit of the state.

Montana Revenue From Filming*

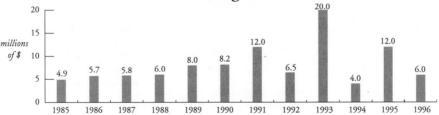

*Dollar amounts given in millions. Data reflects only expenditures directly related to production costs.
Source: Travel Montana, Montana Film Office, Montana Department of Commerce.

Feature Films & TV Productions, Scenes Filmed in Montana

Year	Film	Company	Location
1920	Devils Horse		Hardin area
1920	Where the Rivers Rise		Columbia Falls
1950	Red Skies Over Montana	20th Century Fox	Missoula area
1951	Timberjack		Missoula area
1951	Warpath	20th Century Fox	Billings area
1954	Cattle Queen of Montana		East Glacier
1958	Dangerous Mission		Glacier National Park
1970	Little Big Man		Virginia City/Billings
1972	Evel Knievel		Butte
1973	Route 66		Butte
1973	Thunderbolt and Lightfoot	United Artists	Malpaso/Livingston/Great Falls
1973	Winterhawk	Charles Pierce Prod.	Kalispell area
1974	The Killer Inside Me	Cyclone Productions	Butte
1974	Potato Fritz	Horizon Productions	Helena area
1974	Rancho Deluxe	Frank Perry Films	Livingston
1975	Missouri Breaks	Jack Sherman Prod.	Billings/Virginia City/Red Lodge
1975	Winds of Autumn	Charles Pierce Prod.	Kalispell
1976	Beartooth	ESI Productions	Red Lodge area
1976	Damnation Alley	20th Century Fox	Lakeside
1976	Pony Express Rider	Doty Dayton Prod.	Virginia City/Nevada City
1977	Christmas Miracle in Caulfield USA	20th Century TV	Roundup
1977	Grey Eagle	Charles Pierce Prod.	Helena area
1977	The Other Side of Hell	Aubrey/Lyons Prod./NBC	Warm Springs
1977	Telefon	MGM-Siegel Film	Great Falls
1978	Rodeo Red & The Runaway	Highgate Pictures/NBC TV	Billings
1978	The Shining	Warner Brothers	Glacier National Park
1979	Heartland	Wilderness Woman/Filmhaus, Inc.	Harlowton area
1979	Heaven's Gate	United Artists	Kalispell/Glacier National Park/Butte area
1979	The Legend of Walks Far Woman	EMI Productions/CBS	Billings/Red Lodge/Hardin
1979	South by Northwest	KWSU/Washington State	Virginia City/Nevada City
1982	Firefox	Warner Bros.	Glasgow/Cut Bank area
1980	Continental Divide	Universal Pictures	Glacier National Park
1982	Fast Walking	Lorimar Productions	Deer Lodge
1983	The Stone Boy	Roth Productions	Great Falls area
1983	Triumphs of a Man Called Horse	Sandy Howard Prod.	Cooke City/Red Lodge
1985	Runaway Train	Cannon Films	Butte/Anaconda area
1986	Amazing Grace and Chuck	Tri-Star Productions	Bozeman/Livingston/Helena
1986	Amy Grant: Home for the Holidays	NBC/Smith-Hemion Prod.	Kalispell/Glacier National Park
1986	Stacking	Nepenthe Prod.	Billings area
1986	The Untouchables	Paramount Pictures	Cascade area
1987	Powwow Highway	Handmade Films	Hardin area/Northern Cheyenne Reservation/Colstrip
1987	War Party	Hemdale Productions	Browning/Cut Bank/Choteau
1988	Cold Feet	Avenue Pictures	Livingston area
1988	Disorganized Crime	Buena Vista	Hamilton/Darby/Missoula
1989	Always	Amblin Entertain./Universal	Libby
1989	Bright Angel	Hemdale Prod.	Billings

Feature Films & TV Productions, Scenes Filmed in Montana, (cont.)

Year	Film	Company	Location
1989	*Montana*	HBO Prod./TNN	Bozeman area
1989	*A Thousand Pieces of Gold*	Motherlode Prod.	Nevada City
1990	*Common Ground*		Columbia Falls
1990	*Son of the Morning Star*	Republic Pictures/ABC	Billings area
1990	*True Colors*	Paramount	Big Sky
1991	*A River Runs Through It*	Columbia	Livingston/Bozeman areas
1991	*Diggstown*	MGM	Deer Lodge
1991	*Far and Away*	Imagine Entertain./Universal	Billings area
1991	*Keep the Change*	Tisch Prod./TNT	Livingston area
1991	*Season of Change*	Sterling Films	Bitterroot Valley
1992	*The Ballad of Little Jo*	JoCo Productions	Red Lodge area
1992	*Josh and S.A.M.*	Castle Rock	Billings area
1993	*Beethoven's 2nd*	Universal Pictures	Glacier National Park/Flathead
1993	*Forrest Gump*	Momentum Films/Paramount	Glacier National Park/ Blackfeet Reservation
1993	*Holy Matrimony*	Interscope Prod.	Great Falls area
1993	*Iron Will*	Walt Disney	West Yellowstone area
1993	*The Last Ride*	HKM	Bozeman/Deer Lodge
1993	*Return to Lonesome Dove*	RHI	Virginia City, Butte/Billings area
1993	*The River Wild*	Universal Pictures	Libby, Flathead area
1995	*Amanda*	Family Channel/Cinergi Pictures	Red Lodge area
1995	*Broken Arrow*	20th Century Fox	Lewistown
1995	*Livers Ain't Cheap*	W. T. Entertainment	Deer Lodge
1995	*Under Siege II: Dark Territory*	Warner Bros.	Missoula
1996	*The Horse Whisperer*	Double Divide Inc.	Big Timber/Livingston

Source: *Travel Montana, Montana Film Office, Montana Department of Commerce.*

$\mathcal{M}$ notable ontanans

Myrna Loy (1905-1992)

Born Myrna Adele Williamson in Radersburg, in Broadwater County, Loy made her stage debut as a Hollywood chorus girl in 1925 and made her film debut the following year. Her signature role was Nora Charles in *The Thin Man*, but she starred in more than eighty films, including *The Best Years of Our Lives* (1946), *Libeled Lady* (1936), and *The Bachelor and the Bobby-Soxer* (with Cary Grant, 1947). The Myrna Loy Center in Helena was named for the "Queen of the Movies."

Montana Historical Society

My Favorite Parts
of Montana's Arts

by Beth Lo, Missoula

Beth Lo teaches ceramics at The University of Montana and plays bass for the Big Sky Mudflaps, the popular combo that dishes out jazz, blues, and dance music.

Montana has an abundance of talented individuals who have contributed to the rich artistic identity of the state. Some of these artists were born here, others are transplants, some have merely passed through; but for each of them, there has occurred a lasting mutual impact—the artist upon the state and the state upon the artist.

Of all the artists, art events, monuments, and projects that make up Montana's artistic legacy, the best part of the arts in Montana is an intangible one: the network among these individuals that has evolved over the years. Despite (or maybe because of) the large geographical distances that these artists need to cover when they want to get together, communication, hospitality, humor, and generosity characterize our gatherings.

My own personal work in art and music has given me an opportunity to have an intimate connection with this arts network, particularly in ceramics and jazz music. In both of these artistic realms, there is a strong sense of openness and sharing that I associate with Montana's cultural atmosphere.

The communities that make up these and the other arts, such as writing, dance, and theater, all seem to feel a powerful sense of pride in being affiliated with Montana. We have been fortunate to have the land to turn to for inspiration and solitude when we need to do our work, and then when we have the opportunities to share, we have found support and camaraderie from our institutions and peers.

Media Arts Organizations

Organization	Address/Phone
Blackfeet Media Department	Box 850, Browning 59417
Helena Presents/Myrna Loy Center	15 N. Ewing, Helena 59601 443-0287
International Wildlife Film Festival	802 E. Front St., Missoula 59802 728-9380
High Plains News Service	2401 Montana Ave #301, Billings 59101 252-9673
Montana Teen Video	315 S. 4th E., Missoula 59801
Montanans for Quality TV	P.O. Box 8355, Missoula 59807 543-6333
Montana Film Office	1424 9th Ave., Helena 59620 444-3762 or 444-3960
Watershed Foundation	c/o Bitterroot Films, Hammond Arcade Missoula 59802 728-2261

Statewide Arts Organizations

Montana Arts Council

The 1967 Legislature created the Montana Arts Council to provide citizens of all economic and geographic circumstances with an equal opportunity to have the best of arts in their lives. The governor appoints the Montana Arts Council's fifteen members from the various geographical areas of the state and from those who have a keen interest in one or more of the arts and a willingness to devote time and effort in the public interest. The council's duties are to encourage the presentation of and participation in the arts—including music, theater, dance, painting, sculpture, architecture, and allied arts and crafts—and to foster public interest in and expansion of the state's cultural heritage and resources. Since 1970, the Artists in Schools program has provided thousands of public school children in even the most remote communities of the state the opportunity to learn about all aspects of the arts.

The council also publishes *ArtistSearch*, a bimonthly publication providing information to the Montana arts community.

Montana Arts Council
316 North Park Avenue, Suite 252
P.O. Box 202201
Helena, MT 59620-2201
444-6430
Internet address: MAC montana@tmn.com

Other Statewide Arts Organizations

Montana Art Education Association
1218 Dickinson
Missoula 59801
549-9806
— Provides professional information and development for art teachers in all areas.

Montana Arts Foundation
P.O. Box 1872
Bozeman 59771
585-9551
— Provides administrative services for statewide organizations and some local groups and acts as a fiscal agent for emerging arts organizations.

Montana Committee for the Humanities
P.O. Box 8036
Missoula 59607
243-6022
— Presents programs, awards grants, maintains a speakers bureau, hosts reading-discussion groups and teacher workshops in history, literature, philosophy, and other disciplines.

Montana Community Foundation
Arcade Building, Suite 3-D
208 N. Montana, Suite 207
Helena 59601
443-8313
— Maintains endorsements for and makes grants to nonprofit organizations.

Montana Cultural Advocacy
P.O. Box 1872
Bozeman 59771
585-9551
— A coalition of arts, libraries, and historical agencies that lobbies the State Legislature to maintain funding of cultural agencies and oversees legislation affecting Montana's cultural sector.

Montana Institute of the Arts
P.O. Box 1872
Bozeman 59771
585-9551
— Assists artists in all disciplines through an annual art fair and workshops.

Montana Performing Arts Consortium
P.O. Box 1872
Bozeman 59771
585-9551
— Supports performing arts in large and small communities; sponsors an annual conference showing performing arts; facilitates block-booking; and provides grants to rural presenters.

Very Special Arts Montana
221 East Front
Missoula 59802
549-2984
— Provides information, technical assistance, and workshops on working with people with special needs.

Cowboy CARTOON

Montana cartoonist Stan Lynde created the comic strip *Rick O'Shay*, based on a lawman and his gunslinger pal, Hipshot. The strip was distributed to 20 million readers through 100 newspapers via the *Chicago Tribune-New York News* service from 1958 to 1977. Lynde's second syndicated cartoon, *Latigo*, ran from 1979 to 1983 in the same papers.

Montana Arts Online

Computer users can experience art online via the Montana Artist Gallery and the World Wide Web. The gallery can be found on the Office of Public Instruction's METNET (Montana Educational Telecommunications Network) computer bulletin board and its related web site. To access the site, all you need is a computer, a phone line, a modem, and a copy of some special free software distributed to each of the 823 public libraries in Montana. Web users can view the site at *http://161.7.114.15/opi/opi.html* .

Further Reading:

ArtistSearch. Bimonthly newsletter published by the Montana Arts Council, 316 North Park, Helena, Montana.

Catlin, George. *Letters and Notes on the North American Indians.* New York: Clarkson N. Potter, Inc., 1975.

Kittredge, William, and Annick Smith, eds. *The Last Best Place: A Montana Anthology.* Helena: Montana Historical Society/Falcon Publishing, 1993.

Lively Times. A monthly arts and events magazine published at 1152 Eagle Pass Trail, Charlo 59824, 644-2910.

Montana Calendar of Events. Brochure published annually by Travel Montana, 444-2654 or (800) VISIT MT (out-of-state).

Montana's Cultural Treasures, A Guide to Montana's Museums, Art Galleries & Studios. Brochure produced by Lee Enterprises, the Montana Arts Council, the Montana Historical Society, and Travel Montana, updated each year.

Newby, Rick, and Suzanne Hunger, eds. *Writing Montana: Literature under the Big Sky.* Helena: Montana Center for the Book, 1996.

Rostad, Lee. *Honey Wine and Hunger Root.* Helena: Falcon Publishing, 1985.

Index

Discover Montana with Books from Falcon

PHOTOGRAPHY

Enjoy the beauty and spirit of Montana with quality full-color giftbooks. Each book combines the best writings with spectacular photography to create an unforgettable portrait of Montana, The Last Best Place.

Montana on My Mind
Montana: The Last Best Place
Glacier on My Mind

Last Best Place: A Montana Anthology
A guided tour of Montana's literature, including Native American stories, autobiographies, journals, fiction, and poetry.

The Montana Calendar
Published annually The Montana Calendar features the natural wonders—wildlife, wild lands, and wildflowers—that make the state one of the most stunning places on earth.

The Montana Cookbook
Sample Montana's distinctive flavor with these 500 recipes. Also includes historical anecdotes from Montana's early days.

VIDEO

Beartooth Highway Video
Montana on My Mind Video

FOR YOUNG HISTORIANS

Battle of the Little Bighorn
Colter's Run

 TwoDot is the name of a small town in Montana's Wheatland County. The TwoDot line features classic western literature and history.

Bozeman & the Gallatin Valley: A History
Flight of the Dove: The Story of Jeannette Rankin
Four-Legged Legends of Montana
Growing Up Western
It Happened in Montana
Jeannette Rankin: Bright Star in the Big Sky
Montana Campfire Tales: Fourteen Historical Essays
More Than Petticoats: Remarkable Montana Women

FALCON®

To order check with your local bookseller or call Falcon at 1-800-582-2665.
Ask for a FREE catalog featuring a complete list of titles on nature,
outdoor recreation, and the West.

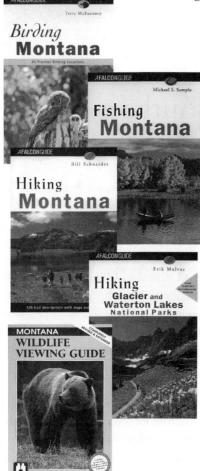

About the Authors

Andrea Slosson Merrill, a native of Anaconda, Montana, spent her twenties in Missoula and has made Helena her home for the past twenty years. Her Montana ancestral roots include great-grandparents who ranched in the Boulder Valley more than one hundred years ago and grandparents and parents who lived most of their lives in various western Montana counties. Ms. Merrill has a BA in Elementary Education and a Masters of Education from the University of Montana. From 1981 to 1995, she served the Montana Legislature as a researcher, bill drafter, and committee staffer with the Montana Legislative Council. That experience, coupled with an interest in collecting and appraising books on Montana and the West, provided the inspiration for this publication. Andrea is currently the Executive Director of the Mental Health Association of Montana.

Judy Jacobson has made Montana her home for the past twenty-five years. After having served on the Democratic Central Committee for several years, in 1980, she was appointed to the Montana Senate to succeed Senator Bob Peterson. She then went on to serve in the Senate for sixteen more years. As a senator, Ms. Jacobson chaired the Public Health, Welfare, and Safety Committee, served as the Democratic Whip, and chaired both the Senate Finance and Claims Committee and the Legislative Finance Committee. She left the Senate to join gubernatorial candidate Chet Blaylock as his running mate in the 1996 election. When Blaylock died of a sudden heart attack, she was chosen by the Democratic Party to take his place, and made history by appearing on the ballot as the candidate for both governor and lieutenant governor. She lives in Butte and has started a business offering technical writing services on a contractual basis.